Psychological and Political Strategies for Peace Negotiation

Francesco Aquilar • Mauro Galluccio
Editors

Psychological and Political Strategies for Peace Negotiation

A Cognitive Approach

Springer

Editors
Francesco Aquilar
Center for Cognitive Psychology and Psychotherapy
Via Guido de Ruggiero 118
80128 Napoli
Italy
francescoaquilar@tiscali.it

Mauro Galluccio
European Association for Negotiation and Mediation (EANAM)
Square Ambiorix 32/43
B-1000 Bruxelles
Belgium
mauro.galluccio@eanam.org

ISBN 978-1-4419-7429-7 e-ISBN 978-1-4419-7430-3
DOI 10.1007/978-1-4419-7430-3
Springer New York Dordrecht Heidelberg London

Printed on acid-free paper

Springer is part of Springer Science+Business Media (www.springer.com)

To our parents and to our children

Foreword

"The best of humanity doesn't wait for the storm to pass. They dance in the rain."

Anonymous

For as long as human beings have walked the earth, conflict has been a part of the landscape, whether over food, property, power, control, or relationships. Much of this conflict may come under the general concept of territoriality, which appears to be an implicit trait in human kind. The literature in anthropology is replete with studies dating to early scientific investigations of human beings' intrinsic need to define specific territory as a way to establish and maintain autonomy and to enter into conflict with others. During the course of history, most wars have been fought between neighbors and usually over issues involving power and domain. The question of proximity is generally less likely the cause of conflict than the means for it. Proximity fosters interaction, and interaction can bring differences to the foreground. As the number of interactions between parties increases, the opportunities for disagreements between them also increase.

However undesirable it may be, conflict is inevitable between human beings; it is simply part of the human condition. Power, wealth, and resources are not distributed equally, and the scramble to gain them or protect them or broker them invites conflict, both petty and profound.

The common denominator in many conflicts appears to comprise several components. One aspect is a sense of vulnerability and perceived threats to the integrity to one's existence. This concept typically evokes an emotional reaction for a fight/flight response. When the fight response manifests, it usually leads to anger and retaliation in the other. This pattern can also thwart communication and narrow the pathway for negotiation. This problem may occur despite the fact that both sides actually desire to reach a level of agreement or homeostasis. In many conflict situations, the amount of animosity and distrust that builds up is antithetical to the type of cooperation that is essential for negotiation to be possible. And although these negative feelings may be a matter of perception that has been somewhat distorted by circumstances, they may seem entirely real to the endangered party. Parties that become so mired in the notion of standing their ground or winning often become entrenched in the mechanics of the struggle, sometimes even forgetting the original issue, much like disgruntled marital partners who become gridlocked in a power struggle.

The Harvard psychologist, Daniel Gilbert, writes that one of the things that bring human beings unhappiness is uncertainty about the future. Conflict brings uncertainty; thus, one way to avoid uncertainty is to avoid conflict. But if, as we said, conflict has existed as far back as recorded history and in virtually every culture, what can be done to ameliorate the situation? It appears that much of the reconciliation perspective presented in this beautifully edited text is predicated upon the removal of the emotional barriers between the warring parties. These include the emotions that are associated with perceptions of having been victimized by an adversary and feelings of distrust that have accumulated during the conflict period. Conflict usually becomes increasingly difficult to resolve when distrust dominates the communication, leaving adversaries waiting for each other to concede.

This unique text presents important discussions of the concept of optimism and finding mutually acceptable agreements between adversaries. This optimism depends on perceptions that have their roots in what cognitive therapists refer to as "schema."

Traditionally, cognitive therapy has focused on three levels of cognitive phenomena, namely: automatic thoughts, cognitive distortions, and underlying assumptions. The underlying assumptions of schemas constitute the deepest and most fundamental level of cognition. They are viewed as the basis for screening, differentiating coding stimuli that individuals encounter during the course of their lifetime. Schemas are typically organized elements of task reactions and experiences that form a relatively cohesive and persistent body of knowledge that guides subsequent perceptions and appraisals. They may also include a set of rules held by an individual that guides his or her attention to particular stimuli in the environment and shapes the types of inferences that individuals make from unobserved characteristics.

Schemas in conflict lend to the ingrained images that individuals or groups have in their minds about their adversaries. These images may go on to develop into collective schemas that are jointly held by populations or cultures, such as is the case with countries that have been at odds for centuries. These schemas are often affected in one way or the other by cognitive distortions about one's self or one's adversary and can contribute to an emotional impasse that is enduring.

Many of the chapters in this text underscore the process of negotiation and offer various useful methods to implement it. Negotiation requires a social mentality that accommodates a cultural sensitivity for both sides, which is often very difficult to achieve. Most important are some of the motivational and cognitive areas that are found in the decision-making process during negotiation. The contrasting aspects of comparison and callous indifference that characterize the relationship between adversaries are often targets of interest. The effects of brain activation are also discussed with regard to some of the engagement in the negotiation process.

Neuroscientists tell us that our primate brain through cold reasoning constantly tries to make sense of our environment and pursues new meaning. This is particularly so when we face a complex problem with disparate facts, such as is the case with any conflict. Our brains try to find a solution that explains all facts. As a result, adversaries caught in the most severe of conflicts may still maintain a certain amount of vulnerability to being influenced by cognitive restructuring and the type of mediation that exists with a cognitive approach. Cognitive therapy offers a new dimension to negotiation, particularly in overriding the heated emotion that often gets in the way of attempts to pursue effective negotiation strategies, which is clearly outlined in the overreaching theme of this textbook. The impetus for this work is born out of the dire need for an effective intervention to quell conflict during a time when the world is in serious turmoil.

It is my hope that this book will sow the seeds to new thinking with regard to forging successful reconciliation agreements between conflicting nations now and in the future.

Department of Psychiatry, Frank M. Dattilio
Harvard Medical School

Preface

Why This Book on Psychology and Politics of Peace Negotiation: Objectives and Approach

The subject of international negotiations, and especially peace negotiations, is considered particularly relevant for the entire planet. The rapid changes that occurred after the fall of the Berlin Wall have proved not only to be heralds of a new and more democratic global balance, but also capable of provoking further outbreaks of war. Today wars are different from those of the last century, but not less painful for people and nations who are affected by them.

Politics, using and taking internal advantage of diplomacy, negotiation, and mediation modalities, has so far been "busy" managing the difficult relationship between governments and people of different cultural anthropology and different geographical, economic, religious, and social conditions, with results that in good and bad times are there for all to see. Our proposal, presented in this volume, concerns the possibility of a concrete and operational integration of the acquisitions of the psychology and psychotherapy of cognitive orientation into the international political and negotiating process, aiming to provide a set of additional tools for the construction of peace processes that may be useful not only for individual human beings sensitive to these topics, but also for public opinion, citizens, negotiators, and governors/rulers.

This text is the second step of our project. In 2008, we published a book titled *Psychological Processes in International Negotiations: Theoretical and Practical Perspectives*, which aimed to draw the boundaries of a new area of study, research and application, resulting from the integration of political science and cognitive psychology/psychotherapy, to analyze and try to change negotiating processes and to outline some modalities of psychologically oriented training for negotiators in the future.

In 2006, during the writing of the previous book, Albert Ellis (1913–2007), one of the most important psychologists and psychotherapists of the twentieth century, encouraged our work with a supportive foreword to our book (Ellis, in: Aquilar and Galluccio 2008) and "authorized" us to continue the path he traced (Ellis 1992). We had already planned to ask, as editors, some of the leading scholars and experts in cognitive psychology, psychotherapy, and political science for a contribution that would aim at a scientific construction of peace processes.

However, at that time we did not imagine that we would receive such an exciting response from the extraordinary authors who now we have the honor of hosting in this volume. Each author has developed some important aspects of psychological and political strategies for peace negotiations, and every contribution is much richer and more complex than we could fairly present in this introduction. However, it can certainly help to shape our conversation with the reader, and to highlight some strengths of the general context, by providing a rough approximation, as follows:

Intelligences – How to Change Mind	Gardner
Values – Evolution – Compassion	Gilbert
Personal Schemas	Leahy
Emotional Competence	Saarni
Tacit Knowledge	Dowd, Roberts Miller
Thinking Errors – Decision-making	Meichenbaum
Images of the Conflict – Negative Escalation	Faure
Communication in Intractable Conflicts	Pruitt
Practical Cooperation Between Science and Society	Nauen
Decision-Making – Thrusts – Constraints – Collective Action	Druckman, Gürkaynak, Beriker, Celik
Negotiating Practice	Kremenyuk
War Experiences	Zikic
Rebuilding Experiences	Karam
Political Strategies Psychologically Oriented	Galluccio
Psychological Strategies Politically Oriented	Aquilar

More specifically, the book starts with a contribution from Howard Gardner, who presents possible applications of his famous theory of multiple intelligences to peace negotiation, with particular attention to processes related to "changing minds." What kinds of intelligence should be developed and how can we train minds to be open to creative and effective solutions? What processes should be encouraged so that people can develop new ideas, acquire relevant information, and check the accuracy of their views objectively?

Paul Gilbert, a scholar who is particularly experienced in processes of "compassion," has contributed a chapter that looks at how the evolution of humans has developed towards a prospective of peace, and through what kind of values. How we could develop a "compassionate mind" and what individual, social, and political benefits might result from this development, are among the topics we can find in his work, with constant reference to the implications of the psychobiology and to the theory of values on past, present and future international negotiations and mediations.

Robert L. Leahy describes the concept of "Personal Schemas," which is well known to cognitive psychotherapists, presenting an application of this concept to negotiation processes. His contribution clearly shows the effectiveness of the extension of theories and techniques derived from cognitive psychotherapy to the negotiating context, specifying and detailing various operational steps and implications.

Afterwards, Carolyn Saarni shows the functions that emotional factors play in the negotiation process. These factors have long been neglected, ignored, or misinterpreted in past studies and research on the subject of international negotiation. Emotional competence, however, is proving to be a key factor both in negotiations (especially particularly delicate or dangerous ones) and in social communication, as well as interpersonal communication.

Factors beyond cognitive and emotional processes, such as the so-called "tacit knowledge," may implicitly influence the minds and behavior of negotiators, and especially of political leaders. The forms in which tacit knowledge is expressed are the subjects of E. Thomas Dowd's and Angela N. Roberts Miller's chapter.

It is interesting to understand how this psychological knowledge could operationally improve politicians' decisions, and of which thinking errors they should be warned. This is the subject of Donald Meichenbaum's chapter, which presents a precise application of theories and techniques of cognitive-behavioral psychotherapy to be applied in key moments when situations may go from bad to worse: that of the decision-making process.

Negotiation processes are embedded in social contexts and raise specific reactions in public opinion. Such reactions "bounce" on governments and negotiators and to some extent tend to influence them. To this end, social images of international conflicts are meant to be studied for their fundamental importance, and are analyzed in the chapter written by Guy Olivier Faure, who pays close attention to distorted images of the conflict that may lead to its escalation.

Unfortunately, conflict escalation sometimes becomes uncontrollable and it is easy to face situations where the conflict is instead characterized by a serious long-term hostility. The modalities used to resume an effective negotiating communication in these dramatic cases are the subjects of Dean G. Pruitt's chapter. He proposes, after a historical and psychological analysis, an operational method for a reassessment of the motivations of each actor. This, through a specific sequence of communication that uses as its first steps back-channel communication and many unofficial channels of communication, and only then passing to the official channels of communication.

But how could we transfer information resulting from scientific research and psychotherapeutic practice to the real world? Why, despite the efforts of generations of scholars, are we still witnessing a disconnection between knowledge and social applications? The aim of Cornelia E. Nauen's chapter, which homogenizes the experience arising from sustainable efforts in the field of international cooperation, is to try to establish a functional link between science and society, encouraging the construction of peace processes.

Another key issue is the constraints faced by politicians and negotiators. These often represent an insurmountable obstacle to peace negotiations. This topic is the central subject of Daniel Druckman's, Esra Çuhadar Gürkayanak's, Betul Celik's and Nimet Beriker's chapter. In particular, the authors focus their attention on the interaction between political decisions and processes of collective action, which may be, for better or for worse, decisive in promoting or destroying peace processes.

Viktor Kremenyuk, starting from the concept of "practical negotiator," focuses his attention on the description of an ideal model of negotiator that would better fit present and different times (compared even to the recent past). This means not being misled either by unfounded hopes or pessimistic temptations. The negotiation practice, in fact, even in light of recent studies, brings implications with it, which are not always taken into account by pure theorists.

Moreover, to focus on practical experiences, we have contributions from two cognitive psychotherapists who have experienced the plight of the war and the strenuous reconstruction modalities of acceptable political and interpersonal environments in two countries that suffered the most tragic consequences of failed peace negotiations: Serbia and Lebanon.

In Olivera Zikic's chapter the reader is conducted through the human experiences and the tragic consequences of the dissolution of former Yugoslavia from the perspective of a Serbian psychiatrist. The topics analyzed include: possibilities and failures of the prevention policy, management modalities of the conflict period and its consequences, and reconstruction processes.

In her chapter Aimee Karam highlights the opportunities arising from the use of cognitive psychotherapy techniques in negotiations following the acute phase of the war in Lebanon. She makes a careful analysis of some real episodes and frames the planning of possible further psychological interventions aimed at a concrete and peaceful rationalization of negotiation processes.

The possible political strategies for peace negotiations, in light of psychological processes outlined all along this book, are the subject of the study made by Mauro Galluccio, who after having reviewed the results achieved so far, outlines possible future scenarios. To make the chapter more readable and up-to-date, he critically examines some of US President Barack Obama's speeches, identifying strengths and weaknesses and proposing and advising actions oriented to "changing minds." From this analysis, the author derives a four-part operative model for peace negotiation, which includes: (a) awareness, (b) sustainability, (c) inclusiveness, and (d) balancing. Moreover, in the chapter there are some specifications of the elements needed for a functional and permanent training of leaders, politicians, and negotiators, which could constitute, empower, and systematically update their skills and abilities for understanding, communication, and negotiation.

The evaluation of the possibility of cognitive psychotherapy intervention in promoting peace concretely is presented in Francesco Aquilar's chapter, with respect to different units of analysis and intervention. Following in the footsteps of Albert Ellis (1992), he distinguishes three possible levels of action: (a) the construction of a peace attitude in individuals; (b) the social dissemination of some constructive modalities for peace, in order to structure and organize a cognitively based peace movement, which would be aware of the magnitude and seriousness of the variables involved (obvious, tacit or hidden); and (c) the training of politicians and negotiators who would be able to influence not only decisions and collective actions, but would also aim to constitute a public opinion that offers significant support to peace and to a motivated war deterrence and of ideologies that tend to produce war.

Finally, as editors, we will try to draw some conclusions from the analysis of the issues addressed, as well as identifying potential scenarios for an integrated application of the issues and strategies mentioned above.

In this way, we hope that the discussion on psychological and political strategies for peace negotiations, through a cognitive approach, is addressed from different points of view that are compatible and integrated. However, we need more specific research, and we know that other relevant aspects of international negotiation were not addressed on this occasion. However, we hope that the wide range of topics and issues addressed, which outlined some key components, could lead to a range of practical applications and operational suggestions for implementing peace processes. As soon as possible!

Francesco Aquilar
Center for Cognitive Psychology and Psychotherapy
Via Guido de Ruggiero 118
80128, Napoli, Italy
francescoaquilar@tiscali.it

Mauro Galluccio
European Association for Negotiation
and Mediation (EANAM)
Square Ambiorix 32/43
B-1000 Bruxelles, Belgium
mauro.galluccio@eanam.org

Acknowledgements

We wish to thank those who helped us most in the delicate phases of the conception, drafting, and implementation of this volume, with their original ideas, their critical suggestions, and their moral and material support: partners, relatives, and personal friends. Without them and their valuable contributions, this volume would never have been written.

We thank with affection and gratitude our colleagues of the Italian Association for Social and Cognitive Psychotherapy (AIPCOS) and of the European Association for Negotiation and Mediation (EANAM), who discussed, criticized, and improved our work with their comments and their input in the workshops and Training Groups that we have organized and done with them. Also a heartfelt thanks goes to the colleagues of the Italian Society of Behavioral and Cognitive Therapy (SITCC), the European Association for Behavioral and Cognitive Therapies (EABCT) and the International Association for Cognitive Psychotherapy (IACP), who have encouraged and supported our work, collaborating with enthusiasm on our project in the Working Groups and Symposia Congresses.

Special thanks go to Sharon Panulla at Springer Science+Business Media, who showed a continuing interest in our work from the start of our project. We valued her support for our efforts to promote pro-social collaboration between psychology, cognitive psychotherapy and political sciences. We are also grateful to her for accompanying us with competence, affection, efficiency, and professionalism throughout this creative, heuristic process.

Contents

Contributors

Nimet Beriker received her Ph.D. degree in Conflict Analysis and Resolution from George Mason University. She is an Associate Professor in the Conflict Analysis and Resolution Program at Sabanci University, Istanbul. Among her research interests we find international negotiation, mediation, conflict resolution, and foreign policy. Her publications appeared in several journals, and she often provides training on conflict resolution and negotiation to the Turkish Ministry of Foreign Affairs, the Turkish General Staff, local governments and NGO's.

Betül Çelik received her Ph.D. from the State University of New York at Binghamton. She is an Assistant Professor at Sabanci University in Istanbul, where she teaches Political Science and Conflict Resolution. Her research areas include ethnicity, civil society, forced migration, and post-conflict reconstruction and reconciliation. She has published several articles and an edited book on Turkey's Kurdish Question.

Frank M. Dattilio, Ph.D., ABPP, is a board certified clinical psychologist and marital and family therapist. He maintains a dual faculty position in the Department of Psychiatry at both Harvard Medical School and the University of Pennsylvania. Dr. Dattilio is one of the leading figures in the world on cognitive-behavioral therapy. He is the author of 250 professional publications, including 17 books. He is also the recipient of numerous state and national awards. His works have been translated into 28 languages and are used in 80 countries.

E. Thomas Dowd, Ph.D., ABPP, DSNAP is Professor of Psychology at Kent State University, USA, and Professor at the Postdoctoral International Institute for Advanced Studies of Psychotherapy and Applied Mental Health at Babes Bolyai University in Romania. He holds a board certification in Cognitive Behavioral Psychology and Counseling Psychology through the American Board of Professional Psychology and is a Fellow of the American Psychological Association in the divisions of International Psychology and Counseling Psychology. He has made numerous presentations in Europe, South America, and the Middle East. Dr. Dowd has been very active over the years in external professional governance. He currently serves as President of the American Board of Cognitive and Behavioral Psychology and President of the Behavioral and Cognitive Psychology Specialty Council.

Daniel Druckman is Professor of Public and International Affairs at the George Mason University and at the Australian Center for Peace and Conflict Studies at the University of Queensland in Brisbane, Australia. He has been the Vernon M. and Minnie I. Lynch Professor of Conflict Resolution at George Mason. He is also a member of the Faculty at the Sabanci University in Istanbul and has been a visiting professor at many universities around the world. Professor Druckman has published widely on topics like negotiating behavior, electronic mediation, nationalism and group identity, human performance, peacekeeping, political stability, nonverbal communication, and research methodology. He is the recipient of the 2003 Lifetime Achievement Award from the International Association of Conflict Management.

Guy Olivier Faure is Professor of Sociology at the Sorbonne University, Paris V, where he teaches International Negotiation, Conflict Resolution, and Strategic Thinking and Action. Professor Faure is a member of the editorial board of three major international journals dealing with negotiation theory and practice: *International Negotiation* (Washington), *Negotiation Journal* (Harvard) and *Group Decision and Negotiation* (New York). He is a member of the PIN Steering Committee (Program on International Negotiations) in Vienna, an international organization with 4,000 members, scholars, practitioners and diplomats. He has authored, co-authored and edited a dozen of books and over 80 articles, and his works have been published in twelve different languages. He is referenced in the *Diplomat's Dictionary* published by the United States Peace Press, in 1997. He is also quoted as one of the "2000 outstanding Scholars of the 21st century" by the International Biographical Center, Cambridge, UK.

Howard Gardner is the John H. and Elisabeth A. Hobbs Professor of Cognition and Education at the Harvard Graduate School of Education. He also holds positions as Adjunct Professor of Psychology at Harvard University and Senior Director of Harvard Project Zero. Among numerous honors, Professor Gardner received a MacArthur Prize Fellowship in 1981. He has received honorary degrees from 22 colleges and universities, including institutions in Ireland, Italy, Israel, Chile, and South Korea. In 2005 and again in 2008, he was selected by *Foreign Policy* and *Prospect* magazines as one of the 100 most influential public intellectuals in the world. The author of over 20 books translated into 27 languages, and several hundred articles, Professor Gardner is greatly known in the education society for his theory of multiple intelligences, a critique of the notion that there exists but a single human intelligence that can be assessed by standard psychometric instruments.

Paul Gilbert received his Ph.D. in Edinburgh in 1980 for his studies on depression. He is Professor of Clinical Psychology at the University of Derby and visiting Professor at the University of Fribourg (Switzerland) and Coimbra (Portugal). He has degrees in both Economics and Psychology. Professor Gilbert has conducted research in the areas of mood disorders, social anxiety and psychosis with a focus on evolutionary models and the nature of shame. He's been interested in working with people who have a very negative experience of self, are self-critical, and come from neglectful or hostile backgrounds. He recognized that many such people had experienced little compassion in their lives and found it difficult to be self-compassionate. Over the last 15 years he has been exploring various standard psychotherapy and Buddhist practices to develop an integrated therapeutic orientation to help people develop self-compassion, particularly those who are frightened of it. He was made Fellow of the British Psychological Society in 1992 and was President of the British Association for Behavioral and Cognitive psychotherapy in 2003. He has written 16 books and over 150 academic papers and book chapters.

Esra Çuhadar received her Ph.D. from Syracuse University. She is currently an Assistant Professor at the Department of Political Science in Bilkent University, Ankara. Her research interests include evaluation of peace-building initiatives and third party intervention processes, political psychology of inter-group conflicts, foreign policy decision-making, and track two diplomacy. She has published several journal articles and book chapters on these topics.

Aimée Karam received her Ph.D. in Clinical Psychology from St. Joseph University in Beirut, Lebanon. She is actually working as a Clinical Psychologist at the Medical Institute for Neuropsychological Disorders (MIND) in the Department of Psychiatry and Clinical Psychology at the St. George Hospital University Medical Center, Beirut, Lebanon. Dr. Karam is a member of the Academy of Cognitive Therapy (ACT) and the President of the Lebanese Society for Cognitive and Behavioral therapy. She is also a researcher and a member of IDRAAC (Institute for Development Research, Advocacy and Applied Care), an NGO specialized in Mental Health.

victor Kremenyuk is a Russian historian and political scientist. His area of academic interest is international relations, decision-making, and conflict management. He has published around 300 works in Russia and abroad: USA, UK, France, Germany, Sweden, as well as China, Lebanon, and India. Dr. Kremenyuk is a Deputy Director at the USA and Canada Studies Institute of the Russian Academy of Sciences, head of chair of World Politics and International Relations at the Moscow Human Sciences University, member of the Processes of International Negotiations (PIN) Program at the International Institute for Applied Systems Analysis (IIASA) in Austria. He has taught at the Salzburg Seminar for American Studies and Vienna Diplomatic Academy in Austria, NATO School at Oberammergau in Germany, NATO Defense College in Italy, as well as at several universities in Paris and Beirut. He is a winner of the Soviet National Prize for Science and Technology (1980), Russian Government Prize for Strategic Risk Analysis (2005) and other Russian and foreign awards.

Robert L. Leahy, Ph.D., is the Director of the American Institute for Cognitive Therapy, President of the Association for Behavioral and Cognitive Therapies, President of the International Association for Cognitive Psychotherapy, and Past-President of the Academy of Cognitive Therapy. Dr. Leahy is Clinical Professor of Psychology at the Department of Psychiatry of the Weill-Cornell University Medical College. He is the author or editor of 18 books, and he has been particularly interested in the application of cognitive therapy to understand therapeutic relationship, personality, and anxiety.

Donald Meichenbaum, Ph.D., is Distinguished Professor Emeritus at the University of Waterloo, Ontario, Canada. He is currently the Research Director of the Melissa Institute for Violence Prevention, Miami, Florida (www.melissainstitute.org). Dr. Meichenbaum is one of the founders of cognitive behavior therapy and in a survey of North American clinicians he was voted "One of the ten most influential psychotherapists of the twentieth century." He has consulted and presented in many countries, and his work on stress inoculation training and resiliency building is now focused on work with service members and their families (www.warfighterdiaries.com). He recently received a Lifetime Achievement Award from the Clinical Division of the American Psychological Association.

Angela N. Roberts Miller is currently pursuing a Ph.D. in Clinical Psychology, emphasis in Health Psychology, at Kent State University. She holds an M.A. in Clinical Psychology, also from Kent State, and a M.P.H. from Wichita State University. Her research focuses on the effects of the progression and treatment of chronic illness on neurocognitive function and adherence to complex medical protocols.

Cornelia E. Nauen received her Ph.D. from the University of Kiel, Germany. She is a trained marine ecologist and fisheries scientist. Dr. Nauen worked in international cooperation, first at the FAO, then in different departments of the European Commission of the European Union, currently as policy officer for scientific relations with South Africa. Among her research interests are peaceful transitions to sustainability, increasing the impact of international scientific cooperation, social dimensions of knowledge and its use in different societies with particular emphasis on restoration of healthy ecosystems.

Dean G. Pruitt received his Ph.D. in psychology from Yale University. He is Distinguished Scholar in Residence at the Institute for Conflict Analysis and Resolution at George Mason University and SUNY Distinguished Professor Emeritus at the University at Buffalo: State University of New York. He is Fellow of the American Psychological Association and the American Psychological Society and has received the Harold D. Lasswell Award for Distinguished Scientific Contribution to Political Psychology from the International Society of Political Psychology as well as the Lifetime Achievement Award from the International Association for Conflict Management. He is author or co-author of many books and more than 100 articles and chapters.

Carolyn Saarni received her Ph.D. from the University of California at Berkeley, specializing in developmental psychology. In 1980 she joined the Graduate Department of Counseling at Sonoma State University (California) where she trains prospective marriage and family therapists and school counselors. She is currently the Department Chair. Dr. Saarni's research has focused on children's emotional development. Her most important and influential work describes the development of specific skills of emotional competence that are contextualized by cultural values, beliefs about emotion, and assumptions about the nature of the relationship between the individual and the larger society. Her work has been published in many periodicals as well as in other edited volumes.

Olivera Zikic, MD, Ph.D., is a psychiatrist and cognitive behavior therapist. She works at the Department for Psychiatry of the Medical Faculty in the University of Nis as well as at the Clinic for Mental Health of the Clinical Center Nis. Dr. Zikic is one of the founders of the Serbian Association of Cognitive Behavior Therapists, and a founder of the journal *Psihologija Danas,* edited by the Association. She is also the establisher and one of the supervisors in cognitive behavior therapy education within this Association as well as Teaching Assistant at the Medical Faculty. Her promotion to Assistant Professor is currently in process. She is author and co-author of more than 80 papers.

About the Editors

Francesco Aquilar received his Dottore in Psicologia degree from the University of Rome, Italy. He is a psychologist and a cognitive-behavioral psychotherapist in private practice in Naples, Italy. Dr. Aquilar is the President of the Italian Association for Social and Cognitive Psychotherapy (AIPCOS), and Supervisor of the Italian Society for Behavioral and Cognitive Therapy (SITCC). For more than 15 years he has been a member of the Governing Body of the European Association for Behavioral and Cognitive Therapies (EABCT). He has more than 60 professional publications in the areas of anxiety disorders, eating disorders, marital and family discord, social psychology, and interpersonal negotiations, and has also given numerous international presentations on the cognitive-behavioral treatment of psychological problems and couple distress. Among his many publications, Dr. Aquilar is author of *Test psicologici e pubblicità* (Psychological testing and advertising, Rome 1982), *Riconoscere le emozioni* (Identifying emotions, Milan 2000), *Psicoterapia dell'amore e del sesso* (Psychotherapy for love and sex problems, Milan 2006a), *Le donne dalla A alla Z* (Women from A to Z, Milan 2006b); he is editor or coeditor of *La coppia in crisi: istruzioni per l'uso* (Couples in crisis: operating instructions, with S. Ferrante, Assisi 1994), *La coppia in crescita* (Couples in growth, Assisi 1996), *Psicoterapia delle fobie e del panico* (Psychotherapy for phobias and panic, with E. Del Castello, Milan 1998), *Psicoterapia dell'anoressia e della bulimia* (Psychotherapy for anorexia and bulimia, with E. Del Castello and R. Esposito, Milan 2005). He is co-author of *Psychological processes in international negotiations: theoretical and practical perspectives* (with M.Galluccio, New York, 2008).

Mauro Galluccio received his Ph.D. in Political Science from the Free University of Brussels, Belgium. He is the President of the European Association for Negotiation and Mediation (EANAM), based in Brussels. Dr. Galluccio studied for a long time in Italy and has a degree in both political sciences and psychological sciences and techniques for the persons and the community. He has given many speeches, presented numerous papers and symposia at international conferences and congresses on the subject of International Relations, with a particular interest in the application of cognitive-behavioral psychotherapy principles to the field of political sciences. As lecturer on behalf of the Directorate-General Communication of the European Commission he gives conferences to many international universities, enterprises, and national administrations from different countries. Dr. Galluccio has worked within the European institutional framework as political analyst and adviser. He was political coordinator at the Directorate-General of the European Commission for Development and Relations with African, Caribbean, and Pacific States. Previously he was Spokesman to the President of COPA and coordinator of the Crisis Management Unit at the COPA-COGECA. Among Dr. Galluccio's research interests are those on applied cognitive psychology and psychotherapy; interpersonal negotiations; specific training for negotiators and politicians; preventive diplomacy and conflict resolution; common foreign and security policy for the European Union; the European Union internal negotiation processes and institutional external communication. He is co-author of *Psychological Processes in International Negotiations: Theoretical and Practical Perspectives* (with F. Aquilar, New York, 2008).

Chapter 1
Changing Minds: How the Application of the Multiple Intelligences (MI) Framework Could Positively Contribute to the Theory and Practice of International Negotiation

Howard Gardner

Mind Changing

Two Instances of Mind Changing

On a bus trip in upstate New York, writer Nicholson Baker fantasized about how he might furnish his apartment. He thought about an imaginative way in which to seat people: He would purchase and install rows of yellow forklifts and orange backhoes throughout his apartment (A backhoe is an excavating machine in which a bucket is tied rigidly to a hinged stick and can be pulled toward the machine). Visitors could sit either on the kinds of buckets used in excavating backhoes or the slings hanging between the forks of the forklifts. Finding whole vision quite intriguing, he began to calculate how many forklifts the floor in his apartment would sustain. But when his thoughts turned again to this exotic form of furnishing some years later, Baker reflected, "I find that, without my knowledge, I have changed my mind. I no longer want to live in an apartment furnished with forklifts and backhoes.... Yet I did not experience during the intervening time a single uncertainty or pensive moment in regard to a backhoe" (p. 5, 1982). Baker uses this experience to ponder a topic that has come to engage my own curiosity: What happens when we change our minds? Baker suggests that seldom will a single argument change our minds about anything really interesting or important. And he attempts to characterize the kinds of significant mind changing that he seeks to understand: "I don't want the story of the feared-but-loved teacher, the book that hit like a thunderclap, the years of severe study followed by a visionary background, the clench of repentance:

H. Gardner (✉)
Hobbs Professor of Cognition and Education,
Harvard Graduate School of Education, 13 Appian Way,
Longfellow Hall 224A, Cambridge, MA 02138
e-mail: howard@pz.harvard.edu

F. Aquilar and M. Galluccio (eds.), *Psychological and Political Strategies for Peace Negotiation*, DOI 10.1007/978-1-4419-7430-3_1,

I want each sequential change of mind in its true, knotted, clotted, viny multifariouness, with all of the color streams of intelligence still tapped on and flapping in the wind" (p. 9).

The phrase "to change one's mind" is so common that we may assume its meaning to be self-evident. After all, our mind is in state 1 – we have a certain opinion, view, perspective, belief; some kind of mental operation is performed; and, lo and behold, the mind is now in state 2. Yet clear as this figure of speech may seem on superficial consideration, the phenomenon of changing minds is one of the least examined and – I would claim – least well understood of familiar human experiences. In this essay I outline my theory of mind changing, and suggest how it may relate to earlier work on the theory of multiple intelligences.

To complement the idiosyncratic example introduced by Nicholson Baker, let's consider change of mind that many individuals have experienced over the years. From early childhood, most of us have operated under the following assumption: When we are confronted with some kind of task, we should work as hard as we are able and devote approximately equal time to each part of that task. According to this 50–50 principle, if we have to learn a piece of music, or master a new game, or fill out some role at home or at work, we should be sure to spread our effort equally across the various components.

Early in the century, the Italian economist and sociologist Vilfredo Pareto put forth a proposition that has come to be known as the 80/20 rule. As explained by Richard Koch in a charming book (*The 80/20 Principle* 1998), one can in general accomplish most of what one wants – perhaps up to 80% of the target – with a modest amount of effort – perhaps only 20%. One must be judicious about where one places one's efforts, and alert to "tipping points" that abruptly bring a goal within (or beyond!) reach. One should, defying common sense, avoid the temptation to inject equal amounts of energy into every part of a task, problem, project, or hobby; or to lavish equal amounts of attention on every employee, every friend, or every worry.

Why should anyone believe the apparently counterintuitive 80/20 Principle? Studies show that in most businesses, about 80% of the profits come from 20% of the products that are offered to the public. Clearly it makes sense to devote resources to the profitable products while dropping the losers. In most businesses, the top workers produce far more than their share of profits; thus one should reward the high producers while trying to ease out the unproductive ones. Complementing this notion, 80% of the trouble in a workforce characteristically comes from a small number of troublemakers – who should promptly be excised from the company. The same ratio applies to customers; the best customers or clients account for most of the profits. The 80/20 Principle even crops up in current events. According to *The New York Times* (Moss 2001), 20% of baggage screeners at airports account for 80% of the mistakes.

It seems, then, that even if you have never before heard of the 80/20 Principle, it is worth taking seriously. And yet, what would it take for a person actually to change her mind, and begin to act on the basis of that principle? Would it be the same factors that persuaded Nicholson Baker that he did not, after all, want to furnish his apartment with forklifts and backhoes? And how do these forms of mind changing compare to other instances – for example, a person changing his political allegiance, a therapist affecting the self-concept of a patient, a teacher educating her classroom, a chief executive office altering the employees' understanding of their business, or a political leader catalyzing a change of attitudes or loyalties in a population?

To begin to answer these questions, one should take three steps. First, one needs to introduce a way of thinking about the human mind. Second, one needs to identify a set of factors that, individually or jointly, are likely to effect a mind change. Finally, one should apply this explanatory apparatus to a range of examples. To these steps I now turn.

The Forms and Contents of the Human Mind

Let me begin by invoking the psychologist's term "mental representation." A mental representation is any kind of thought, idea, image, or proposition about which a person can think. Needless to say, all of our minds are filled with all manner of mental representations. Indeed, our thinking *is* the ensemble of our mental representations. Some of these representations – such as our name, the identity of our relatives, the location of the North Star, the multiplication tables – remain pretty much the same once they have become consolidated. Other representations – the daily weather, our friendship networks, the condition of the stock market, the nature of relations between the United States and Russia, or Iraq and Iran – change from time to time.

Each of these representations has content. Roughly speaking, the content is the propositional information that can be captured in ordinary language, or in some other widely accepted symbol system. We can express our name or the names of our friends in spoken or written (or signed) language. We can express the location of the North Star on a map of the nighttime sky; we can draw a family tree; we can graph the ups and downs of the stock market. Often we remember content (such as the plot of or the public reaction to a film) without being certain where or how we assimilated that content.

Some contents are strongly associated with a particular mode of presentation. For example, anthropologists have created kinship trees in order to reflect the relations that obtain among members of a clan. Meteorologists have developed weather charts that they use in their own work and feature in the newspaper or on television. But most contents can be presented or represented in a variety of formats or forms. If we were to ask individuals about the location of the North Star, one person might draw a picture; another might describe its location with reference to the Big Dipper; another with reference to the Little Dipper or Cassiopeia or Pegasus; still others would consult a map of the sky, or go to a telescope, or look it up in the dictionary, an encyclopedia, or astronomy book; and some might actually wait till the evening, walk around their garden with their head tilted up, and search for a particularly luminous celestial body. One person might refer to Polaris, a second to the star closest to the north celestial pole. The content remains the same; the form in which it is presented differs markedly from one person to another. And of course, the same person – or the same reader – is capable of thinking about (or, if you prefer, just thinking) the North Star in a variety of alternative ways or formats.

Let's apply the distinction between content and form to my two opening examples. In the case of Pareto's principle, the 80/20 Principle can be stated in a straightforward way: One can accomplish 80% of one's goals using a mere 20% of effort. However, the ways in which individuals might represent this principle for themselves or others are varied. Some might put it into words, as I have just done; others would present it as a chart or graph; others would view it in terms of mathematical equations, the way that Pareto stated it; still others would embody it in a vivid example, such as firing most of the staff in a firm, or pushing only a few best selling items in a store, or rearranging one's stock portfolio so that only the most profitable items are maintained or monitored. A variety of forms or representations all convey the same general idea.

In the case of Baker's hypothetical furnishing of his apartment, we have only his brief verbal description to go by. But that very terseness provides a rich opportunity for each of Baker's readers to create his or her own mental representation – which would include calculating how many forklifts would be sustained by the floor. In my own case, I am color-blind and have scant visual imagery, so I retain mostly the verbal traces of what he has written (I had to look up "backhoe" in an unabridged dictionary and was disappointed that there was no drawing). However, it is evident that other readers, with richer and more colorful visual imagery, could create a quite vivid picture in their own minds. For some, the picture would be static, for others quite dramatic. For some, the chairs would occupy only a small part of the apartment, for others, the chairs would dominate the scene like stools in a kindergarten class or rows in a Broadway auditorium. Some would experience the feeling of sitting in one of these chairs, or of it pushing back and forth, or relaxing in it, as in a hammock. And for all I know, some individuals would create scenes that are complete with cuisine, background music, and a collection of desired friends or befuddled strangers strewn across the living room.

Seven Mind Changers

If one wants to think about mind change in the manner of a psychologist or cognitive scientist, one must first posit an initial state – for example, a 50–50 principle or an ordinary apartment with plush padded chairs or plain bridge chairs. Then one has to posit some kind of mental operation upon that initial representation. Finally, one has to posit a final state or at least an altered second state: In the above cases, an 80–20 principle, or an apartment furnished with forklifts and backhoes. In any particular case, the mind change could be brought about by a fluke: In Nicholson Baker's phrase, it could involve "sudden conversions and wrenching insights." My own studies have suggested that the likelihood of mind change is determined by seven factors – and it happens, conveniently, that each of these mind-changing factors begins with the letters RE. I will introduce each factor and indicate how it might figure in our two opening examples.

1. *Reason*: Especially among those who deem themselves to be educated, the use of reason figures heavily in matters of belief. A rational approach involves identification of relevant factors, weighing each in turn, making an overall assessment. Reason can involve sheer logic, use of analogies, creation of taxonomies. Faced with a decision about how to furnish his apartment, Nicholson Baker might come up with a list of pros and cons before reaching a judgment. Encountering the 80/20 Principle for the first time, an individual guided by rationality would attempt to identify all of the relevant considerations and weigh them proportionately: Such a procedure would help him to determine whether to subscribe to the 80/20 Principle in general, and whether to apply it in a particular instance.
2. *Research*: Complementing the use of argument is the collection of relevant data. Those with scientific training can proceed in a systematic manner, perhaps even using statistical tests to verify promising trends. But research need not be formal – it need only entail the identification of relevant cases and a judgment about whether they warrant a change of mind. Writer Baker might conduct formal or informal research on the costs of various materials and on the opinions of those who would be likely to sit in his newly furnished apartment. A manager who has been exposed to the 80/20 Principle might study whether its claims – for example, those about sales figures or difficult employees – are in fact borne out on her watch. Naturally, to the extent that the research confirms the 80/20 Principle, it is more likely to guide behavior and thought.
3. *Resonance*: Reason and research appeal to the cognitive aspects of the human mind; resonance denotes the affective component. A view or idea or perspective resonates to the extent that it feels right to an individual, seems to fit the current situation, and leads to the conclusion that further considerations need not be taken into account. It is possible, of course, that resonance follows upon the use of reason and/or research; but it is equally possible that the fit occurs at an unconscious level, and that the resonant intuition actually conflicts with the more sober considerations of Rational Man or Woman. To the extent that the move to forklifts and backhoes resonates for him, Nicholson Baker may proceed with the redecoration. To the extent that 80/20 comes to feel like a better approach than 60/40 or 50/50, it is likely to be adopted by a decision maker in an organization.
4. *Representational redescriptions*: The fourth factor sounds technical, but the intuition is simple. A change of mind becomes convincing to the extent that it lends itself to representation in a number of different forms, with these forms reinforcing one another. I noted above that it is possible to present the 80/20 Principle in a number of different ways; by the same token, as I've shown, a group of individuals can readily come up with different mental versions of Baker's proposed furnishings. Particularly when it comes to matters of formal instruction – as occurs at school or in a formal training program – the potential for expressing the desired lesson in many compatible formats is crucial.
5. *Resources and rewards*: In the cases discussed so far, the possibilities for mind changing lie within the reach of any individual whose mind is open. Sometimes, however, mind change is more likely to occur when considerable resources can

be drawn on. Suppose, say, that an enterprising interior decorator decides to give Baker all of the materials that he needs at cost, or even for free. The opportunity to redecorate at little cost may tip the balance. Or suppose that a philanthropist decides to bankroll a nonprofit agency that pledges to adapt the 80/20 Principle in all of its activities. Again, the balance might tip. Looked at from the psychological perspective, the provision of resources is an instance of positive reinforcement. Individuals are being rewarded for one course of behavior and thought rather than the other. Ultimately, however, unless the new course of thought is concordant with other criteria – reason, resonance, representational redescription – it is unlikely to last beyond the provision of resources.

Two others factors also influence mind changing, but in ways somewhat different from those outlined so far.

6. *Real world events*: Sometimes, an event occurs in the broader society that affects a great many individuals, not just those who are considering a mind change. Examples are wars, hurricanes, terrorist attacks, economic depressions – or, on a more positive side, eras of peace and prosperity, the availability of medical treatments that prevent illness or lengthen life, the ascendancy of a benign leader or group. An economic depression could nullify Baker's plans for refurnishing his apartment, even as a long era of prosperity could usher it in easily (He could even purchase a second "experimental" flat!). Legislation could also impact policies like the 80/20. It is conceivable that a law could be passed (say, in Singapore) that would permit or mandate special bonuses for workers who are unusually productive, while deducting wages from those who are unproductive. Such legislation would push businesses toward adopting an 80/20 Principle, even in eras where they had been following a more conventional course.
7. *Resistances*: The factors identified so far can all aid in an effort to change minds. However, the existence of only facilitating factors is unrealistic. Indeed, one of the paradoxes of mind changing is this: While it is easy, natural, to change one's mind in the first years of life, it becomes very difficult to alter one's mind as the years pass. The reason, in brief, is that we develop many strong views and perspectives that are resistant to change. Any effort to understand the changing of minds must take into account the power of various resistances. Such resistances make it easy for Nicholson Baker to retain his current pattern of apartment furnishing, and for most of us to adhere to a 50/50 principle, even after the advantages of 80/20 division of labor have been made manifest.

Without saying so explicitly, I have suggested the formula for mind changing. To the extent that the first five factors all weigh in one direction, the "real world" factors are held constant, and the resistances are not too powerful, mind change is likely to happen. It can come about even when the weights on both sides of the scale are more equally balanced. On the other hand, to the extent that most of the first five factors are aligned against change, or the resistances are very powerful, or the "real world" does not cooperate, status quo is likely to prevail.

Levels of Analysis

I have now outlined a general framework for the analysis of mind changes. But mind changes occur at all levels of a society and involve a great variety of individuals and conditions. Can we go beyond a simple assertion that mind changing entails these set of seven or so factors?

I believe that the answer to this question is a qualified "yes." Mind changing occurs at a number of different levels of analysis. As a rough approximation, the first five factors are associated, respectively, with these different levels. In contrast, the latter two factors are wild cards: they can occur with equal probability at any level and to any degree.

Let me unpack this claim. Mind change can occur with respect to entities ranging from a single solitary individual to a whole nation or even the whole planet. While each of the aforementioned factors can be brought to bear on any entity, a rough association obtains between level and factors.

Within an Individual Mind

One of the most dramatic examples in the America of the 20th century involved the writer and intellectual Whittaker Chambers. Chambers began his life as a rather conservative individual from an impoverished and dysfunctional family. As a result of his studies and travels, he became attracted to left wing politics. Ultimately in the early 1930s, he became an active member of the Communist party. After a wrenching analysis, he reluctantly broke from the party in the late 1930s; and a decade later, he famously accused the public servant Alger Hiss of having been a communist. The resulting trial of Hiss brought both fame and obloquy upon Chambers and affected the views of communism held by many Americans. We find that factors of Reason and Research are potent when we examine mind changes that occur within individuals: Whittaker Chambers, who abandoned communism; physicist Andrei Sakharov, who first developed the hydrogen bomb and then became an advocate of peace; the anthropologist Lucien Levy Bruhl and the philosopher Wittgenstein, who renounced theories that they had developed earlier in their lives.

One Individual Affecting the Mind of Another

A principal goal of psychotherapy is to change the thoughts and behaviors of the patient. The psychoanalyst Erik Erikson engaged in the successful treatment of a young seminarian whose development had been stunted because of difficulties in forming a coherent identity. In a dramatic session of dream analysis, Erikson was able to depict to the seminarian the sources of incoherence in his life and to suggest a way in which to bring these elements together productively. The analysis given by Erikson resonated with the young seminarian, and a course of healing commenced.

An unsuccessful example of mind changing occurred when newly appointed Harvard President Lawrence Summers sought to convince star Professor Cornel West to alter his course of behavior. At issue, according to various reports, were the quality of West's scholarship, his involvement in extra-campus activities, and his grading policies. Summers wanted West to set an example for high-profile professors but instead he alienated West, who soon decided to relocate to Princeton University. Summers sought to use rational arguments but these did not resonate with West, who construed them as an effort to denigrate him and his scholarship. Mind changing across two individuals, or within a family, rarely rests on purely rational factors; Resonance proves crucial.

Teaching and Training

Whether in a classroom, or at a place of work, the purpose of instruction is to change the minds of those who are being educated. At special premium here is the potential to express the lesson or message in a number of different congenial and complementary formats. It is easy to state and memorize the principles of natural selection in biology or the laws of thermodynamics in physics. But to understand these scientific laws deeply, the student must be able to represent them in a number of ways and discern them at work in the laboratory and/or in the world. By the same token, any supervisor or trainer can put into words a new mission or mode of operation in a business. But the success of the new regime is likely to depend on the capacity of the firm to reinforce the message by capturing it in a number of powerful formats – ranging from the "live" models provided by leaders to effective video presentations. Such Representational redescriptions, when present throughout the day and throughout the place of work, can prove crucial in helping workers to assimilate the desired message.

Mind Change in the Political Sphere

For the most part, changes of mind within a population occur quite gradually. However, one can point to occasions when a major change of mind has occurred within a relatively brief sphere of time. One such example is the movement under the leadership of Prime Minister Margaret Thatcher from socialist to market beliefs in Great Britain during the last quarter of the 20th century. Other instructive examples include the transition from an apartheid to a democratic society in South Africa under the leadership of Nelson Mandela; and the birth and recent growth of the

European Union as catalyzed by the French economist Jean Monnet. Without detracting from the charisma and mastery of the individuals involved, such mind change is facilitated when appreciable resources are available. These resources can be financial – the support of wealthy individuals groups, or nations; they can also involve personal traits – the willingness of key individuals to risk their livelihood or even their lives in order to support a course in which they believe (social or human capital).

Mind Change in the Cultural Sphere

Some of the most powerful changes of mind occur almost invisibly, far from the corridors of power. Consider the changes in political thought brought about by the writings of Karl Marx; or the changes in our understanding of the human psyche wrought by Sigmund Freud; the changes in our understanding of the physical world brought about by Albert Einstein or in our understanding of the natural world by Charles Darwin; or the changes in our artistic sensibilities wrought early in the 20th century by Pablo Picasso, Martha Graham, Igor Stravinsky, and Virginia Woolf, just to mention a single representative from the four major art forms. These changes begin with a crucial set of changes in the mind of the individual creator. These new perspectives are then captured in various symbolic forms in the arts, sciences, or policy analysis. If successful, the mind of informed individuals will have been irrevocably altered for posterity by the creations of these individual geniuses.

How does such mind change occur? Fundamentally, as the result of a competition between earlier entrenched views of society, psyche, the external world, the world of the imagination, on the one hand, and these new and initially jarring views, on the other. Just because these changes are ultimately so pervasive and powerful, it is likely that they draw upon the full range of propelling factors – including real world events – even as they must overcome some of the most powerful resistances.

Real World Interventions

When George W. Bush took office in January 2001 there was little reason to think that he would be a transformational leader. Until the age of 40, he had coasted through life, benefiting mostly from the connections with family and family friends; and as Governor of Texas, he had consistently compromised with his political adversaries. However, the events of September 11, 2001, had an enormous impact on Bush. Not only did his presidency had a mission – the defeat of terrorism. But he was propelled into a position of world leadership, induced to master many complex issues, and to become his own person and principal decision maker in the sphere of foreign affairs. It seems reasonable to assume that the changes in George Bush were brought about chiefly by powerful and inherently unpredictable events in the external world.

Resistances

Were our minds blank slates, it would be very easy to alter them. One would simply present the new and desired content, in one or more formats, and wait for that content to take. However, from a very early age, all of us human beings develop quite powerful representations. Some of these are correct and serviceable; some are inaccurate but charming; but all too many are fundamentally erroneous and yet difficult to change. And with every passing year, these early conceptions, theories, representations become more consolidated. No wonder it is difficult to teach new tricks to an old dog.

Like real world events, resistances are genuine factors with which the agents of mind change must contend. No magic formula or spray exists to remove them. Indeed, it is advisable to identify the resistances, to allow them to be expressed, and to take them seriously. Ultimately mind change involves a struggle between the old and the new representations, with the old representations often containing powerful resistances. The potency of these resistances most not be underestimated; yet the fact that mind change does occur, at all the levels and units identified, means that these resistances are not omnipotent.

And what of our own minds? No one is in complete control of how his or her mind changes or remains the same. There is some truth to the adage that, like the proverbial lightbulb, it is advisable for us to want to change and to be aware of the factors that propel or inhibit change. And by the same token, if we wish to change the minds of others – be it a single family member, a class, a company, or an entire culture – it is helpful to have some mastery of the facilitating and the inhibitory forces. As for this essay, my primary goal has been to open up your mind to the fascinating puzzles of mind changing – and to move "mind change" from an assumed but poorly understood phenomenon to one what should not be taken for granted but that can benefit from study and elucidation. As for the particular taxonomy introduced here, it will prove useful for individuals who resonate to that kind of account; and it will stimulate those who prefer to resist it.

Multiple Intelligences Framework

If one is concerned with mind changing in the real world, then it is useful to have a working notion of the mind – its development and its organization. In earlier work I developed the theory of multiple intelligences. (Gardner 1983/2004; Gardner 2006). Briefly stated, the theory is a critique of the notion that the mind is a single, all purpose computer – and that the power of the computer is measured by an individual's general intelligence. Rather, I claim that the mind is better thought of as a number of relatively independent computational devices, which I call the "multiple intelligences." The intelligences include linguistic, logical-mathematical, spatial, musical, bodily-kinesthetic, naturalistic, interpersonal and intrapersonal intelligences. There may also be a ninth intelligence – the intelligence of "big questions – which

I term "existential intelligence." Each of us possesses the several intelligences, but we differ in our profiles of intelligence. Thus one individual might be strong in linguistic and interpersonal intelligence, while another might exhibit comparable strength in spatial and musical intelligences. Anyone concerned with changing minds ought to be aware of the spectrum of intelligences, and bear them in mind as they/we seek to change minds on issues of consequence.

International Negotiation and Multiple Intelligences Framework

The international political world is extraordinarily complex, incoherent, and changing. International negotiations seem to provide eminent examples of structural uncertainty (Aquilar and Galluccio 2008; Galluccio 2007). It could be interesting to understand how negotiators could better face this uncertain environment. I think that certainly Multiple Intelligences (MI) theory and practice could help to negotiate in the uncertainty. As noted, MI theory asserts that individuals have many different cognitive faculties. We all possess the range of faculties, or intelligences, but no two of us have exactly the same profile. That is, no two persons, not even identical twins, have exactly the same strengths and the same weaknesses. Of course, on the one hand, this makes negotiation difficult, because we can't assume that everyone thinks about things in the way that we do. On the other hand, it can also be a sign of hope. Because if one approach does not work, we are free to try other ones, and to put the approaches together in novel ways – and perhaps ultimately a fresh and generative solution will emerge. Indeed, the most impressive breakthroughs in negotiation – for example, when an apparent logjam is broken – occur when someone thinks outside the box.

It also seems evident that in situations when leading nations are locked in a direct confrontation with a counterpart they consider potentially dangerous, there is a tendency to adopt very cautious attitudes and behaviors. That is what happened in the Cuban Missile crisis of 1962 when President Kennedy deliberately tried to give his Soviet counterpart more time to react, and chose a less aggressive, but still effective, course of action. In the end, Robert advised his brother, the President, to ignore Khrushchev's second, more belligerent message and just respond to his first, more conciliatory one. We are not concerned just with individual and group outcomes of cooperation and competition but also with the social psychological processes that would give rise to these outcomes. In a way we could help to better frame international decision-making processes, because social psychological processes take into account the very different assumptions that may be made from different cultural backgrounds or with different socialization experiences. Sensitivity to these differences can be crucial. If President George W. Bush had responded seriously and sensitively to the literary overtures from President Ahmedinejad of Iran, rather than ignoring them and ridiculing them, he might have improved the chances for a genuine dialogue. But Bush was unable to take seriously the very different background and orientation of this less-well-educated and less-diplomatic Islamic leader. Like many arrogant leaders, Bush expected everyone to adjust to his style.

In these cases, third parties could be used to prevent conflicts from becoming destructive or to help deadlocked or embittered negotiators move toward a more constructive management of their conflicts. People can be educated to manage their conflicts more constructively. The whole idea behind involving a third party is that he/she does not have a stake in a particular outcome, but just in an outcome that is acceptable to both parties. The third party is more likely to be able to think outside the box, as above described.

It is important to understand why ethnic, religious, and identity conflicts frequently take an intractable, destructive course. How applicable in other cultural contexts are the theories related to conflict that have largely been developed in the USA and Western Europe. Theory and practice of MI have a role to play in cross-cultural negotiations. Individuals from different cultural backgrounds can bring quite different considerations to the table. Only diplomats with an anthropological–psychological frame of mind, who are able to understand issues from a very different perspective, are likely to be successful under these circumstances. A dosage of Lawrence of Arabia would be welcome for almost all negotiators – just as less George W. Bush narcissism would have been a boon to negotiation. Western and US perspectives often get in the way, particularly when they lead to a feeling of triumphalism, as has been particularly the case with the USA in the last years.

MI theory could help to undermine entrenched habits in the negotiation context. The most important intelligences for negotiation are the personal intelligences and the existential intelligence. Interpersonal intelligence involves an understanding of other persons, groups, perspectives – it is the most crucial capacity for negotiation. But also crucial is intrapersonal intelligence – an understanding of yourself, your goals, your anxieties, the traps into which you may fall, and how best to avoid them. Finally, existential intelligence involves an appreciation of the fact that most individuals are interested in answers to the most important questions of life. Whenever a statesman, politician, diplomat, or negotiator can help parties feel that he/she is responsive to the issues that truly matter to them, then progress is possible. Nelson Mandela has understood that lesson, probably better than anyone else alive on the planet. Jimmy Carter has also been sensitive to these issues, though he seems to have lost patience and/or judgment in recent years.

Another important intelligence is that of linguistic intelligence, crucial when individuals speak the same language, and nuances can be invoked. But when translation is needed, then language is a weak reed on which to build – and other, less linguistic means (like maps, numbers, perhaps metaphors) are needed. Chinese Prime Minister Zhou en Lai was a great diplomat because he could get points across, even when there was not a common language.

The best way to connect with other persons in a negotiation is to listen carefully and with an open mind. In the Middle East negotiations, only the rare persons with this capacity – Anwar Sadat, Yitzhak Rabin – made progress. Yassir Arafat failed because he was too interested in listening to himself and not enough to those on the other side of the negotiating table – that is, assuming he wanted some kind of resolution. The same was true for Ariel Sharon, except perhaps at the very end of his prime-ministership. Bill Clinton tried hard, but was not able to break the stalemate, perhaps because time ran out.

Cognitive processes and emotions can interact, inadvertently causing negotiators to process information in a way that will lead to either negative or positive spirals and avoid escalation (Aquilar and Galluccio 2008). MI may help in breaking out destructive negative spirals in giving to the parties' new and different motivations. MI theory is valuable because it insists that, in a negotiation, one pay attention to the emotional tone and tenor of an exchange. Individuals with this kind of sensitivity know when to ask for a break or an adjournment, when to press on for an agreement, when to change the tone. Apparently Tony Blair was able to do this with the Northern Ireland negotiations. Lyndon Johnson was also brilliant at this in the US senate, but it did not rescue him in the case of the Vietnam War, where he was locked into the Cold War ways of thinking and assumed that all Communist nations were marching to the same drummer.

A MI training for negotiators could be based on scenarios and exercises, to increase the strength, the predisposition to use, and the cooperation among intrapersonal, interpersonal, and linguistic intelligences of participants. I would not speak about training the intelligences per se. That is like training individual muscles, rather than the skills needed to succeed in athletics or dance. In negotiation one needs to train individuals to listen carefully, to put oneself in the place of the other, to be patient, to have a sense of the emotional tone and direction of the interchange, to respond to the biggest and deepest (existential) concerns of all involved. Of course, these different skills draw on different intelligences. But the challenge for the trainer is to improve the skills, not to obsess about which particular intelligences are being used. Put differently, the intelligences are a convenient categorical system, helpful to me and to many others (Chen et al. 2009). But at the end of the day, we want the skills to be enhanced, and we don't really care whether it is intelligence #1, or intelligence #8 at work. That is, often the same skill can be acquired and nurtured using different intelligences or combinations of intelligences.

MI framework may help to overcome cognitive egocentrism and communicative egocentrism. Egocentrism or narcissism is of course a huge obstacle to any dilemma, and particularly one involving "buy in" from other persons (Aquilar and Galluccio 2008). MI theory is helpful in two ways. First, of course, the more one learns to read, listen to, and understand others, the better. But second, and equally important, is simply the recognition that not all individuals think the way that you do, and that makes them neither better nor worse, just different. Like a good therapist, the skilled negotiator learns about the different typologies of humans, keeps them in the background, does not label them explicitly, and draws on that knowledge to make the optimal move, given a particular, in a particular situation seated on the opposite side of the table. In other words, the good negotiator displays a respectful mind (see Gardner 2007).

References

Aquilar, F., & Galluccio, M. (2008). *Psychological processes in international negotiations: Theoretical and practical perspectives*. New York: Springer.

Baker, N. (1982). Changes of mind. In Baker, N. (1996). The size of thoughts: Essays and other lumber. Random House, New York: pp. 5–9.

Chen, J.-Q., Moran, S., & Gardner, H. (2009). *Multiple Intelligences around the world*. Jossey Bass, San Francisco.

Galluccio, M. (2007, July). *Cognitive psychotherapy and international negotiation: An overview*. Paper presented at the V World Congress of Behavioural and Cognitive Therapies (WCBCT), Barcelona, Spain,July 2007.

Gardner, H. (1983/2004). *Frames of mind: The theory of multiple intelligences*. New York: Basic Books.

Gardner, H. (2006). *Multiple intelligences: The theory in practice*. Basic Books New York.

Gardner, H. (2007). *Five minds for the future*. Harvard Business School Practice Boston.

Koch, R. (1998). *The 80/20 principle: The secrets of achieving more with less*. Currency New York.

Moss, M. (2001, November 23). A nation challenged: Airport security. US Airport task force begins with hiring. *New York Times*.

Chapter 2
International Negotiations, Evolution, and the Value of Compassion

Paul Gilbert

Introduction

Conflicts occur in all aspects of life, even genes compete for expression. Human conflicts tend to follow archetypal themes. Like other animals we battle over resources and access to resources, power and status, and sexual opportunities. Many of our human motivational systems have evolved over many millions of years and are key drivers for the emotional urgency by which we pursue conflicts, seek to gain an advantage or subdue or even destroy competitors. Around 2 million years ago a species leading to humans began to evolve capacities for high level cognitive processing which eventually gave us opportunities to pursue our motivational systems in totally new ways. Whereas animals may fight and think about getting revenge humans can use their intelligence to manipulate the minds of others, called them to war, and focus resources and scientific efforts to the building of the most destructive weapons. Humans like other animals are also a highly tribal species and intergroup and intertribal conflicts are extremely easy to stimulate. When this happens we have certain kinds of mindsets. These mindsets are mostly about seeking an advantage in some way, so that the powerful always dominate the week. In contrast compassion focuses on the plight of the weak, with a desire to improve their life situation and facilitate justice and fairness We can contextualise International Negotiations as part of the process by which different archetypes are playing out their dramas for competitive edge or compassionate engagement. This chapter will explore these dynamics in detail and argue that facilitating compassion in international negotiations probably requires us to recognise, the complex archetypal dramas we are trapped in, and the need for international law and third-party independent arbitration of conflicts.

There can be little doubt that while humans are capable of great compassion they are also capable of callous indifference to the injustices and suffering of others, and of perpetuating horrendous cruelty (Gilbert 2009). Part of the reason for this is the way our brains have evolved and now operate. Basically we now know that our

P. Gilbert (✉)
Mental Health Research Unit, Kingsway Hospital, DERBY DE22 3LZ, UK
e-mail: p.gilbert@derby.ac.uk

F. Aquilar and M. Galluccio (eds.), *Psychological and Political Strategies for Peace Negotiation*, DOI 10.1007/978-1-4419-7430-3_2,

brain is made up of different motive systems and processing competencies that do not always work well together (Ornstein 1986), and we can go into different states of mind where we think and feel quite differently (Carter 2008). Different patterns of brain functioning get activated as we engage with our environments. One brain pattern can make another unavailable. So, for example, it is difficult to be anxious and relaxed at the same time or vengeful and loving. It seems relatively easy to love our own children in the morning and bomb someone else's in the afternoon. It can be hard to see one's enemies, whom we see as a threat, as also human beings requiring basic justice and compassion – the current Middle East conflict shows this most tragically and clearly. It's because we have a brain that creates these states of mind, and can become so intent on pursuing its own selfish, defensive, retaliatory and group-focused goals, that negotiators, arbitrators, and other mediators are so vital for the pursuit of peace and justice in the world.

So the call to compassion must start with a reality check that not only places the brain, and the social contexts in which it operates, central to our understanding of how conflicts emerge and can be resolved, but also the enormity and urgency of the tasks before us. The reasons are not hard to articulate. While diseases and famines haunt the Earth, causing immense suffering, some of the greatest suffering is perpetrated by humans on other humans. Over the last few thousand years humans have been responsible for many billions of deaths through wars and have spent many trillions of dollars inventing and trading in weapons. Some nations have crippled their economies in a race to purchase arms. As a result of long-running tribal conflicts in various parts of the world, and particularly at present in North Africa, there are millions of displaced people, subjected to atrocities and suffering starvation. It is estimated that the USA alone has spent over $600 billion on the Iraq war – which as one commentator noted, is over $121,000 per person, and at that rate it would have been better just to bribe everyone! The cost in human misery is tragic with varying estimates of loss of life, but some put at over 700,000 (over 2.5% of the population) – (http://en.wikipedia.org/wiki/Lancet_surveys_of_casualties_of_the_Iraq_War). Unknown numbers have been maimed for life, losing limbs and senses, and whole sections of society have been traumatized, left with deep psychological and mental health problems, thrown into grief, not to mention resentment. In the wake of wars many anti-personnel mines are scattered like confetti waiting for children yet to be born to have limbs blown off, and whole areas can become uninhabitable.

Failure of negotiations to reduce, contain or resolve conflicts that lead to group violence (war) also sets the contextual conditions for humans (especially those actually doing the fighting) to enter into barbaric and cruel states of mind. From these flow mass raping, cutting off the limbs of children, forcing one's enemies to batter their relatives to death – to name just a few. Cruel practices such as torture, crucifixions, mass executions, and holocausts have flourished for centuries as ways to impose dominance through fear and power. Because the weak cannot easily negotiate with the powerful, or defend themselves, slavery, economic exploitation and injustice are still tragically prevalent.

In addition, because we live in a world of desperately unequal power, there are serious problems with failures in the negotiating processes that are not just related to violent conflicts but to the whole process of how we share resources as a species (Aquilar and Galluccio 2008). For example, a casual look at Wikipedia (http://en.wikipedia.org/wiki/Distribution_of_wealth) suggests that

> A study by the World Institute for Development Economics Research at United Nations University reports that the richest 1% of adults alone owned 40% of global assets in the year 2000, and that the richest 10% of adults accounted for 85% of the world total. The bottom half of the world adult population owned barely 1% of global wealth. …Moreover, another study found that the richest 2% own more than half of global household assets. Despite this, the distribution has been changing quite rapidly in the direction of greater concentration of wealth.

Inequalities have major effects on all health indices and crime (http://www.equalitytrust.org.uk/). So we live in a world of serious violence, cruelties and inequalities in trade, health and wealth, of haves, have-nots and have-lots, where children die from lack of clean water or a 50 cent vaccination, and where each year millions are vulnerable to starvation. There are many areas where failures to negotiate the settlement of conflicts, needs and trade deals are a disaster. So why can negotiated settlements be so difficult to achieve – when it is so obvious to any outside, logical person that their failure is tragic, often catastrophic and perpetrates intense injustice, from which resentment and conflict seed the next generations of wars and violence.

The Challenges of the Evolved Brain and the Evolutionary Processes

The reasons for this sad state of affairs are many. One is that conflicts and inequalities have arisen from the history of wars and conquests, suppression, oppression and exploitations of people and their resources. These may have arisen a few thousand years ago as isolated groups started to come into contact with each other, and found benefit in raiding (rather than trading) resources. This led eventually from village to tribal to nation and religious wars with efforts to steal and exploit resources – modern day imperialism (Armstrong 2006). So we are caught in cycles of modeling what previous generations have done and defending our positions – conflicts are historically and socially constructed around us. Another (not competitive) view starts from the fact that conflicts are endemic to all organic life. Indeed, conflicts of interest between individuals and between groups, and the evolution of (genetically stable) strategies to pursue and cope with them, have been one of the main driving forces of the evolution process (Buss 2003; McQuire and Troisi 1998).

One such strategy (offering evolved solutions to conflicts over resources) pertains to the development of social hierarchies based on displays of strength and controls of territory and resources (MacLean 1990). Individuals within groups can engage in various, ritualized, threat and submissive behaviors which avoid serious conflict and injury. Subordinates are vigilant to, and express submissive behaviors towards those who have more power than they do. Abilities to make the appropriate social comparisons and work out one's place/rank, what kinds of alliances to form, whom to submit to and whom to avoid, are all part of the strategy for the navigation of "conflicts of interest" within groups (Gilbert 2000).

In contrast to individuals, when *groups* come into conflict with each other there are also evolved defensive strategies such as awareness of boundaries, scent marking and preparedness to exit the territories of other groups. For the most part such defensive strategies evolved *to reduce* aggression with avoidance. However there are various species of monkeys where inter-group violence is common and is a major source of injury and mortality. For inter-group violence there is no equivalent to submissive behaviors that turn off aggression. Indeed, one group of chimpanzees split into two and were found to actually kill members of the other (now) separate group in what looks like war-like behavior (Goodall 1990). Keep in mind that before the group split they would have known each other and may even have been allies.

The fact is that humans can pursue the same motives. We have brains that can be easily stimulated to pursue aggressive goals, can override aggression regulation strategies (e.g., fear, moral concerns, or compassion), and are more destructive, violent and cruel to our own kind than any other species. What this means is that our brains can perceive, construct, and feel relationships in quite different ways. The way we think about friends is quite different from how we think about strangers or opponents. Concerns about the well being and welfare of opponents can be inhibited or turned off as a psychological motive – especially if they are seen as a threat. This is because compassionate concerns turn off or tone down aggressive and self-focused competitive desires – and that could leave one at a disadvantage and vulnerable to injury, loss, or defeat. So the brain is constructed in such a way that compassionate goals are inhibited in competitive and threat-based contexts. This is precisely why, of course, psychologies such as Buddhism argue that we must train our minds with and for compassion and that in some sense the unenlightened mind "is insane" (Vessantara 2003, p. 150). Without awareness of the power of such evolved archetypes and strategies we are liable to repeatedly fall victim to them, and believing that we're "in the right" with what we do – as destructive as that may be (Bandura 1999).

Social Mentalities

So one source of our difficulties lies in how and why our brains have evolved in the way they have (Gilbert 1998a, b; 2009). The human brain is the product of many millions of years of evolution and a long line of adaptations stretching back to the reptiles and beyond (Bailey 1987). The implications of this fact are only just beginning to impact on the psychological sciences (Barrett et al. 2002; Buss 2003; Dunbar and Barrett 2007). There is much debate about these implications (Li 2003; Lickliter and Honeycutt 2003) and on the way social conditions stimulate non-conscious strategies for social living (e.g., trusting vs mistrusting (Cohen 2001)). Coming to understand the implications of the fact that national and international negotiations are guided by powerful evolutionary strategies operating within them can be hard. We like to think we know ourselves and are "in control" of our own minds, and that we're not just automatons to underlying archetypal forces. Numerous psychotherapists from Freud, Jung and many others have seriously questioned this assumption, and recent evidence suggests that our conscious thoughts are often latter stage outputs of many non-conscious processes – our emotion systems can make decisions that our cognitive processes will then justify (Haidt 2001; Hassin et al. 2005).

Indeed, there is increasing agreement that evolved strategies and archetypes are readily observed and include such things as identifying strongly with one's own particular group (Baumestier and Leary 1995); submissiveness to leaders (Gilbert 2000); power abuses by leaders (Keltner et al. 2003); tendencies to a variety of cognitive biases such as seeing one's own group as special in some way, or more deserving or more threatened – called self-serving biases (Aquilar and Galluccio 2008; Tobena et al. 1999); and preparedness to obey orders in the service of one's groups including those associated with atrocities – a process Kelman and Hamilton (1989) call "crimes of obedience." Indeed, our human preparedness to obey and show excessive loyalty to our leaders, group, subgroups, and elites, which easily overrides concerns about fairness or even morality, remains a serious problem in human social life and specially on the international stage. Leaders can exert destructive influence because their subordinates obey.

So when we look deeper into our evolved brain we can see that we are a species capable of multiple and often contradictory behaviors and feelings (Carter 2008; Ornstein 1986). A popular undergraduate textbook on psychology attempts to stimulate the interest of potential students with the following statement (Coon 1992, p. 1).

> You are a universe, a collection of worlds within worlds. Your brain is possibly the most complicated and amazing device in existence. Through its action you are capable of music, art, science, and war. Your potential for love and compassion coexists with your potential for aggression, hatred...Murder?

This focus, on the great variation of potentials *within* an individual (in contrast to variation *between* individuals) is of course the starting point for much psychotherapy. Most clinicians are familiar with clients describing themselves as having "different parts," or experiencing "intense inner conflicts." And clinicians themselves also view the psyche as made up of different elements that can be labeled in different ways.

One reason for this is that the evolution of the brain has gone through various stages that can be traced back to reptilian life forms (Bailey 1987; MacLean 1990). Reptiles are concerned with dominance, spacing, territory, and mating. These are basic archetypal forms. For example, the threat display of reptiles with stiff limbs and eyes staring can still be used in humans as a threat display. With the mammals, however, came a new range of archetypes and social mentalities – new psychologies come into the world. First mammals engaged in investment in their offspring and developed caring and attachment systems. Importantly, they developed capacities for alliances. These abilities evolved partly through the process of inhibiting fight/flight tendencies when in close proximity to each other (Porges 2007). So our brain has evolved to feel, think, and "do differently" in different contexts. However, these different potentials can be in conflict – for example a negotiator might follow a line of argument but be personally very opposed to it. How they cope with that conflict could influence their negotiating style.

One way of thinking about the fact that our brain can think, feel, and do differently in different contexts and "states of mind" has been with the development of social mentality theory (Gilbert 1989, Gilbert 2005a, b). A social mentality has been described as an organizing process that brings together motives, emotions, attention, thinking, and behavior for the purpose of creating a certain type of dynamic reciprocal interaction and role. For example, the evolution of caring behavior was a solution to infant mortality. Rather than disperse at birth, mammalian infants are helpless and remain in contact with the parent. But caring has evolved with a particular psychology and brain pattern and organization – that is, the "carer" and "cared for" must form a reciprocal interacting relationship (e.g., the parent is motivated to provide care and respond to infant distress signals, and the infant responds to care and prospers rather than (say), runs away). Various psychological mechanisms could not evolve unless this reciprocal interacting process, where each is mutually influencing the mind of the other, occurs.

In regard to the organization of our minds we can see that if one has a care-giving mentality then we feel *motivated* to care for and look after another (e.g., a child, adult, or pet), to pay *attention* to their needs, to *feel* distressed by their distress, to have sympathy and empathy, and to *think* of what they might need, or of ways to relieve that distress or enable their growth.

Another form of relating that has been extremely beneficial to many mammals has been co-operative behavior where individuals coordinate their actions for mutual gain. Once again evolution has evolved this type of interaction with reciprocal relationships. With humans, cooperative behavior is complex and requires a monitoring of oneself in relationship to others. But notice how our minds are organized when we are in a cooperative mentality. We are motivated to seek others similar to us, to share and engage in reciprocal roles (e.g., playing in an orchestra, participating on a football team, working on a project). We praise and value others and feel valued by others in this cooperative dynamic. We think about our contribution, how it will be valued, and how it will link with others. Cooperative behavior tends towards more egalitarian ways of thinking and feeling, and pursuit of justice. But keep in mind that this requires one's brain to be in a particular mentality and pattern, and it is easy to disturb that pattern with threats to the self or one's group. It is also easy to disturb it if the competitive mentality becomes powerfully triggered.

The competitive social mentality is of course very old and has undergone various evolved adaptations by the time we get to humans. Nonetheless there are some continuities of attention, thinking and behavior that underpin competitiveness. First there has to be a *motive* to compete with others in such a way that one either avoids an inferior position or gains a superior one. Hence self-promotion (or that of one's group), in contrast to caring or cooperation, is the primary motive. One's attention is directed to what others are doing and thinking, and one's thinking is linked to social comparison and working out how to gain a competitive edge. This may be strategic thinking. One enacts those behaviors that will give one the advantage.

Note how we can contrast the social mentality of caring with the social mentality of competing. In caring the focus is on the other and how to help them; the emotions of empathy and sympathy are prominent, and the focus on the self is reduced. In competing, however, the organization of mental mechanisms is quite different.

The focus is on the self, whilst empathy and sympathy are reduced (particularly if competitors are seen as enemies). Desires to seek an advantage, defend a position or even harm others are increased. The point is, then, that our minds become organized in very different ways according to the motives and mentalities that operate. This relates directly to the way we conceptualize and engage in our relationships with others. The key question then is what kinds of mentalities do your negotiators bring to their negotiations and how does this influence the reciprocal dynamic process of the negotiation? We can see that there is likely to be quite a different dynamic reciprocal process emerging if participants are in a competitive mentality, a cooperative mentality, or indeed a compassionate caring one. What influences the mentality individuals activate is itself complex and needs be understood within a biopsychosocial framework.

Evolution, Culture and Learning: The Biopsychosocial Model

According to evolutionary psychology many of our basic motives, emotional dispositions, and cognitive competencies are the result of *distal* pressures (meaning selective pressures operating in the past and over the long term). One can think here of motives to form attachments to parents, to want to develop alliances and friendships, distinguish in-group from out-group, to take an interest in sexual relationships, to compete for position, to gain status, and so on. These are socially motivated behaviors that are observed the world over in multiple species. All species need to be able to detect threats and defend themselves, and for many of the higher mammals there are three major defensive emotions of anger, anxiety and disgust – with relatively similar triggers.

However, these evolved psychologies interact with various competencies for learning and form the *proximate* factors (factors that operate during an individual's life). We learn in a variety of ways, of course. Relatively simple organisms learn via classical and instrumental conditioning and so do we, but we also have a whole range of language and symbolic-based learning competencies. These provide for the social and cultural shapers of human psychology; they provide for us to acquire a sense of values and self-identify (Taylor 1989). Most now agree that it is *the interaction* between evolved dispositions, learning, and socio-cultural contexts that creates the complexity of the human mind. We can depict this with a simple model as shown in Fig. 2.1.

The interaction of the three circles simply suggests that our internal physiological states, how we behave within our relationships and our beliefs and values, are all mutually influencing each other. For example, we physiologically operate in different ways if we are in conflict situations or in loving supportive situations – cortisol is higher in the former; oxytocin is higher the latter (Carter 1998). Even genetic expression can be influenced via relationships (Harper 2005). Similarly our states of mind give rise to behaviors which impact on relationships. Our thoughts, beliefs and values influence our behaviors and affect our relationships and our physiological states.

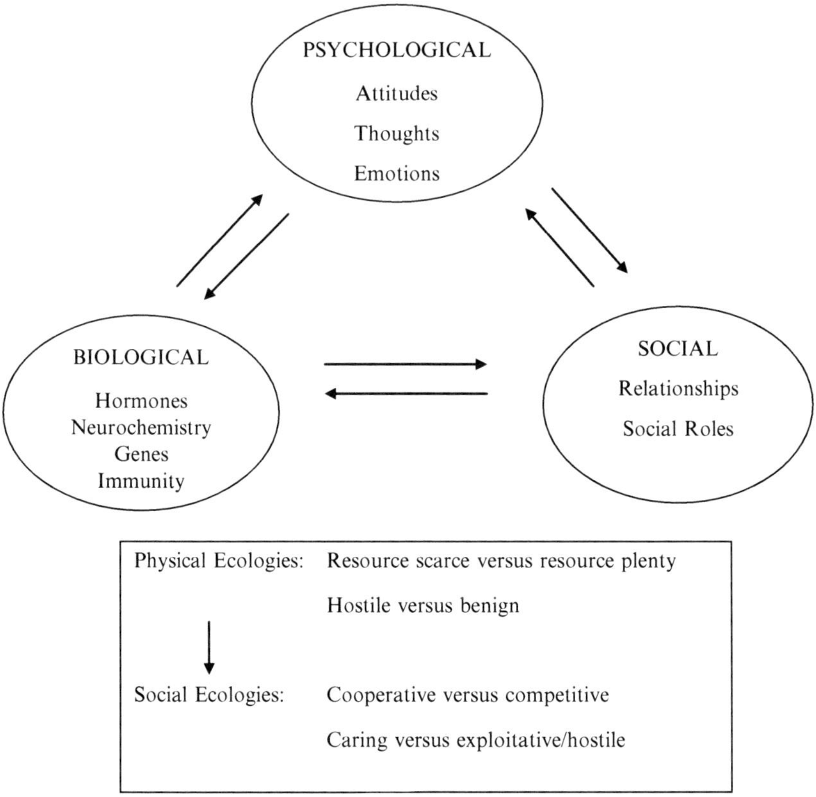

Fig. 2.1 Biopsychosocial and ecological interactions

This is also related to *genotype–phenotype* interactions (Barrett et al. 2002). Phenotypes are the way traits (genotypes and potentials) are expressed by virtue of how they have been shaped by experience. For example, we have genotypes for learning an aural language, but how well we learn, what we learn, and the actual way we use language is the phenotype and is dependent on experience. Recent work has shown that environments can influence the expression of genes and in some cases may actually turn genes "on and off." This is partly because different genes underpin the development and operation of different strategies and competencies to fit different niches. All of these interactions influence the prototypical social mentalities people will use in their social relationships.

Cultures, cultural discourse, and narratives also play huge roles in the way in which people construct their self-identities, create conflicts, activate social mentalities, and influence various strategies played out between participants. For example, in some cultures the use of violence as a solution to conflict and insults is regarded as honorable whereas in others it is regarded as showing lack of self-restraint (Gilmore 1990). As outlined by Cohen et al. (1998), there are variations within the USA (a single country) as to the acceptance of the use of violence in defense of honor;

southern states are far more accepting of aggression if seen as defensive, than northern states. So while aggression is an evolved strategy for dealing with conflicts, culture and group pressure play a major role in how much people seek to develop this strategy within themselves, feel socially valued in doing so, observe others engaging in these behaviors, and submit to the social norm. This raises the importance of contextualising the interactions, beliefs, and values within ecological parameters. As depicted in Fig. 2.1 these can be social and physical and impact on three interacting processes in dynamic reciprocal ways.

These kinds of models open us to complex ways for thinking about international negotiations, negotiators, and the kinds of processes that are likely to be played out in that process.

The Cognitive World

The human mind is equipped with a whole range of motives and emotions that go back many millions of years. However, about 2 million years ago there was a rapid expansion in a range of cognitive abilities. It was around this time that early humanoids known as *Homo habilis* first appeared on Earth with a brain capacity of 650–700 cc. They walked upright, lived in family groups, developed simple tool use, followed a hunter–gatherer way of life, and may have built shelters. After them evolution came up with *Homo erectus*, Neanderthals, and *Homo sapiens* (us), and today our brain capacity is around 1,500 cc. So in just two million years the expansion of the brain, and especially the cortex, has been rapid and dramatic. The ratio of cortex to total brain size is estimated to be 67% in monkeys, 75% in apes, and 80% in humans (Bailey 1987).

This new brain has opened us to a whole range of capacities for thinking, imagining, planning and ruminating. The expansion of the frontal cortex has given us the capacities for empathy, mentalizing, theory of mind, and the ability to have a sense of self and self-identity (Goldberg 2002). All these have proved fantastically valuable in the struggle for survival and reproduction. Along with them, of course, are language and symbol use, which have created completely new ways of thinking and communicating. These abilities give rise to science, culture, the communication of ideas across generations, and more besides.

However, evolution can never go back to the drawing board and push a delete button, so complex and important cognitive abilities sit on top of much more primitive motivational and emotional systems. Indeed, this is perhaps our biggest threat to our species. Our primitive motivational and emotional brains, which run many of the archetypes and strategies, can simply hijack our cognitive abilities and direct them to the fulfillment of their own programs. So, for example, humans don't just live in the moment, responding to signals around them, submitting or fighting if threatened. Rather humans can lay plans to achieve status, to work out how over the long-term one might outperform competitors or even undermine them, to avoid inferiority, and to only create alliances that advance one's goal. Or consider how the archetypal processes that lead us to be very group orientated and defensive, submissive to dubious leaders, can recruit our intelligence and motivate us to design and create weapons of destruction. Through a process of symbols and values and the way our self-identities form within our social groups, we can associate with others we have never met and have no personal relationship with whatsoever – we may not even like them – and yet can link up and form allies and go to war with them because they seem to have the same values or religion, etc. Chomsky (1992) has repeatedly pointed out how Western countries have supported all kinds of unpleasant dictatorships, undermining indigenous resistances, because they see them as conducive to their own interests and having similar values.

Inter-group Conflicts

Over a number of years Sidanius and Pratto and their colleagues have been developing an important theory and research base on what they call Social Dominance Theory. This is based on the fact that groups in conflict for resources will compete and try to win advantage over each other and exploit that advantage. Sidanius and Pratto (2004) argue,

> Most forms of group conflict and oppression (e.g., racism, ethnocentrism, sexism, nationalism, classism and regionalism) can be regarded as different manifestations of the same basic human predisposition to form group-based social hierarchy (p. 319).

Social dominance theory blends evolutionary dispositions with socially constructed belief systems that make certain behaviors acceptable. These can be offset by spiritual religious beliefs, but very often those belief systems themselves can become another means for ascribing dominance and specialness (Gay 1995) – religious wars. Indeed, one of the important roles that group-focused social identities and communication networks can do is provide narratives to legitimize inequalities (e.g., to see others are less deserving or inferior in some way) and create fears and terrors around differences. Gay (1995), for example, suggests that the political rhetoric can easily stimulate audiences into fear, and from fear a hatred of the outsider. So for all kinds of reasons there can be socially constructed values and beliefs or what Pratto et al. (1994) call hierarchy-legitimizing myths – ways of justifying our special positions and the subjugation of others.

Competitions and Conflicts: Negotiating to Get the Best Deal for Oneself

We are living in a world of increasing expansion of population, desires for more resources, rising expectations linked to the internet, sharing of values and display of lifestyles of the rich around the world, and an environment that is slowly choking itself to death. Negotiations to create fair trading between the developed and less developed countries, limit the exploitation of resources (destruction of rainforests), control CO_2 emissions, or resolve conflicts in major areas such as Palestine, Afghanistan and Sudan are failing tragically. The problem and reasons why are well known. Leaving aside corruption of course, currently most groups negotiate with other groups with the motives of seeking the best deal for the home team. They come to the table in a competitive (seeking a superior advantage), protective (avoiding giving up any advantage or privilege), defensive (a preparedness to be intransigent), or even a vengeful frame of mind. Not only may they be unaware of the archetypal forces playing through them, but the reciprocal dynamic interplay stirs emotions linked to different mentalities they may struggle with too. As Galluccio (this volume and Galluccio 2007) points out, negotiators are subject to the same motives and emotions as all humans, and their ability to understand and regulate their emotions during what can be arousing conflict situations will play an important role in their interpersonal style, their ability to create the experience of safeness and trust, and how they handle their negotiations.

There are serious problems with the competitive mentality being the primary organizing process by which individuals engage in negotiations. Such outcomes are often influenced by differences in power of the parties and the compromises one party can enforce on another. "Gaining the competitive edge" *is seen as a virtue* no matter how unfair or exploitative that outcome may be. Is it a "good deal for us?" is the primary judgment, and this is true for international business (Bakan 2004) and nation states negotiating with other nation states (Aquilar and Galluccio 2008). Politicians all over the world endorse these sentiments quite happily, ignoring that what might be "good for us" may be a disaster for other countries, especially those with little power – e.g., Western trade agreements with the developing countries, or forcing arms sales (Keegan 1993). The tendency for the powerful to subjugate or subordinate the less powerful is well known.

In conflict situations people have various (not mutually exclusive) choices. They can threaten and fight, seek out helpful support from others, back down and acquiesce, run away, or try to negotiate. In the latter, compromises may be resentfully accepted (mostly if people feel in a submissive position), or compromises might be seen as offering mutually beneficial positions. Agreements that seem to be mutually beneficial are associated with positive emotion for both sides, and that builds relationships (De Dreu et al. 2006). Resentful compromise can create the conditions for cheating, revenge, and the next conflict.

The Problem of Leaders

It is very important to recognize that most negotiators are not free agents, but operate as a directed arm of government and leaders (Aquilar and Galluccio 2008). This presents us with major problems. It is now well known that leaders can inspire us to compassion, reconciliation, and peacemaking or violence and cruelties (Crook 1986; Lindholm 1993). Although we often put great emphasis on the importance of personal freedom, we often fail to recognize just how much of our behavior is directed at seeking approval, fitting in with our social groups, and *subordinating* ourselves to various individuals, doctrines, traditions, and values (Cohen 2003). In a fascinating study, Green et al. (1998) looked at the historical records for the link between unfavorable economic conditions (e.g., high unemployment) and hate crimes (lynching and beatings) directed at minorities. Current wisdom had it that with increases in relative poverty, envy and frustration build up, leading to increases in hate crime. But this link proved weak. Green et al. believe that an important factor in the rise of hate crimes is the emergence of leaders, or power elites that direct and orchestrate violence for their own ends or reasons. Their work is important because we can certainly see the same psychologies at work all over the world – not least in the Palestinian Israeli context.

Although fear and hatred of the outsider is an all-too-familiar aspect of our behavior, such feelings are typically mixed in cauldrons of social values that literally cultivate it, as Gay (1995) had so fully described, and Nelson Mandela demonstrated by his refusal to endorse such. Is it possible that the human race has been burdened and scared in the way it has (and is still being) partly because there are certain types of personality (enacting certain strategies) who seek and get power and then are able to inflame people to violence because of our compliant and submissive tendencies, need for belonging and tribal identity, and fear of shame by "breaking ranks?" Can leaders inflame violent strategies to outsiders for political ends to impress others and/or to deflect attention from their failed leadership and internal economies? Many political commentators believe so. Grabsky (1993) offers many examples of how leaders have manipulated situations for their own ends. One wonders what would've happened had the Middle East or Zimbabwe found a Gandhi or a Nelson Mandela.

A major problem is that leaders require certain personalities in order to navigate the stages of acquiring leadership positions. They in turn need to be supported by various financial backers and power groups. These are not necessarily individuals who facilitate the best or fairest negotiations. Indeed Western governments have been more intent on using other nations to support their fight against communism or support selfish trade agreements, often keeping unpleasant regimes in place (Chomsky 1992).

In a recent review of Patrick Tyler's book *A World in Trouble*, Martin Woollacott (2009) notes how successive leaders have dealt with the Israeli–Palestinian conflict and comments: "It is the most dismal chronicle of incompetence, ignorance, ineffectiveness, indecision and inefficiency imaginable…." (p 6). He goes on to make the shocking revelation that in 1973 Kissinger was entrusted to give a message from Nixon to Brezhnev for joint superpower action to end the Arab–Israeli war and to try for a just settlement in the region. Apparently Kissinger decided mid-flight simply not to deliver it. He later encouraged Israel to violate the cease-fire (p 6). Group and tribal loyalties cross nations, but such behavior shows just how serious the consequences are, and are paid for in the suffering and lives of the many.

Although subordinates can defy leaders, it is much more usual that they are willing to enact policies – be they just or not. In pursuit of their own self-interest leaders can be rather contemptuous and lose interest in the concerns of the subordinates; their main concern is that subordinates do as they are asked (Keltner et al. 2003). Leaders can play their subordinates off against each other (as Adolf Hitler and

Saddam Hussain were well known to do) making each insecure and more ready to do the bidding of the leader. Leaders can also lack abilities for self-reflection – as in the case of Margret Thatcher, who always believed her downfall was due to treachery and not her own behaviors. And of course leaders can simply lie and manipulate for their own ends.

Leaders can also be mentally ill and seriously disturbed – but subordinates (including negotiators) may still enact their orders (Freeman 1991; Green 2005; Owen 2007, 2008). Indeed subordinates can still follow and obey leaders even when *they know* they are incompetent, fakes, bad, or even mentally ill – because if the leader falls so does the group and the sense of belonging protection and identity (Lindholm 1993). The submissive process is complex and involves a range of motives to try to please those higher in power than oneself, to seek security under their wing (Kelman and Hamilton 1989) and because, as Lindholm (1993) suggests, the subordinates have linked their sense of identity and future prospects to that of the leader – so if she/he goes down, so do they. In addition they operate in subgroups whose narratives seek to maintain biased and self-justifying views of themselves and their world (Lindholm 1993). Any analysis of negotiator behavior and the negotiation process must therefore be set in social contexts of real life and reflect both the present and distal pressures that operate at the negotiation table.

The Pressures on Negotiators

Negotiators who come from the "home team" are not free agents and should not be regarded as such, so we need to recognize that individuals engaging in (international) negotiations are under a range of pressures (Aquilar and Galluccio 2008). Some examples of these can be depicted in Fig. 2.2.

First is the negotiator's primary motivation or social mentality. Two major ones are (1) the cooperative social mentality, involving seeking mutual benefit, recognizing

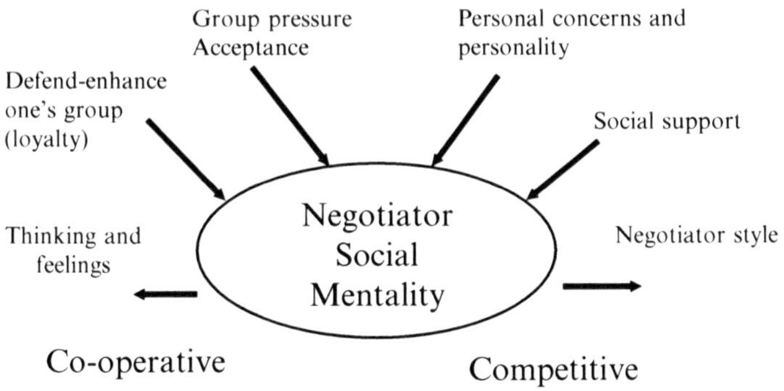

Fig. 2.2 An interactive model of some of the pressures on negotiators

a need to work together to achieve a common goal. In contrast is (2) the competitive social mentality, which will orientate negotiators in a completely different way – as noted above – for some advantage or defense of a position. Occasionally the social mentality could be one of care seeking where one group is seeking help and support from another. It's also possible that negotiators could be in a caring frame of mind, where they are sympathetic to the complexity of the task or the distress of participants. This is more likely in the minds of the third party mediators.

We can then move around the circle (of Fig. 2.2) and note that the negotiators' ability to think and reflect, to be able to recognize and regulate their own emotions as they arise moment by moment, to have "theory of mind" and mentalize, to be empathic in their thinking and feeling – all of these will influence the process of negotiation (Aquilar and Galluccio 2008).

Related to the competitive mentality are issues related to the degree to which negotiators start from the premise of trying to defend a position or enhance a position and out of a sense of loyalty to a position. The negotiator's personal identification with the arguments is important. Conflicts, where negotiators believe their group is pursuing an unfair position that they are not fully behind, can create difficulties for negotiators and the process.

Pressures to conform to the dictates of their leaders and political parties, be these Democratic or other forms, can be intense. Negotiators can feel quite stuck if distal power groups, who have a fragile understanding of the issues or no real interest in "a fair settlement," put pressure on negotiators. They may be caught between the degree to which they wish to express their personal preferences versus simply being a mouthpiece for power groups behind them. In these contexts the negotiator may have to face both ways, working with groups at the table but also negotiating and trying to persuade power groups back home (Aquilar and Galluccio 2008). In democratic societies power groups back home may have little interest in a fair deal but simply in how the deal will play to their electorate (Cohen 2003). In this sense neither the power group nor the negotiator has a free hand because they must balance and be cautious of how their own group will respond to any loss of advantage.

The state of mind of negotiators; the degree to which they handle pressure, if they are slightly depressed or anxious, worried about maintaining their position and careers; the degree to which they are narcissistic or affiliative, a shallow or complex thinker, have good social skills, especially non-verbal skills, are patient and able play a "long game" versus impatient – will influence the reciprocal dynamic nature of the negotiation process.

Negotiations can of course be stressful, and a key issue then is the degree of social support and opportunities for debriefing and reflection that are provided outside of these forums themselves. Opportunities to explore one's own thoughts and feelings may be crucial to working them through. This is to use a psychotherapeutic model. Individuals operating in these mental support roles would ideally be skilled in psychological support.

Finally there is the negotiator's style, which really is the outcome of all the above. Some individuals can create a sense of trust and safety whereas others portray a sense of closed-off-ness, distrust and wariness. In all social encounters humans automatically respond to non-verbal communication, more powerfully at times than verbal communication. Problems in setting a tone that creates a possibility for openness, frankness, and safety can lead to parties focusing primarily on defensive positions. Negotiators can look and sound anxious, frightening, contemptuous, or angry – or open, friendly, and patient. Even listening to them on radio interviews can indicate which they seem to be.

Solutions

The chapter has focused mostly on conflicts. However within in-group psychology there are also evolved advantages for egalitarianism and sharing (Ridley 1997). Buddhists believe that our basic nature is compassionate – in part because compassion creates the greatest chances of us flourishing and calms our easily disturbed minds. There are therefore key research question as to how these mentalities and ways of thinking can be harnessed.

Socio-political

Given the complexities and clear importance of modern-day negotiations there have been a number of solutions to these problems, especially those of negotiators operating from the home team. Now *within* countries and individual societies the way the powerful will try to exploit their position over the weak is well known – and in conflict situations people will have their own personal self-serving biases. It is precisely to put limits around the abilities of the powerful to exploit the less powerful, and get around self-serving biases, that humans have also developed the concept of *law and arbitration by independent third parties*, be these juries or judges (Grady and McGuire 1999; Lewis 2003). Of course cynics can sometimes suggest that the law and policing can be used to punish the crimes of the poor and hide the crimes of the rich. Be that as it may, the profession of the law operates as a way to take decisions about conflicts out of the hands of the participants. Law provides for independent, third-party decisions and legislation, which are binding on the parties involved. For indigenous laws this works fairly well.

Unfortunately despite efforts of the United Nations, we are a long way from developing an *international* constitution and being able to utilize "third-party independent" legal systems. This is partly because democratic states believe that democracies would not accept "giving up power to such systems." Nation states still believe they can and should negotiate for and on behalf of themselves. However nation states can simply refuse to obey the dictates of international United Nations mandates and resolutions, and there's no evidence that arbitration would have any greater enforcement potential. This is clearly the case in the current Palestinian–Israeli dispute. As a result, international negotiators operate from a background of not having an independent, third-party legal system that can enforce compliance to agreements. Clearly, however, one can make powerful arguments as to why this will be necessary in the decades to come.

Training

Another solution is much better training in the psychology of negotiations. For example, all over the world there is a growing awareness that our evolved human brain is very difficult to regulate and understand, and that we need to train our minds carefully. It's an old view stretching back over 3,000 years now, notably within the Buddhist tradition. Learning how to be reflective and mindful provides many benefits in the ability to regulate one's emotions and keep "a calm mind." From this position one can use one's intelligence and is much more likely to be able to spot the operation of different archetypes and mentalities within oneself (Didonna 2009).

We can also take the view that we need a complete change in the dominant social mentality (competitive) that has come to percolate though all aspects of our lives (Gilbert 2009). Currently we are dominated by self-focused competitive edge psychology – that is causing increasing difficulties and creating rather than resolving them (Gilbert 2009). Over 3,000 years ago Buddha argued that only through a process of developing and practicing compassion would we be able to transform our minds and regulate our relationships. Compassionate mind training is now seen as a way in which we can move forward on these issues. It is unclear what introducing "compassion focused negotiations" would achieve but this is potentially a helpful research area (Gilbert 2009). When our minds are orientated for compassion, we can more easily recognize that all of us simply find ourselves on this Earth, with these lives, and not of our choosing. From there we may be able to see beyond our differences, identify with our common humanity, and more easily reconcile our conflicts. We may tire of acting out, over and over, old archetypal dramas like unpaid actors.

As to how one trains negotiators, much depends on what you want them to do. Clearly, if you want your negotiators to be tough and maximize the benefits flowing to your own group, this is a very different remit and with different required skills than if you want your negotiators to focus on fairness and justice. Although empathy training can be recommended, wherein the negotiator learns to be sensitive to the feelings and aspirations of others, there is no guarantee (without a compassion focus) that these enhanced qualities will be used for good. Indeed, on the Internet one can find many advertised programmes in empathy training that are specifically designed to enable you to be better at selling and marketing. Empathy without a sense of caring for the other person(s) one is interacting with can be used exploitatively.

However, if we wish to pursue justice and fairness then empathy training is certainly a key skill. There are various ways to do it. One is for negotiators to be trained by spending some time negotiating from the other person's point of view. For example, in an Israeli–Palestinian conflict the Palestinians would take on an Israeli position and vice versa. Learning how to see the world through the eyes of the other requires time and formal and structured practice. But once again the motive determines what is learnt. People could do this exercise simply to gain insight into the weak points of their participants, so as to exploit that weakness, rather than to facilitate the fairer compassionate understanding and approach.

Compassion focused empathy also requires one to think carefully about the impact of one's behavior on "the other": to think about the impact of what one does – not just for those present but for those on whom the outcome will have a major impact – and not just today or tomorrow, but for the future. To understand the impact on children growing up in a society that may have been significantly influenced by the outcome of negotiations, training programmes also need to consider how individuals deal with issues of vengeance and forgiveness because these can play a major role in the success or failure of negotiations.

It is possible (although more research is required) that there are actually different types of personalities here. It is to the genius of Nelson Mandela that he anticipated these issues and set his country on course for proper confrontation with the tragedies and abuses of the past with a focus on reconciliation, not vengeance. It is difficult to know what would happen in, say, the Israeli–Palestinian conflict if the international community decided to push for *reconciliation processes*, perhaps modeled on the South African system, for this conflict – or maybe we are too far away from that stage. However negotiation processes and skills to cope with histories of violence and vengeance are clearly desperately needed. Even if one keeps a cease-fire or peace, the future may perhaps only be secured in negotiating longer-term reconciliation and trade.

It is very unclear if the negotiators who have been trained to be tough and resistant could easily become more compassion focused – even assuming that their leaders would allow it – unless of course that was their directive. It is possible compassionate individuals may not make the best new negotiators. It is possible that one needs different types of negotiators for different phases in the negotiation.

Short Term Versus Long Term

More consideration could be given to training in mutual benefit as opposed to maximizing one's own advantage. This is because an advantage can be short-lived. For example, the advantages extracted by the Allies at the end of the First World War in terms of German remunerations and occupation of the Rhine coalfields are believed to have sown the seeds for the Second World War. Selling arms to third world countries (for short term gains of employment in one's own country) can result in great human tragedy as well as floods of refugees and immigrants – and these arms can come flooding back against one. Had Kissinger put pressure on Israel in 1973 then it is possible (no more than possible) that both countries would have got into a more sustainable settlement and thus both sides would have been saved much pain and tragedy. Looking only to the short-term interests can be a disaster. It is sometimes said that political careers are relatively short, and so are their vision and concerns. There are questions as to how we can move beyond this situation.

Indeed there are so many areas where negotiators need to make distinctions between long-term and short-term benefits. In the world of economics, for example, the recent banking crisis has shown the stupidity of deregulating markets – aided by right-wing politicians interested in pursuing the short term self-interest of the wealthy. Also note in these days of climate change that we see that businesses are still allowed to prosper despite the costs they are passing to future generations. One obvious example is that when governments negotiate with logging businesses as they deforest the world, they do not take account of the costs "to the world" of climate change 10 or more years down the line. Logging companies are allowed to get away with only addressing short-term, local problems associated with logging. Indeed, one could ask how negotiators would factor in such long-term economic costs. Currently they are simply ignored.

We are a long way from establishing what the core skills of negotiators should be, how they should be acquired and how they should be enacted. As noted above, much depends upon the goals that they are pursuing, and many of these goals are not fairness- and justice-focused, but seek the greatest advantage for oneself. It is also clear that they operate in wider political systems and with political wheeler-dealers who have their own agendas. Only when we, as a world, move beyond these circumstances and set up appropriate independent international law for the regulation of international conflicts and business ethics are we likely to see much progress. Our human psychology is too complex and powerful to rely on self-interest.

Conclusions

Increasingly today we are coming to terms with the fact that we did not arrive on this planet "de novo," but we are an evolved species, with an evolved brain, guided by certain motives that had developed to achieve certain goals, such as acquiring resources conducive to survival and reproduction. I have focused on the evolutionary dimensions here because it is from the potentials lurking in our evolved brain that our disposition for wars, cruelties, and the creation of inequalities arise. It is partly understanding the challenges of our evolved brain with which national and international negotiators will need to grapple if they are to move our world forward with decisions based on fair and moral principles. However, to make negotiators, and the elites that guide them, operate with fair and moral principles is itself a major challenge (Aquilar and Galluccio 2008).

Evolutionary psychology has revealed many important problems that we need to face as a result of our evolutionary history (Gilbert 2009). One of the key messages of this chapter, therefore, is that negotiators and all of us who support them a need to understand the pull of the archetypes within ourselves and that they can hijack our cognitive processes. We like to think that we run the show, but actually it's mostly our motivational systems that utilize our cognitive competencies – and cause us problems. If we reflect and train our minds for compassion and fairness, we might find ways to make more conscious choices about the world we want to create. But we must also bear in mind that good negotiators might be relatively easy to select and train but they are not free agents. Rather they are often negotiating on behalf of their groups and leaders, and it is here that most of the problems lie.

References

Armstrong, K. (2006). *The great transformation: The world in the time of Buddha, Socrates, Confucius and Jeremiah*. New York: Atlantic Books.

Aquilar, F., & Galluccio, M. (2008). *Psychological processes in international negotiations: Theoretical and practice perspectives*. New York: Springer.

Bailey, K. (1987). *Human paleopsychology. Applications to aggression and pathological processes*. Hillsdale, NJ: Lawrence Erlbaum.

Bandura, A. (1999). Moral disengagement in the perpetration of inhumanities. *Personality and Social Psychology Review, 3*, 193–209.

Bakan, J. (2004). *The corporation: The pathological pursuit of profit and power*. London: Constable & Robinson.

Barrett, L., Dunbar, R., & Lycett, J. (2002). *Human evolutionary psychology*. London: Palgraave.

Baumeister, R. F., & Leary, M. R. (1995). The need to belong: desire for interpersonal attachments as a fundamental human motivation. *Psychological Bulletin, 117*, 497–529.

Buss, D. M. (2003). *Evolutionary psychology: The new science of mind* (2nd ed.). Boston: Allyn & Bacon.

Carter, R. (2008). *Multiplicity: The new science of personality*. London: Little Brown.

Carter, C. S. (1998). Neuroendocrine perspectives on social attachment and love. *Psychoneuroendocrinology, 23*, 779–818.

Chomsky, N. (1992). *Deterring democracy*. New York: Vintage.

Cohen, D. (2001). Cultural variation: Considerations and implications. *Psychological Bulletin, 127*, 451–471.

Cohen, G. L. (2003). Party over policy: The dominating impact of group influence on political beliefs. *Journal of Personality and Social Psychology, 85*, 808–822.

Cohen, D., Vandello, J., & Rantilla, A. K. (1998). The sacred ad the social: Culture of honour and violence. In P. Gilbert & B. Andrews (Eds.), *Shame: Interpersonal behaviour, psychopathology and culture* (pp. 261–282). Oxford: Oxford University Press.

Coon, D. (1992). *Introduction to psychology: Exploration and application* (6th ed.). New York: West.

Crook, J. H. (1986). The evolution of leadership: A preliminary skirmish. In C. F. Graumann & S. Moscovici (Eds.), *Changing conceptions of leadership*. New York: Springer Verlag.

De Dreu, C. K. W., Beersma, B., Stroebe, K., & Euwenma, M. C. (2006). Motivated information processing, strategic choice, and the quality of negotiated agreement. *Journal of Personality and Social Psychology, 90*, 927–943.

Didonna, F. (2009). *Clinical handbook of mindfulness*. New York: Springer.

Dunbar, R. E. M., & Barrett, L. (2007). *The Oxford handbook of evolutionary psychology*. Oxford: Oxford University Press.

Freeman, H. (1991). The human brain and political behaviour. *The British Journal of Psychiatry, 159*, 19–32.

Galluccio, M. (2007, July). *Cognitive psychotherapy and international negotiation: An overview*. Paper presented at the V World Congress of Behavioural and Cognitive Therapies, Barcelona, Spain.

Gay, P. (1995). *The cultivation of hatred*. London: Fontana Press.

Gilbert, P. (1989). *Human nature and suffering*. London: Lawrence Erlbaum.

Gilbert, P. (1998a). Evolutionary psychopathology: Why isn't the mind better designed than it is? *British Journal of Medical Psychology, 71*, 353–373.

Gilbert, P. (1998b). The evolved basis and adaptive functions of cognitive distortions. *British Journal of Medical Psychology, 71*, 447–463.

Gilbert, P. (2000). Varieties of submissive behaviour: Their evolution and role in depression. In L. Sloman & P. Gilbert (Eds.), *Subordination and defeat. An evolutionary approach to mood disorders* (pp. 3–46). Hillsadale: Lawrence Erlbaum.

Gilbert, P. (2005a). Compassion and cruelty: A biopsychosocial approach. In P. Gilbert (Ed.), *Compassion: Conceptualisations, research and use in psychotherapy* (pp. 9–74). London: Routledge.
Gilbert, P. (2005b). Social mentalities: A biopsychosocial and evolutionary reflection on social relationships. In M. W. Baldwin (Ed.), *Interpersonal cognition* (pp. 299–335). New York: Guilford.
Gilbert, P. (2009). *The compassionate mind. A new approach to life's challenges.* London: Constable Robinson.
Gilmore, D. D. (1990). *Manhood in the making: Cultural concepts of masculinity.* New Haven: Yale University Press.
Goldberg, E. (2002). *The executive brain: Frontal lobes and the civilized mind.* New York: Oxford University Press.
Goodall, J. (1990). *Through a window. Thirty years with the chimpanzees of gnome.* London: Penguin.
Grabsky, P. (1993). *The great commanders.* London: Boxtree and Channel Four.
Grady, M. F., & McGuire, M. T. (1999). The nature of constitutions. *Journal of Bioeconomics, 1*, 227–240.
Green, V. (2005). *The madness of kings.* London: Sutton.
Green, D. P., Glaser, J., & Rich, A. (1998). From lynching to gay bashing: The elusive connection between economic conditions and hate crime. *Journal of Personality and Social Psychology, 75*, 82–92.
Haidt, J. (2001). The emotional dog and its rational tail: A social intuitionist approach to moral judgment. *Psychological Review, 108*, 814–834.
Hassin, R. R., Uleman, J. S., & Bargh, J. A. (2005). *The new unconscious.* New York: Oxford University Press.
Harper, L. V. (2005). Epignetic inheritance and the intergenerational transfer of experience. *Psychological Bulletin, 131*, 340–360.
Keegan, W. (1993). *The spectre of capitalism.* London: Vintage.
Keltner, D., Gruenfeld, D. H., & Anderson, C. (2003). Power, approach and inhibition. *Psychological Review, 110*, 265–284.
Kelman, H. C., & Hamilton, V. L. (1989). *Crimes of obedience.* New Haven: Yale University Press.
Lewis, J. E. (Ed.). (2003). *The new rights of man: An anthology of the events, documents and speeches that have shaped western civilisation.* London: Robinson.
Li, S. C. (2003). Biocultural orchestration of developmental plasticity across levels: The impact of biology and culture in shaping the mind and behaviour across the life span. *Psychological Bulletin, 129*, 171–194.
Lickliter, R., & Honeycutt, H. (2003). Developmental dynamics: Toward a biologically plausible evolutionary psychology. *Psychological Bulletin, 129*, 819–835. Plus peer commentary, pp. 836–872.
Lindholm, C. (1993). *Charisma.* Oxford: Blackwell.
MacLean, P. D. (1990). *The triune brain in evolution.* New York: Plenum.
McGuire, M. T., & Troisi, A. (1998). *Darwinian psychiatry.* New York: Oxford University Press.
Ornstein, R. (1986). *Multimind: A new way of looking at human beings.* London: Macmillan.
Owen, D. (2007). *The hubris syndrome: Bush, Blair and the intoxication of power.* London: Politicos.
Owen, D. (2008). *In sickness and in power: Illness in heads of government during the last 100 years.* London: Methuen.
Porges, S. W. (2007). The polyvagal perspective. *Biological Psychology, 74*, 116–143.
Pratto, F., Sidanius, J., Stallworth, L. M., & Malle, B. F. (1994). Social dominance orientation: A personality variable predicting social and political attitudes. *Journal of Personality and Social Psychology, 67*, 741–763.

Sidanius, J., & Pratto, F. (2004). Social dominance theory: A new synthesis. In J. T. Jost & J. Sidanius (Eds.), *Political psychology* (pp. 315–322). London: Routledge.
Ridley, M. (1997). *The origins of virtue*. London: Penguin.
Taylor, C. (1989). *Sources of the self: The making of the modern identity*. Cambridge: Cambridge University Press.
Tobena, A., Marks, I., & Dar, R. (1999). Advantages of bias and prejudice: An exploration of their neurocognitive templates. *Neuroscience and Biobehavioral Reviews, 23*, 1047–1058.
Vessantara. (2003). *Meeting the Buddhas*. London: Windhorse.
Woollacott, M. (2009, July 2). *Manic moments: A Review of a world in trouble by Patrick Tyler*. UK: Guardian.

Chapter 3
Personal Schemas in the Negotiation Process: A Cognitive Therapy Approach

Robert L. Leahy

It is inevitable that at some point individuals will recognize that they may have conflicting interests with one another. These apparently incompatible differences may lead to an attempt to reconcile the differences so that some agreement may be reached. This is the process of negotiation. It affects all areas of our lives. We may negotiate the price of a car, the rent we pay, the hours and tasks we work on, the division of labor in our families, access to sexual pleasure, a parking space, and a replacement of a side dish on the blue-plate special. But negotiation also can be a matter of life or death, such as the negotiation of a treaty to avoid armed conflict or the reduction of genocidal warfare.

A "rational" approach to negotiation would be based on consideration of the value of reaching an agreement between two parties that would have a likelihood of being honored in the future. It does not help to negotiate a settlement if when negotiation is completed the other party is unwilling to follow through on the agreement. Thus, if the other party feels coerced or humiliated, then the follow-through on a negotiated settlement may be ephemeral. Or, if there is no way to enforce compliance on the other party, then opportunistic and unilateral abandonment of the agreement will be more likely. The parties to a negotiation attempt to persuade the other side in order to achieve an optimal outcome for the self. Rational negotiators recognize that the other side is also pursuing these goals and will not be easily dissuaded. The participants in a negotiation will consider the interests, options and "personalities" of the disputants in a negotiation, attempting to maximize their own position, often at the expense of the other participants.

Except in the case where sheer force is applied to coerce compliance, the negotiator attempts to persuade. Fisher and Ury have proposed a model of principled negotiation that sets out certain guidelines (Fisher 1991). A principled and rational model of negotiation is guided by the following ideas: (1) We will rely on facts and logic. Thus, persuasion should be based on reference to information and to logical inference rather than to appeals of emotion or personal need; (2) We attack the problem, not the person. This implies that ad hominem attacks in negotiation

R.L. Leahy (✉)
Director, American Institute for Cognitive Therapy, New York City
e-mail: Leahy@CognitiveTherapyNYC.com

F. Aquilar and M. Galluccio (eds.), *Psychological and Political Strategies for Peace Negotiation*, DOI 10.1007/978-1-4419-7430-3_3,

only interfere with the process and obscure the reliance on facts and logic; (3) Compromise is acceptable. Negotiation is not unilateral power-assertion, but rather an understanding that both parties may have to give up something to gain agreement; (4) Participants may want to continue the relationship later. This is an important point for disputants to consider since future interaction may depend on how the current differences are resolved. If one side feels humiliated, then resentments and distrust may interfere with future capability to cooperate. For example, the Treaty of Versailles created conditions of humiliation and economic hardship on Germany following the First World War, resulting in non-compliance and later attempts to retaliate (Keynes 1920). Furthermore, if the future relationship requires compliance as a result of the current negotiated settlement, there need to be ongoing persuasive reasons for cooperation; (5) Both parties recognize that they both have other possible desirable alternatives. This is known as the Best Alternative to a Negotiated Agreement (BATNA). Thus, in negotiating we recognize that the other side may have a better alternative than reaching an agreement with us. In addition, we need to consider our own alternative to a negotiated settlement. Our power over the other is also dependent on the degree to which they view themselves dependent on us for outcomes (Kim and Fragale 2005).

Negotiation and the View of the Self

Negotiators consider their view of themselves and of others in this interpersonal process. Rational negotiators take into consideration a number of factors about themselves before entering the negotiation (Of course, negotiators are not rational and may sacrifice a potential advantage by failing to consider these factors). The individual assesses for himself the following:

- Specific goals and values: What am I trying to accomplish? Am I trying to get a raise, buy a house, or reduce the threat of being attacked? Do I want to uphold certain values, such as freedom, fairness and human dignity? What am I looking for?
- What is the *most* desired alternative: Of all of the possible outcomes, what would be the most desirable for me?
- What am I willing to accept? Perhaps I will not achieve the outcome I most desire. What would I be willing to accept that is progress over the current situation?
- Rationale for my position. How do I justify my position? What is the logic, precedent, or justification behind my position?
- Best alternative to negotiating: If I don't accept the alternative offered by the other party, what is my alternative elsewhere?

Research on negotiation indicates that the process is far from rational. Negotiators suffer from anchoring effects of initial offers, framing effects, egocentric biases, emotional effects, confirmation biases, over-reliance on recent and easily accessible information, and distortions in what is considered to be fair (Aquilar and Galluccio 2008; Babcock and Loewenstein 1997; Babcock et al. 1995; Bazerman 1998; Forgas 1998). Moreover, negotiators may differ as to the mental models that they hold of the process of negotiators. Some negotiators view the pie as fixed and thereby are more inclined to take a winner-loser approach, while others take an integrative approach allowing for tradeoffs or even expanding the range of negotiated points (Thompson and Hastie 1990). Some negotiators employ a model of cooperative negotiation, attempting to find a solution that meets the needs of all relevant parties, while others employ an individualistic model, attempting only to maximize the position of the self. Individualistic negotiators are less flexible and tend not to adjust to the behavior of disputants (Weingart et al. 2007).

Although the foregoing research has emphasized general processes in negotiation, it is argued in the present chapter that individual differences in personality may exacerbate these processes. We will see shortly how cognitive distortions and personality disorders interfere in the process of negotiation (Aquilar and Galluccio 2008; Galluccio 2004). It is difficult for individuals whose personal schemas are problematic to achieve a rational and principled negotiated settlement, especially when the problem is compounded by emotional dysregulation.

These foregoing guidelines in evaluating the self's position may become compounded with problematic views of the self. As we shall see, personal schemas about the self may include the view that the self is weak, incompetent, overwhelmed, helpless, or defective. This will affect the negotiation process. Or the individual may view himself as superior, entitled to special treatment or, in the alternative, he may view himself as vulnerable to being controlled, his autonomy is threatened, or driven by his emotions. In everyday life, it is humans who negotiate, and we bring to the process all our strengths and vulnerabilities.

Negotiation and the View of the Other

Just as principled and rational negotiation assumes that one has evaluated the position for the self, it also assumes that one has a clear view of the other. In considering the other person, how do I evaluate their point of view, their needs and their alternatives? I might consider the following.

1. What are their specific goals and values? What do they value, what do they want and what are they trying to accomplish?
2. What are their most desired alternatives? What do they see as the most desirable outcome? Why is this desirable to them?
3. What are they willing to accept? Do I know what their "bottom-line" is? What is the minimum that they are willing to accept?
4. What is their rationale for their position? How do they justify their position? Is it based on logic, reasons, evidence, power, better alternatives?
5. What is their best alternative to negotiating? If they do not accept my offer, what is their best alternative?

Negotiation requires a social mentality that is often very difficult to achieve (see Gilbert in this book). When we enter the negotiation process we may be overwhelmed with our own emotions, we may have felt personally injured or treated unfairly, and we may want to humiliate the other side. Negotiation attempts to accomplish an apparent contradiction – to achieve an agreement with a person we do not trust. It is naïve to encourage one to "think positively" or "trust," since these are the very problems that are under negotiation. But just as we may have "issues" with the other side, they also have their point of view.

For example, consider the American efforts in Iraq. Initially, there appeared to be a global view that the other side was a unilateral group of deranged militants or fascist holdovers from Saddam's regime. Even if there were individual examples that might verify that position, it was an unhelpful way to go out about thinking about the "enemy." A more rational and sophisticated approach unfolded for the American intelligence community. Different groups had different interests. They saw things from their perspective and from their historical context. Some wanted security, some wanted jobs, others wanted participation in the political process. Others wanted to drive allied forces out and punish any collaborators. Some wanted an Islamic Caliphate. By recognizing what the diverse positions were of the various participants in the conflict, American intelligence became smarter. They could then form alliances, for example, with the Sunni nationals who wished protection, participation and jobs. They could attempt to marginalize the al-Qaeda insurgents and pit them against the Sunni tribal leaders.

Consider how the negotiation of this important conflict benefited from (finally) understanding the interests of the other side. By understanding the interests, goals, concerns, and "rational" basis of the positions taken by Sunni tribal leaders, it was possible to understand why it might "make sense" for Sunnis to be fearful of Shiite power and threats from fundamentalist insurgents. As a result of this new understanding, the allied forces were able to offer a better alternative to conflict – and that was protection, alliance, "your enemy is my enemy," participation in the political process and autonomy. People will generally stop fighting if they believe they can get what they want through less costly means.

An important step in negotiation is to write out the strongest case for the other side. The rational negotiator can step outside of his or her own point of view and write a detailed description of the rationale for the other side, the best alternatives to negotiation, the audience or base of the other side, what their schemas are of "us," and how they can maintain their sense of dignity if they do reach an agreement. Simply asserting the self's position from a position of power, humiliation, or bravado will seldom convince the other side to reach an agreement. Indeed, people are often willing to die – not to achieve land or money – but to avoid humiliation (Kagan 1995). One can also have a schematic view of the other. Again, personal schemas (and personality disorders) may affect how we see the other in the negotiation process. For example, the other may be seen as persecuting, strong, weak, inferior, benevolent, or even as someone who will rescue and take care of the self. These problematic schemas may over-ride any attempt to be rational and principled in the negotiation process.

Impediments to Negotiation

Automatic Thoughts in Negotiation

The cognitive therapy model asserts that dysfunctional negative thoughts contribute to anger, anxiety, and depression (Beck 1976, 1996). If we view negotiation as a common process in relationships, we can see from the literature on couples that problematic styles of attribution, communication, automatic thought distortions, withdrawal, punishment, escalation, and schematic thinking can influence any relationship (Epstein and Baucom 2002). Distraught couples often have problematic ways of seeing their partner. They may think, "The problem is my partner," or they may engage in personalizing, mind-reading, catastrophizing, all-or-nothing thinking, and a series of endless should statements (Aquilar and Galluccio 2008; Galluccio 2004). When differences are discussed, distraught partners bring up the kitchen sink, label their partner, go off task, threaten, pout, or withdraw. One can make a good case that the same dysfunctional patterns of thinking and behaving characterize participants in the process of negotiation. For example, consider the following negative (or overly positive) thoughts about the self and how they might impact in achieving a negotiated settlement:

Labeling: "I am a loser." (Alternatively, "I am all powerful") The negative label of the self may underestimate the ability to achieve goals. For example, the dependent individual with low self-esteem may believe that he has no ability to press his point. Alternatively, overly positive views of the self may lead one to over-state one's position, leading the other side to call the bluff and to the collapse of negotiation. Labeling is often a major impediment in negotiation. This is why I recommend writing out a justification of the other's point of view. Understanding the historical context of the conflict may be part of this. For example, in Iraq how have Westerners and Christians been viewed in the historical context of Islam or the Arab world? Even if American intentions may, at times, be driven by a desire to "extend democracy" as a human right, this is hardly the history of Western European involvement in the Middle East. Realizing that westerners (which, by proxy, includes Americans) were viewed alternately as the origins of the Crusades, an attack on Islam, infidels, those who defeated the Ottomans, who arbitrarily divided up the Ottoman empire and established "states," who exploited oil reserves, and backed repressive regimes – all of these historical "contexts" of the "invader" need to be viewed from the perspective of the Islamic or Arab world. One might argue the justification of any one of these views, but the views exist regardless of whether one sees them as valid. Thus, the imposition of control and the assertion of power, coupled with the unfortunate use of the word "crusade" by the President of the United States, further compounded what for millions in the Middle East had been experienced as centuries of humiliation (Lewis 2003, 2009 March/April).

As with all automatic thoughts, we can utilize a range of traditional cognitive therapy techniques to test and challenge them (Leahy 2003). For example, in regard to labeling the other side, we can look at the advantages and disadvantages of labeling.

An advantage is that it may make us feel morally superior and may allow us to justify whatever nefarious means we will employ. The disadvantage is that we may miss our opportunity to form an alliance with a complicated "adversary." For example, what would the outcome have been if the United States had refused to form an alliance with the Soviet Union during the Second World War? We can look for information to disconfirm our view. Keeping in mind the tendency toward confirmation bias in any labeling, we may want to look for evidence that the other side is not always "stupid," "backward," or "evil." We might want to examine the impact of communicating this all or nothing thinking to the other side – does it help the process of negotiation?

Fortune-telling: "Nothing will work out for me" or "I will get exactly what I want." Rational negotiators recognize that the future is hard to predict and that outcomes may or may not work out. The depressive negotiator does not foresee any possibility of success and may either cave in or refuse to negotiate. The overly optimistic and narcissistic negotiator may ignore the possibility that the outcome will be negative and, thereby, is ill prepared for other contingencies. Perhaps a prudent model would be "Hope for success, but plan for failure." The Secretary of Defense, Donald Rumsfeld, would have been well advised to take this precautionary approach.

Fortune-telling often follows the path of one story that will unfold inevitably. If the story is bleak, then we may feel that our position in negotiation is forlorn. But there may be a series of other paths that we can follow before we throw in the towel. For example, we might begin to build some common ground with the other side by negotiating minor issues (Nixon, for all his personal foibles, was wise to begin the process of rapprochement with the Chinese communist leaders by encouraging an international table-tennis competition). The element of uncertainty is part of any negotiation – which is why we negotiate (Galluccio 2007). We negotiate to explore alternatives – each alternative with a separate branch of other alternatives.

Distorted automatic thoughts often characterize the way we may think about the other disputants in the process. Indeed, we may label the other side as "evil," "the enemy," or "stupid" and fail to recognize that they also have feelings, past histories, moral principles, and families just like we do (Beck 1999; Hofstadter 1965). Labeling the opposition in a negotiation interferes with understanding how they might see alternatives, how they might justify their position, or how they might consider facts and logic. Indeed, labeling the other side interferes with the process of role-taking, validation, joining, compromising, and, of course, trusting in compliance. Nefarious labels may contribute to a tendency to rely on power-assertion, intimidation, or humiliation. This then leads to a backlash and retaliation that may, ironically, reinforce the label, "They are just rigid in their ways. You can't negotiate anything with them."

Labeling can be reversed by employing the processes that labeling jeopardizes. For example, it is hard to hold onto a rigid label if we empathize and validate the other side. "I can understand how hard it has been for your people to have to experience these difficulties that we are experiencing at this time." Appealing to the opposite of the label also helps disconfirm the label and facilitate the negotiation: "I know that our side has said some tough things, but I also know that you want the best for your people and that you are respected and trusted by them." Moreover, looking for initial points of simple compromise, which are not costly to either side, helps dissuade both sides from labeling.

Negotiation can also be impeded by unjustified mind reading ("They think we are idiots"), personalizing ("Their policies are out to ruin us"), dichotomous thinking ("Either you are with us or against us"), and discounting the positive ("Their cooperation on controlling terrorism isn't relevant to this issue"). Of course, it may be that mind reading may be accurate (they may think we are fools), but like any thought that the other side has, it may depend on the information that is provided. It may be that past cooperation may not be directly relevant to the current content of the crisis at hand, but past cooperation may be used as an argument that we can cooperate, even if we have other differences. Building common ground in negotiation may be impeded by automatic thoughts and may be facilitated by the process of differentiating thoughts and situations, so that the self and other can be viewed flexibly and less in terms of attributions fixed forever in stone. These fixed attributions have been shown to impede effective negotiation (Morris et al. 1999).

Problematic Styles of Persuasion

Participants in the negotiating process often bring to the table their own personal schemas and assumptions about how to persuade others. As noted earlier, principled and rational negotiation relies on logic, facts, mutual interests, principles and respect. However, negotiators may harbor underlying theories about "persuasion" that may get in the way of rational and principled negotiation. These may include problematic styles of communication, such as the following:

- Power assertion: "Do this, or else!"
- Humiliation and personal attacks: "Only an idiot would say such a thing"
- Stonewalling: "I won't talk to you"
- Emotionalizing: Crying, yelling, dramatizing.
- Pleading: "You don't realize how much I need this."
- Surrender: "OK. You win."

There are consequences of interpersonal styles that deviate from the principled and rational approach to negotiation. For example, power assertion may lead to a stiffening of the stance of the other side so that both sides become "positional" rather than "principled" negotiators. Indeed, power assertion often leads to reciprocity of negatives and escalation of conflict. However, power assertion may be a "backup" position that can be used to enforce an agreement, so that the other side (failing to be persuaded by principles) may be persuaded by the credible threat of force. But if the threat of force is not credible, then power assertion may reveal an ultimate weakness in the position of the side that attempts to force an agreement. Humiliation and personal attacks are often styles of communication when negotiators forget that they are trying to reach an agreement. These provocative statements often lead to retaliatory name-calling or counter-attack. Stonewalling, which may be a "negotiating" strategy, may be used to find out if the other will initiate a compromise simply to get things moving. However, stonewalling usually leads to mutual withdrawal and the destruction of trust.

Emotionalizing the discussion may intimidate the other side, but it seldom serves the purpose of convincing anyone of the legitimacy of the position taken. Individuals who use emotionalizing as a tactic run the risk of undermining their credibility in the eyes of the other. However, emotionalizing may be a useful tactic for propagandists who wish to appeal to their base by showing how determined and passionate they are. Pleading for mercy and pity reveals one's weakness and only works if the other has a conscience. Pleading is based on an assumption that the other will feel empathy or guilt and will try to resolve the differences by sacrificing a powerful position. However, if the other side wishes to assert power, then pleading becomes an invitation to that endeavor. Finally, capitulation ("OK, you win") is a tactic that some people will use to put an end to the "agony" of negotiation. Caving in and giving the other what he or she wants may end the process of negotiation, but will usually leave one with a settlement that will be resented later.

These foregoing problematic styles of negotiation may be issues to put on the table for the negotiators. For example, the individual who says, "Do this, or else!" may be confronted with the following query: "It sounds like you are making an intimidating statement to us at this point in time. Will this help us work together or will this impede our work together? I ask you to consider, if you were in my position and the other side made this kind of provocative comment, how would you react?" Similarly, statements that are provocative and humiliating may also be placed on the table as issues to be negotiated "before negotiation begins." "If you call me names and attempt to humiliate me, it will make it hard for us to reach a settlement that we can both agree to. I understand that you have a lot of reasons to be upset – just as our side does. We can empathize with one another about those differences. But I think we will get further working together if we refrain from calling each other names."

Now it may be that the use of humiliating and provocative language is not meant to persuade the other side, but rather to persuade the allies that are driving the negotiator. For example, a politician may find it convenient in building his base of support to attack the disputant in a negotiation – consider the present leaders of Venezuela, Korea, and Iran. Indeed, he or she may have little interest in reaching any settlement and may simply want to use the negotiation as a tool for political propaganda. For years the "negotiation" in the press between the Bush administration and the Iranian leader were simply mutual posturing and statements of public humiliation. It even appeared from an outsider's point of view to be an international "game of chicken" ("Chicken" is a game of driving your car toward the edge of a cliff, screaming in a frenzy, to see which one "chickens out" until one jumps out of the car first before the car goes over the cliff. Unfortunately, as amusing as this game may seem to high-testosterone teenage males, it often leads to both cars going over the cliff ending in an explosion as the chickens are barbecued at the bottom of the cliff).

When the negotiator has come to the table with little interest in reaching a settlement and more of an interest in proving a point to a base, negotiation is difficult. However, the rational negotiator can go to the opponent's base and obviate the attacks: "Our side is sincerely interested in having rational and reasonable and respectful talks. We believe that calling each other names will not help the situation. I ask each of you who is hearing the personal attacks made by your leader if this is going to help us reach an agreement between our nations. If not, then what purpose could it be serving?" The rational negotiator can view the rants as a tactic that distracts and, thereby, widen the negotiation to go to the base of political support. Ironically, however, ranting on one side leads to ranting on the other side which then gets us back to the game of chicken as both sides go over the cliff in a blaze of glory (Aquilar and Galluccio 2008).

Personal Schemas and Negotiation

How do personal schemas express themselves in negotiating? The cognitive model proposes that each personality disorder is characterized by schemas about self and other (Beck et al. 2003). Moreover, any one individual may endorse schemas that cut across personality disorders (Leahy et al. 2005; Young et al. 2003). The avoidant personality fears negative evaluation and rejection and approaches negotiation with the following vulnerabilities: Fearing conflict, underestimating his own position, and hesitating to enter negotiation. The avoidant individual believes that he is defective or inferior and believes that negotiation will be another experience for humiliation. Consequently, he will hesitate to negotiate or may simply give in so as to avoid further conflict. This then leads to resentment that unfair conditions have been imposed. The dependent personality, fearing abandonment and believing that he is unable to take care of himself without the support of a stronger individual, views negotiation as threatening or as an opportunity to plead his needs. The dependent person does not recognize potential strengths he may have, or that there may be alternatives to offer, and therefore is often unwilling to assert the self in negotiating. Because they fear rejection and termination of relationship dependent people may often cave in and compromise. For example, a woman with a dependent personality believed she could not survive without her husband's love and support. This was followed by humiliation, manipulation, and eventual physical abuse. When she finally initiated separation and divorce proceedings, she was surprised both by her ability to cope without his support and by his desperate pleas to maintain the relationship. She had never realized that he was far more dependent on her than she was on him.

The histrionic personality views negotiation as a form of psychodrama. This individual may crave attention and emotional expression and turns negotiation into dramatic displays by trying to seduce and impress the other side. The histrionic relies on emotion, not rationality and facts. Hoping to impress the other with an exciting personality, the histrionic may sometimes succeed but at the eventual risk of undermining any credibility. The hardest thing may be to overcome the view that others do not take you seriously any more. Borderline personalities, beset by demands for validation, dichotomous thinking, and emotional dysregulation, approach negotiation as invalidating, feel oppressed, manipulated, and rejected. Their emotions override compromise and they may find themselves so angry, anxious, and confused that they either escalate the process with threats or withdraw completely. Often the borderline will view negotiation in all-or-nothing terms.

Obsessive–compulsive individuals often get hung up on the minute details of agreements, often missing the bigger picture and failing to realize that the other side may have personal schemas and emotional needs. This litigious, picky style of negotiation focuses on issues such as responsibility and logic, often nit-picking the smallest issue. The obsessive compulsive often appears to feel bewildered by emotional and irrational statements by the other side, simply dismissing them as "absurd," without exploring the personal meaning that others bring to the table. It is sometimes hard for the obsessive to empathize and validate, since emotional needs may be viewed as messy, off-task, and a sign of immaturity and irresponsibility.

The Special Case: The Narcissist as Negotiator

In this chapter I have chosen to focus on one particular personality style in the negotiation process, namely the "narcissistic personality." It is my view that over the course of history political and military disasters have ensued because of the dominance of narcissistic approaches to negotiation. One can make a case that some narcissism might be helpful in negotiation, since the narcissist may show substantial self-confidence, lack genuine empathy for the other side, be less "hampered" by feelings of guilt, and be more willing to use power to make a point. However, narcissism can sometimes have devastating consequences in negotiation. This will be my focus here.

Let us examine the underlying assumptions and views that the narcissist holds in interpersonal functioning and how this impacts on negotiation. The narcissist often holds personal schemas of moral rigidity ("I'm right, you are wrong") and sees the self as a superior person. By viewing the self as superior, entitled and always occupying the moral high ground, the narcissist is likely to view the other in a condescending manner. This condescension may then provoke the other side to retaliate and escalate the conflict, leading the narcissist to fall back on power assertion, humiliation, and bravado.

Moreover, the narcissist's sense of superiority may obscure recognition of vulnerabilities that others can readily see. Since the narcissist views the other as inferior and as, at best, a need-gratifier for the narcissist, he will often overlook the alternatives that are available to the other side. He will also underestimate the determination, resources, and moral suasion that the other side has for its own position. In a domestic dispute during divorce, a narcissistic husband believed his wife would never follow through with her threats of separation and believed that he was entitled to his aggressive and hostile behavior. This led him to place himself into greater legal and financial liabilities with her, which eventually led to a costly divorce. Overestimating his own power, he underestimated her resources, which included her intelligence, her legal position, and her support network.

The narcissist – believing that "God is on my side" – may take unusually provocative and ill-advised approaches to attack the other side, not recognizing that the other side may have military superiority. One can argue that in the past the Pakistani government has overestimated its ability to win an armed conflict against India, resulting in costly defeats. The narcissist often believes that he can utilize control, intimidation, and even emotional blackmail in relationships, which may, in some cases, lead to serious impasses in negotiation. The narcissist may take a "win everything" approach, believing "I am entitled to get my way, I should always win, I am a superior person." This view of winning everything makes negotiation extraordinarily difficult and makes conflict even more costly. It is very difficult to get other people to accept that you are a superior person and that they are inferior need-gratifiers. By violating a basic tenet of principled negotiation – preserving the self-respect of all parties – the narcissistic insistence on winner take all will lead to a collapse in the process and escalation of hostilities.

Narcissistic schemas that one is a special, superior person conflict with flexibility, role taking, compromise, and principled negotiation. Narcissists often view flexibility as arbitrating against their own entitlement: "Why should I compromise? I'm right." Inflexible negotiation runs the risk of an inflexible and mutually escalating conflict. Viewing mutual respect and flexibility as part of the process can enhance the position of both parties, but the narcissist has difficulty recognizing and respecting the value of both parties. Their difficulty in taking the role of the other – seeing the legitimacy of the other point of view, the historical context, the personal needs, and the value of respecting differences in style – hampers negotiation. The condescending, often dictatorial and didactic role of imposing one's will on the subservient other only reinforces the belief of the other that one is being oppressed and exploited once again. Dictating to others what they must accept, believe and do is seldom a successful strategy in negotiating. Others have alternatives to accepting humiliation – and one alternative may be a counter-attack.

The narcissist often has impasses to compromise. He views relationships in terms of winner-loser orientation. Rather than viewing compromise as a satisfactory solution to competing interests, the narcissist views it as losing. Indeed, compromise may be a narcissistic injury, reminding the narcissist that he is not special and superior and, so, must share the distributive pie with "inferiors." For some narcissists, compromise is equated with humiliation: "If I let her win, then I am a loser, just like everyone else." Thus, the narcissist has difficulty going beyond the zero-sum game model of negotiation, having difficulty expanding the pie or negotiating a less than perfect settlement.

As I noted, the narcissist has a negative view of the other as an inferior person. Others are viewed as need-gratifiers "for me," inferior, and as obstacles to getting "my way." Since the narcissist is focused on gratification, he has difficulty recognizing that there may be legitimate concerns presented by the other side. These legitimate concerns are viewed as problems for others to contend with, rather than thinking of the self and other as solving each other's respective problems. Moreover, the narcissist has deficits in skills that could be useful in negotiation such as an inability to understand the other person's perspective, reliance on control and threat, and rigidity in taking a position. Viewing the self's position from a "moral perspective" of entitlement, the narcissist may be hampered in perspective taking, unable to understand that the other side has an equally compelling "moral" position. Ironically, the narcissist may oppose reasonable settlements, claiming, "I won't compromise. It's a matter of principle." Failing to understand that both sides have their principles, the narcissist may conclude that the failure of the other side to give in to the principles and entitlement of the narcissist is part of the sad story that the inferior "losers" control the universe. For example, one businessman, driven by his narcissistic entitlement and grandiose visions of his investment acumen, would readily get on his high horse and claim he would not reach deals with other investors as a matter of principle. This made it impossible for him to reach deals.

Narcissists often go into a rage at the positions taken by other disputants. Using anger to intimidate, the narcissist may believe that they can make the other cower before their angry display, thereby proving that the other is weak and inferior. Indeed, rage is a negotiating tactic, very much like a temper-tantrum, and it may work at times. The intimidated avoidant, dependent, or threatened disputant may give in promptly simply to quell the anger. This fuels the reliance on rage and intimidation.

Turning the Narcissist into a Negotiator

Narcissists can become excellent negotiators if they view principled and rational negotiation as in their interests. I have worked with many highly successful and powerful individuals who were able to benefit from a cognitive therapy approach to negotiation. These are individuals who pursued therapy because they were having difficulty with their spouse, their children, staff members in their business, or partners and executives. My experience has indicated that focusing on developing the "advanced skill-set" of negotiating enhances "one's interest." Ironically, the strategy in helping a narcissist may be to appeal to his narcissism in order to overcome the impediments of the narcissism. Let's take a closer look.

We can contrast the narcissistic view with the adaptive view, where adaptive implies a more effective, rational, principled, and flexible approach. It is helpful to have the narcissist identify impasses in the negotiating process. For example, in marital negotiation, a narcissistic husband attempted to use threats ("You won't get any money if you divorce me"), self-promotion ("I'm an excellent husband. I'm faithful and I support you") – all to no avail. He then turned to making promises that lacked credibility: "I will change completely." Having failed in his negotiation endeavors and feeling helpless and fearful of divorce, he realized that his prior attempts did not work. I suggested to him that the goal at this point was to develop an entirely different approach to negotiating with his wife, based on a new model of a relationship. This new model would place his narcissistic needs of being special, superior, and entitled on the back burner and place his wife's needs for respect, validation, and independence in the front. We contrasted the costs and benefits of continuing with the old style with the potential benefits of a new style.

We began by contrasting the narcissistic view with the adaptive view as shown in Table 3.1.

By contrasting the less "effective" narcissistic style with the professional, effective, and empowering adaptive style, the narcissist can see that it is in his interests to be more adaptive. Thus, the appeal here is to rise above the skill deficits that one has to become a "special kind of negotiator," one who truly understands the process and is able to stay within his game. The goal is also not simply about winning (by defeating the other side); the goal is changed to being a skilled negotiator. This new goal of "skilled negotiator" is contrasted with entitlement, moralistic claims, and claims of being superior. Consider the contrasts depicted in Table 3.2 as reflecting the strategy of turning the narcissist into an "expert" on negotiation.

Negotiation becomes an odd game in this new view. Although there is always an adversarial quality to negotiation, its cooperative aspects are now emphasized.

Table 3.1 Narcissistic View of Compromise

Narcissistic view	Adaptive view
• Winner-loser orientation	• Effective negotiation enhances the position of both sides. Otherwise, why would anyone bother to negotiate?
• Views compromise as losing	• Compromise is a sign of professionalism. Winning-losing is childish.
• Compromise = Humiliation	• Compromise allows movement and opportunities for future relationships.
• Lack of flexibility	• Flexibility shows how professional you are. It empowers you to do more things.

Table 3.2 Narcissistic Assumptions in Negotiation

Narcissistic view	Adaptive view
1. Difficulty in using rational persuasion	5. Rational persuasion will be more convincing and is more likely to lead to agreements that are honored
2. I am entitled to get my way	6. Negotiation is about balanced interests. Even if you were entitled, you might not be able to get your way
3. I should always win	7. Winning is a self-defeating goal because compromise is the heart of negotiation.
4. I am a superior person	8. Even if you were superior it's irrelevant to negotiation.

In order for you to be effective in negotiating, you need to partly be a team player with the other side. You work together rather than work against each other.

This cooperative and "co-constructing" model of negotiation obviates the labeling and marginalization of the other. By understanding the other person's perspective, one enhances one's own position in negotiating (Table 3.3). In this new model, the other becomes a source of information, even "curiosity," so that the skilled negotiator may still harbor wishes to exploit the other side, but his or her attention is deployed to gaining information about the needs, historical context, perceptions, and emotions of the other side. In order to be more effective in negotiating you must do the non-narcissistic thing – you must look beyond yourself into the minds and hearts of others. Consider the contrast between the narcissistic view and adaptive view of the others. By ignoring the other person's point of view (history, needs, perspective, value system) you risk ignoring important motivating factors for the other in agreeing to a solution. Imagine that you are a quarterback and you had the option of knowing what the defense thought would be the best strategy for them. The more you know about how the other side plays the game – and why – the better you will be at achieving an optimal strategy. Indeed, by gaining more information about the other side by asking them what they need, how they see things and how they view their position, the more the other side "gives away its strategy." Rather than dictating to the other side the conditions of "surrender," the skilled negotiator attempts to inquire and listen carefully to how the other side views compromise. Perhaps they are willing to give more than you think they would. Perhaps you can achieve a solution that is optimal for both sides without sacrificing too much.

The narcissistic negotiator may view the other as a need gratifier. This may be the desire of the narcissist, but it may be unrealistic. The other side may have better options for themselves. Recognizing that they can "go elsewhere" – or that they have a better alternative to a negotiated settlement, may help one avoid being blind-sided by one's own superiority. For example, cutting off imports of oil from an "undesirable" state may lead to the sale of oil on the world market and to alliances with other "undesirable states." The narcissistic husband who attempts to demand that his wife be a need gratifier may not recognize that there may be others whose needs will be more appealing than his. Indeed, if the narcissist could stand back and assume that

Table 3.3 Narcissistic View of the Other

Narcissistic view of the other	Adaptive view of the other
• Inability to understand the other person's perspective	• Understanding the other's view empowers you in negotiating.
• Others are need-gratifiers for me	• Others are players with possible equal or superior options to negotiating with me.
• Inferior	• Underestimating the "opposition" can defeat my goals. Understanding their strengths enhances my strategy.
• Obstacles to getting my way	• The other side has its own goals, values, needs, and options. Rather than view them as obstacles we may be able to complement each other's needs.
• I should be in control	• They may not "need" me.

each participant will attempt to maximize his or her options, then it places the narcissist in the position of competing against more desirable alternatives than the self.

Narcissists may view control as an all-or-nothing phenomena. "Either she is in control or I am," or "Who is going to enforce the agreement?" Mutually assured checks and balances – and opportunities for feedback – may be more desirable than authoritarian and rigid styles of control. Just as the narcissist does not wish to be controlled, it is reasonable that the other side does not relish being controlled. The alternative to autonomy and control may be flexible cooperation. For example, on certain tasks one partner may be more effective being in control, whereas in other tasks the other partner could be better. Or control can be referred to a third agent. In the case of nations, an international arbiter may be invoked.

Special Traps for Narcissists

Just like the rest of us, narcissists may find themselves at impasses in the negotiation process. There are four that stand out as potentially problematic.

1. The victim trap. Here the narcissist focuses on how unfair it all is and views negotiation as a way to rectify the injustice of having been treated unfairly. The narcissist may demand apologies or restitution and fail – at all costs – to see his role in the problem. "How can you do this to me?" The problem with the victim trap is that – even if it is true – it is not a useful strategy for negotiation. Certainly, bringing up past wrongs may be an important part of setting the groundwork for why one's position is what it is, but the victim trap fails to address the interests of the other disputant. Challenging the victim trap may involve validating that the unfairness did occur, but then refocusing on how one can make things better in the future (Leahy 2001). Again, practical utility rather than past injury becomes the focus.
2. Commitment to sunk costs. Here the narcissist has invested a great deal in a past decision that is now (from the perspective of others) a failure. For example, Lyndon Johnson committed hundreds of thousands of troops to Vietnam, only to see this strategy fail. Rather than abandon the strategy he escalated it in an attempt to redeem the sunk cost of the prior sacrifices. Narcissists may be particularly vulnerable had to the sunk-cost effect since they are most concerned with "losing face." I have previously outlined a number of techniques to reverse the sunk-cost effect, including focusing on future utility rather than past costs, recognizing that abandoning a sunk cost is a sign of good decision-making, reflecting on what decision one would make now if one had never made the prior decision, and examining the advantage of cutting one's losses (Leahy 2001, 2004).
3. Ignoring risks. Narcissists often are viewed by others as tough, strong, determined, even – oddly – courageous. Sometimes this may be true, but it also may be the case that narcissism leads one to underestimate realistic risks. For example,

in my view Rumsfeld was driven by a narcissistic overestimation of his own wisdom in the Iraq War. Rather than listen to his generals, who advocated a larger troop commitment, he vetoed their recommendations and assumed that American forces had to face the risk of invasion with a smaller, compromised force. He ignored the risks precisely because he overestimated his own capacity. Similarly, a narcissistic husband may overestimate his position in a marriage, thereby risking losing it because he fails to recognize that his wife has better alternatives. Clear, practical, and transparent evaluation of risk is an essential ingredient in good negotiation.

4. Confirmation bias. Finally, narcissists are better than the rest of us at surrounding themselves with people who will tell them what they want to hear. Although they may point to the consensus that they have obtained for their position, they fail to recognize that they are, in fact, a victim of group thinking (See also Aquila and Galluccio 2008). Their strategy in building a consensus to justify their position is to turn to people who will agree with them. They stack the audience and believe the applause. An alternative to group-think is to assign someone the role of devil's advocate – someone who will find holes and vulnerabilities in the viewpoint that is offered. Although the narcissist may view this as disloyal, it is ultimately in his interests to check the facts and logic against a vigorous critic. This is part of cognitive therapy as well, engaging in a role-play to challenge the initial position. It is quite helpful to have the narcissist challenge his own position – and attempt to win the argument.

Conclusions

I recall when I first read the classic book, *Getting to Yes,* by Fisher and Ury I was immensely impressed with the clear, immediately empowering wisdom contained in that approach. It also occurred to me how much of this was consistent with a cognitive therapy approach. As I thought about it more I could see the value of the principled model of negotiation, but I could also see how cognitive distortions, maladaptive assumptions, problematic theories of how to persuade others, and personal schemas would interfere with negotiation. The present chapter attempts to integrate the cognitive therapy model with the Fisher and Ury model.

When one editors of this book, Mauro Galluccio, invited me to participate in a symposium titled "International Negotiation and Cognitive Psychotherapy" in 2008 in Rome at the International Congress of Cognitive Psychotherapy, I was eager to agree. I believe that cognitive therapists can make a significant contribution to this important area. As I looked out in the audience (where the room was packed) I could see people from all over the world. There were people there listening attentively whose fathers and grandfathers participated in wars against one another. Past enemies were present friends. It made me recognize the urgency of this moment in time that we use our tools to break down the barriers that unnecessarily divide us.

Indeed, it may be that narcissistic approaches to international relations have been the bane of our existence. Think about how many cognitive distortions have failed to stand up to experience. Labels such as "fascist," "racist," "communist," "terrorist," or "fanatic" have become passé in many circles. If negotiation is an interpersonal process then understanding the minds and needs of others should be a first requirement. Unfortunately, if we look at negotiation from the perspective of our own needs, demands, entitlement, and superior position we fail to understand that others have their own history, their own story, and their own solutions. If we attempt to intimidate, we will meet with resistance. If we attempt to dictate, we will find rebellion. But if we attempt to understand, empathize, validate, and find common ground we may find more than we bargained for. We may find peace.

References

Aquilar, F., & Galluccio, M. (2008). *Psychological processes in international negotiations: Theoretical and practical perspectives*. New York: Springer.

Babcock, L., & Loewenstein, G. (1997). Explaining bargaining impasse: The role of self-serving biases. *The Journal of Economic Perspectives, 11*, 109–126.

Babcock, L., Loewenstein, G., Issacharoff, S., & Camerer, C. (1995). Biased judgments of fair ness in bargaining. *The American Economic Review, 85*, 1337–1343.

Bazerman, M. H. (1998). *Judgment in managerial decision making* (4th ed.). New York: Wiley.

Beck, A. T. (1976). *Cognitive therapy and the emotional disorders*. New York: International Universities Press.

Beck, A. T. (1996). Beyond belief: A theory of modes, personality and psychopathology. In P. Salkovskis (Ed.), *Frontiers of cognitive therapy* (pp. 1–25). New York: Guilford.

Beck, A. T. (1999). *Prisoners of hate: The cognitive basis of anger, hostility, and violence*. New York: HarperCollins.

Beck, A. T., Freeman, A., Davis, D. D., Pretzer, J., Fleming, B., Artz, A., et al. (2003). *Cognitive therapy of personality disorders* (2nd ed.). New York: Guilford.

Epstein, N. B., & Baucom, D. H. (2002). *Enhanced cognitive-behavioral therapy for couples: A contextual approach*. Washington, DC: American Psychological Association.

Fisher, R., & Ury, W. (1991). *Getting to yes: Negotiating agreement without giving in*. New York: Penguin.

Forgas, J. P. (1998). On feeling good and getting your way: Mood effects on negotiator cognition and bargaining strategies. *Journal of Personality and Social Psychology, 74*(3), 565–577.

Galluccio, M. (2004, July). International negotiation: Cognitive, emotional and communicative aspects. Paper presented at the 27th Annual Scientific Meeting of the International Society of Political Psychology, Lund, Sweden.

Galluccio, M. (2007, July). Cognitive psychotherapy and international negotiation: An overview. Paper presented at the V World Congress of Behavioural and Cognitive Therapies, Barcelona, Spain.

Hofstadter, R. (1965). *The paranoid style in American politics and other essays*. New York: Alfred A. Knopf.

Kagan, D. (1995). *On the origins of war and the preservation of peace*. New York: Doubleday.

Keynes, J. M. (1920). *The economic consequences of the peace*. New York: Harcourt, Brace & Howe.

Kim, P. H., & Fragale, A. R. (2005). Choosing the path to bargaining power: An empirical comparison of BATNAs and contributions in negotiation. *Journal of Applied Psychology, 90*(2), 373–381.

Leahy, R. L. (2001). *Overcoming resistance in cognitive therapy*. New York: Guilford.
Leahy, R. L. (2003). *Cognitive therapy techniques: A practitioner's guide*. New York: Guilford.
Leahy, R. L. (2004). Decision making processes and psychopathology. In R. L. Leahy (Ed.), *Contemporary cognitive therapy: Theory, research, and practice* (pp. 116–138). New York: Guilford.
Leahy, R. L., Beck, J., & Beck, A. T. (2005). Cognitive therapy for the personality disorders. In S. Strack (Ed.), *Handbook of personology and psychopathology* (pp. 442–461). Hoboken: Wiley.
Lewis, B. (2003). *What went wrong? The clash between Islam and modernity in the Middle East*. New York: Harper Perennial.
Lewis, B. (2009, March/Aprail). Free at last: The Arab world in the twenty-first century [Electronic Version]. Retrieved March. *Foreign Affairs, 13*, 2009.
Morris, M., Larrick, R., & Su, S. (1999). Misperceiving negotiation counterparts: When situationally determined bargaining behaviors are attributed to personality traits. *Journal of Personality and Social Psychology, 77*(1), 52–67.
Thompson, L., & Hasti, R. (1990). Social perception in negotiation. *Organizational Behavior and Human Decision Processes, 47*, 98–123.
Weingart, L., Tepper, D. A., Brett, J. M., Olekalns, M., & Smith, P. L. (2007). Conflicting social motives in negotiating groups. *Journal of Personality and Social Psychology, 93*(6), 994–1010.
Young, J. E., Klosko, J. S., & Weishaar, M. (2003). *Schema therapy: A practioner's guide*. New York: Guilford.

Chapter 4
Emotional Competence and Effective Negotiation: The Integration of Emotion Understanding, Regulation, and Communication

Carolyn Saarni

The construct "emotional competence" was first introduced by the sociologist Steve Gordon (1989) and subsequently elaborated by the author as consisting of eight skills that developed interdependently and were also very much tied to the emotionally evocative context (Saarni 1999). Table 4.1 presents the eight skills, and I shall refer to these skills in my discussion of how they influence the negotiation process as well as the negotiators themselves.

Emotional competence can be succinctly defined: It is the demonstration of self-efficacy in emotion-eliciting social transactions, but this brief definition belies its complexity. Self-efficacy essentially means that one possesses the capacity and confidence in one's abilities to reach one's goals (Bandura 1977, 1989), and goals in emotion-laden situations refer to the motivating aspects of the situation facing the individual in which various emotions are evoked (Lazarus 1991). Competence is judged relative to: (1) the cultural standards that are indicative of appropriate developmental mastery and maturity and (2) the functional adaptiveness of the individual's response (Campos et al. 1994) in a particular cultural context. We experience emotions when we have a stake in the outcome of our encounter with the environment, and to make matters even more complicated, our appraisal of the environment may vary across several levels of conscious awareness. This means that we may respond emotionally to the environmental encounter in ways that are not deliberate, not rational, and without a conscious sense of volition. Indeed, most emotion processes operate without consciousness (Clore et al. 2005), although once we are experiencing the emotion itself, we are generally aware of our feeling state and tend to attribute it to something in the environmental encounter (but not always accurately).

Because of the unconsciousness of many processes in emotion generation, on occasion we will behave in ways, when examined in retrospect, that were not especially emotionally competent and did not serve our healthy self-interests adaptively in the *long run*. How should we understand such a contrary outcome? Using the concepts "declarative" and "procedural knowledge" helps to explain how this might

C. Saarni
Department of Counseling, Sonoma State University, Rohnert Park, California, USA
e-mail: saarni@sonoma.edu

F. Aquilar and M. Galluccio (eds.), *Psychological and Political Strategies for Peace Negotiation*, DOI 10.1007/978-1-4419-7430-3_4,

Table 4.1 Skills of emotional competence

1. Awareness of one's emotional state, including the possibility that one is experiencing multiple emotions, and at even more mature levels, awareness that one might also not be consciously aware of one's feelings due to unconscious dynamics or selective inattention.
2. Skills in discerning and understanding others' emotions, based on situational and expressive cues that have some degree of consensus as to their emotional meaning.
3. Skill in using the vocabulary of emotion and expression in terms commonly available in one's subculture and at more mature levels to acquire cultural scripts that link emotion with social roles.
4. Capacity for empathic and sympathetic involvement in others' emotional experiences.
5. Skill in realizing that inner emotional state need not correspond to outer expression, both in oneself and in others, and at more mature levels the ability to understand that one's emotional-expressive behavior may impact on another and take this into account in one's self-presentation strategies.
6. Skill in modulating emotional reactions by using strategies that modify the intensity, duration, or aversiveness of such emotional responses as well as skill in coping adaptively with distressing circumstances.
7. Awareness that the structure or nature of relationships is in part defined by how emotion is communicated, for example, by the degree of emotional immediacy or genuineness of expressive display and by the degree of reciprocity or symmetry within the relationship; e.g., mature intimacy is in part defined by mutual or reciprocal sharing of genuine emotions, whereas a parent-child relationship may have asymmetric sharing of genuine emotions.
8. Capacity for emotional self-efficacy: The individual views her- or himself as feeling, overall, the way he or she wants to feel. That is, emotional self-efficacy means that one accepts one's emotional experience, whether unique and eccentric or culturally conventional, and this acceptance is in alignment with the individual's beliefs about what constitutes desirable emotional "balance." In essence, one is living in accord with one's personal theory of emotion when one demonstrates emotional self-efficacy that is integrated with one's moral sense.

Note: Adapted from Saarni (2000), pp 77–78. Copyright 2000 by Jossey-Bass. Reprinted by permission of the author.

come about. Declarative knowledge refers to explicit concepts of *what* one knows, and procedural knowledge refers to *how* one tacitly applies what one knows. To illustrate, we can have explicit (declarative) knowledge of words that represent different emotions, but in a given instance, we may not be immediately aware of how we actually appraise an emotion-eliciting situation and respond to it with, for example, surprise versus happiness, fear versus anger, or sadness versus anxiety, among many other possible emotional reactions. That appraisal process, the subsequent regulation of the emotions themselves, and how one copes with the emotion-evoking situation are largely reflective of well-rehearsed procedural knowledge, which functions much like the application of non-conscious event scripts. In short, we do not always act in an emotionally competent manner if the situation facing us exceeds our resilience, our knowledge, and/or our coping capacity, and we may not even be aware of it until a later point in time (North Americans sometimes refer to this as having "stuck one's foot in one's mouth" after having impulsively expressed an emotional reaction).

From the standpoint of effective negotiation, emotional competence skills serve the negotiator, and such skills also influence the dynamic transactions that are part of the communication and interpersonal influence between negotiators. I shall discuss these two inter-related phenomena in this essay relative to the specific skills of emotional competence, but first I elaborate on some of the theoretical assumptions of emotional competence and what we know about its development (further details are available in Saarni (1999) and Saarni et al. (2006)).

Theoretical Assumptions

Reciprocal Influence Between Emotions and Relationships

When we think about how humans develop emotionally, it is through the relationships that we have with others. Granted, we are also biologically wired to be emotional, but the meanings, the language, the appraisals we make of emotion-evocative situations have all been filtered, so to speak, through our relationships with others. Even when we are alone and face an emotion-evocative situation, our appraisal of it is still made meaningful through our prior immersion in relationships. However, as we develop from infancy through adolescence and into adulthood, we also contribute to those relationships. Whether it be from a temperamental "bias" (e.g., introversion versus extraversion) or from simply how young children attend to some features of relationships and not to others due to cognitive limitations, those emerging relationships with parents, siblings, kin, and peers are also influenced by what the individual child brings to the dynamic transaction (Anybody who is a parent is very aware of how even the newborn – and quite profoundly so – influences its relationship with its parents). What is important to emphasize here is that the *way* that the developing child influences its relationships with others is through emotion-laden communication: crying, smiling, screaming as in temper tantrums, gaze avoidance or intent eye contact, laughing with pleasure, and coyly tilting its head. Leach and Tiedens (2004) have summed up very well the perspective that I take here: "Emotions are one channel through which the individual knows the social world, and the social world is what allows people to know emotion" (p. 2).

Of course, this social world is saturated with cultural beliefs, artifacts, and practices, and if we extend Leach and Tieden's thinking, then emotional experience, considered both within the individual and collectively across groups of people, reciprocally influences the cultural context. As we can see in the globalization of information via the Internet, cultural beliefs do indeed change, albeit change is more evident in superficialities and nuance than in deeply held values. The emotions that are evoked in people may lead them to question culturally approved practices and beliefs, and thus the dynamic fluidity of a society is manifested in this reciprocal influence of emotions and cultural beliefs and practices. Faure (2002) wisely predicted that growing exchanges between nations (via media, trade, etc.) would result in both cultural transcendence as well as a heightened sensitivity to cultural distinctiveness; indeed, a celebration of cultural and ethnic differences may be what we see ensuing in our current international climate. In sum, emotions are dynamic psycho-physiological processes that occur "in" the individual, but they cannot be understood without taking into account the individual's transaction with an environment (especially a social environment). Thus, emotional experience, by definition, is a *bio-ecological* experience as well. We are, after all, organisms who inhabit a dynamic habitat (Saarni 2008).

Emotion Generation and Ethno-Psychology

A Western model of "mind" assumes that mental processes are linked to the generation of emotional states through appraisal of events and their meaningfulness for the "self." In other societies emotions may be construed as directly caused by ancestral spirits, by dreams, as well as by others' actions. In this sense, cultural beliefs (folk theories) about emotion may actually mediate emotion *generation*. Emotions may be manifested or described as "illness" or as bodily responses (e.g., jumping livers, dizzy spells), as well as in expressive behavior, and thus, cultural context also mediates emotional *experience* or how we make sense of our felt emotions, which is a subjective process for each individual with regard to awareness of one's own emotions or in trying to understand others' emotions.

The functionalist theory of emotion generation and experience is a western theory (Campos et al. 1994), and it emphasizes goals that are meaningful to the individual as the impetus for emotion evocation. Granted, these goals may be relational, collectivist-oriented, and/or individualized, and it is this flexibility of the functionalist theory of emotion that makes it attractive for examining emotional experience in a variety of societies. There has also been a convergence within both developmental psychology and social psychology to emphasize the inter-penetration of emotions and relationships; see, for example, Campos et al. (1994) or Saarni (1999) for the developmental perspective, and for the social psychology perspective, Lazarus (1991) and Morris and Keltner (2000). For the latter, the function of emotions is "to guide interactions between individuals" (Morris and Keltner 2000, p. 3).

For international negotiators to come together in productive meetings, both are better served if they are knowledgeable about the emotion folk theories or ethno-psychologies of their counterpart's culture. It is my hope that the discussion of emotional competence in this essay will serve as a vehicle for assisting non-Western negotiators to understand the ethno-psychology of their counterparts who come from Western or individualist societies. Given the globalization of information, we are also seeing "hybrid" cultures emerging in diverse societies in which both collectivist and individualist values and beliefs are endorsed (e.g., compare urban Beijing or Shanghai with rural western Sichuan Province). Faure (2002) again embraces cultural factors as active elements in the negotiation process that competent negotiators can make use of, understand, and develop as "integrative cultural blends" (p. 413) and bridges to improve the outcome of negotiations that encompass two or more distinctive societies.

Moral Disposition or Identity

In addition to one's developmental and relational history, another very significant contributor to emotional competence, especially by adolescence and continuing into adulthood, is one's moral disposition or identity. I have been influenced in this regard by the philosopher Wilson (1993) and by various psychologists (Colby and Damon 1992; Walker and Hennig 1997), who have convincingly argued that personal integrity comes with a life lived in accord with one's moral sense or disposition. Colby and Damon, in their case-oriented research on moral action and moral ideals, studied individuals who were characterized by their commitment to truth-seeking, open-mindedness, compassion, flexibility, and a sensitivity to "doing the right thing" in their daily lives. Personal integrity was deeply valued by these individuals. Walker and Hennig (1997), in their review of moral development as part of personality, also argued that moral commitment and personal identity are inextricable from one's social-emotional experience. I believe that those individuals, whose lives reflect integrity, compassion, and open-mindedness, are simultaneously characterized by mature emotional competence. They can readily access the skills listed in Table 4.1 and deploy them in both ordinary and challenging situations. Surely effective international negotiations are among the latter, and those negotiators who can apply these various skills in the context of their own personal integrity should also be those negotiators who are perceived by their counterparts as trustworthy, honorable, and respectful.

Negotiation Theory and Emotion Research

In the last decade a rich and increasingly large body of research has been published on emotion-related processes in negotiation. I will not attempt a review of that literature here but instead refer the reader to Aquilar and Galluccio (2008) and Barry et al. (2006). The former authors conducted their review of emotion-related research in negotiation from the standpoint of interpersonal motivation systems, including affective neuroscience and psychotherapy research as well. Thus, their viewpoint is explicitly consistent with the social-emotional functional platform advocated by both developmental and social psychologists in recent years (e.g., Campos et al. 1994; Morris and Keltner 2000). Barry et al. (2006) constructed their review in four parts, namely, (a) research on emotion as a predictor of other processes or outcomes (e.g., positive affect usually predicts more cooperative negotiation), (b) emotions as outcomes or products (e.g., an impasse results in negotiators feeling more dissatisfaction, frustration, anger), (c) emotion as mediator (e.g., interpersonal rapport between negotiators facilitates cooperation and more positive outcomes), and d) emotion as an expressive strategy (e.g., positive expressive behavior, even if dissembled, might yield more positive agreements).

Emotional Intelligence and Negotiation

What is interesting to me is that the construct "emotional intelligence," either as an information processing ability about emotions (Mayer et al. 2008) or as a personality style (e.g., Bar-On 2004), only occasionally appears in the emotion-related negotiation research. Fulmer and Barry (2004) developed a well-reasoned set of arguments as to how an emotional intelligence construct ought to be useful for examining individual differences among negotiators, and indeed, Mueller and Curhan (2006) found that those partners with greater ability to understand emotion were more likely to have counterparts reporting greater satisfaction with the negotiated outcome as well as greater desire to negotiate in the future with the emotionally intelligent partner. In contrast, Foo et al. (2004) found that emotional intelligence in the one partner predicted a positive emotional experience, but did not result in greater objective gains in the negotiated outcome for that partner (the counterpart gained more instead). Foo et al. report a number of limitations to their study, so it is not clear how this "tension between creating and claiming value" came about, but it does raise some significant methodological questions about most of the research done on negotiators and their experienced emotion: The vast majority of the studies are done with *simulated* negotiation exercises, relatively low-intensity evoked emotions, and with students in business or management schools or training units, who do not expect to have future negotiations with their research study counterparts. An exception is the empirical work done by Galluccio (2007), who surveyed and interviewed 120 experienced negotiators for the European Union (the European Commission negotiators) about their perception of emotion processes in negotiation (see also Aquilar and Galluccio (2008)). I return to the results of his research later in this essay.

Distinguishing Emotional Competence from Emotional Intelligence

There are substantial overlaps between the construct of emotional competence as described above and the construct of emotional intelligence, but there are three significant conceptual differences. The first is that emotional competence is seen as a set of skills that develop interdependently; there is no developmental platform for the construct of emotional intelligence. The second is that emotional competence is inextricable from the emotion-evocative context – there can be situations in which we respond with less adequate application of our emotional competence skills – whereas emotional intelligence is seen by Mayer and his colleagues as an ability that resides within the individual and is applied across diverse situations, much like a trait. The third is the emphasis in emotional competence on personal integrity as a contributor to mature emotionally competent functioning. The earlier discussion on moral disposition or "doing the right thing" as a component of emotional competence has no analogue in the conceptualization of emotional intelligence. Indeed, in an early paper by Salovey and Mayer (1990) the "dark side" of emotional intelligence could be found in those individuals who use emotion management to manipulate others or "lead others sociopathically to nefarious ends" (Salovey and Mayer 1990, p. 198). I have thought of this outcome as something like an emotionally intelligent Machiavellian character, whose chief goal is to obtain and retain power, perhaps using unjust and cruel strategies to do so, yet appearing on the surface or in public as above moral reproach. Such characters have been readily apparent on the political stage of the United States in recent years, not just in the writings of Machiavelli in the sixteenth century of Florence.

In summary, negotiators and those who train prospective negotiators would be wise to address personal integrity as a contributor to effective use of emotional competence skills and to adopt a degree of humility in recognizing that there will always be those occasions when we respond stupidly and incompetently. Complex negotiations entail ambiguity, multiple counterparts or teams, time pressure, perception of crisis or high risks, and dynamic interpersonal influences (Fulmer and Barry 2004). In addition, complex negotiations include multiple layers of culture – for example, professional culture, corporate culture, societal culture, and family culture – which may all interact in the negotiation process (Faure 2002). Acknowledging one's counterpart with respect and applying one's own skills of emotional competence with humility and resilience will go a long way toward keeping the negotiation process moving along a trajectory of flexibility and creativity in developing jointly gainful outcomes.

Skills of Emotional Competence as Applied to Negotiation

I turn next to a series of brief discussions of how the skills of emotional competence as listed in Table 4.1 can be seen as contributing to negotiation effectiveness. In some cases, I will combine various skills, as they are indeed inter-dependent, but also for the sake of brevity.

Awareness of One's Own Emotions

To have an explicit awareness of one's emotional response entails self-reflection: One can articulate what evoked one's emotional reaction in terms of what is meaningful to the self; i.e., "I am disappointed because I did not get the outcome I wanted," or "I am frustrated because my counterpart's offer is extremely ambiguous" and so forth. At more complex levels of awareness, one also realizes that one can have multiple emotions about the same event or relationship, resulting in ambivalence or a rich mixture of feelings that make more ambiguous how one will subsequently cope with the situation or relationship. When this occurs, one must also reflect on the complex presenting situation and analyze its constituent parts that evoke the different emotional reactions. In English we have phrases such as "bitter-sweet" or "Pyrrhic victory" to describe these mixed emotional responses. This awareness of mixed feelings develops typically in middle childhood; for example, a 9-year-old girl with divorced parents is aware that she is happy about having a birthday party, but she is also aware that she feels sad that her father did not show up at her birthday party. By adulthood, we can evaluate a complex relationship or situation and recognize that we might have any number of emotional reactions, but we also can prioritize what is most important to us, and that is where personal integrity plays a role: Do we privilege an emotional reaction that ultimately is petty or vengeful or do we give greater weight to a reaction that serves our long-term adaptive goals, a response that "keeps the doors open" rather than shutting them?

Mature application of this particular skill of emotional competence would also entail that one is aware of the cultural construction of one's emotional response and that there may be aspects to one's emotional reaction that one is not conscious of (as in procedural knowledge or even in the case of self-deception). Thompson et al. (2004b) reviewed how various kinds of bias influence negotiators' behavior and decision-making, and such biases are generally not conscious. Specifically, they examined cognitive biases, motivational biases, and emotional biases, and relative to this last bias, they addressed misperception and misinterpretation ("faulty beliefs") in negotiators' emotion-related judgments, predictions, and actual behavior. They divided these emotional biases into two broad categories in terms of impact on negotiation: the bias of positive affect and that of negative affect, more specifically, anger. They cited research that addressed how negotiators who experienced positive affect were more likely to show more compliance (Forgas 1998a), more cooperative interaction (e.g., (Forgas 1998b), but also over-confidence and inflated self-evaluation (Kramer et al. 1993). If negotiators experience negative affect, they may refuse perfectly good offers out of a sense of wounded pride, spite, or misperception of unfairness.

As an illustration of awareness of one's emotions and effective negotiation, I mention here briefly one complex study on the effects of self-attributed emotion and counterpart-attributed emotion on negotiation outcome. Butt et al. (2005) used a simulation negotiation exercise with 322 participants, all of whom were either attending an executive education program ($N = 214$) or were graduate students in a MBA program ($N = 108$) at Lahore University (Pakistan). The participants were divided into same-sex negotiating dyads. The investigators manipulated performance feedback to four subgroups of the sample such that one group was induced to feel their negotiation success was self-caused, a second group was induced to feel their success was caused by the counterpart, a third group was led to feel that their failure was self-caused, and the fourth group was led to feel that their failure was caused by the counterpart. This manipulated feedback was delivered individually such that the two members of the dyad might have received differing feedback. They were then immediately given a self-report emotional reaction questionnaire, and the four types of manipulated feedback statistically differentiated the kinds of emotion felt: Pride/achievement was reported if given self-caused success feedback, gratitude was reported if given other-caused success feedback, guilt/shame was reported if given self-caused failure feedback, and anger was reported if given other-caused failure.

Butt and his colleagues had the dyads undertake a second negotiation task after which the participants evaluated their own negotiation behavior as well as their perception of how their counterparts felt and behaved. Distributive and joint gains were also assessed for the second negotiation task. Their analytic strategy was complex: Hierarchical linear models were calculated to examine various predictors of the negotiator's behavior (specifically: integrating, compromising, dominating, or yielding) and predictors of joint or personal gain. Their predictors included the felt emotion noted above, the perception of the counterpart's emotion, and several other control variables (e.g., gender). What was intriguing about their results was that the attribution that the counterpart was somehow at fault (in Task 1) was what led to awareness of feeling angry, and then in Task 2 acting in a dominating way toward that counterpart. Dominating behavior in the negotiator and yielding behavior in the counterpart was also associated with increased personal gain for the negotiator; when this was reversed (yielding negotiator, dominating counterpart), personal gain was reduced for the negotiator. Overall joint gain was best predicted by counterparts feeling pride/achievement and the negotiator reporting feeling gratitude. The authors concluded that from a pragmatic perspective, it would do one well as a negotiator to induce pride/achievement in one's counterpart and to appear to be graciously receptive (albeit not yielding). It is important to note here what the authors included as subscale items for "gratitude" when negotiators reported their awareness of emotions: thankful, grateful, obligated, appreciative, liking, and happy. These affective characteristics, when self-ascribed but felt as a result of being given feedback that one's success was the result of the counterpart's action, can be viewed as building blocks for a cooperative exchange that is less likely to become competitive and more likely to yield higher joint gains.

In conclusion, awareness of one's own emotions facilitates one's understanding of what led up to one's emotional response. Rather than responding automatically to the emotion-evoking situation, one self-reflects, and that moment of self-reflection may be what is critical to emotion regulation, which I discuss under the topic of Skill 6. Recall that the skills of emotional competence operate interdependently, and indeed, the next skill, understanding others' emotions, builds one's own self-awareness of emotion just as one's own awareness facilitates understanding others' emotional experience.

Understanding of Others' Emotional Experience and Capacity for Empathy/Sympathy

I will combine these two skills in my discussion since they are obviously linked. Both require being able to take the perspective of the other – with the capacity for empathy and sympathy being more emotionally-laden and often implicated in undertaking prosocial action. Seeing and even feeling an emotion-evocative situation from another person's perspective is critical to effective negotiation, and research by Elfenbein et al. (2007) verified that skill in accurately recognizing posed facial expressions was associated with enhanced positive outcomes in a negotiation exercise of selling and buying (specifically, in creating value, indicating cooperation between negotiators, and in getting a greater share of a commodity, indicating individual claimed value achieved via competition). The authors point out a number of limitations to their work, but most notable to me was the reliance on posed facial expressions and not on dynamic facial expressions (e.g., on video) as a way to try to index skill at recognizing facial expressions. One technique used by researchers investigating marital couples' interaction—noteworthy for its pervasive negotiation – has been to ask the couple to look at a video tape of their interaction and to try to recount what they were feeling at specific critical moments during the taped interaction (Gottman 1999). This could be extended methodologically in negotiation research to include asking a negotiator what he/she thinks their counterpart was feeling during a critical moment in a taped negotiation session. A comparison of the negotiator's emotion judgment with what the counterpart judges his/her emotion to have been during some critical moment in the taped interaction could be an indicator of approximate "accuracy" or concordance in judgment of emotion. Perhaps such a study has been done, and I am simply not aware of it.

Empathy with and sympathy for one's counterpart appear to promote cooperative exchanges that also communicate respect. Some research on outcome gains suggests that yielding or giving too many concessions may be associated with empathy, whereas being able to take the perspective of others is critical to improved individual outcomes (Galinsky et al. 2008). These authors conducted two studies in which they attempted to manipulate empathy versus cognitive perspective-taking by simply asking the participants to focus on either "getting into the heart" of their counterpart versus "getting into the head" of their counterpart. The latter stance, emphasizing cognitive perspective-taking, appeared to pay off in both studies in terms of individual and joint gain, but the authors suggest an important caveat: "...The outcome benefits of empathy may emerge over time...for example, in disputes, negotiators often come to the table angry and with a desire to be heard, and empathy may help calm them and soften outburst that can escalate conflict" (Galinsky et al. 2008, p. 383). Many negotiations are repeated or revisited, frequently using the same negotiators, and insofar as moderate empathy and sympathy for one's counterpart contributes toward relationship-building, future negotiations may be more productive if each negotiator believes they have been genuinely understood, even as they recognize that both sides must also thoughtfully consider and promote their own interests and positions. Galluccio (2007) also found in his survey of experienced negotiators from the EU that the majority expressed an empathic orientation toward promoting the negotiation power of African, Caribbean and Pacific nations and wanted to help the negotiators from these countries to improve their skills so that their needs and goals might be better achieved (see also Aquilar and Galluccio 2008).

Skill in Using the Vocabulary of Emotion and Expression

This skill of emotional competence builds on the other skills as well as contributes to their further development. The interdependence of the skills of emotional competence is, in my opinion, especially evident in having access to an emotion lexicon and then being able to use that lexicon to understand and use social scripts that invariably entail emotional and expressive behavior (think here of how declarative knowledge can render procedural knowledge explicit). For example, if negotiators perceive a stalemate, an impossibility of resolution, their distress may escalate into an emotional downward spiral, and the negotiation is broken off. Now, assume that the negotiators access their emotional lexicon and knowledge of how emotional-expressive behavior is embedded in social roles (including the role of negotiator), and they respectfully verbalize what is going on at the meta-level of exchange: "We are on the verge of a downward spiral in our interaction that leads no-where; let's return to the original platform and examine what we as negotiators may have overlooked." Granted, this is very simplistic, but acknowledging and making verbally explicit what is occurring in the interaction will function to repair the rift in the relationship to the extent that interaction can at least continue for the time being. This type of relationship repair has been examined in research on married couples (Gottman 1999; Johnson et al. 2001), and it can be seen as either social influence or as a strategy of effective negotiation in that it "keeps the door open." Indeed, ethologists have even determined that wild chimpanzees use relationship repair when aggression disrupts interaction (Wittig and Boesch 2005).

Few studies have examined emotion lexicon in negotiators, but Galluccio (2007) also included this feature in his survey of experienced negotiators for the EU. Surprisingly, he found that their meta-cognitive understanding of emotion-related verbal communication was "defensive, confused, unclear" (p. 7; see also Aquilar and Galluccio (2008)). What this implies, from my perspective, is that negotiators may need some further training in how to manage and evaluate (and alter if needed) their emotion-related language as well as learn more explicitly how their emotion lexicon can be strategically deployed (e.g., when, with whom, and why). When negotiators have access to meta-cognitive understanding of their communication, both verbal and nonverbal, then they can better regulate systematically how they approach their communicative exchanges with their counterparts. Obviously, if one throws cross-cultural communication into the emotion-laden exchanges of negotiators, then having a well-developed meta-cognitive understanding of when, why, and how to deploy one's emotion-related language will be critical to the structure, strategy, and process of negotiation (Aquilar and Galluccio 2008; Faure 2002).

One study worthy of mention in this context of emotion lexicon was undertaken by Schroth and her colleagues (Schroth et al. 2005), who examined how words can evoke emotional reactions in counterparts and how this affects interpersonal perception. Their results were qualified by gender of negotiator and counterpart and whether the negotiation was over a personal issue or over an issue at work or in business. What I will focus on is their exploratory study on what sorts of words trigger emotional reactions. They developed six categories of phrases and words that: (a) label the other person negatively (e.g., "you are lying"), (b) tell the other person what to do (e.g., "you need to give me a better deal…"), (c) blame or abdicate responsibility (e.g., "it's not my fault"), (d) express rudeness or sarcasm (e.g., "this is frivolous and insignificant"), (e) label one's own behavior as superior (e.g., "I should get more…"), and (f) imply a threat (e.g., "we are going to form a coalition without you") (Schroth et al. 2005, pp. 107–110). Their results indicated that anger and frustration were most reliably elicited by being the target of such categories of verbal communication and were most likely to be evoked by being negatively labeled and by being told what to do (categories a and b above). It is also important to note that the research participants were students in an organizational behavior course in California, so we do not know the generalizability of these results. As these researchers also acknowledged, I would like to see more research that takes into account the contextual and script nuances of emotion-laden language when one negotiates with another. Schroth et al. (2005) did indeed take into account work setting versus personal negotiations and gender script and stereotype differences in their research, but by using hypothetical examples and inexperienced negotiators, we really do not know how a strategic knowledge of an emotion lexicon is accessed by experienced negotiators *in vivo*. Again, I think a useful method would be to videotape real negotiations and then have the participants afterwards report qualitatively what they believed was going on for them meta-cognitively when they used emotion-laden language (and nonverbal displays, which will be elaborated below under the topic of self-presentation).

Emotional-Expressive Behavior Management and Regulation of Emotion Regulation

I have linked together here skills 5 and 6, whereby Skill #5 entails recognition that inner emotional state need not correspond to outer expression, both in oneself and in others, and at more mature levels the ability to understand that one's emotional-expressive behavior may impact another and take this into account in one's self-presentation strategies. Skill #6 entails modulation of emotional reactions by using strategies that modify the intensity, duration, or aversiveness of such emotional responses as well as skill in coping adaptively with distressing circumstances. In many instances of research on emotion regulation these two skills are combined, but I prefer to maintain some distinction between them. Whereas Skill #5 has to do with managing one's overt, visible to others, emotional-expressive behavior (e.g., one's intentional self-presentation), Skill #6 has to do with regulating one's internal or covert emotional arousal (but not always covert – as in visible perspiration, flushing throats and faces, respiration rate, etc.). The implications of this distinction have much to do with interpersonal communication: When we manage our emotional-expressive behavior, we are most often doing so because we want to convey a particular impression to a social target. Granted, we may also manage our external expression as a way of coping with a particular challenging situation, and this is when Skills #5 and #6 begin to overlap. For example, when little boys in the USA learn the social script of "crying makes it worse" or "crying is only for babies," they struggle mightily to control their emotional displays when hurt, especially in front of their peers; however, they are also attempting to modify their internal distress as well. When we regulate our emotional arousal by cognitively reframing the emotion-evocative situation facing us or by trying to self-soothe as in using slow/deep breathing or reassuring self-talk, our behavior may or may not hold communicative information for others (often depending on others' sensitivity in noticing subtle emotion regulating cues), but the function of such emotion regulation is to allow us to cope with emotionally evocative circumstances more effectively than if we respond with high emotional arousal (e.g., panic, intense anger). In order to solve an emotion-laden problem, we have to be able to take in and *use* relevant information, which requires attending and reflecting for the sake of appraisal, decision-making, and contingency planning.

Management of Emotional-Expressive Behavior

Relative to Skill #5, I briefly discuss an intriguing series of laboratory experiments undertaken by Kopelman et al. (2006) on emotional-expressive displays in negotiations with a North American sample of graduate business students. They systematically varied positive, neutral, or negative facial displays within three types of negotiation (dispute, ultimatum, and distributive). For the sake of brevity, I will not go into their methodology here of how facial expressions were conveyed in the negotiations; however, their results indicated that overall, positive facial displays facilitated the likelihood that negotiators would build longer-term business relationships with counterparts. Relative to an impasse in the dispute situation, negotiators displaying negative facial expressions were as successful as those displaying positive or neutral expressions in avoiding outcomes such as bankruptcy or being sued. An important caveat to this result is that the counterparts were not as accurate in judging the negative facial expressions compared with positive expressions. Thus, negotiators may try to express feigned negative displays, but their displays may not be perceived that way. In the second experiment, an ultimatum or zero-sum setting, negotiators displaying positive expressions were twice as likely to close a deal than those displaying negative expressions. In the final experiment, a distributive setting in which counter-offers could also be made, positive displays once again garnered more advantage: Concessions were more often made to the negotiator who displayed positive emotion compared to the condition in which negative emotions were expressed. Interestingly, when the negotiator expressed negative emotion, the counterpart was more likely to respond with extreme counter-offers, suggesting that the original offer from the negotiator had become "devalued." As the authors prudently point out, emotional-expressive behaviors are highly scripted by culture, and positive displays may be more valued in the USA than in other societies.

Relative to cross-cultural negotiation, once again it pays off for the negotiator to know the emotion folk theories of the society with whom one will be negotiating and to understand how norms of emotional-expressive behavior may differ from the norms of one's own society.

In contrast to the results of the preceding research, two experiments undertaken by Sinaceur and Tiedens (2006) indicated that negotiators' angry facial displays appeared to convey "toughness," and such a display successfully influenced the counterpart to concede more, but only when the counterpart had poor alternatives. The authors also cautioned that this strategy may be effective only in single instance negotiations and not when there are protracted or repeat negotiations. Given the current volume's emphasis on international negotiation, which is invariably either protracted or repeated or both, then this particular study seems limited in its practical utility. Lastly, a thoughtful review chapter on emotion displays in negotiation by Thompson et al. (2004a) concluded that negotiators often have to deal with exchanges that entail finding common positions of agreement and yet also compete to maximize one's own gains. As a result, positive displays are important for developing agreement between negotiators, but "poker face" or neutral displays may be more useful in distributive zero-sum exchanges. These authors also discussed the "irrational" negotiator who is more likely to be unpredictably aggressive, hostile, and threatening. Their example was Hitler negotiating with the Austrian Chancellor von Schuschnigg (based on an analysis by Raven 1990), who succeeded possibly by eliciting escape behavior in Schuschnigg (i.e., escape from or avoidance of an aversive stimulus – the threatening and hostile negotiator – is negatively reinforcing).

Emotion Regulation

Relative to Skill #6, perhaps the most important feature for negotiation that emotion regulation facilitates is the de-escalation of emotional reactivity to the negotiation process (e.g., intense frustration) and to the counterpart's potential provocations (e.g., reciprocating with anger and counter-threats). As mentioned above, emotion regulation also facilitates problem solving by enhancing the individual's ability to attend and reflect on how to consider the problematic situation. But if one remains in a heightened emotionally reactive state, it is difficult to attend to possible reappraisals of the challenging situation. Adler et al. (1998) provided a comprehensive review of how to regulate anger and fear in negotiation. Their review pragmatically suggests steps for dealing with one's own anger and fear as well as dealing with one's counterpart's anger and fear. They highlight self-awareness of what triggers our anger or fear (i.e., Skill #1) as well as self-monitoring whether one should display these emotions or not (i.e., Skill #5). Additionally, they suggest behavioral techniques to regulate one's emotional reactivity that range from self-soothing strategies (e.g., systematic relaxation of muscle groups, breathing, taking a break, etc.) to cognitive reframing (e.g., begin to write what one wants to discuss later so as to maintain one's organizational focus as well as give oneself time to "cool off"), and appropriate use of humor (and I would add judicious use of irony that is not accusing or deprecating). They also suggest that in dealing with a counterpart's intense or destructive anger that a mediator or impartial third party be brought in. In fear-eliciting negotiations they suggest making sure that one's fearful counterpart can save face, and if oneself feels fear, in addition to the strategies noted above, they suggest that the negotiator can reduce anxiety by careful preparation, acting confidently, and to consult with another before reaching a possibly premature agreement.

Awareness of How Emotion Communication Differentiates Relationships and Capacity for Emotional Self-Efficacy

I will combine these two skills in my discussion of their relevance to negotiation. Briefly, Skill #7 (awareness of emotion communication) requires that the individual minimally recognize that emotions are communicated differently depending on one's relationship with an interactant, but this particular skill goes beyond that of impression management or self-presentation strategies as defined in Skill 5. With this skill I also want to include the awareness and use of emotional experience to differentiate the organization of one's relations with others. Implied then are the following capabilities: (a) recognition of the interpersonal consequences of one's emotion communication, not only in how the other is impacted, but also how the relationship itself is affected, (b) the ability to distinguish among different sorts of relationships and thus tailor one's emotion communication accordingly, and (c) an understanding of how emotion communication is a vehicle for social influence and thus has the potential to shape the "relational space" between the interactants. Note that the use of the term "emotion communication" entails verbal statements as well as all channels of nonverbal expression that can convey affective information to an on-looker or interactant. Mature use of this skill entails the ability to access one's understanding of meta-communication, both how it influences one's own construal of the interaction but also how it might be affecting one's counterpart as well (e.g., judicious hunches that one diplomatically suggests may be useful). Aquilar and Galluccio (2008) are particularly emphatic in advocating this sort of meta-communicative understanding in that it also facilitates negotiators not becoming trapped in their own potential cognitive distortions (i.e., biased appraisal). Furthermore, this meta-communicative awareness can be used to infuse the dialogue between negotiators with a sense of hope or optimism about the outcome of the exchange. As noted previously, when negotiations occur in an atmosphere of positive communication, then both the relationship between the negotiators is improved, the likelihood of mutual satisfaction with the respective outcomes is increased, and future negotiations are looked forward to as facilitating progress rather than ending in a stale-mate or a downward spiral.

Skill #8, emotional self-efficacy, overlaps with resilience in the face of adversity and entails well-developed skills of emotional competence as described in the preceding sections. I have also argued that emotional self-efficacy must entail a moral sense and a willingness to make choices that support one's beliefs that one is doing "the right thing" even if it is uncomfortable or unpopular (Colby and Damon 1992; Saarni 1999; Walker and Hennig 1997; Wilson 1993). Obviously, such moral choices require thoughtfulness and self-reflection and very likely a sense of moral justice tempered with sympathy and compassion. Social effectiveness is also part of emotional self-efficacy: One needs to be aware that one's emotion-directed information processing while engaged in a social encounter, especially a challenging or emotionally evocative one, will be influenced by one's memory associations of similar past encounters as well as by one's current emotional state. If we add to this social effectiveness one's understanding of how meta-communication operates in any interpersonal interaction, then the challenging social encounter should unfold with minimal defensiveness, appropriate assertiveness, and demonstration of personal integrity.

Relevance to Negotiation

In thinking about how these two skills, Skill #7 (awareness of emotion communication) and Skill #8 (emotional self-efficacy), respectively, could be integrated into theoretical work on negotiation processes, I considered them more generally in the context of interpersonal conflict – whether the conflict is between spouses, between employer and employee, or between negotiators. I found Rubin's classic article on models of conflict management (Rubin 1994) useful in understanding how these two skills of emotional competence could be applied to yield effective conflict resolution. Rubin discusses conflicts as being dealt with constructively or non-constructively. The former include negotiation strategies (exchanging ideas, positions, and interests so as to generate a mutually acceptable outcome) as well as third-party mediation, whereby an impartial and mutually agreed upon party works with the disputants to move toward resolution. Non-constructive conflict approaches include domination/coercion, capitulation, inaction, and withdrawal. I argue that negotiators who are keenly aware of how both verbal and nonverbal communication impacts relationships can access effective strategies for dealing with conflicts that will avoid the non-constructive conflict approaches. For example, being aware of conveying positive responsiveness verbally and nonverbally (and this does not mean adopting a vacuous pasted-on smile), acquiring knowledge about the cultural expressive displays and scripts of one's counterpart, and acknowledging the interdependence of one's interests is much more likely to result in mutually agreeable negotiated outcomes. Such a negotiation is also likely characterized by optimism rather than pessimism, and that optimism is important for conveying the outcomes to the negotiators' respective constituencies and superiors.

Maintaining one's personal integrity and explicitly communicating the significant moral values attached to one's interests will also facilitate one's maintenance of self-confidence and resilience, in spite of possible counterpart provocations. Emotional self-efficacy means that one believes oneself to be capable of reaching one's goals even as one recognizes the necessity of weathering an adverse "emotional storm," particularly when such "storms" may not be under one's control (e.g., one's counterparts are threatened and/or negatively coerced by their nation state's political leaders or constituencies). Negotiators who are emotionally self-efficacious have no need to resort to the non-constructive conflict "strategies" mentioned above. Rubin (1994) also discusses how "principled problem solving... requires lots of effort and skill" (p. 39). International negotiators often face the dilemma of how to work out mutual benefits in complex multi-layered disputes or trade agreements, which cannot be resolved with simple bargaining tactics such as "scratch my back and I'll scratch yours" or "I'll high-ball and you low-ball the price, and then we'll converge in the middle." I argue that the emotional competence skills of awareness of emotion communication in differentiating relationships and the capacity for emotional self-efficacy are embedded in principled problem solving, and in support of this argument, I address next a recent relevant research study.

Steinel et al. (2008) used students as research participants in a laboratory simulation of an offer and counter-offer negotiation. The authors systematically manipulated feedback to the participants such that they were led to believe that their counterpart was either angry at (or pleased with) them personally or was angry about (or pleased by) an offer. The former they referred to as person-directed emotions and the latter as behavior-oriented emotions. In essence, Steinel et al. manipulated the meta-communication within the interaction with predictable results when one applies Aquilar and Galluccio's (2008) analysis of how meta-communication operates within negotiation. Not surprisingly, Steinel et al. found that when the counterpart (the buyer in their study) expressed that they were pleased with the offer, they received few concessions. However, if buyers said they were really angry about an offer, then the sellers (the negotiators) were more likely to concede, but if buyers expressed personalized anger toward the negotiator, then the latter was more likely to reply with competitive responses and concede less.

What I perceive as a dilemma here is how cultural differences could cloud one's understanding of whether one's counterpart meant their responses to be personally attacking as opposed to strongly expressing opposition to the offers advanced by the negotiator. Once again, we are back to the importance of advance preparation and a degree of transparency as well as humility in checking in with one's counterparts as to how the interaction is progressing (or not) (Kremenyuk, 2002). The importance of mutual feedback about the process of interaction cannot be understated (also echoed in Aquilar and Galluccio (2008)) for the effectiveness not only of outcomes but also for future negotiations with the same or parallel counterparts. Given that many other societies value relationship building over the concrete mentality of "we got what we want versus you got what you deserve" type of distribution, then meta-communicative awareness is crucial to complex, multi-layered international negotiation that extends over time.

Conclusions

In closing and in summary, the skills of emotional competence can be cultivated through education, exposure, humble recognition of and learning from mistakes (i.e., when one was emotionally "incompetent"), and careful looking-and-learning from expert negotiators (more video-taped records, please). Of course, we need more empirical research to verify best practices overall and strategic interventions that are specific to particular negotiating contexts (e.g., Allred (2000)). It is my belief that the thoughtful negotiator, if well-prepared with facts, cultural knowledge, respect, basic emotional competence skills (Skills #1–6), meta-communicative awareness (Skill #7), and emotional self-efficacy in conjunction with personal integrity (Skill #8), will likely be far more effective in creating mutually shared value in the negotiation process and simultaneously managing the tension that is inevitable in also trying to maximize one's own outcome (i.e., claiming value; see Allred (2000)). As usual, we need empirical research that teases apart these components of the person, of the process, and of the situational context facing the negotiators. We most definitely need empirical data based on real-life negotiations, which could be recorded for detailed analysis, but I do realize that many (most?) negotiations have a degree of covertness to them, whether for competitive or political reasons or from fear of reprisal. As a developmental psychologist attempting to bring a different perspective to understanding international negotiation processes, these fears and apprehensions speak to the poorly developed meta-communicative awareness of the constituencies behind the negotiators. I suspect the negotiators themselves often sigh with exasperation as they try to reason with those whose positions and interests they are expected to represent. This has also been assessed by Galluccio's research on this issue (2007). He found in his sample that negotiators face two kinds of pressures when they negotiate: external pressure represented by the counterpart and the internal pressure represented by their constituencies and superiors. An emotionally competent negotiator should be aware of this dichotomy and be able to detect diplomatically delicate issues, which if not adequately assessed, could bring the negotiation process toward the brink of a disastrous outcome (see Aquilar and Galluccio (2008), pp. 81–82).

References

Adler, R. S., Rosen, B., & Silverstein, E. M. (1998). Emotions in negotiation: How to manage fear and anger. *Negotiation Journal, 14*, 161–179.

Allred, K. G. (2000). Distinguishing best and strategic practices: A framework for managing the dilemma between creating and claiming value. *Negotiation Journal, 16*, 387–397.

Aquilar, F., & Galluccio, M. (2008). *Psychological processes in international negotiations: Theoretical and practical perspectives*. New York: Springer.

Bandura, A. (1977). Self-efficacy: Toward a unifying theory of behavioral change. *Psychological Review, 84*, 191–215.

Bandura, A. (1989). Human agency in social cognitive theory. *The American Psychologist, 44*, 1175–1184.

Bar-On, R. (2004). The Bar-On Emotional Quotient Inventory (EQ-i): Rationale, description and summary of psychometric properties. In G. Geher (Ed.), *Measurement of emotional intelligence: Common ground and controversy* (pp. 115–145). Hauppauge: Nova Science.

Barry, B., Fulmer, I. S., & Goates, N. (2006). Bargaining with feelings: Emotionality in and around negotiation. In L. L. Thompson (Ed.), *Negotiation theory and research* (pp. 99–127). New York: Psychology Press.

Butt, A. N., Choi, J. N., & Jaeger, A. M. (2005). The effects of self-emotion, counterpart emotion, and counterpart behavior on negotiator behavior: A comparison of individual-level and dyad-level dynamics. *Journal of Organizational Behavior, 26*, 681–704.

Campos, J., Mumme, D., Kermoian, R., & Campos, R. (1994). A functionalist perspective on the nature of emotion. In N. Fox (Ed.), *The development of emotion regulation. Monographs of the society for research in child development* (Vol. 59, pp. 284–303). Hoboken: Wiley.

Clore, G., Storbeck, J., Robinson, M., & Centerbar, D. (2005). Seven sins in the study of unconscious affect. In L. F. Barrett, P. Niedenthal, & P. Winkielman (Eds.), *Emotion and consciousness*. (pp. 384–408). New York: Guilford.

Colby, A., & Damon, W. (1992). *Some do care: Contemporary lives of moral commitment*. New York: Free Press.

Elfenbein, H. A., Foo, M. D., White, J., Tan, H. H., & Aik, V. C. (2007). Reading your counterpart: The benefit of emotion recognition accuracy for effectiveness in negotiation. *Journal of Nonverbal Behavior, 31*, 205–223.

Faure, G. O. (2002). International negotiation: The cultural dimension. In V. Kremenyuk (Ed.), *International negotiation* (2nd ed., pp. 392–415). San Francisco: Jossey-Bass.

Foo, M. D., Elfenbein, H. A., Tan, H. H., & Aik, V. C. (2004). Emotional intelligence and negotiation: The tension between creating and claiming value. *International Journal of Conflict Management, 15*, 411–429.

Forgas, J. P. (1998a). Asking nicely? The effects of mood on responding to more or less polite requests. *Personality and Social Psychology Bulletin, 24*, 173–185.

Forgas, J. P. (1998b). On feeling good and getting your way: Mood effects on negotiator cognition and bargaining strategies. *Journal of Personality and Social Psychology, 74*, 565–577.

Fulmer, I. S., & Barry, B. (2004). The smart negotiator: Cognitive ability and emotional intelligence in negotiation. *Internation Journal of Conflict Management, 15*, 245–272.

Galinsky, A., Maddux, W., Gilin, D., & White, J. B. (2008). Why it pays to get inside the head of your opponent: The differential effects of perspective taking and empathy in negotiations. *Psychological Science, 19*, 378–384.

Galluccio, M. (July 2007). *Cognitive psychotherapy and international negotiation: An overview*. Paper presented at the V World Congress of Behavioural and Cognitive Therapies, Barcelona, Spain.

Gordon, S. L. (1989). The socialization of children's emotions: Emotional culture, competence, and exposure. In C. Saarni & P. Harris (Eds.), *Children's understanding of emotion* (pp. 319–349). Cambridge: Cambridge University Press.

Gottman, J. (1999). *The marriage clinic*. New York: Norton.

Johnson, S. M., Makinen, J. A., & Millikin, J. W. (2001). Attachment injuries in couple relationships: A new perspective on impasses in couples therapy. *Journal of Marital and Family Therapy, 27*, 145–155.

Kopelman, S., Rosette, A., & Thompson, L. (2006). The three faces of Eve: Strategic displays of positive, negative, and neutral emotions in negotiations. *Organization Behavior and Human Decision Processes, 99*, 81–101.

Kramer, R., Newton, E., & Pommerenke, P. (1993). Self-enhancement biases and negotiator judgment: Effects of self-esteem and mood. *Organization Behavior and Human Decision Processes, 56*, 110–133.

Kremenyuk, V. (2002). The emerging system of international negotiation. In V. Kremenyuk (Ed.), *International negotiation: Analysis, approaches, issues* (pp. 22–39). San Francisco: Jossey Bass.

Lazarus, R. S. (1991). *Emotion and adaptation*. New York: Oxford University Press.

Leach, C., & Tiedens, L. (2004). Introduction: A world of emotion. In L. Tiedens & C. Leach (Eds.), *The social life of emotions* (pp. 1–16). Cambridge: Cambridge University Press.

Mayer, J. D., Salovey, P., & Caruso, D. (2008). Emotional intelligence: New ability or eclectic traits? *The American Psychologist, 63*, 503–517.
Morris, M. W., & Keltner, D. (2000). How emotions work: The social functions of emotional expression in negotiations. *Research in Organizational Behaviour, 22*, 1–50.
Mueller, J., & Curhan, J. (2006). Emotional intelligence and counterpart mood induction in a negotiation. *International Journal of Conflict Management, 17*, 110–128.
Raven, B. H. (1990). Political applications of the psychology of interpersonal influence and social power. *Political Psychology, 11*, 493–520.
Rubin, J. Z. (1994). Models of conflict management. *Journal of Social Issues, 50*, 33–45.
Saarni, C. (1999). *The development of emotional competence*. New York: Guilford.
Saarni, C. (2000). Emotional competence: A developmental perspective. In R. Bar-On & J. D. Parker (Eds.), *The handbook of emotional intelligence* (pp. 68–91). San Francisco: Jossey-Bass.
Saarni, C. (2008). The interface of emotional development with social context. In M. Lewis, J. Haviland-Jones, & L. Feldman Barrett (Eds.), *The handbook of emotions* (3rd ed., pp. 332–347). New York: Guilford.
Saarni, C., Campos, J., Camras, L., & Witherington, D. (2006). Emotional development: Action, communication, and understanding. In N. Eisenberg (Ed.), *Handbook of child psychology: Social, emotional, and personality development* (6th ed., Vol. 3, pp. 226–299). New York: Wiley.
Salovey, P., & Mayer, J. D. (1990). Emotional intelligence. *Imagination Cognition and Personility, 9*, 185–211.
Schroth, H. A., Bain-Chekal, J., & Caldwell, D. F. (2005). Sticks and stones may break bones and words can hurt me: Words and phrases that trigger emotions in negotiations and their effects. *International Journal of Conflict Management, 16*, 102–127.
Sinaceur, M., & Tiedens, L. (2006). Get mad and get more than even: When and why anger expression is effective in negotiation. *Journal of Experimental Social Psychology, 42*, 314–322.
Steinel, W., Van Kleef, G. A., & Harinck, F. (2008). Are you talking to me?! Separating the people from the problem when expressing emotions in negotiation. *Journal of Experimental Social Psychology, 44*, 362–369.
Thompson, L., Medvec, V., Seiden, V., & Kopelman, S. (2004a). Poker face, smiley face, and rant 'n' rave: Myths and realities about emotion in negotiation. In M. B. Brewer & M. Hewstone (Eds.), *Emotion and motivation* (pp. 70–94). Malden, MA: Blackwell.
Thompson, L., Neale, M., & Sinaceur, M. (2004b). The evolution of cognition and biases in negotiation research. In M. J. Gelfand & J. M. Brett (Eds.), *The handbook of negotiation and culture* (pp. 7–44). Stanford: Stanford University Press.
Walker, L. J., & Hennig, K. (1997). Moral development in the broader context of personality. In S. Hala (Ed.), *The development of social cognition* (pp. 297–327). East Sussex: Psychology Press.
Wilson, J. Q. (1993). *The moral sense*. New York: Free Press.
Wittig, R. M., & Boesch, C. (2005). How to repair relationships – Reconciliation in wild chimpanzees. *Ethology, 111*, 736–763.

Chapter 5
Tacit Knowledge Structures in the Negotiation Process

E. Thomas Dowd and Angela N. Roberts Miller

International negotiations, like all interpersonal processes, are shaped by the knowledge structures and cognitive assumptions of each of the participants. These cognitive processes are generally tacit or implicit in nature, that is, they are not identifiable and describable by those who hold them. Perhaps for that reason they exert an especially powerful influence on both the process and outcome of negotiations because they cannot easily be countered. In this chapter we identify and describe certain aspects of tacit knowledge structures that may play a large, but not understood, part in the negotiation process.

At the outset, we would like to suggest that behavioral principles of reinforcement, punishment and extinction are important aspects of negotiations. Fundamentally international negotiations are about the acquisition of power, influence, and resources. Nations and groups, like individuals, are concerned about maximizing these attributes for themselves and minimizing them for others. Or, as one negotiator said (in perhaps an unusual moment of candor), "If I am strong, why should I compromise? If I am weak, I can't afford to compromise." Many parties to negotiations are concerned essentially with obtaining as much as possible for themselves while conceding as little as possible to the other side. It is important under these conditions to find some reinforcer desired by the respective negotiation partners that will encourage them to compromise while extinguishing oppositional forces opposing compromise. Because reinforcers vary somewhat between and among individuals, especially those of different cultural groups, it is important to discover the reinforcers that are significant to the members of each group.

Nevertheless, cognitive assumptions and constructs play a important, although often undetected, part in the negotiation process. It is not uncommon to discover that negotiators seem perversely to work against what appears to be their own best interests, at least as a rational observer looking at reinforcing and punishing

E.T. Dowd (✉)
Board Certified in Cognitive & Behavioral Psychology and Counseling Psychology, Professor Emeritus, Department of Psychology, Kent State University, Kent, Ohio 44242, USA
e-mail: edowd@kent.edu

F. Aquilar and M. Galluccio (eds.), *Psychological and Political Strategies for Peace Negotiation*, DOI 10.1007/978-1-4419-7430-3_5,

consequences and what is reasonably obtainable might judge. At the end of a protracted negotiations process, certain groups or nations might possess less than they had previously or even less than they might have obtained had they compromised in certain areas. There are many examples of this outcome now and in the past, and where and when they occur tacit knowledge structures of the negotiators may be implicated.

Cognitive Products, Processes and Structures

In examining human cognitive functioning we would first like to distinguish among cognitive products, cognitive processes, and cognitive structures. Cognitive products are the automatic self-statements that people say to themselves (e.g., "I'll never understand this!) and are concerned with *what* people think. They are close to surface consciousness and usually readily identifiable. All people use automatic self-statements but individuals with psychological difficulties tend to have more negative ones.

Cognitive processes are processing distortions and are essentially concerned with *how* people think. It is important to emphasize that these processes are shared by all people, the only difference being how strong and pervasive they are and consequently how much difficulty they cause us. Judith Beck (1995) has identified 12 cognitive distortions: dichotomous ("all-or-nothing") thinking, catastrophizing, discounting the positive, emotional reasoning, labeling, magnification/minimization, mental filter, mind reading, overgeneralization, personalization, using imperative statements, and tunnel vision. These are more difficult to identify and several have important implications for the negotiation process. Aquilar and Galluccio (2008) have applied these to the negotiations process and have provided examples.

Negotiators who engage in dichotomous thinking may tend to see an agreement as either perfect or fatally flawed. They may also adopt cognitive heuristics such as, "The friend of my enemy is my enemy" or "The enemy of my friend is my enemy" or even "The enemy of my enemy is my friend." Those who catastrophize may see all the bad outcomes, no matter how improbable, that might occur as a result of any agreement. Those who discount the positive may see only negative results from any agreement. Those who engage in magnification/minimization may maximize difficulties and minimize positive aspects of an agreement. Those using a mental filter may allow only information into their cognitive system that favors one outcome and screen out information favoring other outcomes. Those using imperative statements and labeling may believe that others *must* or *should* see things their way or be labeled as "stupid," "incompetent," or worse if they do not. Those engaging in tunnel vision may see only one possible outcome to negotiations from the start.

Cognitive structures have also been called cognitive schemas (or core beliefs) and can be thought of as tacit networks of rules and assumptions that organize and give meaning to one's prior experience. They are predispositions to think, interpret, and respond in certain ways and are outside of conscious awareness. They are close to what Freud referred to as "the unconscious." Cognitive structures are advantageous in that they enable people to process information rapidly but that very ability may result in entrenched maladaptive thinking patterns that are resistant to change. They are also heavily influenced and shaped by the culture in which one lives. All of us, because we grow up in a particular culture, have cultural knowledge, which is the tacit (or implicit) knowledge that is derived from the unspoken (and often unspeakable) rules and assumptions we learned from our culture. Tacit knowledge is acquired largely from one's experience in one's environment (which includes other people) and it is deeply conservative and not easily changed.

Dowd and Courchaine (2002) have identified several aspects of tacit knowledge that have implications for the negotiation process. Implicit learning systems hold evolutionary primacy over explicit learning and are therefore more resistant to change. Implicit learning is acquired faster than explicit learning. Implicit learning is especially useful for learning complex material. Tacit knowledge precedes and cognitively is less available to people than explicit knowledge. The implication for negotiations is that the rich tacit (especially cultural) knowledge that negotiators bring to the table profoundly influences their world view and assumptions in ways that cannot be discerned by them and often by others. The difficulty occurs when negotiators with widely differing world views and cultural assumptions talk with each other.

The role of "encoding algorithms" plays a significant part in the acquisition and maintenance of tacit knowledge (Lewicki et al. 1997). These are essentially "rules in the head" that organize and classify incoming stimuli and therefore enable them to be noticed and used. The result is a cognitive filter (similar to the "mental filter" identified by J.S. Beck 1995) that screens in information consonant with an individual's existing schemas and world view and screens out information discrepant with the existing schemas and world view (Dowd 2006). Over time these algorithms become self-perpetuating as the inferential rules become stronger and more elaborated because they are repeatedly strengthened. This strengthening process occurs as confirming information is noticed and processed while disconfirming information is discounted, ignored or not noticed. This process is especially pronounced in ambiguous situations – which most negotiations are – where a variety of explanations might be plausible. Over time, therefore, we gradually come to "see what we expect to see" and "find what we expect to find," thus further strengthening these algorithms. Perhaps rather than "seeing is believing," a more accurate phrase might be, "Believing is seeing."

There is also a phenomenon known as "hasty encoding" in which people use very little supporting information before imposing a particular interpretation (which is derived from the existing algorithm) on an event. Essentially speed is substituted for accuracy; what we might call "jumping to conclusions." There appear to be individual differences in whether people use a more internal (hasty) encoding style or a more external encoding style, in which outside data are used. Those who use an internal encoding style are more likely to use their pre-existing inferential rules and expectations and are less likely to use external information in arriving at their conclusions. Given all of this, it is perhaps surprising that people change their cognitions (mind) at all!

Cognitive structures have been organized into categories based on one's early learning by Jeffrey Young and his colleagues (Young et al. 2003). These are known as Early Maladaptive Schemas (EMSs) and consist of 18 schemas organized into five domains. Space precludes a detailed examination of the implications of all 18 EMSs for the negotiation process but interested readers are urged to consult this book. Here we will examine a few of the most relevant schemas for the negotiation process.

Mistrust/abuse. Individuals with this EMS have an expectation that others will abuse and take advantage of them and therefore have a profound distrust of other people and their motives. They avoid becoming vulnerable or trusting anyone about anything. Their preferred strategy is to use and abuse others, with an implicit rule of, "Get others before they get you" (or, "Do unto others before they do unto you!"). The schema is laid down early in life (Dowd et al. 2001) and is very difficult to overcome. The implications of this schema for the negotiations process are obvious; these negotiators simply cannot trust their counterparts on the other side to be reasonable and rational.

Defectiveness/shame. Individuals with this EMS have a profound sense of themselves as somehow inferiour, defective, and shameful. Consequently they avoid expressing their true thoughts and feelings and letting others get close to them. Their strategy is often to criticize and reject others while trying to appear perfect themselves. Many of their actions are primarily devoted to attempting to feel better about themselves. Negotiators with this EMS may have difficulty accepting any less-than-perfect agreements.

Vulnerability to harm or illness. Individuals with this EMS possess an exaggerated fear that an imminent catastrophe will befall them at any time, a fear that an outside observer would see as unrealistic. They therefore may avoid going to places or engaging in activities that are not completely safe. Ironically, they may overcompensate on occasion by behaving recklessly. Negotiators with this EMS often anticipate events of very low probability that might result from an agreement.

Approval seeking/recognition seeking. These individuals have an excessive need for gaining recognition and approval from others, at the expense of developing a true sense of themselves. In negotiations they may act to impress others rather than to reach an agreement. Occasionally, as overcompensation, they may deliberately provoke others in order to demonstrate their power – power they do not normally see themselves as possessing. Negotiators with this EMS may be more interested in calling attention to themselves and their abilities than in actually reaching an agreement.

Unrelenting standards/hypercriticalness. These individuals have extremely high standards that they and others must meet, usually to avoid criticism. In the negotiation process they may unduly procrastinate and avoid tasks by which they might be judged. Only a perfect negotiation process and outcome is acceptable to them.

Memory Processes in Cognitive Functioning

To a large extent, interpersonal processes, such as negotiations, depend on accurate memory (See Dowd (2002) for a discussion). Negotiators must be able to remember the content of previous negotiations and the points agreed upon if the process is to proceed. The metaphor often used is that of the computer; information is assumed to be stored in the mind much as information is stored on a computer disk. The only problem is access – how to help people recall as much as they can of the information in storage.

But what if memories were not necessarily accurate? What if memories were constructed as much or more than they were recalled? What if these memories changed over time in responses to people's life experiences and changing life circumstances? What if memories were at least partially and sometimes mostly constructed in response to their fears, wishes, and hopes? In that case, we could not assume that what negotiators remembered about previous sessions or their own personal or cultural history was necessarily true. Recent research has indeed suggested that memories do change over time, usually in self-enhancing directions to help us feel better about ourselves and our societies. These memory distortions have been described by the phrase, "We remember what we want to remember," as if deliberate dissembling were the mechanism. It is more likely, however, that nonconscious distortions in memories, fueled perhaps by people's wishes, hopes, or fears, are the problem, not deliberate distortion.

For decades experimental psychologists have known that memories can be manipulated. They know that people can be guided to recognize or recall events they might not otherwise recognize or recall by using such techniques as distracter words or hints. Memories can also be modified by the way the information is encoded. If the information is *under-encoded* (that is, if not enough information is processed and too little distinguishing information is present), a negotiator may attend only to one or two salient aspects of an event or a negotiation agreement and not remember other important details. If information is *over-encoded*, however, they may remember events differently because they have come to expect certain things to occur by prior learning. If, for example, in the past a negotiator has experienced the negotiators on the other side as deceitful, they may see and remember deceit later when it may not occur. In under-encoding one knows too little for accurate memory to occur; in over-encoding one knows too much.

Memories can also be changed by current beliefs and emotions. It has been long known that depressed people have great difficulty remembering times when they were happy. Conversely, people who are sad may spontaneously remember other sad times in their lives. People often reconstruct their earlier memories of a relationship according to their current beliefs about that relationship; if they thought the relationship was bad now they tended to think it had always been bad. Thus, one's memories of past experiences can be shaped by one's current beliefs, a phenomenon known as *retrospective bias*. These can be seen as examples of the mood-congruence effect, in which one's current mood or reactions (the context) manipulate one's memory of a past event. Therefore, people tend to remember the past in terms of the present and negotiators who have bad experiences with their counterparts may remember that previous negotiations were also bad.

Context and the number of times an event is recalled also manipulate memory (Fleming et al. 2002). Thus, an experienced negotiator in a new negotiations process may spontaneously remember previous failed negotiations. In addition, the number of times an event is recalled (e.g., failed past negotiations) increases one's confidence in that memory but perversely decreases its accuracy.

Memories of past events can also be deliberately, as well as spontaneously, changed. It has been found that providing misleading postevent information can change the memories of the previous event. The effect of misleading postevent information on memories has been clearly documented, especially in forensic settings. Postevent information may consist of misleading or inaccurate subsequent questions.

Repetition of the postevent information can enhance the effect. Repetition of a false or partly false statement or a story can increase one's belief in the truth of that story, a phenomenon known as the *illusory truth effect*, and the more the story is repeated, the more firmly it is believed. Concomitantly, the accuracy of the story often decreases with repetition. Indeed it has been stated by some political cynics that anything said many times becomes true! Thus, not only can beliefs shape memories but also memories can shape beliefs. If negotiations have failed in the past it is easy to believe they will fail in the future. And memories of historical grievances may be gradually modified and enhanced over time and can become part of historical cultural memories in a self-enhancing fashion. All societies carry cultural stories or "myths" within their collective memories that say more about what individuals within that society want to believe than what actually happened historically.

Misleading postevent suggestions or information may lead individuals to remember events they did not experience, a phenomenon known as the *source misattribution effect*. The source misattribution effect can also lead people to remember something correctly but think it came from a different source. It is often very disconcerting to discover that an idea we like came from a source we do not like and people have been known to repudiate the idea upon discovering that. We tend to discredit the message if we discredit the source, so that any idea coming from a negotiator on the other side may be discredited on that basis – even if we may have liked the idea before we knew who said it. If we cannot recall the source of a memory or if our attention is divided between two tasks, we may not even be able to distinguish memory from imagination or fantasy. Did a prior negotiation really happen and in the way we remember it, or did we just imagine it did, perhaps because we wanted to remember it that way?

Engaging in more elaborative thought processes, in other words thinking about something repeatedly and in more detail has been shown to result in more source misattribution effects and more false memories. It has been found that more elaborative perceptual processing tends to lead to the greater creation, with increased confidence, of false memories. It has been hypothesized that this occurs because people are encouraged to create more specific and detailed representations of the suggested items or events than they otherwise would have done.

There are other types of misattribution effects. People sometimes misattribute a spontaneous thought to their own imagination when in fact they are retrieving it from their memory. Many people can even, under some conditions, falsely recall or recognize events that never happened or did not happen exactly as remembered.

Fast and Frugal Heuristics

Decision-making, whether in the negotiation process, or elsewhere is often thought to be a logical, rational, and time-consuming process. We assume that the more information we have about the relative merits and demerits of a decision we must make and the more thoroughly we consider them, the better decisions we will make. However, Gigerenzer (2001) has pointed out that if individuals were actually required to follow these cumbersome processes, humans probably would not have survived. Many decisions must be made quickly and accurately for survival purposes.

Classical decision-making is based upon models of *unbounded rationality*, in which all information relevant to the situation is assumed to be known by everyone (Gigerenzer 2004). It also assumes that individuals must completely know the environment in order to make good decisions. These are common assumptions in decision-making, whether the decision involved is accepting a new job, choosing a mate, or negotiating a political settlement. However, for humans who have limited time and knowledge and who must often make rapid decisions the model of *bounded rationality* is more applicable. The term can refer to constraints in the environment, such as incomplete information, or constraints in the mind, such as limited memory or the cognitive biases discussed earlier. Essentially we must make decisions rapidly and with limited information. Under conditions of *bounded rationality,* decisions that first appeared to be reasonable turned out to be cognitive illusions. For example, individuals who were 100% confident of providing a correct answer were found to give a lower number of correct answers, labeled the *overconfidence bias*. Other examples include an *overestimation of low risks and an underestimation of high risks, contingency illusions* (seeing contingencies where none exist), and *the false consensus effect* (overestimating the degree to which our own behavior, attitudes, or beliefs are shared by other people). Under conditions of bounded rationality, which are the conditions negotiators typically face, several heuristics can prove especially useful in understanding the negotiation process.

Heuristics

A heuristic is essentially a cognitive rule. Although a detailed consideration of the exact conditions under which people select one heuristic over another is beyond the scope of this chapter, Gigerenzer (2008) points out that people select different heuristics intuitively as they tacitly evaluate their ecological rationality. The selection seems to involve elements of their learning and reinforcement history, their social learning history, and evolutionary learning. This heuristic selection process is better in new situations, and the utility of any one heuristic tends to deteriorate when it is used habitually. We would now like to describe different heuristics used by individuals under conditions of bounded rationality (see Gigerenzer 2004, 2008).

Recognition heuristic. The rule here is that one selects the alternative that is recognized over those that are not. Individuals who have heard some, but not all, of the alternatives can actually do better than individuals who have heard of all the alternatives. In this instance, "less is more" because those people with less information provide more correct answers. A related heuristic is the *"fluency heuristic,"* in which the alternative that is recognized faster is chosen, often with the same "less is more" effect. Thus negotiators with limited information may actually do better than those with more detailed and comprehensive information.

"Take the best" heuristic. The rule here is, terminate the search for a decision when the first good reason is found that favors one alternative over another. Interestingly, research studies have indicated that the "Take the best" heuristic is at least as good as more complex decision-making strategies, for example multiple regression. In addition, it is more efficient because people do not have to process many and complex cues. But many negotiators search for the ideal solution rather than the best obtainable under the circumstances.

Satisficing heuristic. Using this rule, individuals search through the available alternatives and choose the first one that exceeds their level of aspiration, then terminate their search. Essentially, rather than attempting to maximize their choice, they pick the first one that is good enough. Research has indicated that satisficers score higher on measures of happiness, optimism, self-esteem, and life satisfaction and lower on measures of depression, perfectionism, and regret (Schwartz et al. 2002). Satisficing is usually how people select their mates, eventually if not necessarily immediately. The implications for negotiators are clear. Rather than attempt for an optimal outcome (and potentially obtaining no outcome), both sides would likely be happier and more satisfied by working towards (and accepting) a "good enough" solution. The utility and validity of compromise is once again confirmed.

Tallying heuristic. In this model, solutions are adopted by simply tallying the number of cues favoring certain outcomes. Unlike more complex decision-making, it is not necessary to weigh the value of each cue. Interestingly, this model performed better than more complex models, such as unit-weight and weighted linear models and as well as multiple regression and was only marginally less effective than the "*Take the Best*" heuristic (Gigerenzer and Goldstein 1996). The reason appears to be the use of the recognition principle, useful in environments where recognition is strongly correlated with the target variable. The tallying algorithm ignores negative information, focusing instead on positive information (i.e., cues favoring a particular decision). Too often negotiators look for negative information precluding certain outcomes, but perhaps they would be better served by looking for positive information favoring those outcomes.

There are other cognitive heuristics as well. Aquilar and Galluccio (2008) discuss two other, more general, cognitive heuristics and their effect on the negotiation process. Cognitive efficiency refers to the tendency to ignore unique aspects of a particular situation if it is familiar to previous situations in other ways and is similar to what Dowd (2006) referred to as "hasty encoding." While it tends to result in faster cognitive processing, it may also result in significant inaccuracies because individuals use their pre-existing rules and inferences rather than data unique to the situation. Exacerbating this tendency is the need for cognitive consistency, or the general tendency to explain the present in terms of the past.

Aquilar and Galluccio (2008) also refer to cognitive maps or "a mental representation of some area of one's environment" (p. 30), showing awareness of how they "could be generally distorted" (p. 30) and not consistent with the reality. As Alfred Korzybski (1994) has pointed out, the map is not the territory and significant cognitive errors can result if one assumes that it is. The mental perception is not necessarily veridical in nature with actual reality and can diverge from it in many ways.

Practical Implications for Negotiations

International negotiation is by its very nature complex. As discussed above, it necessitates a reliance on information and influences that are variable, expansive in scope, and frequently underestimated. Successful negotiation requires more than a mere understanding of political theory. It requires psychological savvy and interpersonal finesse. For the negotiator, this translates into viewing the process of negotiation as the mutual creation of a unique, evolving entity, an unseen, yet significant third party. This "third party" comprises shared and conflicting experiences, competing cognitive assumptions and structures, heuristics, and combined individual and cultural memory. It is the individual negotiator's multifaceted interaction with this "third party" that can and does dictate immediate and long-term outcomes as this "third party" will far outlive the temporal confines of the current issues. With this in mind, it is important to consider the following five keys to unlocking this relationship.

- Acknowledge that tacit psychological knowledge influences all interpersonal interactions in distinctive and pervasive ways and that the perception and memories of past, present, and future events are malleable and subject to emotional modification. This may require training yourself and your staff in what tacit knowledge is and how it affects human cognition. It is important to "normalize" this by carefully explaining that all people possess tacit knowledge, and it does not indicate a defect of any kind. Perhaps certain individuals would benefit from participating in a therapeutic process themselves to gain knowledge of their own biases and perceptions, again with the explanation that this is common to all people. This is, in fact, what a training analysis in psychoanalysis education and training is supposed to accomplish and thereby enables new analysts to conduct better therapy with awareness of their own biases.

- Identify the verbal, nonverbal, and material reinforcers that serve as cultural currency in the context of the specific interpersonal "transaction." It is important to study and analyze the other person's cultural background in order to understand their modes of communication, rules of etiquette, body language, and cultural history and values. It may also be useful to practice (role play) interactions in the context of other cultural systems and utilize members of other cultures if possible because they would be able to understand and describe subtleties that may be missed by non-natives.
- Develop a heightened level of self-awareness regarding your own tightly held tacit core beliefs and early maladaptive schemas because these have the potential to hinder negotiations by enhancing undue cognitive rigidity and a myopic world view. As described in the first point, it may be useful to undergo a therapeutic experience in order to understand your own tacit cognitive assumptions. An exercise that might be helpful involves using videotaped negotiations and role-plays, with a subsequent review by yourself and/or a peer group, in which group members are asked to identify your core beliefs. It may also be helpful to make use of a technique frequently employed in marriage therapy: arguing from the point of view of the other party. This can be a powerful and experiential way of understanding at a deeper level another person's world view and tacit assumptions. One can then develop action plans on how to approach similar situations in the future.
- Cultivate a healthy skepticism regarding the veridicality of personal memory and instead pursue objective sources of issue-related external information to the extent possible. Do not rely on your own memory because that is likely to be tainted by your tacit assumptions. When approaching negotiations, research the situation from a variety of sources from both cultures. It is important to obtain the services of someone familiar with the other culture in this process.
- Take a cue from heuristics and keep the interactions as simple as possible. While it may be prudent to consult important shareholders, the value of their input must be weighed against their potential to intentionally or unintentionally confound the process through the introduction of additional interests and biases. The quickest and most parsimonious is often the best. Include only those arguments and negotiation points that are absolutely necessary, keeping in mind that the fewer the people involved in the negotiation process the better.

Ultimately, success in international negotiations, as in any relationship, centers on the individual's ability to manage conflict and encourage a spirit of reciprocity within the context of mutual trust and respect. To the extent that the parties involved are unwilling and/or incapable of this level of collaboration due to tacit psychological or more tangible impediments, difficulties will develop. By utilizing the keys gleaned from tacit knowledge structures, it is possible for the negotiator to make considerable strides toward overcoming these barriers.

References

Aquilar, F., & Galluccio, M. (2008). *Psychological processes in international negotiations*. New York: Springer.

Beck, J. S. (1995). *Cognitive therapy: Basics and beyond*. New York: Guilford.

Dowd, E. T. (2002). Memory processes in psychotherapy: Implications for integration. *Journal of Psychotherapy Integration, 12*, 233–246.

Dowd, E. T. (2006). What changes in cognitive therapy? The role of tacit knowledge structures. *Journal of Cognitive and Behavioral Psychotherapies, 6*, 141–148.

Dowd, E. T., & Courchaine, K. (2002). Implicit learning, tacit knowledge, and implications for stasis and change in cognitive psychotherapy. In R. L. Leahy & E. T. Dowd (Eds.), *Clinical advances in cognitive psychotherapy*. New York: Springer.

Dowd, E. T., Pepper, H. F., & Seibel, C. A. (2001). Developmental correlates of psychological reactance. *Journal of Cognitive Psychotherapy, 15*, 239–252.

Fleming, K., Heikkinen, R., & Dowd, E. T. (2002). Cognitive therapy: The repair of memory. In R. L. Leahy & E. T. Dowd (Eds.), *Clinical advances in cognitive psychotherapy*. New York: Springer.

Gigerenzer, G. (2001). The adaptive toolbox: Toward a Darwinian reality. In J. A. French, A. C. Kamil, & D. W. Leger (Eds.), *Evolutionary psychology and motivation. Nebraska symposium on motivation* (Vol. 48, pp. 113–143). Lincoln: University of Nebraska Press.

Gigerenzer, G. (2004). Fast and frugal heuristics: The tools of bounded rationality. In D. J. Koehler & N. Harvey (Eds.), *Blackwell handbook of judgement and decision making*. Oxford: Blackwell.

Gigerenzer, G. (2008). Why heuristics work. *Perspectives on Psychological Science, 3*(1), 20–29.

Gigerenzer, G., & Goldstein, D. G. (1996). Reasoning the fast and frugal way: Models of bounded rationality. *Psychological Review, 103*, 650–669.

Korzybski, A. (1994). *Science and sanity: An introduction to non-Aristotelian systems and general semantics*. Fort Worth: Institute of General Semantics.

Lewicki, P., Czyzewska, M., & Hill, T. (1997). Nonconscious information processing and personality. In D. C. Berry (Ed.), *How implicit is implicit learning?* Oxford: Oxford University Press.

Schwartz, B., et al. (2002). Maximizing versus satisficing: Happiness is a matter of choice. *Journal of Personality and Social Psychology, 83*, 1178–1197.

Young, J. E., Klosko, J. S., & Weishaar, M. E. (2003). *Schema therapy: A practitioner's guide*. New York: Guilford.

Chapter 6
Ways to Improve Political Decision-Making: Negotiating Errors to be Avoided

Donald Meichenbaum

Foreword I have been nurturing a "fantasy" for over a decade, and it is now time to go public with this preoccupation. I am sure some readers will characterize this "fantasy" as nothing more than an unrealistic "fairy tale" that would never ever come true. But as the popular entertainer Frank Sinatra used to sing, "Fairy tales can come true if you are young at heart," and I would add optimistic and practical. By the end of this chapter, you can determine if there is any basis for my hopefulness. Perhaps, my "fantasy" will inspire other young-at-heart dreamers.

Origins of the Fantasy

In order to understand the roots of this "pipe dream" it is relevant to describe how I spend my professional time. For the last 35 years I have been conducting research on the development of cognitive-behavior therapy, and in particular, I have been studying the thinking processes of an array of clinical populations. In fact, I have characterized myself as a "cognitive ethologist" who studies how individuals make decisions, especially under conditions of uncertainty and stress. Like the behavioral ethologist who is an astute and informed observer of animal behaviors, I am an observer (perhaps, even a voyeur) of how individuals tell "stories" to themselves and to others, and the implications this has for how they behave. In turn, I am eager to see how they behave and the resultant consequences, and the subsequent impact on their story-telling behaviors.

For instance, with colleagues we have studied how individuals who have experienced traumatic events construe such events and construct "stories" that they tell themselves and others and what are their accompanying coping behaviors. What factors will determine if they will develop post traumatic stress disorder (Meichenbaum 2000), or whether they will evidence post traumatic growth and evidence resilience (Meichenbaum 2006a). I have also explored the heuristic value of adopting such a

D. Meichenbaum (✉)
Distinguished Professor Emeritus, University of Waterloo,
Ontario, Canada

F. Aquilar and M. Galluccio (eds.), *Psychological and Political Strategies for Peace Negotiation*, DOI 10.1007/978-1-4419-7430-3_6,

constructive narrative perspective in analyzing the thinking processes that contribute to such behaviors as becoming angry and aggressive (Meichenbaum 2002), attempting suicide (Meichenbaum 2006b), and not complying with medical procedures and engaging in treatment non-adherence (Meichenbaum and Fong 1993).

In short, I work with varied psychiatric and medical clients to develop a supportive, nonjudgmental, compassionate therapeutic alliance so they can better appreciate how they make decisions that impact their lives and the lives of others. I help them learn how to conduct cognitive, affective, and behavioral chain analyses and how to consider the motivational, developmental, functional, and consequential aspects of their decision-making processes. During the course of therapy with individuals, couples, families, and groups, I try to help educate them by means of the "art of questioning," discovery-based procedures, guided instruction, generalization and relapse prevention procedures, on how they construct their "realities" and make decisions. I help them learn how they can use feedback to make more informed and adaptive decisions in the future. I work to have my clients "take my voice with them." I ask them the following question:

> "Do you ever find yourself, out there, in your day-to-day experiences, asking yourself the questions that we ask each other right here in our sessions?"

A major objective of my work with clients is to establish a trusting, supportive, confidential relationship where they can collaboratively develop behavioral, achievable, and measurable, short-term, intermediate, and long-term goals that can help nurture "hope," and that can lead to behavioral changes (See Meichenbaum (1994, 2002, 2007) for examples of how to conduct such psychotherapeutic interventions).

My Fantasy

Here is my fantasy. Could one provide a similar supportive service to politicians who make critical decisions that have widespread impact such as going to war, or decisions that impact the nation's economic well-being, or that impact global ecological concerns? Imagine for a moment, *what would happen if* every political leader included a cognitive-behavior therapist as an integral member of his or her closest advisory team. I told you this was a "fairy tale."

But hold on! There is a research literature on decision-making that could be brought to bear. In the same way that behavioral economics has emerged as a field, as reflected in the research program of Nobel Prize winner Daniel Kahneman and his colleagues (Kahneman et al 1987) and in the recent book by Akerlof and Shiller (2009) on how "irrational exuberance" and misperceptions drive economic decision-making, could we develop a similar discipline called behavioral politics? In fact, some fine examples of this approach are already evident (see George 1980; Houghton 2008; Iyengar and McGuire 1993; Janis 1982; Jervis 1976; Staub 2007).

Just how far-fetched are these ideas? Appointed commissions, historians and journalists often analyze after-the-fact (post-hoc), the decision-making processes of politicians that contribute to their decisions to go to war. They highlight how these politicians framed questions, selectively attended to certain aspects of data, held confirmatory beliefs (the drunkard's search), engaged in a wide range of cognitive and motivational errors, engaged in impulsive cognitive shortcuts, employed mental heuristics (or habits of thought) and stereotypes, used analogical and metaphorical thinking that distorted and compromised problem-solving efficiency, and used wishful thinking and "denial" procedures that contribute to their failure to both consider the credibility of the sources of information and the long-term consequences of the decisions to be taken. In addition, misperception-induced failures to empathize and perspective-take and group-think processes as well as "gaming the system" procedures may also undermine decision-making efficiency. See Tables 6.1 and 6.2 for examples of these cognitive errors and distortions that need to be avoided.

My fantasy is why wait until *after* such decisions have been made to write post-hoc analyses. Imagine what would be the impact if a politician had someone in his or her cabinet who could observe the group decision-making process in action and in a non-threatening, supportive, and confidential manner could provide in situ feedback on the possible impact of cognitive distortions and cognitive errors. For a moment, think through how this could be done both on a preventative basis and on an ongoing feedback basis.

Preventative Interventions

Since I have done a good deal of work on stress-inoculation training (Meichenbaum 2007), I fantasize how political decision-makers (as well as military decision-makers) can be encouraged to invite psychological researchers who have expertise in decision-making, as well as presidential historians and journalists to present the lessons to be learned from such events as the Cuban Missile Crisis, the Bay of Pigs invasion, and the invasion of Iraq. The examples need *not* be limited to U.S. historical episodes. One could find similar examples from many international conflicts. For example, consider the failure of U.N. members to act to prevent genocide in Rwanda (see Dallaire (2003)). In fact, what would be the impact of such ongoing workshops, seminars, invited address for world leaders at the United Nations? What would be the impact if all key advisers (members of the "kitchen cabinet") to the president had to take a course in decision making? Surely, this fantasy is getting out of hand.

Two immediate sets of questions emerge. What should be the content of such presentations? What do we know about decision-making under conditions of uncertainty and stress that could inform world leaders and politicians? Could one generate a "decisional checklist" for politicians and their advisors so they could self-monitor the efficacy of their decision-making efforts? The second set of questions concerns whether world leaders and their advisors and politicians would be interested and open to such feedback. Is this a naïve proposal?

As a clinician, I can attest to the fact that I am quite often confronted with unmotivated clients, and even mandated clients, who are uninterested in changing their behavior. Fortunately, there is a good deal of research on how to work effectively with such unmotivated clientele, subsumed under the research heading of motivational

Table 6.1 List of motivational and cognitive errors in decision-making "What to watch out for"

I. Use of cognitive shortcuts

1. Tendency to use the most *salient* or most *readily available examples* and the tendency to take them as being most *representative* of a whole class of events. Such "mental heuristics" (habits of thought) may be emotionally charged and be selectively retrieved in a mood-congruent fashion (Tversky and Kahneman 1974, 1981, 1986).
2. Tendency to use *stereotypes* and *black-white prejudicial dichotomous thinking* in formulating decisions (Kahneman et al 1987).
3. Tendency to use *metaphors* and *analogies* that may oversimplify and misrepresent the complexity of the present situation. Tendency to draw an experience that is familiar from a historical analysis, but that *distorts the present situation* (Dodge 2008; Dyson and Preston 2008; Khong 1992; Lakoff and Johnson 1980).
4. Tendency to reason by *historical analogies* by turning to history to justify policies that have already been settled on by misreading historical parallels and engaging in "rhetorical jujitsu." As Lakoff and Johnson (1980) observe, "Frames trump facts."

II. Desire for cognitive consistency

5. Tendency to employ a *confirmatory bias* and seek information that is only consistent with prior views or existing hypotheses. This is also known as the "drunkard's search" to characterize someone who looks for his key at night time under the lamp post because the light is best there, even though he has lost his key in the alley way. The directive to seek information that "fits" what you are looking for, or to only ask those who concur with your opinion for their views illustrates this confirmatory bias (Houghton 2008).
6. Tendency to *stubbornly hold a mind-set* and to "cherry pick" for consistent data and to manipulate information to fit pre-existing notions that may be anchored to faulty suppositions. Desire to hear what one wants to hear and disregard incompatible information and to view non-agreeing participants as not being part of "the team" (Suskind 2004).

III. Cognitive deficits and distortions

7. Tendency to engage in informational processes that *fail to* consider how the questions or situations were *framed* (posed); *fail to* consider multiple non-violent options or alternatives; and *fail to* consider the full range of possible consequences; not think through the "aftermath" of decisions; and *fail to* calculate which course of action is in your and others' best interests and that are most consistent with your values (Brooks 2008; Dodge et al 1990; Jervis 1976; Tversky and Kahneman 1986).
8. Tendency to hold a *hostile attributional bias* whereby you readily view each perceived provocation as a sign of "intentionality," which contributes to aggressive counter reactions. Tendency to misperceive and misinterpret interpersonal cues and *fail to* consider *alternative interpretations* (Dodge 2008).
9. Tendency to *fail to demonstrate empathy* with one's adversary and *fail to* perspective take on what may contribute to the decision-making processes of others. Putting oneself in the shoes of another in order to better understand his/her actions can contribute to conflict avoidance and conflict resolution (Houghton 2008; White 1968).
10. Tendency to engage in *impulsive* and *snap decisions* when handling complex problems, thus failing to adequately weigh consequences (Gladwell 2005; Houghton 2008). As the adage goes, "If there is a simple solution to a complex problem, it is usually wrong."
11. Tendency to make the *fundamental attribution error* of overestimating the extent to which *one's actions* are viewed as the result of situational factors, while someone else's actions are viewed as being the result of their disposition. This attribution error can lead to over and under estimation of behavioral responsibility and lead to misconceptions of how alterable an individual's or a group's behavior may be (Fiske and Taylor 1984; Ross and Nisbett 1991).

(continued)

Table 6.1 (continued)

12. Tendency to engage in *stereotyped fallacies* in their thinking. Decision makers may make unwise decisions because they believe they are so smart, so powerful, and so invincible. Out of "fear," "hubris," and "irrational exuberance," this can lead to tunnel vision and immoral choices. (Sternberg 2002, 2007).
13. Tendency to make *schema-related errors* or the tendency to make decisions based on personal and developmental issues ("hidden agenda") that go well beyond the demands of the present situation (e.g., prove one's manhood, not appear weak, win an election, improve popularity, a distraction procedure) (Houghton 2008; Iyengar and McGuire 1993; George 1980).
14. Tendency to *lack curiosity*, avoiding debates and confrontations among advisers, engaging in denial, and engaging in wishful thinking, reflecting a failure in question posing (Woodward 2006).
15. Tendency to *reason defensively* when failure occurs (blame others, or extraneous events, or chance), rather than evidence the emotional maturity to ask the anxiety arousing challenging questions (e.g., about the validity of deeply held assumptions or about personal flaws in diagnosis or execution). Leaders need support and guidance on how to learn from errors and failure (Hackman and Wageman 2007).
16. Tendency to depend on *group think processes* that strive for unanimity and high group cohesiveness and that contribute to group homogeneity and solidarity and feelings of correctness and invulnerability. The insulation of the decision-making group contributes to self-censorship, collective rationalization, and self-reinforcing self-analysis, as some group members act as "guardians" of decision makers. These processes are exacerbated when decisions have to be made under time pressure. Such group-think processes can lead group members to proceed along a path that in retrospect was obviously wrong-headed. Group-think tends to be closed to outside ideas and decision makers and fails to ask or encourage difficult and challenging questions. Group-think can skew and close down the decision-making process (Brown and Paulus 2002; Janis 1982; Stroebe and Diehl 1994).
17. Tendency to use *gaming the system procedures* whereby advisors intentionally and strategically decide to avoid, bypass, misrepresent, and selectively distort other advisors' opinions and positions in order to manipulate the decision outcome. This type of "bureaucratic combat" may take the form of using back channels and proxies that can undermine the decision making process.

Interviewing (Miller and Rollnick 2002). There are a number of intervention strategies that can be used and evaluated in an effort to teach decision-making procedures to politicians. The research field on instruction has learned a great deal about how to teach decision-making and problem-solving procedures to all types of professionals such as doctors, researchers, students, and negotiators (see Kelman 2008; Kirschner et al. 2006). Can we bring this research literature to bear in training politicians on decision-making? Perhaps, there is some basis to this fantasy?

Translating a "Fantasy" into a Practical Intervention

What does the research indicate are the major motivational and cognitive errors that contribute to faulty decision-making? Table 6.1 provides a summary of many of these decisional errors. In working with policy decision makers there would be a

Table 6.2 Examples of "thinking errors"

Type of error	Definition	Examples
1. Use thinking shortcuts	Tendency to use well-worn "mental habits." Pick out most readily available other past examples and take them as a general representative example.	It is the same as..., just like...
2. Thinking by historical analogy	Tendency to seek historical analogies that misrepresent and do not fit present circumstances or situations.	Watch out for "Like a" statements. This is like Lord Chamberlain giving into Nazism.
3. Drunkard's search. use of "confirmatory bias"	Tendency to seek information that is only consistent with prior views. Seek information that "fits" what you are looking for.	Looks for keys at night under the lamp post because the light is best there, although he had lost his keys in alley way.
4. Mindset that leads to tunnel vision	Tendency to stubbornly hold firm beliefs that lead to selecting and manipulating data to "fit" what one wants to hear and believe.	"Cherry pick" the data. Frames always trump facts. How one frames questions influences decision making.
5. Lack of consequential thinking	Tendency to fail to consider short-term, intermediate and long- term consequences of one's actions.	Little or no planning and forethought. "State of Denial."
6. Make snap decisions	Tendency to engage in impulsive decision making.	"If there is a simple solution to a complex problem, it is usually wrong."
7. Use black-white thinking	Tendency to be prejudiced in your judgement.	"You are with us or against us." You did it "on purpose" without checking this out.
8. "Arrogance"	Exaggerated pride, wins "irrational exuberance," and unquestioned self-confidence	Know-it-all. No need to check with others.
9. Reason defensively	Tendency to blame others, events, chance.	Failure to learn from errors or failures. Use "psychobabble" to explain failures.
10. Lack of curiosity	Avoid debate, minimize confrontation, not question the accuracy of the data.	"What we have here is a failure to communicate and question."
11. Use group think processes	Strive for unanimity and high group cohesiveness, focus on group solidarity, homogeneity of decision.	Self-censorship, closed to outside ideas, close down decision making process.
12. Game the system	Strategically bypass, and misrepresent other advisor's positions.	Jumping chain of command.

need to provide multiple case examples of each error, and moreover, there is a need to have participants, in any workshop, generate their own examples of each of these errors. They can then develop strategies and skills to counter each motivational and cognitive error. The first step in changing behavior is to increase awareness. The second step is to teach strategies and skills in effective decision-making using a combination of guidance-directive exercises and experiential training trials (Kirschner et al 2006). Kelman (2000, 2008) describes a way to use integrative problem solving as a means to nurture negotiation, mediational, and communicative decision-making skills. Brooks (2008), George (1980) and Thaler and Sunstein (2008) highlight that training in effective decision making should include:

- A search and analysis of the presenting situation or problems and a careful consideration of how questions are being framed.
- A consideration of the major goals, values and interests that will be affected by the proposed decisions.
- A generation of a wide range of options and alternatives and a consideration of the likely and unlikely consequences of each – namely, the ability to ask critical questions and "think through" the problem and decision-making processes.
- A careful consideration of the problems and potential barriers that may arise during the implementation and the back-up plans should these be needed.
- A built-in evaluative and corrective feedback process and a willingness to change course, if necessary.

There is a difference between having policy makers be able to articulate these decision-making steps and their actually using them on a regular basis while under pressure. This is when the cognitive behavior trainer comes into play. Like a good coach who is present during a game, the trainer or decision-making consultant can act like a supportive coach or "cognitive ethologist" and provide feedback in private about the decision-making process. For example, a conversation with a President might go like this:

> "I noticed something and I wonder if you noticed this as well?"
>
> *"How did you judge the credibility of the information that was presented?" "Whom else did you rely on for advice?*
>
> *Do you think it would be useful to solicit any other opinions of how you should proceed? Whom else do you think you should hear from?*
>
> *I noticed that in today's Press Conference you stated that "One of the lessons we learned from...(historical analogy) was..." I wonder if we could take a moment and examine the exact similarities that you were referring to and whether there are any important differences between the present situation and the historical example you offered? (e.g., Chamberlain in 1938)? Moreover, if these important differences do indeed exist what are the implications for the decisions you are now considering?*
>
> *With regard to possible options, what are the pros and cons of taking such actions, both the short-term and the long-term consequences, including the historical consequences of the chosen option?*
>
> *What potential barriers or obstacles might arise and what will be the back-up plans that you should have in place?*

How did you come to the decision to do X? Could you take me through the decisional steps you took to come to this decision?

What were your goals in this situation and how will undertaking these steps help you achieve your goals? How will you know if you are making progress?

How do you feel about our chatting like this about the decision-making process? Do you believe this is helpful? Whom else in your cabinet would you like me to see next?

The need for such an ongoing consultation on the decision-making process was highlighted by Barton Gellman, who in his 2008 Pulitzer prize winning book on the vice presidency of Dick Cheney in the United States, describes in detail how decisions are made at the highest levels of government. One critical feature that he highlights is the way politicians "game the system" by selectively manipulating the type of information that is input into the decision-making process and how this information is framed (Gellman, 2008). Gellman describes how politicians would intentionally and strategically avoid, bypass, and misrepresent the views of other advisors whose opinions may differ. Such actions can clearly undermine and bias the decision-making process.

Such "gaming the system" behaviors may arise out of a desire to exert influence, pursue a "hidden agenda" policy position, or avoid admitting a mistake. Whatever the motivational origins of such behaviors, the end result can be quite catastrophic, as Gellman documents.

How can the decision-making consultant help a president avoid such "traps"? The President can be encouraged to ask each of his or her advisors such questions as:

"I appreciate your advice and input, but I am wondering if you have "gamed the system" in presenting your position? Can you tell me which other advisors (members of our team) you have intentionally avoided discussing your views with?"

"How would their views differ from your position? What steps, if any, have you already taken to implement your position?"

By the way, note that most of the questions asked by the decision making consultant are "How" and "What" questions and not "Why" questions. The consultant wants to help decision makers become more aware and knowledgeable about possible motivational and cognitive errors and cognitive distortions that can undermine the decision making process. Tables 6.1 and 6.2 provide examples of the kind of motivational and cognitive errors that have been identified in the research literature that can be incorporated in any training program or consultative session. Such training would have to include concrete historical examples of each type of error and have participants offer their own examples of each type of error and strategies of ways to notice and change them in the future.

A Touch of Reality Testing

No "fairy tale" would be complete without an element of reality testing. Some readers may find this "fairy tale" as being too far-fetched. Consider some possible objections.

1. The decision-making processes are not as rational and linear as being depicted in this fantasy. Decision-makers often make emotionally charged, impulsive, intuitive, "gut" decisions based on incomplete information.
2. Decision-makers are often selecting options based on implicit (perhaps, unconscious) influences that act as "hidden agendas," guiding their decision-making processes.
3. Decision-makers often do not have the luxury of time to engage in such a reflective analysis.
4. There are too many critical decisions to be made in a short time and there is little or no time and little interest to analyze how decisions are being made.
5. Decision-makers believe they already engage in such steps and are thus unlikely to be open, nor ready, to invite such ongoing probing and feedback. They may feel that they already have such decision-making skills in their repertoire or they would not have been chosen to be political leaders.
6. Decision-makers may be uninterested, feel embarrassed and threatened, and closed to receiving feedback on their decision-making processes. Their job is already very stressful. Why add more stress by receiving such feedback on a regular basis? Moreover, they do not want to be accused of being a "flip-flopper."
7. "Saving face" may be viewed as a critical feature and promoting a self-enhancing image may be considered as being central to political leadership. Such ongoing decisional feedback may compromise one's self-esteem and undermine self-confidence. Which political leader would want to learn that his or her cognitive errors and cognitive distortions contributed to the loss of life, economic downturns, or ecological endangerment? Political leaders have the ability to cognitively reframe events so they do not have to admit errors: "History will prove me correct!"
8. This reflective process involves a level of trust that would allow the observer (psychologist) to be "embedded" with decision-makers. The observer needs to focus on the integrity of the decision-making process and be neutral and dispassionate and not have "hidden agendas." Similarly, a life-time commitment to confidentiality is essential to gain such trust.

Any intervention to improve political decision-making would have to anticipate and address each of these potential barriers. How to anticipate and address these likely obstacles can constitute the basis for yet another fantasy for the young-at-heart. But such barriers are addressed on a day-to-day basis by cognitive-behavior therapists and their clients, with some success. Could the same intervention procedures be employed with world leaders and politicians? Dream on!

References

Akerlof, G. A., & Shiller, R. J. (2009). *Animal spirits: How human psychology drives the economy and why it matters for global capitalism*. Princeton: Princeton University Press.

Brooks, D. (2008, October 28). The behavioral revolution. *New York Times*, p. A23.
Brown, V. R., & Paulus, P. B. (2002). Making group brainstorming more effective: Recommendations from an associative memory perspective. *Current Directions in Psychological Science, 11*, 208–212.
Dallaire, R. (2003). *Shake hands with the devil: The failure of humanity in Rwanda*. Toronto: Random House Canada. (Also see DVD www.microfilmsinc.com)
Dodge, K. A. (2008). Framing public policy and prevention of chronic violence in American youth. *The American Psychologist, 63*, 573–590.
Dodge, K. A., Bates, J. E., & Petit, G. S. (1990). Mechanism in the cycle of violence. *Science, 250*, 1678–1683.
Dyson, S., & Preston, T. (2006). Individual distractions of political leaders and the use of analogy in foreign policy decision making. *Political Psychology, 27*, 265–288.
Fiske, S., & Taylor, S. (1984). *Social cognition*. Reading: Addison-Wesley.
Gellman, B. (2008). *Angler: The Cheney vice presidency*. New York: Penguin.
George, A. (1980). *Presidential decision making in foreign policy: The effective use of information and advice*. Boulder: Westview.
Gladwell, M. (2005). *Blink: The power of thinking without thinking*. New York: Little Brown.
Hackman, J., & Wageman, R. (2007). Asking the right questions about leadership: Discussion and conclusions. *The American Psychologist, 62*, 43–47.
Houghton, D. (2008). Invading occupying Iraq. Some insights from political psychology. *Peace and Conflict, 14*, 169–192.
Iyengar, S., & McGuire, W. (Eds.). (1993). *Explorations in political psychology*. Durham: Duke University Press.
Janis, I. L. (1982). *Group think: Psychological studies of policy decisions and fiascoes* (2nd ed.). Boston: Houghton Mifflin.
Jervis, R. (1976). *Perception and misperception in international policies*. Princeton: Princeton University Press.
Kahneman, D., Slovic, P., & Tversky, A. (Eds.). (1987). *Judgment under uncertainty: Heuristics and biases*. Cambridge: Cambridge University Press.
Kelman, H. C. (2000). The role of the scholar-practitioner in international conflict resolution. *International Studies Perspectives, 1*, 273–288.
Kelman, H. C. (2008). Evaluating the contributions of interactive problem solving to the resolution of ethnonational conflict. *Peace and Conflict, 14*, 28–59.
Khong, Y. (1992). *Analogies at war: Korea, Munich, Dien Bien Phu and the Vietnam decisions*. Princeton: Princeton University Press.
Kirschner, P. A., Sweller, J., & Clark, R. E. (2006). Why minimal guidance during instruction does not work: An analysis of the failure of constructivist, discovery, problem-based, experiential and inquiry-based teaching. *Educational Psychologist, 41*, 75–86.
Lakoff, G., & Johnson, M. (1980). *Metaphors we live by*. Chicago: University of Chicago Press.
Meichenbaum, D. (1994). *Treatment of adults with posttraumatic stress disorder: A clinical handbook*. Clearwater: Institute Press.
Meichenbaum, D. (2000). Treating patients with PTSD: A constructive narrative perspective. *NC-PTSD Clinical Quarterly, 9*, 55–59.
Meichenbaum, D. (2002). *Treatment of individuals with anger-control problems and aggressive behavior*. Clearwater: Institute Press.
Meichenbaum, D. (2006a). Resilience and posttraumatic growth: A constructive narrative perspective. In L. G. Calhoun & R. G. Tedeschi (Eds.), *Handbook of posttraumatic growth* (pp. 355–368). Mahwah: Lawrence Erlbaum.
Meichenbaum, D. (2006b). Trauma and suicide: A constructive narrative perspective. In T. Ellis (Ed.), *Cognition and suicide: Theory research and practice* (pp. 333–354). Washington: American Psychological Association.
Meichenbaum, D. (2007). Stress inoculation training: A preventative and treatment approach. In P. M. Lehrer, R. I. Woolfolk, & W. E. Sime (Eds.), *Principles and practice of stress management* (pp. 497–518). New York: Guilford.

Meichenbaum, D., & Fong, G. (1993). How individuals control their own minds: A constructive narrative perspective. In D. M. Wegner & J. W. Pennebaker (Eds.), *Handbook on mental control*. New York: Prentice Hall.
Miller, W. R., & Rollnick, S. (2002). *Motivational interviewing: Preparing people for change* (2nd ed.). New York: Guilford. Also see www.motivationalinterview.org.
Ross, L., & Nisbett, R. E. (1991). *The person and the situation*. New York: McGraw Hill.
Staub, E. (2007). Preventing violence and terrorism and promoting positive relations between Dutch and Muslim communities in Amsterdam. *Peace and Conflict, 113*, 333–360.
Sternberg, R. J. (Ed.). (2002). *Why smart people can be so stupid*. New Haven: Yale University Press.
Sternberg, R. J. (Ed.). (2007). A systems model of leadership: WICS. *American Psychologist, 62*, 34–42.
Stroebe, W., & Diehl, M. (1994). Why groups are less effective than their members: On productivity losses in idea-generating groups. In W. Stroebe & M. Hewstone (Eds.), *European review of social psychology* (Vol. 5, pp. 271–303). Chichester: Wiley.
Suskind, R. (2004). *The price of loyalty: George W. Bush, the White House and the education of Paul o'Neil*. New York: Simon & Shuster.
Thaler, R. H., & Sunstein, C. R. (2008). *Improving decisions about health, wealth and happiness*. New Haven: Yale University Press.
Tversky, A., & Kahneman, D. (1974). Judgment under uncertainty: Heuristics and biases. *Science, 221*, 453–458.
Tversky, A., & Kahneman, D. (1981). The framing of decisions and the psychology of choice. *Science, 211*, 453–458.
Tversky, A., & Kahneman, D. (1986). Rational choice and the framing of decisions. *Journal of Business, 59*, 251–278.
White, R. K. (1968). *Nobody wanted war: Misperception in Vietnam and other wars*. Garden City: Doubleday.
Woodward, B. (2006). *State of denial: Bush at war. Part III*. New York: Simon & Shuster.

Chapter 7
Escalation of Images in International Conflicts

Guy Olivier Faure

A negotiation process is a process of construction: a modification of representations that goes far beyond what can be drawn from rational actor models. If reality is considered unattainable, perceptions are the data with which negotiators have to work. Perceptions and their associated evaluations relate to values and judgments that influence behavior, and also strategic choices. As indicated in Confucius' Analects, without common principles, there is no point in negotiating. Even when parties only agree to disagree, their disagreement concerns issues, offers, suggestions, problem framing, and methods that go through their own perceptions. Representations may take a dramatic turn, for example in the case of the escalation of negative images of the counterpart – leading, for instance, to demonization. Negotiators act not on the basis of facts, but on the basis of their perception of facts. Thus, subjectivity plays an essential role – and rather than being static, that role can evolve during the negotiation process. This can be a key element in the evolution of the problem's perception, its framing, and possibly its transformation. Changes in the perception of the other party, in the perception of one's own subjective utility function or that of the other party, or in the perception of the context, may greatly facilitate the reaching of a common solution. However, the same phenomenon may also work the other way round. Those changes may contribute to an increase in the level of conflict and the perceived incompatibility of goals. In that case, they become highly counterproductive (Faure 2009).

The perception of negotiations as strictly distributive, zero-sum games has led to a great deal of failures in negotiations. This fixed-pie bias (Bazerman and Neale 1983) stems from inadequate information processing or erroneous and/or insufficient data collection. Organizations are subject to the same kinds of cognitive bias as individuals (Jervis 1976). They can be victims, for instance, of attribution, stereotypes, the polarization of images, or the misperception of signals.

The purpose of this research is: to explore the question of representations in negotiation activities in international relations, taking into account the role of stereotypes;

Guy Olivier Faure (✉)
Professor of Sociology, Université la Sorbonne de Paris, 202 Bd Saint Germain, 75007 Paris, France
e-mail: guyolivierfaure@yahoo.fr

F. Aquilar and M. Galluccio (eds.), *Psychological and Political Strategies for Peace Negotiation*, DOI 10.1007/978-1-4419-7430-3_7,

to observe their consequences in conflict and escalation situations; and to analyze the demonization process and its consequences for negotiation practices. Disinformation, especially in its conspiracist form, may be anchored in the quest for a subjective rationale for events and actors. Finally, the temporal dimension of the life of images will be observed and commented on.

The Negotiation Process: Metaphors and Images

Negotiation can be defined as a process by which parties aim to combine their diverging positions into a commonly agreed outcome. Parties engage in a negotiation process because they believe that this will allow them to improve upon the status quo. A number of conditions must be met in order to allow a negotiation process to begin. These include a minimum level of trust, without which any offer, commitment, or suggestion from the other side will not be considered credible (Faure 2003).

A negotiation process may include three distinct types of activity: sharing a resource, compensating on other issues, and transforming the problem. Sharing a resource relates to needs, merits, and fairness. Subjectively expected outcomes also play an important role, for they depend upon the actors' representation of the game and on their counterparts' needs or objectives. A similar process takes place when the negotiation reaches another level of complexity through the build-up of packages in which compensation is offered in return for possible gains. The image of the counterpart may then play a critical role in the way the logic of the game and the counterpart's willingness to cooperate is understood. The transformation of the game or problem is based on similar conditions. When the rationale of the game has no solution, it is necessary to reconstruct the game in such a way that a solution acceptable to all parties exists or may be devised. On top of the basic conditions already established comes a common representation of the situation, which means a similar interpretation of the conflict.

Parties to the dispute may ask themselves about the type of game in which they are involved. In other words, what are the metaphorical representations of negotiation on which each party is basing its approach, defining its strategy and tactics? If, for instance, negotiation is perceived as a game, the action will be based on a win–lose rationale and the related images will belong to the world of competition. If the negotiation is perceived as a fight, the aim is no longer to defeat the other party, but rather to inflict damage on that other party, possibly to destroy it. War metaphors can apply to such an activity. The rationale of such an action is win–lose, and sometimes even lose–lose.

Negotiation may also be regarded as a joint project, a common task to which each party makes its own contribution. The game can also be viewed as a problem to be solved jointly, as was the case with the setting-up of the European Union after the Second World War. The aim is then to implement approaches that are likely to facilitate cooperation. This type of game is based on a win-win rationale. There are also other negotiation metaphors, such as that of social interaction that favors the relationship itself over the substance of the deal and the subsequent outcome. Thus, retribution belongs to another level: the relational level. The negotiation activity may also be perceived as a human adventure, an opportunity to encounter previously unknown situations, to meet new people, and to face uncertainty with surprise, astonishment and the many other emotions that are associated with discovery. Negotiation is then a personal itinerary, a part of life, and a way of being.

Images and Unachieved Negotiations

There are numerous negotiations that do not reach an outcome. Some of them have dreadful consequences. Representations also play their part in these dramatic events Aquilar and Galluccio. The causes of the failure of negotiations – or at least the non-achievement of their objectives – include cognitive issues such as the processing of information. Negotiators process information through pre-established knowledge structures. These structures provide ready-made explanations and are particularly useful where the available data are complex. As a consequence, negotiators may face the unconscious – but substantial – distortion of their perception of the situation. The fixed-pie bias (Bazerman and Neale 1983) is another cognitive cause of failing to reach an agreement. Parties may tend to see negotiations as distributive, win-lose situations, in which, where there is no possibility of clearly winning, the only outcome is to incur a loss. The zero-sum assumption deters parties from accepting an offer or even negotiating in a cooperative way. In negotiations, parties are required to work on the basis of assumptions and forecasts regarding the other party and its intentions. To that end, they have to infer conclusions from behavior and signals. Sometimes people even tend to think that the weaker a signal is, the more reliable it must be. The problem is that this may give rise to the misperception of signals sent by the counterpart, thereby leading to an erroneous assessment of reality and the adoption of an inadequate strategy.

For example, the last-ditch US–Iraqi negotiations in Geneva prior to the first Iraq war (1991) may have failed because the US representative, James Baker, did not send a strong enough signal to the Iraqi side that the USA remained committed to using force if Iraq did not withdraw from Kuwait. The Iraqis continued to regard Kuwait as a local issue to be dealt with among Arab neighbors, thinking that the USA would not go beyond threatening.

Another cause of failures is when concessions from the other side are viewed as tactical ploys intended to lower one's level of vigilance. They can also be underevaluated and thus not effective in triggering reciprocity (Ross and Ward 1995). Sincerity in the attitude of the counterpart can also be systematically questioned or regarded as a manipulative trick. Sometimes, biases may go as far as considering that the other party is too prejudiced or even irrational to be able to understand any reasonable offer. Parties may go so far as to consider that their counterparts are not even able to take proper care of their own interests. Once rationality has been challenged, there is no solid ground left on which to build an agreement (Faure 2008, Faure G.O. and Zartman 2010).

Historical analogies, whether conscious or unconscious, may play a role in hampering any potential agreement (Jervis 2007). Once the Soviet Union had signed a secret accord with Nazi Germany with the Molotov-Ribbentrop Pact (1939), it became very difficult to place any trust in Soviet government commitments. Traumatic events in the past may also render any agreement difficult, if not unlikely. For instance, the constant reluctance of the Turkish authorities to acknowledge the Armenian genocide of 1915 renders complicated any attempt, even one made in good faith, for Turkey to enter the European Union. The Turkish authorities acknowledge only "relocation" or "deportation." They claim that the massacres, labeled the "events of 1915" by Prime Minister Erdogan (2005), were not deliberate or were not governmentally orchestrated. They were, in their view, justified because the Armenians, sympathizing with the Russians, posed a threat to Turkish integrity. The Turkish Penal Code, which prohibits the "insulting of Turkishness," is used on occasion to silence Turkish intellectuals who speak of the atrocities suffered by the Armenians. With this historical trauma systematically revived by the Armenian diaspora, the negotiation of Turkey's accession to the European Union continues to lag, with no clear prospects as regards the final outcome.

Stereotyping is another cause of negotiations failing, because such a phenomenon may promote a caricature of the people concerned. Stereotypes are usually an over-generalization of certain traits and are based on social biases, not individual judgments. They make for an easy understanding of other people because they operate as pre-perceptions of reality. However, they often reflect an unfair and one-sided image that can be very critical and tends to spoil personal relationships. They can trigger a growing hostility among parties. If a counterpart is viewed as tough and tricky, the negotiator will resort to tough tactics to protect him or herself that will elicit tough responses from the other party. Thus, the stereotype will be validated and will lead to self-fulfilling prophecies.

These predictions that come true as a result of the act of predicting may lead a party to consider the situation hopeless, or at the very least lower that party's level of expectations so much that it ceases to be worthwhile trying to continue negotiating. This begins with a false interpretation of behavior, which influences negotiators in such a way that their actions ultimately fulfill the once false prophecy. The prediction, as a belief, becomes an influential part of the situation and affects future developments – like the placebo effect in medicine. A self-fulfilling prophecy works in such a way that people who expect to be successful are more likely to succeed and people who expect to fail are more likely to fail.

Stereotypes, as rigid images describing a group, contribute functionally to the reduction of uncertainty. Thus, they intervene in decision-making and guide behavior. However, although they enhance one's own sense of identity, they also instigate prejudice and may de-legitimize the other party as a counterpart. Stereotypes may, in specific contexts, go as far as triggering violence, destruction, killing, and even genocide.

Stereotypes are rife in the areas of nationality and gender. Fortunately, most of the time they do not lead to dramatic consequences, just questionable social judgments. For instance, Americans are often depicted as brash, ignorant, and self-important. The English are phlegmatic, obsessed by social status, and convinced of their own superiority. Germans are defined as humorless, extremely organized, bureaucratic, and mechanical. The French are described as culturally arrogant, pathologically reluctant to speak English, and romantic. The Chinese are viewed as cunning, tricky, and hypocritical. Other categories of people have their share of biased over-generalizations. For instance, blondes are stupid, athletes are idiots, politicians are professional liars, women are superficial and overly talkative, and men are devoid of feelings and unable to listen.

Causal attribution may also play an important role in the failure of negotiations, as it introduces a bias in the perception of the reasons why a particular event occurred. Dispositional factors are put forward to explain the actions of the other party, especially if these are negative, and situational factors are emphasized when one has to explain one's own unconstructive conduct. Put simply, a negotiator will think that the other party did something wrong on purpose, while he himself did something similar because he was bound by circumstances. There is also a need for consistency that pushes people to interpret or judge behavior in accordance with the image of the counterpart. If the counterpart is viewed as a cooperative person, positive moves will be interpreted as consequences of dispositional factors, while negative moves (in other words, inconsistent behavior) will be explained by situational factors.

Escalation in Negotiation

A conflict can be defined as a state of friction because of an opposition of interests, beliefs, or values. Interests usually relate to objective data and, even if originally framed as a zero-sum game, they can be dealt with through fair sharing, compensation, or problem transformation. Beliefs refer to a totally different category of causes that are often rooted in culture, history, and religion. As a consequence, they are subjectively shaped. This layer of social reality does not leave much room for negotiation. One does not normally negotiate when it comes to one's own beliefs or the beliefs of one's group, or what constitutes one's own identity, as one does not negotiate one's own destruction.

Values tell us what is desirable and what is not acceptable. They thereby draw an invisible line between good and bad and thus guide actors as to what they should do. Relatively intangible, values also cannot be negotiated. A value is either complied with or not complied with. For instance, in conflict resolution, one of the most difficult challenges is achieving peace and justice simultaneously (Zartman and Kremenyuk 2005). Peace – in other words, the restoration of harmony and cooperation – requires a solution beneficial to both parties, whereas justice demands the punishment of the offender. In a tribal dispute, a tribe may feel bound by the obligation to take revenge, but abiding by this tradition may completely destroy any hope of a lasting peace.

Conflict may also stem from personal factors, such as the absence of chemistry. Sometimes conflicts continue for the same reason when representatives of the disputing parties meet at the negotiating table. For instance, this was the case with Ehud Barak and Yasser Arafat at the Camp David Summit negotiations (2000). The dramatic lack of chemistry between these two major decision-makers simply helped to draw out and feed the conflict.

In negotiations, conflicting positions may lead to tensions, aggressive verbal exchanges, and open disagreements, unless a solution is devised. Conflicts in social settings often elicit emotions and stress in the parties to the dispute. In political life, diverging interests may lead to rows, fights, wars, and even revolutions. A major phenomenon affecting conflicts and leading to such dramatic consequences is escalation. Escalation is an expression of conflict in its dynamic form. It can be framed as a move from parties having incompatible static views to having dynamically incompatible views. Escalation expresses a clear increase in conflict that can have an impact on the qualitative dimension of the interaction. It has been defined as a mutually coercive mechanism resulting not just in simple intensification but also in a particular type of intensification: a change in nature, rather than in magnitude (Zartman and Faure 2005).

A classical escalation rationale is the conflict spiral model (Pruitt and Kim 2004), which develops into a vicious circle of action and reaction. A party's contentious tactics encourage a contentious retaliatory reaction by the counterpart, which provokes further contentious behavior by the first party. The motivation can be revenge, defense, or even the deterrence of hypothetical moves by the other party.

As concepts and as practices, escalation and negotiation are closely related. Competitive behavior, commitments, and threats are strategic and tactical moves belonging to both domains. Escalation is a mutually coercive mechanism that pertains to the domain of conflict. Once the negotiation has started, competitive strategies may lead to the escalation of tactical methods in order to achieve a more favorable outcome and thus destroy the negotiation process. However, escalation may at some point also provide incentives for starting to negotiate, especially if the current outcome is of the "lose–lose" type.

Escalation also tends to take on a life of its own. It works as a lethal mechanism leading both parties into a situation where they never anticipated being and never wanted to be. A typical example can be found in the First World War and its unforeseeable consequences. The Austro-Hungarian Empire viewed it originally as a short trip south to teach the Serbs a good lesson. Because of the system of alliances in place, it turned into global slaughter with a death toll of almost ten million and no fewer than 39 countries involved, including unexpected parties such as the Philippines, Siam, China, and Japan. At the end of the war, even the Austro-Hungarian Empire did not survive that fatal escalation process. Three more empires disappeared: the German, Ottoman, and Russian empires. Negotiation attempts were made, but all failed. For instance, in 1916 US President Wilson offered "peace without victory," but in response Germany announced, "unrestricted warfare."

Escalation of Images: First Level

There are many different types of escalation, and these are not limited to means and ends (Zartman and Faure 2005). The escalation of images is a common expression of a qualitative increase in conflict. The other party may be viewed first as a counterpart, then as an obstacle, then as an opponent, then as an enemy, and finally as evil. This process can be frequently observed and has characterized many crises and disasters. The cold war between the two super-powers offered fertile ground for turning enemies into devils. Ethnic conflicts and genocides may result from such deadly processes. The escalation of images may lead to an escalation of goals in response to the new subjective balance. The aim is no longer to achieve the initially defined objectives, but to counter-balance the other party or to defeat it. Threats will not be considered sufficient or sufficiently effective, and parties will move to a "fait accompli" nullifying any hope of negotiation.

The representation of the Egyptian leader Nasser in British and French perceptions, leading to the Suez crisis, is a typical case of the escalation of images. The "Munich Syndrome" (1938) led both countries to launch a senseless military campaign against Egypt (1956) when Nasser nationalized the canal. Anthony Eden, the British Prime Minister, had drawn a parallel between Nasser and Hitler: both dictators facing Britain and France; two men with a dark complexion and a small moustache; charismatic leaders delivering highly emotional public speeches. Nasser's nationalization of the Suez Canal by force and Hitler's re-militarization of the Rhineland were perceived as similarly aggressive moves. Furthermore, Nasser had recruited former Nazi scientists with the aim of building an atomic bomb. This historical analogy (Jönsson 1990) led to the conviction that Nasser's initiative was just the beginning of a long-planned process to expel Western influence from the Middle East and dramatically harm British and French interests. The logical consequence of this perception was to immediately counter Nasser's strategy.

The escalation of images may be triggered and fed by cognitive problems, poor information, or distorted data. Much of the literature on escalation insists on the leading role played by judgmental and perceptual biases. Cognitive dissonance can produce escalation, because, once a negotiation process has been started, feedback that is inconsistent with the initial beliefs is kept away and the party then escalates, thinking that such a step is necessary in order to strengthen its position and maintain the consistency of its perceptions. Expectations that are not met may equally feed the escalation process. An effort on one side that is not followed by any attempt to reciprocate on the other may be seen as a threat (Jervis 1984). The escalation of images and portrayals also leads to increasingly negative images, resulting in a challenge to the counterpart's very identity – an attack on the self. Thus, the most sensitive layer of the cultural dimension of negotiation is reached.

A paranoid attitude on the part of the producer of fantasized negative representations may help to feed the whole escalation process. A similarly paranoid stance may be elicited in its counterpart. Each proponent may consider the other a sworn enemy. A kind of obsessive focus is placed on the adversary, and all difficulties are attributed to that party. Paranoid people suffer from permanent anxiety. For instance, they develop an imaginary vision of someone – or some group – spending their time trying to destroy their life. They experience this as a permanent threat. As a result, they are obliged to resort to strong self-defense measures. Furthermore, paranoid people seek to protect themselves against any intrusion into their cognitive mapping. Since they feel vulnerable, they react by building a protective barrier, which results in an increase in the rigidity of their views. They tend to develop mental models of the thought processes of the other party in order to read their enemy's hidden intentions and to predict future behavior. Thus, they have no way of finding peace with themselves unless they annihilate their enemy. They have to act radically to clean up the situation. This phenomenon touches upon the essence of terrorism.

A Further Stage in the Escalation of Images: Demonization

Beyond a certain level of negativity, one has to speak about a process of a different nature, that of demonization (Faure 2007). Such a process can be defined as the characterization of people as evil or subhuman. Demonizing an individual usually implies the suspension of the normal considerations of human behavior and respect. This psychological phenomenon may lead to two types of consequence: the rejection of any possibility of entering into discussions with the demonized counterpart or the breaking-off of negotiations. Within the first option, it may even go as far as justifying an attack. Any means of "self-defense" is considered legitimate in relation to the magnitude of the perceived threat. For instance, demonizing Saddam Hussein created conditions for taking military action to eradicate him, instead of striving to achieve an agreement that would maintain him at the head of Iraq. Thus, the polarization of images works as a self-serving bias for future action.

Demonization is a typical case of escalation of the image of the counterpart. This is a complex development that addresses first the psychological dimension, by building up on anxiety, and then the strategic dimension, by disqualifying the other party in order to allow any type of action against it. Images have their own lives, their own rationales, and their own ways of escalating when confronting each other (Zartman and Faure 2005). They tend to remain consistent with emotions and beliefs; thus, they feed and strengthen the conflict. The interplay between cognitive factors and emotions has an important function in reinforcing consistency in representations, especially when the enemy is perceived as a demon. The result is an intensification of the conflict, which in some cases is ultimately defined as an irrational fatality.

There is no shortage of devils in our contemporary world. Demonization has been observed on the part of some Western governments, for instance, through their development of a Manichean worldview and the definition of an "axis of evil" comprising Iran, Iraq, and North Korea. Islam religion and Muslims when associated with terrorism are widely demonized in some Western media. Fundamentalists and radical Muslims are categorized as "Islamo-fascists." Muslim activist groups are qualified as "barbarian, monstrous, merciless, and inhuman." Muslims are regarded as "bigots and psychopaths." American leaders have labeled the members of the current government of Iran as "mad mullahs" and "congenital terrorists," also characterizing them as "wild-eyed and irrational."

Muslim fundamentalists are far from being the only ones suffering from demonization. North Koreans have joined them as villains. North Korea's leader Kim Jong Il has constantly been the target of demonization campaigns. Kim and his country have been described as "irrational, unpredictable, secretive, reclusive, and militaristic." President G.W. Bush referred to the North Korean leader as a "tyrant," a statement that did considerable damage to the prospects for negotiations, undoing all efforts to persuade North Korea that the USA would bargain in good faith. Negotiating with Kim Jong Il means holding discussions with a man who holds millions of hostages, a "genocidal maniac." North Korea is described as a "vast and grim concentration camp," where an "evil-minded and abstruse dictator" brainwashes ordinary North Koreans into supporting his "malefic designs" on the world. Kim Jong Il is personally depicted at best as a "bizarre" dictator with a "bad haircut and a funny jacket," and at worse as a "paranoid neo-Stalinist."

Terrorist groups also demonize their designated enemy in irrational ways. The USA is labeled as the "number one rogue state," and the former neoconservative clan in the White House has been called a "group of fanatics." The USA has persistently been named the "Great Satan" by Iran or "the head of the snake" by Al-Qaeda. Westerners are identified as "Judeo-Crusaders" whose basic purpose is to eradicate Islam. The Pope is addressed as "the worshipper of the cross." Heads of moderate Arab countries such as Egypt or Jordan are called "apostates." Israel is not even acknowledged as a country, but simply named the "Zionist entity."

A conflict of interests may, on occasions, turn into a hostile personal relationship and the other party into an enemy. Then, it may become convenient to demonize that party. A typical case was that of Slobodan Milosevic, the Serbian leader, who was assiduously vilified in Western media and presented in a highly emotive way as a "Nazi-like thug." At best he was described as "moody, reclusive, and given to mulish fatalism." References were made to "US psychiatrists" who studied Milosevic "closely" and diagnosed the Yugoslav leader as having a "malignant narcissistic personality," which subsequently paved the way for self-deception. As if it were indispensable to add more weight to such a harsh portrait, he was described as having been under the fatal influence of his wife, Mirjana Markovic, "the real power behind the throne." Nicknamed "Lady Macbeth," she was depicted as absolutely insane, falling into mental states impossible to keep under control. She was also suspected of suffering from schizophrenia, having only a "tenuous grasp on reality." She and her husband supposedly shared the same "autistic relationship with the world." When perceptions of this kind occur, it is no longer useful to consider negotiation as a means of solving problems. There is no basis for the slightest amount of trust and thus no ground for accepting such people as possible counterparts.

Ariel Sharon has had his share of demonization, even on a scale that Yasser Arafat never had in the West. He has been nicknamed the "butcher of Kibya," a Palestinian Arab village raided by the Israeli army in a retaliatory action (1953) in which 69 civilians died. The Sabra and Shatila massacres (1982) carried out by Christian Arabs in Lebanon are often attributed to Sharon personally, as if he had done it himself. He has also often been accused of igniting the intifada by visiting the Temple Mount (September 2000), as if it were a crime for a Jew to so much as set foot there. Even in the Western media, Sharon has been labeled "the truly bad guy of the Middle East" (*Salon*'s Middle East correspondent). He has been accused of "taking on the role of Slobodan Milosevic, the former Yugoslav leader and widely reviled war criminal." His political career has been summarized as follows: "From butcher [...] to Prime Minister" (*The Observer*, UK, 4 Feb. 2001). Sharon has been relentlessly described as a warmonger, violent, and a ruthless leader. His methods have been deeply criticized and caricatured, as in the following statement: "Sharon's motto has been the same – always escalate."

One may be critical of the Taliban and their social philosophy, but Western media have escalated matters much further by systematically demonizing them, despite the fact that the rules they have imposed on the Afghan population that they control are not significantly different from what has been going on in quite a few other Islamic states. They have been accused of heinous crimes and have been the target of intense campaigns in the media against "madrassas," where the Taliban did nothing but primitive brainwashing. They have deprived women of the opportunity to work and have forced them to wear burkas in the street. They have supposedly stoned to death a number people for adultery, for prostitution, for sodomy, and for "corrupting society." They have also been portrayed as puppets of Osama Bin Laden. Mullah Omar has been depicted as an illiterate recluse with a visceral hatred of non-Muslims. The identification badges that non-Muslims have to wear in the places they rule have been compared to the Nazi's tagging of Jews during the Second World War, although in Afghanistan the wearing of badges has not entailed dramatic consequences of any sort.

Demonizing Versus Negotiating

Two types of demonization situations may occur in the context of negotiations. If the negotiations have not yet started, the ongoing demonization will make it very difficult for the process to begin. The demonizing party will certainly not take the risk of sitting at the same table as the devil. In addition, that party might use it as a pretext in explaining why it is refusing to negotiate. If negotiations have already begun, a demonization process, possibly combined with conspiracy theories and aggravated by escalation dynamics, will simply annihilate the negotiation process. The counterpart will be disqualified as such and – both on political and on ethical grounds – it will be impossible to carry on with the negotiations.

Two options normally remain: (a) a standstill, which could result in a situation where no more negotiation attempts can be carried out, and where the problem – the crisis, even – persists with no solution; (b) the situation could be interpreted as a good excuse for going as far as assaulting the other party. In the case of the latter, war becomes the continuation of politics by other means. The situation thus turns into another classic: that of strategic conduct in open confrontation.

Demonization carries with it psychological violence that may extend the pain and the related resentment long after the conflict has regressed or even disappeared. It works as a phantom pain, a type of neuropathic pain that is truly felt even when the cause has been suppressed. For instance, when someone has lost a leg, the pain is still felt in the foot because the nerves keep telling the brain that the leg is still there. Demonization may persist without any objective cause as a phantom pain.

Distorted beliefs produced by the demonization process may stay on even after the real situation has changed. A motivational bias or an emotional commitment can play a role alongside the avoidance of cognitive dissonance. Belief persistence occurs because "(a) people tend to seek out, recall, and interpret evidence in a manner that sustains beliefs; (b) they readily invent causal explanations of initial evidence in which they then place too much confidence; (c) they act upon their beliefs in a way that makes them self-confirming" (Nisbett and Ross 1980).

Distorted Images

Beliefs play an essential role in international relations. They tend to structure understanding and provide a rationale for acting. The demonization of the counterpart may, sometimes, be legitimized and enhanced by another process stemming from the domain of conspiracy theories. Conspiracy theories are based on the belief that many events happening in the world can be explained by the existence of a plot organized by a covert alliance of powerful people manipulating affairs behind the scenes. These theories have far-reaching social and political implications. Conspiracy theories tend to satisfy people's need to find meaning, especially when official explanations remain barely credible or are at least far from satisfactory. Conspiracy theories tend to remedy institutional or societal flaws that operate as sources of dissonance. Individuals naturally respond to events that produce a strong emotional reaction by trying to make sense of those events in what they believe to be rational terms. This general phenomenon has produced a surprising number of social rumors, such as NASA having never landed on the moon. Conspiracy theories insinuate themselves into interpretations of dramatic events, as was the case with the assassinations of John F. Kennedy and, later, his brother Robert Kennedy, which have been often attributed to the Mafia. Many works of fiction are based on conspiracy theories, such as the best-selling novel "The Da Vinci Code," which deals with a supposed conspiracy on the part of the Catholic Church to erase from history some embarrassing "facts" about the life of Jesus.

Insufficient control of uncertainty in causation leaves room for all sorts of interpretations and thus explains the development of conspiracy theories. The purely logical path, through reasoning, would be to never rule out any possibility until it had been proved absolutely impossible, but nothing can ever be proved impossible. A conspiracy theory is based on assumption or speculation, which may on occasion feed the demonization process – for instance the idea that events do not happen by chance, but rather serve a hidden agenda.

Some of the world's best-known dramatic events have been explained by conspiracy theories – for instance the Japanese attack on Pearl Harbor in 1941, of which the US government supposedly had prior knowledge and which it allowed to occur in order to provide a pretext for the USAs' entry into the Second World War.

The destruction of the twin towers of the World Trade Center in New York on September 11, 2001 dramatically feeds anxiety and hate. The need for a scapegoat thus comes to the fore. Moreover, the "real cause" behind any attack is supposed to remain secret for unclear reasons. Originating from dissatisfaction with the mainstream account, theories surrounding this dramatic event have surfaced. Time magazine observed that by November 2008 there were around 150,000,000 web pages dedicated to 9/11 conspiracy theories. The assumptions they carry point to groups such as the Israeli intelligence agency Mossad, the Pakistani intelligence services, or US ultra-neoconservatives having organized the attack. A large proportion of conspiracy theorists also tend, for instance, to believe that the US government was aware of the preparation of the attacks and cynically let them happen.

Conspiracy theories have great appeal and a substantial proportion of people believe them. Several recent surveys have concluded that roughly 50% of Westerners regard them as serious information. Conspiracy theories capture the public imagination and fulfill a sociological function. They can be understood as a narrative form of scapegoating, framing demonized enemies as part of an insidious plot (Berlet and Lyons 2000). The scapegoater is then considered a hero, revealing the truth and sounding the alarm. Assigning a scapegoat is the most effective modus operandi imaginable for mobilizing the energy of people and providing a focal point.

At the beginning of contemporary conspiracy theory literature are the Protocols of the Elders of Zion. These Protocols are an anti-Semitic forgery that purports to describe a Jewish plot to achieve world domination. The Protocols take the form of an instruction manual for a new member of the "Elders," describing how they want to run the world through control of the media and replace the traditional social order with another one based on mass manipulation. Although there is indubitable proof that these were a complete fabrication on the part of the Russian secret service (1917), the Protocols are still a bestseller in quite a few countries, especially in the Middle East.

Since the so-called "Jewish plot," many cabals have taken the floor with the same objective of establishing a new world order. Among them are the Trilateral Commission, the Club of Rome, the Rosicrucians, and the Bilderberg Group. The Trilateral Commission was founded by Rockefeller in 1972 as an organization that could "be of help to government by providing measured judgment." Members of the TLC are carefully selected and represent the absolute elite of world finance and industry. Officially, they promote "cooperation in keeping the peace, in managing the world economy, in fostering economic development, and in alleviating world poverty." Their ultimate aim is to "improve the chances of a smooth and peaceful evolution of the global system." However, observers suspect that the Trilateral Commission is in reality the latest manifestation of an international conspiracy that is aiming to create a one-world totalitarian state.

The Club of Rome is a global think tank described by conspiracy theorists as a committee of 300 subversive influential people. It was founded in 1968 as an alliance between Anglo-American financiers and the old black nobility families of Europe. These elite individuals had a reputation for regarding man as being only slightly above the level of cattle and considering mankind, in any case, as the first enemy of humanity. For the committee, democracy is not an effective formula for world development. Critics have charged the Club of Rome with "Neo-Malthusianism, through wars, diseases, and famines leading to a genocidal reduction of the world population." Some people link the Club of Rome with various conspiracies, especially as regards the New World Order. The key to their successful control of the world is, allegedly, their ability to create and cleverly manage economic recessions and depressions. Thus, the millions of people in trouble all over the world become dependent on their "welfare." They are also accused of having developed a plan to divide the world into ten regions or kingdoms.

The term "Rosicrucian" ("of the Rose Cross") concerns a secret society of mystics, allegedly formed in late medieval Germany. This society has a doctrine built on esoteric truths relating to the ancient past, which are concealed from the average man. This doctrine provides insights into nature, the physical universe, and the spiritual realm. Conspiracy theorists strongly believe that over the centuries this society has developed into a network of highly influential people with a hand in the world's destiny.

The Bilderberg Group started as a conference held at the Hotel Bilderberg near Arnhem in the Netherlands (1954). Leaders from European countries and the USA were brought together with the official aim of promoting understanding between the cultures of the USA and Western Europe. Following that first conference, they have met on a regular basis, and this most elitist group includes representatives of 18 countries. These four secret organizations are depicted by conspiracy theorists as models of malice, amoral groups trying to deflect history from its normal course in the most evil way.

There is a widespread belief that the Great Seal of the USA contains a mass of occult and Masonic symbols. As it appears on the one-dollar bill, this seal is interpreted as tangible proof that Freemasonry rules everything important, particularly in the USA. The USAs' first major politicians were Masons, including George Washington, and the dollar bill contains their symbol: a pyramid, with the All-Seeing Eye above it. This image is symbolic of the Great Architect of the Universe. Above the eye is written "annuit cœptis," and below the pyramid the words "novus ordo seclorum" are understood as announcing the birth of a "New World Order." Conspiracy theorists see this as part of a huge plan to surreptitiously send secret signals by putting them on highly important documents, including presidential proclamations and files on the ratification of treaties. The symbol of the pyramid has always been of fascination for Freemasons, and according to conspiracy theorists, it represents the temple of Satan worship.

Finally, as with conspiracy theories, the wars, disasters, genocides, and other calamities that occur in this world are also considered to have a genuine purpose. A few invisible and highly influential people are believed to have carefully planned these catastrophes. These people supposedly operate behind the scenes and are high above any power structure that the ordinary citizen could ever imagine. This is presumed to be the case with the Illuminati, an organization suspected of conspiring to control world affairs through governments and multinational companies and aiming to impose a new order on the entire planet. It is claimed that they have cleverly managed to infiltrate governments and are behind the most important events in world history. They are believed to have organized the French Revolution, financed Napoleon, manipulated the Congress of Vienna, set up the United Nations, created a number of states, given rise to false religions, and financed the development of communism. They are even believed to have been behind the outbreak of both World Wars.

This kind of paranoid delirium is propagated in the media by experts in pseudo-history who keep disseminating imaginary plots. These beliefs are involuntarily encouraged by the recurrent tendency of governments to provide scarcely credible explanations for dramatic events, as was the case with the assassination of John F. Kennedy. Once accepted, the belief may be reinforced by processes such as the confirmation bias avoidance of cognitive dissonance. Where a conspiracy theory has become popular within a group, communal reinforcement may equally play a part. Some historians have also argued that there might be an element of psychological projection in conspiracism. This projection, according to the argument, takes the form of the attribution to conspirators of undesirable characteristics of oneself (Hofstadter 1964). This would explain why, in some cases, potential victims turn into executioners.

Beliefs created by conspiracy theorists feed the demonization process in a very specific way. Conspiracists promote rumors as if they were revealed truths. The people who come to know these truths get a sense of being "initiated" into a closed circle, of gaining knowledge that others have no chance of getting access to. The "initiated" parties may also feel quite self-important for allegedly being less naïve than ordinary citizens.

World domination by a malevolent group is not the only matter conspiracy theories are dealing with. There are numbers of so-called revelations that relate to events such as conflicts, tribal fighting, or wars. In such cases, responsibility for the dramatic event is attributed to a specific group. The many aborted negotiations in the Middle East are typical examples of this. Viewed as being responsible for the event that has taken place, the counterpart is disqualified as a negotiation counterpart. In that case, alleged responsibility means guilt. This may happen even if, in reality, the event in question was way beyond that party's control. Such a party can be demonized for two different reasons: first, for having done something extremely harmful; and second, for being unscrupulous enough to try to evade its responsibility. Thus, such perception of his counterpart will prompt the negotiator to abandon the idea of negotiating and disregard the other party (an isolation strategy, which is often a by-product of demonization) or switch to another type of action, that is open conflict.

Images and Reality

When parties enter into a potential relationship, stereotypes provide the initial basis for knowledge, thereby shaping expectations. Perceptions derived from direct experience may complete or modify the picture. If conflict increases, the relationship runs the risk of escalating into animosity in terms of means, goals, and images. Thus, a demonization process may begin. The counterpart is no longer even an adversary or an enemy, becoming a devil, and the aim is no longer to attain one's goals, but to defeat that devil, potentially to annihilate him. The party turns into a dragon slayer and negotiation ceases to be a suitable way of handling the conflict. Similarly, mediation is rejected as a procedure giving illegitimate status to the evil group.

Beliefs stemming from conspiracy theories may, in some cases, contribute to the strengthening of the demonized image and the feeding of the hate or fear of those who regard themselves as victims of deliberate disinformation or even malefic designs.

The life cycle of demonization may be divided into three stages. At first, the demonization process continues to develop with the aid of phenomena such as cognitive dissonance or because of an absence of positive moves by the other party. Negative images prevail and reality is reinterpreted in order to support beliefs. However, there are limits to this development, because a reasonable level of credibility must be maintained, because the resulting situation must not be too painful, and because going too far, for instance by making irrevocable commitments, renders any mediation or negotiation most unlikely.

The second stage is characterized by an unusual form of stability, a situation where a mutually hurting stalemate prevails (Zartman and Berman 1982; Zartman 1989). A mutually hurting stalemate is where a conflict has reached a point at which a sort of equilibrium is established, in which neither side is getting any closer to achieving its goals nor is anyone happy with the situation. Both sides come to realize that the cost of continuing the struggle exceeds (sometimes greatly) the benefits to be gained. This kind of painful deadlock creates a window of opportunity – a ripe moment – for the introduction of proposals for settlement.

This is normally a lose-lose situation, and although history provides examples of cases that continue for decades, most of the time an extremely costly or painful situation for both parties helps them to move on to the third stage, that of de-demonization. Judgmental biases and extreme emotional commitments cannot develop endlessly, and so parties may return to more realistic views. Expectations may also fall to a level more acceptable to the other party.

The influence of mediating third parties may help to create the conditions triggering a de-demonization process. Representations and opinions also evolve because of changes in the global context. Less aggressive representations of the counterpart enable both parties to finally reconsider their former positions and contemplate negotiation as an option. The road to negotiation goes through a gradual reduction of antagonism and related images. Sufficient credibility has to be restored such that each party is able to develop enough trust to listen to and accept some of the arguments advocated by the counterpart, regarding them as being delivered in good faith. For instance, Al Sadat's historic visit to Israel (1977), following the 1973 war, resulted in increased personal respect and sufficient credibility regarding his own sincerity in trying to establish more normal neighborly relations. This radical and spectacular initiative paved the way for the subsequent Camp David Accords (1978).

Historic gestures of a highly symbolic nature have sometimes significantly changed the image people have had of foreigners. For instance, when Pierre de

Coubertin, speaking at the Sorbonne in Paris (1894), proposed a revival of the ancient Olympic Games as a celebration of athletic chivalry, he moved humanity much further than any international organization could do. With athletes and spectators from all parts of the world meeting, images of others changed considerably.

Another momentous step was taken, for instance, when German Chancellor Willy Brandt fell to his knees when visiting Warsaw (1970) to commemorate the 500,000 Jews from the city's ghetto who had been massacred by the Germans during the Second World War. Bowing his head and surrounded by silence, he sent an extremely powerful message to the whole world. In so doing, he helped enormously to modify the Germans' image in contemporary history.

At this point, images have their own life, their own rationale. The unconscious dimension of the judgment of the actor assessing them is important. Images can be manipulated for strategic purposes in view of the ongoing negotiation or the negotiation to come. However, there are limits to such an exercise, because the resulting effect remains relatively unpredictable. In the combined conscious and unconscious dimensions, the final word goes to the receiver. Images play an active part in negotiations and conflict resolution. Deliberate strategies and biases feed those images and contribute to them having a role to play. Negotiators are both vectors and victims at the same time, whether it is a matter of perceptions regarding situations, actors, and games, of processes such as demonization and escalation, or of weird beliefs such as conspiracy theories. In all cases, these nourish the negotiator's thinking and actions, thereby helping history to be written.

References

Aquilar, F., & Galluccio, M. (2008). *Psychological processes in international negotiations: Theoretical and practical perspectives*. New York: Springer.

Bazerman, M. H., & Neale, M. A. (1983). Heuristics in negotiations: Limitations to effective dispute resolution. In M. H. Bazerman & R. J. Lewicki (Eds.), *Negotiating in organizations*. Beverly Hills: Sage.

Berlet, C., & Lyons, M. N. (2000). *Right-wing populism in America: Too close for comfort*. New York: Guilford.

Faure, G. O. (2003). *How people negotiate: The resolution of conflicts in different cultures*. Dordrechts, The Netherlands: Kluwer.

Faure, G. O. (2007). Demonization and negotiation. *PIN Points, 28*, 7–10.

Faure, G. O. (2008). Negotiating with terrorists: A discrete form of diplomacy. *The Hague Journal of Diplomacy, 3*, 179–200.

Faure, G. O. (2009). Culture and conflict resolution. In J. Bercovitch, V. A. Kremenyuk, & I. W. Zartman (Eds.), *The Sage handbook of conflict resolution* (pp. 506–524). Thousand Oaks: Sage.

Faure G.O. and Zartman I.W. (2010). *Negotiating with Terrorists*: Strategy, Tactics, and Politics (vol 27). London and New York, Routledge.

Hofstadter, R. The Paranoid Style in American Politics. *Harper's Magazine*, November 1964, 77–86

Jervis, R. *The Illogic of American Nuclear Strategy* (Ithaca: Cornell University Press, 1984)

Jervis, R. (1970). *The logic of images in international relations*. Princeton: Princeton University Press.

Jervis, R. (1976). *Perception and misperception in international politics*. Princeton: Princeton University Press.
Jönsson, C. (1990). *Communication in international bargaining*. London: Pinter.
Nisbett, R., & Ross, L. (1980). *Human inference: Strategies and shortcomings of social judgment*. Englewood Cliffs: Prentice-Hall.
Pruitt, D., & Kim, S. (2004). *Social conflict: Escalation, stalemate, and settlement*. New York: McGraw-Hill.
Ross, L., & Ward, A. (1995). Psychological barriers to dispute resolution. In M. P. Zanna (Ed.), *Advances in experimental social psychology (vol 27)*. San Diego: Academic.
Zartman, I. W. (1989). *Ripe for resolution*. New York: Oxford University Press.
Zartman, I. W., & Berman, M. (1982). *The practical negotiator* (pp. 66–78). New Haven: Yale University Press.
Zartman, I. W., & Faure, G. O. (2005). *Escalation and negotiation in international conflicts*. Cambridge: Cambridge University Press.
Zartman, I. W., & Kremenyuk, V. A. (2005). *Peace vs justice*. Lanham: Rowman & Littlefield.

Chapter 8
Communication Preliminary to Negotiation in Intractable Conflict

Dean G. Pruitt[1]

Intractable conflict is severely escalated, long-lasting conflict. The hostility that occurs in such conflict tends to block association between adversaries and interfere with their communication (Coleman 1957; Sherif and Sherif 1969). For example, for years before the Oslo negotiations that established the Palestinian Authority, communication with the Palestinian Liberation Organization (PLO) was illegal in Israel and PLO members who made contact with Israelis risked assassination (Pruitt et al. 1997). Low communication makes it hard to escape conflict, because misperceptions and misunderstandings are not cleared up (Aquilar and Galluccio 2008; Newcomb 1947), and negotiations to settle differences are not initiated.

Opposition to communication with the adversary has several sources. One is doubts about its usefulness. When conflict becomes severe, zero-sum thinking often sets in (Aquilar and Galluccio 2008; Pruitt and Kim 2004). Anything that is good for the adversary seems bad for us and vice-versa. Hence, there is no middle ground and nothing to talk about. In addition the adversary is often seen as untrustworthy and unchangeable, again blocking serious communication.

Opposition to communication is also partly strategic. People fear that communication will imply recognition of the adversary or approval of its demands and complaints.[2] Or communication may be seen as a sign of weakness, encouraging the adversary to persist in its hostile behavior and undermining the morale of our supporters (Pruitt 2006).

In addition, opposition to communication may be a product of irrational forces. The adversary is viewed as evil and hence not worthy of human contact (Spector

[1] The author wishes to thank Daniel Lieberfeld and Neta Oren for their many useful comments on this manuscript.

[2] In a Washington Post editorial (Zahar and Carter 2008), Former US President Jimmy Carter was chided for meeting with the foreign minister of Hamas. The complaint was that he had "grant(ed.) recognition and political sanction to a leader of a group that advocates terrorism, mass murder or the extinction of another state."

D.G. Pruitt (✉)
Distinguished Scholar in Residence,
Institute for Conflict Analysis and Resolution, George Mason University
e-mail: dean@pruittfamily.com

F. Aquilar and M. Galluccio (eds.), *Psychological and Political Strategies for Peace Negotiation*, DOI 10.1007/978-1-4419-7430-3_8,

2003). Or our group's self-definition may include opposition to the adversary group. In that case, communication other than the delivery of accusations and demands becomes a challenge to group identity and causes the communicator to experience self-doubt or accusations of disloyalty.

This chapter concerns the processes and conditions that encourage adversaries in intractable conflict to move into communication with each other and thence to negotiation. The first topic will be motivation to escape the conflict (called "motivation"), which is usually a prerequisite for the development of communication. After that will be a discussion of optimism about finding a mutually acceptable agreement (called "optimism"), which is another common prerequisite. Then there will be a section on causal relationships between motivation and optimism. Back-channel communication will be discussed in the next section, followed by a discussion of unofficial communication by undesignated elites – so-called Track 2 and Track 1 ½ diplomacy. The conclusions will present a preliminary theory about stages on the way to overt negotiation which postulates that increases in optimism allow communication to become progressively more formal and direct.

Motivation to Escape the Conflict

Movement toward communication and negotiation usually starts with the development of motivation to escape the conflict on one or both sides (Pruitt 2005, 2007). This motivation often arises from pessimism about the strategy one is using, which derives from one or more of three possible sources:

1. Evidence that the conflict is *unwinnable* or that *defeat* is on the way. For example, the white South African government began to explore negotiation with their prisoner, Nelson Mandela, in the mid-1980s when they concluded that they could not forever contain mass black civil disobedience and were unable to persuade other non-white groups into siding against Mandela's party, the African National Congress (ANC) (Lieberfeld 1999).
2. Perception that the conflict has become too *costly*. The costs may be tangible; for example, in the Nagorno-Karabakh War, negotiation began immediately after an abrupt rise in battlefield casualties on both sides (Mooradian and Druckman 1999). Or they may be intangible; for example, Israel's effort to settle the conflict with the Palestinians in the early 1990s may have been partly motivated by a perceived threat to Israeli identity as a democratic state that was posed by this conflict (Oren 2010).
3. Perception that the conflict has become too *risky*. For example, the USA and the USSR moved toward negotiation immediately after the mutually frightening Cuban Missile Crisis. There the risk was possible escalation to a nuclear exchange. In other cases, risk arises because a greater enemy has appeared on the scene and the conflict interferes with efforts to beat that enemy. The greater enemy may be common to both sides, as when the USA and the Soviet Union put aside their differences to fight Nazi Germany. Or the greater enemy may be different

for each side; for example. In 1993, Israel sought negotiation with the Palestinians because of "a growing threat to national security from regional adversaries armed with weapons of mass destruction – notably Iran and a remilitarized Iraq" and the PLO sought negotiation with Israel because of "fear of losing power to Hamas" (Lieberfeld 1999, pp. 120–121).[3]

Motivation to escape a conflict may also result from erosion of the rationale for participating in the conflict. This can be seen in Northern Ireland in the late 1980s and early 1990s when communication developed between Sinn Fein – the political wing of the Irish Republican Army (IRA) – and the British government (see below). Important parts of the rationale underlying IRA terrorist attacks had come into question because (a) the nationalists, whose cause the IRA espoused, were better off than earlier; (b) the breakup of the Soviet Union had weakened the case for establishing a socialist state; and (c) desired alliance partners were vigorously arguing that further progress toward nationalist goals depended not on ejecting the "colonialist" British government but on persuading the unionists to accept a coalition government.[4]

Third parties often encourage the motivation to escape a conflict. As in the Northern Ireland peace process, they may urge the parties to rethink their rationale for perpetuating the conflict. They may also reinforce pessimism about the effectiveness, cost, and safety of efforts to defeat the adversary. In addition, powerful third parties may apply pressure to adopt a new approach, such as the international boycott and freeze on lending money to South Africa in the late 1980s, which helped persuade the white government to open talks with the ANC.

Logically, motivation to escape the conflict should also derive from mutually enticing opportunities[5] – the possibility of engaging in joint projects for mutual gain. This sometimes happens in less escalated conflicts. For example in 2007, the British government sought to encourage unionists and nationalists in Northern Ireland to resume the provincial government that had been abandoned in 2002 by offering them a lot of money to build infrastructure. Negotiations followed this offer and the provincial government was reinstated. However in intractable conflicts, mutually enticing opportunities are much less common as a route to negotiation. This may be because the hostility and distrust engendered by such conflicts is antithetical to cooperation on joint projects.

Even when there is a strong rationale for rethinking a conflict, leaders do not always recognize it because they are so heavily committed to winning or so deeply involved in the mechanics of struggle. It follows that motivation to escape a conflict

---

[3]Zartman (1989, 2000), whose ripeness theory inspired the ideas presented in this and the next section, uses the term "mutually hurting stalemate" to describe a situation in which both sides view a conflict as unwinnable and too costly. He adds that such a stalemate is more likely to produce change when "associated with an impending, past, or recently avoided catastrophe" (Zartman 2000, p. 228), which implies the importance of perceived risk.

[4]The IRA was fighting on behalf of the nationalists, who were mostly Catholic descendents of the indigenous Irish population. The unionists were mainly Protestant descendents of earlier British settlers.

[5]The term comes from Zartman (2000).

may not develop until there is a shock – a sudden reversal of fortunes which commands attention (Goertz and Diehl 1997) – or a change in leadership (Mitchell 2000). In addition, a temporary lull in the fighting may allow leaders to gain sufficient perspective to critique the strategy they are using. Thus Lieberfeld (1999), commenting on cases discussed in this chapter, observes that the Israeli and South African governments only entered negotiation after temporarily thwarting their adversaries militarily. This lull in the fighting may have permitted them to examine the long-term prospects for the conflict, which were unfavorable.

If official decision makers do not recognize the need for rethinking a conflict, non-official elites may do so. Hence, as will be discussed later, communication may begin in the absence of participation or endorsement by top leaders.

Optimism About Finding a Mutually Acceptable Agreement

To embark on a program of communication and negotiation requires more than motivation to escape a conflict. There must also be optimism about finding a mutually acceptable agreement (Pruitt 2005). Without optimism, communication and negotiation seem futile.

There is a time dimension to optimism. Some optimism is required for a party to begin communicating with the adversary – enough to overcome the arguments against communication described in the first section of this chapter. And progressively more is required to enter into and to continue in negotiation. Early on, optimism often derives from what Kelman (1997) calls "working trust," a belief that the other side is also motivated to settle and hence will work hard and make concessions. However, for optimism to be sustained, one must eventually see the outlines of a possible agreement, a formula that bridges the two parties' opposing positions. There will be less of the latter kind of optimism the greater the apparent distance between the parties' positions.

Optimism also depends on a perception that the negotiator on the other side is a valid spokesperson, an individual who can actually commit the other side. Early in the Oslo talks, Israel tested the chief PLO negotiator, Ahmed Qurei, to find out how much influence he had in his organization. He was asked to arrange for a return of the Palestinian delegation to some Washington talks they were boycotting and for removal of one member of that delegation. He passed that test, making Israel optimistic enough to continue the talks with more senior representation (Peres 1995).

The Relationship Between Motivation and Optimism

Motivation to end a conflict and optimism about finding a mutually acceptable agreement are separate entities that have a joint (probably a multiplicative) effect on the likelihood and extent of communication and negotiation. In addition, these entities appear to be closely related, with each encouraging development of the other.

Reasons for optimism can help crystallize motivation to end the conflict by providing ammunition for doves, who want to settle the conflict peacefully and are trying to discredit the arguments of hawks, who want to continue fighting.

Conversely, motivation to end a conflict can encourage the development of some optimism, especially if the other side is also so motivated (Pruitt 2005). At least five mechanisms produce this effect, which can be seen in a number of historical peace processes.

One mechanism is that this motivation implies *scaling down one's aspirations*. The conflict cannot be escaped unless one gives ground on issues that are important to the other party. Doing so should encourage both parties to become more optimistic about the success of negotiation, since lower ambition means less divergence of interest.

A second mechanism is that strong new motives often encourage *information gathering* with results that challenge old views and stereotyped perceptions. Intractable conflicts usually produce well entrenched, heavily distorted "enemy" images of the adversary, which keep the conflict going (Pruitt and Kim 2004; White 1984). "They are the aggressors and all they understand is force. Hence, we must fight them wherever we can, and make no concessions for fear of being seen as weak." Such perceptions help to justify our aggressive role in a conflict. But when motivation to end a conflict develops, they are likely to come under scrutiny because they offer no way out. New information is gathered; and if these perceptions are wrong, as is often the case, they are likely to be challenged and changed (Pruitt and Olczak 1995).

Stein (1996) reports that Gorbachev and Sadat gathered information of this kind at a time of crisis in their conflicts with the West and with Israel. In Stein's words (p. 102):

> The evidence suggests that both leaders were motivated to learn and to change their images of their adversary. Both searched for new information: Gorbachev from experts in academic institutes and government and from American interlocutors, and Sadat through intermediaries and then through secret meetings between high-level Egyptian and Israeli leaders.

Both leaders sought and were receptive to new information because they had become pessimistic about the strategy they were pursuing.

A third mechanism is that a certain amount of *wishful thinking* or grasping at straws often develops in such a search – selective attention to evidence that the other party is reasonable or is also motivated to end the conflict. An example of grasping at straws is described in a book about the beginnings of the 1993 Oslo negotiations by Mahmoud Abbas (1995), foreign minister of the PLO who later became president of the Palestinian Authority. The PLO leaders were desperate for some sort of solution, as a result of losing much of their financial support and the rise of Hamas. Abbas reports the reactions of those leaders when they learned that a well connected Israeli professor (Yair Hirschfeld) was interested in talking with them. Optimism rose abruptly, and PLO Chairman Yasser Arafat sent one of his closest lieutenants, Ahmed Qurei, to the talks. Similarly, during the Cuban Missile Crisis, US President John Kennedy fixed attention on the only conciliatory message received from Soviet Premier Nikita Khrushchev and replied to it in a conciliatory fashion (Allison 1971).

A fourth mechanism is that when a party becomes interested in ending a conflict, it will often "test the waters" by sending *conciliatory signals* or making *secret back-channel contact* with the other side – both forms of communication. In intractable conflicts, such initiatives are usually small and ambiguous at first – a spoken hint or roundabout contact – so that their conciliatory intent can be denied if the other side does not reciprocate (Mitchell 2000). But if people on the other side are similarly motivated and seeking new information, they are likely to notice the initiative, take it seriously, and respond in a conciliatory fashion, enhancing the first party's optimism enough to launch a stronger conciliatory initiative.

Examples of this process abound. Toward the end of the Berlin Airlift, Kremlin watchers in the USA noticed that a Soviet statement had omitted some of the usual invectives against the West. The US government, which was highly motivated to end the conflict, sent a message through diplomatic channels asking whether this omission had been intentional. The answer was "yes," producing enough optimism on the US side to propose negotiations (Jervis 1970). Gorbachev and Sadat exhibited the same kind behavior when they became motivated to end the conflict and began seeking a way to do so. Continuing the quote from Stein (1996, pp. 102–3).

> Both began with a small change in image, moved tentatively to small actions, accepted feedback, learned, and initiated a new series of actions that generated further feedback and change. Gorbachev and Sadat ultimately became confident that their adversaries would reciprocate their acts of reassurance....In both cases, enemy images changed.

The fifth mechanism is that a party's motivation to end a conflict may be noted by *third parties*, who then try to bring the parties together. Such efforts are likely to enhance optimism on both sides. This is what happened during the late 1980s and early 1990s in the Northern Ireland peace process. Learning of some readiness to adopt a new strategy on the part of the IRA/Sinn Fein leadership, John Hume of the SDLP, a moderate nationalist political party, informed the British government which sent back conciliatory messages (Moloney 2002). More about this later.

Back-Channel Communication

Intractable conflict often ends with front-channel negotiation – publicly known meetings between legitimate representatives of the parties who seek to develop a mutually acceptable formula. However, front-channel negotiation is frequently preceded by secret back-channel communication involving officials or their designees (Pruitt 2008).[6]

Back-channel communication takes two forms: direct and indirect. Direct communication involves officials from both sides conversing informally in out-of-the-way places. Third party facilitators are sometimes involved (Nan 2005), but that is not common. Indirect

---

[6]Back-channel communication can also be employed during formal negotiation as an aid to problem solving about the issues under discussion. However, the present chapter will only consider its prenegotiation role.

back-channel communication involves designated intermediaries who shuttle back and forth between officials on both sides. An example of the latter is a communication chain that was developed in the prenegotiation period that led up to the negotiations that settled the Northern Ireland conflict. Gerry Adams, leader of Sinn Fein, talked with John Hume of the SDLP who talked with members of the government of the Irish Republic, who talked with members of the British government, who talked with leaders of the Ulster Unionist Party (UUP) which was the main unionist party (Pruitt 2007). In such a chain, the public may be aware of meetings that are taking place at points in the chain but be unaware that messages and proposals are being passed from one end of the chain to the other.

Communication chains need not be as long as the one just described. Indeed they often involve only a single intermediary, who is either a designated representative of one side talking to leaders on the other side or a neutral party shuttling between two sets of leaders.

Back-channel communication has a number of advantages over front-channel communication, including the following:

Flexibility and future orientation. One of the big problems with front-channel communication during conflict is its lack of flexibility. Participants have a tendency to make prepared statements and to reiterate demands and arguments, which often leads to deadlock. By contrast, back-channel communication encourages informality and frank discussion of motives and concerns. Needs, goals, values and fears about the other's proposals can be revealed more readily, along with information about priorities. Hence, the parties are more likely to discover common ground, identify basic goals that must be met in any solution, and develop win-win solutions.

A related problem with front-channel communication is that participants often spend much time rehashing the past and accusing each other of misconduct. That is much less common in back-channels, where participants are more likely to face the future and discuss ways to resolve the conflict (Egeland 1999). There are four explanations for the improved flexibility and future orientation: reduced audience effects, reduced numbers of people interacting, emotional bonding between the participants, and the non-binding nature of what is said.

The benefits of flexibility and future orientation can sometimes be achieved without full secrecy; for example, by locating publicly known talks at a distance from inquiring constituents or concealing their time and place so that reporters cannot immediately debrief the participants. That is what happened in the 1990 Rome talks that ended the Mozambique civil war (Bartoli 1999).

Political cover. In intractable conflicts, when the parties are fighting each other militarily or otherwise, leaders may get into trouble with their constituents or allies if they openly contact the other side and engage in front-channel talks. Political pressure may force cancelation of the talks (Lieberfeld 2008), and the leaders may risk their reputations, positions, or lives. Even if talks with the adversary are politically acceptable, a leader may get into trouble if these talks are unsuccessful (Lieberfeld 2008). By contrast, back-channel communication provides political cover to leaders who wish to explore the possibility of a negotiated settlement without political jeopardy. Historical leaders who have moved well ahead of their constituents through back-channels include Nelson Mandela of the ANC (Mandela 1994), Gerry Adams of the IRA (Moloney 2002), Anwar Sadat of Egypt (Stein 1989), and Yitzhak Rabin of Israel (Lieberfeld 1999).

Because they are secret, back-channel talks are usually *disavowable* if an outsider finds out about them. The leader may argue that reports about these talks are faulty or a misinterpretation of innocent events, or that the participants in these talks were not authorized to do so. Indirect contacts are easier to keep secret and to disavow than are direct contacts, especially when there are several intermediaries.

Cover is also provided when back-channel communication is accompanied by angry public statements and actions against the adversary. Thus during the time that Gerry Adams was secretly communicating with Britain, his public statements and those of his colleagues continued to be full of fire, and the IRA (on whose Army Council he probably sat) continued its violent campaign (Moloney 2002). Such a tactic may backfire if it hardens the views of constituents who then block later front-channel negotiation. Fortunately this did not happen in Northern Ireland.

Lack of preconditions. Parties in conflict often set preconditions that must be satisfied by the other side before front-channel negotiation can begin, the most common being a cease-fire. However, back-channel communication can occur without satisfying such preconditions. Thus Mandela (1994) reports that front-channel talks between the ANC and the government were scheduled for April 1990, shortly after his release from prison and the legalization of the ANC. But in March, police opened fire on some ANC demonstrators, causing the ANC to cancel these talks. Mandela told President F. W. de Klerk that "he [de Klerk] could not 'talk about negotiations on the one hand and murder our people on the other.'" Nevertheless, he "met privately with Mr. de Klerk in Cape Town in order to keep up the momentum for negotiations" (p. 557).

No acknowledgment of the other side's legitimacy. As mentioned earlier, front-channel negotiation is sometimes avoided because of fear that it will send the wrong signal, according legitimacy to the adversary or seeming to endorse the adversary's complaints and demands (Spector 2003). This is especially a problem in internal war, when insurgents and the government often compete for legitimacy in the eyes of the public and the world. Back-channel talks do not pose this problem, because they are unpublicized.

Unofficial Communication: Track 2 and Track 1 ½ Diplomacy

Another common preliminary to formal negotiation is unofficial communication by undesignated elites (private citizens or government officials acting on their own), who pass on their conclusions either to the public or to policy makers. Two varieties are reviewed here: Track 2 and Track 1 ½ diplomacy.

In Track 2 diplomacy, undesignated elites from each side meet informally as unofficial intermediaries. In Track 1 ½, undesignated elites from one side meet informally with officials from the other side.[7] The meetings in both tracks are seldom secret but always private. Like back-channel communication, they allow flexibility and future orientation, avoid preconditions, and imply no official recognition of the other party. They also permit people on both sides to discover that there are normal human beings on the other side who are interested in resolving the conflict, and they promote an understanding of the other side's "central concerns…(their) basic needs and fundamental fears that any agreement would have to address" (Fisher 1997, p. 60). Joint projects and possible solutions to the conflict may also be developed.

An example of Track 2 diplomacy is the problem solving workshops pioneered by Burton (1969) and Kelman (2002). In these workshops, influential or potentially influential people from both sides meet for several days under the leadership of trained academics to discuss their conflict. Sometimes the meetings are repeated several times with the same participants (Rouhana and Kelman 1994). Problem solving workshops are especially useful in the prenegotiation period, when they can (a) help structure a climate of optimism on both sides about the other party's readiness for meaningful negotiation; (b) provide substantive knowledge about the other party's motives, priorities, and assumptions; and (c) produce knowledgeable personnel who can swing into action once higher officials become motivated to escape the conflict.

Another example of Track 2 diplomacy is the Dartmouth Conferences, in which prominent Soviet and American citizens met periodically over a 30-year period to analyze the Cold War and attempt to narrow the divide between these nations (Voorhees 2002). The governments on both sides encouraged these meetings and used them as a way to gain information about the true nature of the other side. The ideas discussed at these meetings "were shared broadly beyond (them)" (Voorhees 2002, p. 348), contributing to an elite climate of opinion on both sides that was more optimistic about the possibility of peace than it had been.

Examples of Track 1 ½ diplomacy are two unofficial meetings that took place between white South Africans and exiled leaders of the ANC. The first, a 6-h meeting that was held in Zambia in 1985, involved four English-speaking businessmen and three reporters, who came away with very positive impressions of the ANC leaders, "that they were patriots, as deeply and passionately committed to South Africa as any of their white visitors (and) that they were human beings – and moderate ones at that" (Waldmeir 1998, p. 74). This meeting set the stage for a 3-day 1987 meeting in Senegal involving a much larger group of Afrikaaners, who reached similar conclusions. These conclusions were widely publicized by the latter group and appear to have "built [among whites] a reservoir of latent readiness to accept the ANC as a legitimate participant in a negotiated settlement" (Lieberfeld 2002, p. 368).

[7]The term "Track 1 ½" is employed in a somewhat different way by two other authors. Lieberfeld (2005) adds the stipulation that the elite private citizens are authorized by and report back to high political officials (2005). Hence his concept is similar to what was described earlier as back-channel communication by a single intermediary who is authorized by one side to meet leaders of the other side. Nan (2005) uses the same term to refer to facilitated "informal off-the-record workshops on conflict resolution" involving "senior official representatives of the conflict parties" (p. 161).

Conclusions: Growing Optimism and Stages on the Way to Negotiation

Even intractable conflicts must eventually end. One side may defeat the other or the issues may disappear. But these conflicts often end with negotiation and settlement.

There are several way stations on the path to negotiation and settlement. Both sides must become motivated to escape the conflict – to move beyond their current unpopular or counterproductive efforts to defeat the other. They also must become optimistic about the likelihood of finding an acceptable agreement. Fortunately, motivation to escape the conflict tends to encourage optimism, but usually not in sufficient magnitude for the parties to jump directly into negotiation. They must first part with enemy images, extreme hostility, profound distrust, and strong opposition to contact, all of which are generated by intractable conflict. Hence, the parties usually approach negotiation gradually.

Initial contacts between adversaries, if and when they occur, are likely to be hesitant and exploratory – an ambiguous signal from a government official, a mildly conciliatory message sent through an obscure channel, or meetings between undesignated civilians and insurgent leaders. If such initial explorations show promise, the contacts may become less hesitant, and a benevolent circle of increasing optimism may ensue, bringing the parties ever closer to overt negotiation. But that process is likely to move slowly through several stages, with both parties feeling their way, checking and rechecking whether they have a basis for optimism – whether the adversary has changed and there are genuine prospects for an acceptable agreement.

The following is a rough list of seven types of contact ranging from the most informal and indirect to the most formal and direct. The first six can be thought of as stages on the way to the seventh.

- Track 2 diplomacy
- Track 1 ½ diplomacy
- Conciliatory signals from officials
- Indirect back-channel contacts with longer chains
- Indirect back-channel contacts with shorter chains
- Direct back-channel contacts
- Overt (publicized) negotiation

No peace process examined by the author went through all of these stages. But many of them went through some of these stages in the order shown in the list. Three examples are given here, all involving internal war.

The *South African peace process* began[8] with the Track 1 ½ diplomacy described earlier – two unofficial meetings between white South African community leaders and exiled leaders of the ANC, which contributed to broader white optimism about dealing with the ANC. These meetings were followed by indirect back-channel

[8]The point at which these cases are said to "begin" is the first communication between the adversaries that was plausibly antecedent to the final negotiation.

meetings between intermediaries from the South African government and the ANC leadership (the Mells Park House talks) and then by direct back-channel negotiations. The final result was publicized negotiations that produced a representative government (Lieberfeld 2002). Thus Track 1 ½ contacts began a sequence that traversed short-chain indirect and then direct back-channel talks and culminated in overt negotiation.

The *Middle East (Oslo) peace process* (Pruitt et al. 1997) began with Track 2 meetings between Israeli and Palestinian community leaders. This was followed by a Track 1 ½ meeting between an Israeli Cabinet member, acting on his own, Ezer Weizman, and a PLO official (Shamir dismisses Weizman from Israel's government 1990). These informal meetings bore fruit in 1993, when top leaders on both sides became interested in escaping the conflict. A series of highly secret indirect back-channel meetings began in and round Oslo, with the PLO represented by a top official, Mahmud Querei, and the Israeli foreign ministry by two professors, Yair Hirschfeld and Ron Pundak, who were veterans of the earlier Track 2 meetings. These meetings became direct back-channel communication with the arrival of Israeli government officials, and a framework agreement was reached, which was announced by top leaders of the PLO and Israel on the White House lawn. After that, there were several overt negotiations to work out the details. Thus Track 2 meetings were antecedent to a Track 1 ½ meeting, which led to short-chain indirect and then direct back-channel talks which culminated in overt negotiation.

The first step in the *Northern Ireland peace process* (Pruitt 2007) was a conciliatory signal from Gerry Adams, the leader of Sinn Fein, who said publicly in 1988 that "there is no military solution" and that he would be willing "to consider an alternative unarmed form of struggle to achieve Irish independence, if someone would outline such a course" (Taylor 1997, p. 353). A little while later, John Hume, leader of the moderate Social Democratic and Labor Party (SDLP) had a publicized meeting with Adams and then met with him secretly for another 5 years. Hume also met with officials of the Irish Republic, who met with officials of the British government, who communicated with UUP leaders, creating the communication chain that was described earlier. Thus the second step was long-chain indirect back-channel communication. When overt negotiations began, contact between Sinn Fein and the UUP was still indirect, though the communication chain was much shorter than it had been earlier. Once the Good Friday Agreement was reached, the two sides negotiated openly and directly. In brief, a conciliatory signal was followed by long- and then short-chain indirect communication, which culminated in overt negotiation.

There is an interesting three-phase trend in these and other accounts of peace processes: the initial phase involved overt communication, then the parties moved to secret (back-channel) communication, and finally back to overt communication. The move to secret communication can be understood as occurring at the point where leaders start substantive communication with each other across the enmity divide. Back-channel talks allow for political cover, lack of preconditions, and no acknowledgement of the other side's legitimacy. Without these safeguards, most leaders would be unwilling to communicate with the adversary and many intractable conflicts would not be solved. The move back to overt communication may be partially due to the need for broad public support to sustain and implement an agreement.

The stage and phase theory just described is admittedly preliminary and applicable to only certain kinds of cases.[9] The author operates on the premise that a preliminary, non-comprehensive theory is better than none in this early state of knowledge about conflict resolution (Pruitt 2009). The theory needs elaboration and should eventually be tested in a large-sample study.

References

Abbas, M. (1995). *Through secret channels*. Reading: Garnet.

Allison, G. (1971). *Essence of decision: Explaining the Cuban Missile Crisis*. Boston: Little Brown.

Aquilar, F., & Galluccio, M. (2008). *Psychological processes in international negotiations: Theoretical and practical perspectives*. New York: Springer.

Bartoli, A. (1999). Mediating peace in Mozambique: The role of the community of Sant'Egidio. In C. A. Crocker, F. O. Hampson, & P. Aall (Eds.), *Herding cats: Multiparty mediation in a complex world* (pp. 247–273). Washington: United States Institute of Peace.

Burton, J. (1969). *Conflict and communication*. London: Macmillan.

Coleman, J. S. (1957). *Community conflict*. New York: Free Press.

Egeland, J. (1999). The Oslo Accord: Multiparty facilitation through the Norwegian channel. In C. A. Crocker, F. O. Hampson, & P. Aall (Eds.), *Herding cats: Multiparty mediation in a complex world* (pp. 527–546). Washington: United States Institute of Peace.

Fisher, R. J. (1997). *Interactive conflict resolution*. Syracuse: Syracuse University Press.

Goertz, G., & Diehl, P. F. (1997). The initiation and termination of enduring rivalries: The impact of political shocks. *American Journal of Political Science, 39*, 30–52.

Holbrooke, R. (1998). *To end a war*. New York: Random House.

Jervis, R. (1970). The logic of images in international relations. Princeton, NJ: Princeton University Press..

Kelman, H. C. (1997). Some determinants of the Oslo breakthrough. *International Negotiation, 2*, 183–194.

Kelman, H. C. (2002). Interactive problem-solving: Informal mediation by the scholar-practitioner. In J. Bercovitch (Ed.), *Studies in international mediation* (pp. 167–193). New York: Palgrave Macmillan.

Lieberfeld, D. (1999). *Talking with the enemy: Negotiation and threat perception in South Africa and Israel/Palestine*. Westport: Praeger.

Lieberfeld, D. (2002). Evaluating the contributions of track-two diplomacy to conflict termination in South Africa, 1984-90. *Journal of Peace Research, 39*, 355–372.

Lieberfeld, D. (2005). Contributions of a semi-official prenegotiation initiative in South Africa: Afrikaner-ANC meetings in England, 1987-1990. In R. J. Fisher (Ed.), *Paving the way* (pp. 103–125). Lanham: Lexington.

Lieberfeld, D. (2008). Secrecy and "two-level games" in the Oslo accord: What the primary sources tell us. *International Negotiation, 13*, 133–146.

[9]Peace processes led by powerful third parties appear to follow a rather different story line. Examples are the events leading up to the British-dominated Lancaster House agreement that established the country of Zimbabwe (see Stedman 1991) and the events (including NATO air attacks) leading up the Dayton Accord that settled the Bosnian War (see Holbrooke 1998).

Mandela, N. (1994). *Long walk to freedom*. New York: Little Brown.
Mitchell, C. (2000). *Gestures of conciliation: Factors contributing to successful olive branches*. London: Macmillan.
Moloney, E. (2002). *A secret history of the IRA*. New York: Norton.
Mooradian, M., & Druckman, D. (1999). Hurting stalemate or mediation? The conflict over Nagorno-Karabakh, 1990-95. *Journal of Peace Research, 36*, 709–727.
Nan, S. A. (2005). Track one-and-a-half diplomacy: Contributions to Georgian-South Ossetian peacemaking. In R. J. Fisher (Ed.), *Paving the way* (pp. 161–173). Lanham: Lexington.
Newcomb, T. M. (1947). Autistic hostility and social reality. *Human Relations, 1*, 69–86.
Oren, N. (2010). Israeli identity formation and the Arab-Israeli conflict in election platforms 1969–2006. *Journal of Peace Research*, 47, 193–204.
Peres, S. (1995). *Battling for peace*. New York: Random House.
Pruitt, D. G. (2005). Whither ripeness theory? Working Paper #25, Institute for Conflict Analysis and Resolution, George Mason University, Fairfax. http://www.gmu.edu/departments/ICAR/wp_25_pruitt.pdf.
Pruitt, D. G. (2006). Negotiation with terrorists. *International Negotiation, 11*, 371–394.
Pruitt, D. G. (2007). Readiness theory and the Northern Ireland conflict. *American Behavioral Scientist, 50*, 1520–1541.
Pruitt, D. G. (2008). Back-channel communication in the settlement of conflict. *International Negotiation, 13*, 37–54.
Pruitt, D. G. (2009). Foreword. In D. J. D. Sandole, S. Byrne, I. Sandole-Staroste, & J. Senehi (Eds.), *Handbook of conflict analysis and resolution (pp. xix to xx)*. London: Routledge.
Pruitt, D. G., & Kim, S. H. (2004). *Social conflict: Escalation, stalemate and settlement* (3rd ed.). New York: McGraw-Hill.
Pruitt, D. G., & Olczak, P. V. (1995). Beyond hope: Approaches to resolving seemingly intractable conflict. In B. B. Bunker & J. Z. Rubin (Eds.), *& Associates, Conflict, cooperation and justice: Essays provoked by the work of Morton Deutsch* (pp. 59–92). San Francisco: Jossey-Bass.
Pruitt, D. G., Bercovitch, J., & Zartman, I. W. (1997). A brief history of the Oslo talks. *International Negotiation, 2*, 177–182.
Rouhana, N. N., & Kelman, H. C. (1994). Promoting joint thinking in international conflicts: An Israeli-Palestinian continuing workshop. *Journal of Social Issues, 50*, 157–178.
Shamir dismisses Weizman from Israel's government. (1990, January 1). *The New York Times*.
Sherif, M., & Sherif, C. W. (1969). *Social psychology*. New York: Harper & Row.
Spector, B. I. (2003). Negotiating with villains revisited: Research note. *International Negotiation, 8*, 613–621.
Stedman, S. J. (1991). *Peacemaking in civil war: International mediation in Zimbabwe, 1974-1980*. Boulder: Lynne Rienner.
Stein, J. G. (1989). *Getting to the table: The processes of international prenegotiation*. Baltimore: Johns Hopkins University Press.
Stein, J. G. (1996). Image, identity, and conflict resolution. In C. A. Crocker, F. O. Hampson, & P. Aall (Eds.), Sources of and responses to international conflict (pp. 93–111). Washington: United States Institute of Peace Press.
Taylor, P. (1997). *Behind the mask: The IRA and Sinn Fein*. New York: TV Books.
Voorhees, J. (2002). *Dialogue sustained: The multilevel peace process and the Dartmouth Conference*. Washington: United States Institute of Peace Press.
Waldmeir, P. (1998). *Anatomy of a miracle: the end of Arpartheid and the birth of the new South Africa*. New Brunswick: Rutgers University Press.
White, R. K. (1984). *Fearful warriors: A psychological profile of US-Soviet relations*. New York: Free Press.
Zahar, Mr. and Carter. Mr. (2008, April 17). *The Washington Post*, p. A22.
Zartman, I. W. (1989). *Ripe for resolution: Conflict resolution in Africa* (2nd ed.). New York: Oxford.
Zartman, I. W. (2000). Ripeness: The hurting stalemate and beyond. In P. C. Stern & D. Druckman (Eds.), *Conflict resolution after the Cold War* (pp. 225–250). Washington: National Academy Press.

Chapter 9
Negotiating a New Deal Between Science and Society: Reflections on the Importance of Cognition and Emotions in International Scientific Cooperation and Possible Implications for Enabling Sustainable Societies

Cornelia E. Nauen*

Introduction

As someone with an ecological background, it is perhaps not common to venture into the realm of cognition and emotions and even less so to write a chapter in a book that counts leading scientists and practitioners of this field of study among its contributors. The justification, if any, is to approach the argument from the perspective of someone who has been empirically confronted with some of the issues in more than 25 years of professional work in international cooperation and sees the necessity – and possibility – to build greater awareness of emotions into international relations in general and more particularly into the way scientists interact with non-scientists and relate to the human relations and political processes underpinning international cooperation in order to increase the positive impact of science on society. In today's context, this is intimately linked to the imperative to support transitions towards greater sustainability of human societies on our planet.

Because these issues touch on a very wide range of studies, any individual one will be touched upon only in the briefest and most condensed ways. Inevitably, this will leave the specialists unsatisfied, as justice cannot be done to the intricacies of debates in their field, and major parts of the literature will be left out. In other words, in this particular context, no attempt is being made to get to the depth

*The views expressed herein are the personal views of the author and do not necessarily the official views of the European Commission.

C.E. Nauen (✉)
Principal Policy Officer, International Cooperation (INCO),
Research Directorate General (DG RTD), European Commission, 8,
Square de Meeûs – SDME 5/83, B-1049, Brussels, Belgium

F. Aquilar and M. Galluccio (eds.), *Psychological and Political Strategies for Peace Negotiation*, DOI 10.1007/978-1-4419-7430-3_9,

of any individual area of investigation. That would be the purpose of a monograph or disciplinary publication. Conversely, what is being attempted here is to piece together elements from different fields of study to see whether they can hang sufficiently together to be consilient in the sense of Wilson (1999). From there, it is a logical next step to explore whether this can help us build new levels of awareness and understanding in international relations and cooperation, particularly in knowledge-intensive forms such as science, research, technology, education, and social and technological innovation.

Emotions play a fundamental role in all learning processes and the formation of memory. They also precede action. The need for increasing our ability to act together is overriding as we search for more viable forms of organising our relations with each other and with nature. Aquilar and Galluccio (2008) elaborated on theoretical and practical perspectives of cognitive and emotional processes with particular focus on international negotiation situations.

If one looks at a graph that plots the ecological footprint[1] of a country against the human development indicator[2] and further looks at which countries have a reasonably high human development indicator within an ecological footprint that distributes the land space available on earth equally among 6.6 billion humans, one finds that hardly any nation is currently able to meet this fundamental sustainability criterion. Each human being – us all taken together – has about 1.8 ha of all types of land lumped together from the Himalayas to the Gobi desert, with a shrinking trend given continued demographic growth expected to level off only by about 2050. The ecological footprint calculates a country's combined consumption of resources to sustain the economic activities underpinning living conditions and compares this with what is available and renewable. Lifestyles in the United Arab Emirates beat anybody else by requiring almost 12 ha per capita to sustain. Close on their heels, USA lifestyles consume the renewable resources of about 9.5 ha per capita, Finland about 7.5 ha per capita (2003 assessment). The current world average resource consumption is already more than the earth can renew in the cycle of a year. While one may argue about this or that detail in the calculation, the aggregate illustrates that taking no action is not an option. While one can negotiate with other human beings, the parameters of nature are not up to such approaches, even considering significant scientific advances in biotechnology and other fields.

As far as the human development indicator (HDI) is concerned, it shows more than the usual macroeconomic take on life as an estimate of gross domestic product (GDP), which usually includes all economic activity on the asset side of the balance sheet. Measuring also war expenses and reparation after natural or other disasters as positive economic activity ensures that the curve goes up almost uninterrupted over a century, with neither WWI nor the Great Depressing

[1]www.footprintnetwork.org

[2]www.undp.org/hd

making a dent, while WWII is just perceptible (Jaeger C. 2009, personal communication based on Maddison 2001 and others). Some reflections on how to go beyond this influential index supported by global machinery have been voiced, among others, at a Conference in the European Parliament in 2007 with the telling title "Beyond GDP."[3] The human development indicator approach developed and implemented under the auspices of the UN Development Programme (UNDP) is an attempt to capture a broader range of dimensions by including in addition life expectancy, access to education by males, females and different age groups, CO_2 emission and others. African countries with very low ecological footprints also have excessively low human development indicators; the European Union and North America have high human development indicators but excessive footprints. A good number of Asian, Middle Eastern, and Latin American countries are hovering between human development indexes close to or in the high bracket and footprints requiring between 0.5 and 4 earths. Unsurprisingly, the perceptions, cognition, and emotions surrounding these questions vary widely.

The recognition of the strength of emotions – and might we say basic biological traits of humans – even in the context of institutions honed on models of sophisticated industrial technologies and their disciplining and homogenising influence – does not come easily. The training in the natural sciences is quite naturally focused on seeking the most parsimonious rational explanation to any observed phenomenon or mechanism in nature. The ambition is directed at not giving undue room to feelings and social preferences, but rather observe and interpret the facts with a view to validate or reject a hypothesis on the underlying rules. This neither excludes social responsibility nor empathy, but encourages not taking explanations for granted and asking probing questions in one's field of enquiry. However, it is certainly a fiction that scientists are neutral, disconnected, and disinterested persons who go about the pursuit of knowledge entirely objectively.

Such a caricature of scientists opens the way to several types of possible fallacies: A first trap pertains to overextending the explanatory and/or problem-solving power of a narrow disciplinary field in relation to the increasingly complex problems societies face today. A second problem lies in the assumption that scientific results are so self-evident that they will be taken up quickly by others to drive problem-solving and innovations in social and technological fields. A third, somewhat related, challenge pertains to the scale difference between the pursuit of science at individual or group levels, while (public) policies and institutions operate at a different level. The intermediary steps required to reach some higher-level decision in society, and even more so in an international context – and afterwards ensure its implementation – are considerable and involve many forms of negotiations.

---

[3]http://www.beyond-gdp.eu

This chapter examines briefly some of these challenges in the light of several decades of international scientific cooperation, mostly from a European perspective, and reflects on (a) what type of science and scientific cooperation is needed for the transitions towards more sustainable societies in decades to come; (b) the implication of some recent research results from other fields of science for a more effective engagement of science with societal negotiation and mediation processes; and (c) under what conditions such cooperation can increase its contribution to sustainable societies.

Back to Basics: What Type of Science and Scientific Cooperation is Needed for the Transitions Towards More Sustainable Societies?

There is no shortage of international research cooperation, which typically addresses knowledge gaps in relation to agri-food systems, such as the exploration of under-utilised plants and animals with potential for diversifying the food basket or fine-tuning understanding at the molecular level of pathways to speed up and otherwise improve the selection of more desirable traits in crops we already use but need, e.g., to adapt to climate change and associated abiotic stress (e.g., drought, heat). Other common areas of cooperation are infectious and poverty-related diseases, but also diabetes and vasco-circular diseases increasingly common not only in industrial societies. At first glance, such investigations may come across as pretty "disciplinary," though the moment one looks at possible use of such knowledge, any number of additional questions arises.[4]

Other types of international collaborative research projects convey more evidently, from the start, the need to look at multiple dimensions at the same time: Examples may be researching the mechanisms and dynamics of climate change together with mitigation and adaptation strategies as well as strategies for more sustainable use of river basins and coastal zones for reconciling multiple, and often conflicting, demands as well as documenting and conserving biological diversity, tropical rainforests, and much more. What practitioners of international cooperation note is that even in the interaction with their disciplinary peers, there is something more than "just" the discussion of a specific scientific challenge. While laws of nature are universal, and the mathematics of expressing much of it can be understood even when people do not share a vernacular language, the different cultural, institutional, economic and ecological contexts – to mention but a few – add

[4]Overview information about funded international research collaborations supported under successive European Research Framework Programmes can be gleaned from the project database on cordis (http://cordis.europa.eu/search/index.cfm?fuseaction=proj.advSearch) and catalogues of synopses by period, region, or theme (e.g., European Commission 2005, 2007, 1982a; Estrella Santos and Nauen 2008).

dimensions to the way science is done, the type of questions raised, and the way one looks for answers. The greater richness and diversity in perspectives arising from international cooperation is evident at all levels.

In a review of more than 10 years of international water research supported by successive European Research Framework Programmes, Gyawali et al. (2006) estimate that international cooperation is ahead of most national and/or thematic research agendas in framing the issues, encouraging more integrated approaches and enabling pathways to impact on society. It is also obvious from work as a scientific officer in accompanying dozens of international collaborations in water and aquatic systems research that even at similarly high levels of scientific competence, the different cultural, institutional, and ecological perspectives enrich the overall approach. Moreover, everybody acquires greater sensitivities towards the other and a richer repertoire of own behaviour in the daily negotiation of how to frame research questions, how to carry through the research and how to encourage its further use. Much of this positive human development is connected to the emotional and non-conscious level and experiencing in practice that humans have more in common than what divides them (Galluccio 2007).

Numerous European coordinators of international collaborative projects have expressed this additional dimension in one way or the other when they acknowledge, e.g., that in their youth as ambitious scientists they would pay little heed to anything but the next thrilling idea in science, but that with time and practice they have become acutely aware how important it is to learn about the history, culture, and wider context of other societies to be able not only to engage in productive scientific cooperation, but gain greater mutual understanding and through that also open new avenues for the use of its results in society. Such awareness and understanding also enhance the ability to draw in a wider range of actors outside science and its codifications and have been experienced as feeding back positively on what science questions are put forward next and how they are approached. An example of this process can be seen in aquaculture. The ramifications of many years of empirical learning – and building trust and mutual understanding – started out with a small international aquaculture research cooperation involving, among others, Belgian and Vietnamese teams back in the 1980s. It was followed up by criss-crossing networks of collaborations involving ever more partners, which led to a multi-stakeholder platform in the ASEM context (Asia-Europe Meetings). In turn, this has created an enabling environment for a widening spectrum of collaborative activities from higher education and research to industrial and commercial cooperation (European Commission 2008b).

Conversely, working in a narrower mental framework, the temptation is great to get absorbed in one's field of specialisation (not only in research, but in "ordinary" exercise of other professions) and take it as a proxy for a bigger whole as well as making implicit assumptions about the rationality and superiority of some technical solution (Aquilar and Galluccio 2008). The inherent risk of overestimating the possible contribution of a limited field to managing complex systems, particularly in the interface between eco- and social systems has, among others, been empirically investigated by Dörner (2003). He shows the predominance of failure in such narrow approaches to address complex situations. He also elaborates how a seemingly small difference in approach by choosing iterative and reflexive methods, including such basics as systematic checking of results of the sequence of prior decisions, makes all the difference towards successful outcomes. Bazerman and Hofman (1999) lay down much of the environmentally destructive behaviour to a human tendency to attribute problems to a single cause, even when there are many (a typical failure to cope with complexity). Among the other mechanisms of shaping behaviour, they also observe that making implicit assumptions about the interests and motivations of other parties in negotiation situations, particularly when they are being perceived as opponents/enemies, often leads to poor arrangements for failure to see the common ground because they are grounded in mistrust of others and belief in what the authors call "mythical fixed-pie."

Umberto Eco (2002) goes a step further in cautioning against overconfidence in technology, which may almost reach conditions comparable to medieval belief in magic. He invites a clear distinction between technology and science to contrast the blurring perpetuated by most media accounts favouring magical expectations from "science" (read "technology") and obscuring the fact that science is rather the painstaking cumulative process of teething out the rules of processes in nature and society, including the falsification of wrong hypotheses. This daily reality is far removed from the high pitch press releases on the "success story," which appeals so much more to the hope for the miracle solution. One is tempted to assume there is widespread willingness to believe in silver bullets rather than the down-to-earth reality of continuous work in the accumulation and systematisation of knowledge on the one hand and a willingness to pass on responsibility to someone else on the other. Indeed, there may be good evolutionary reasons for believing in stories, as we shall see later.

Jasanoff (2007), synthesising the gist of several of her books, also addressing this widespread phenomenon, invites researchers and politicians to remain conscious about the inherent uncertainty of research results. She underlines the need for keeping in mind "what people value and why they value it" and invites complementary analysis in areas not easily accessible to scientific pursuit. Hers is essentially an argument for remaining critical and questioning in relation to all-out technological "solutions." She indicates that many have already failed and, together with the basics of human demography and temporary disregard for the renewal capacity of natural systems, cannot, in principle, live up to implied substitution of natural systems at a larger scale.

An example may illustrate what such a shift in emphasis from a belief in total "doability" on risk taking and emphasis on market-solutions to greater emphasis on environmental and human safeguards might involve: An estimated 100,106 chemical substances were in the market in 1981 worldwide; they required no formal risk assessment. Since the cut-off year 1981, approximately 3,000 new substances have been introduced into the market. According to a recent report released by the European Commission, since 1993 only 141 high-volume chemicals have been identified for testing; due to capacity problems only 27 have completed the risk assessment (European Commission 2004).

In analysing more than 10 years of international water research cooperation supported under successive European Research Framework Programmes (Gyawali et al. 2006) find an encouraging trend towards integrating more dimensions into the research agenda rather than confining work to what amounts essentially to an engineering approach. These external reviewers from four continents and diverse professional backgrounds, though pointing out considerable room for improvement, show that these types of more integrated approaches increase the relevance of the research for transitions towards sustainability. They also argue that it is the political process of trying to reconcile often-contradictory demands that generates solutions. So, while injection of new knowledge can be extremely helpful and is even a necessity in most situations, the research cannot single-handedly bring about the solution. The implication in the context of our line of argument here is that the political process, akin to constant negotiation, is loaded with emotions, not only "cool analysis." In searching for common ground across a wider range of perspectives than can be provided by a research project, and by bringing in the perspectives (including the emotions) of social solidarities, science can play a very constructive role, but it is not a substitute for the political process. A preliminary analysis of some 10 years of international scientific cooperation in fisheries, aquaculture, and coastal zone issues finds similar trends. It concludes as well that "solutions" are usually only second best from a technical point of view, but are those that are socially and politically acceptable (Nauen 2008). In this societal negotiation process, many other factors beyond rational ponderation play a role. This can be subjected to analysis, but the process itself is not scientific, though it may benefit considerably from scientific inputs as well as from international cooperation.

Today's science is an increasingly international and collaborative endeavour, not so much the work of "loners." This is, among others, expressed in the growing percentage of multi-author publications, not just in international "big-science" projects (Regalado 1995). Publications authored by teams of scientists are 6.3 times more likely to be cited by at least 1,000 other publications compared to single-author papers (Wuchty et al. 2007) and thus are likely to have more impact on other academic research. This does not, however, automatically indicate impact in society, which will be touched upon below.

What types of research should receive more emphasis and resources and attract the best brains and collaborations? From the perspective of sustainability (Bogliotti and Spangenberg 2005) and helping increasingly interdependent societies cope with changing conditions, more integrated forms of study straddling conventional disciplinary boundaries are the most likely to make high-value contributions. This should not, in any way, diminish the rigour of disciplinary training. However, because of the nature of these challenges, the willingness and ability to converse with other fields of knowledge has become particularly important today. Even more than simple conversation, the basic compatibility between different fields of study is itself a measure for the degree to which specialisation can still contribute to understanding the bigger whole. In different measure and from different perspectives, this necessity is emphasised by such authors as Wilson (1999), Mittelstrass (2004), and Hollingsworth et al. (2008).

Gyawali et al. (2006) have developed a robust framework that allows to broadly appreciate whether a research collaboration is making a contribution to sustainability. The method incorporates elements of sustainability principles, political analysis conceptualised as the engagement of the four social solidarities and modernity theory. In a nutshell, the screening method consists of several steps: (a) a quick assessment of the extent of addressing social, environmental and economic dimensions of the problem under study as well as the relationship between them which can facilitate the political process of discursively established sustainability, including the question of whether the research addresses context-specific features and local knowledge; (b) an analysis of communication and critical engagement with non-academic social actors; and (c), associated to this, a search for indications of impact within the academic system and in wider society.

The notoriously difficult issue of impact was further addressed through a questionnaire survey involving the coordinators of international water research projects.[5] This brought to light the importance of time in generating impact. That should not be surprising given the documentation by the European Environment Agency of the long lapse times between scientific identification of a problem and societal action on the problem (European Environment Agency 2001). The analysis of the survey results also pointed to the challenge for creating truly engaging communication, which always involves a degree of emotional arousal and a feeling of being concerned. This is in opposition to simple "broadcasting of information." Such broadcasting of even very valuable and pertinent information fails to establish a sense of personal and/or group concerns and thus cannot trigger impact, at least not directly. Such engaged communication is a necessary intermediary step, but it will only occur if parties concerned are willing to listen to each other and engage. As the reviewers poignantly noted, "There is none so deaf as those who do not want to hear."

The fears that often slow down mutually beneficial relations and cooperation are intimately linked to the imbalance of the parties, e.g., in access and analytical capabilities of information and knowledge. That imbalance has grown as more and more areas of interaction, which used to draw on public resources, are being commodified and subjected to market mechanisms. This can be observed in relation to many public goods, from education, health, and security to water and even the air.

Public goods are characterised by the key feature that consumption by one person or group does not diminish the consumption of others, most strongly visible in the field of knowledge. Knowledge is not governed by the economy of scarcity, but increases the more it is shared. At the same time, public goods are difficult to appropriate privately. Conversely, the higher their availability, the greater is the welfare available to the many.

As Kaul (2008) argues, the predominant model of analysing public economies is based on assumptions of a domestic, closed economy, and thus does not capture the increasingly global nature of public goods. With this premise, in times of

[5]See also http://ec.europa.eu/research/water-initiative/iwrm_review_en.html

difficulties, the reflexes of protectionism and defensive attitudes and policy measures are strong, even irresistible. But the long list of challenges governments and the public face would best be tackled by cooperation and joint action, particularly as the transnational, even global nature makes typically domestic responses blunt and ineffectual. However, so long as international relations are largely based on an outmoded concept, the necessary investment into building trust and mutual understanding is not being made, and even existing positive objectives may be framed in ways that do not lead to positive and effective action.

The point could, therefore be made that international scientific cooperation should on the one hand explicitly address international policy objectives, such as sustainability and its derivatives in climate, biodiversity, freedom from hunger, health, universal access to education, peace, environmental integrity, cultural diversity, and human and dignified development, but also focus on disentangling the conceptual changes needed to cope with the increasingly global nature of public goods on the other. Such disentangling would need to explicitly address the unknowability of many aspects of complex systems that cannot be tamed by statistical and insurance approaches. Given the scale and irreversibility of human intervention and the potential risk of long-term – often unintended and unknowable – "side"-effects of technological manipulations, conventional responses in terms of "more of the same" are inherently ineffectual. Helping us to improve the diagnostic tools and harnessing such collaborations, including those reaching beyond the research community itself, for identifying the most critical areas for cooperation would likely represent the highest social added value to public investment and pave the way for iterative, risk-minimising, precautionary approaches.

The setting of broad goals without interfering unduly in the approach to the research problem has been tried successfully before, even before "big science," such as the Manhattan Project. Among the best-popularised examples is the need to improve navigation standards by developing the ability to identify longitude. The problem had vexed seafarers for centuries, but it was when the British Parliament set a prize in 1714 that it was finally solved in 1759 by John Harrison (Sobel 1996).

What is more, we need reference frameworks to determine where we stand right now and fix objectives. When looking "at the bigger picture," the problem of shifting baselines (Pauly 1995) is one of the most pervasive obstacles to determining positions properly. By taking one's own professional experience of only a few decades at best as the principal reference framework, the creeping erosion, e.g., of land and marine ecosystems goes largely unnoticed and objectives fixed in this respect unwittingly help to administer the degradation. This is why reconstructing past states, as well as documenting and making widely available validated information about historical developments, is so crucial. A key criterion for determining whether there is real advancement in understanding, even when paradigm changes are involved, is that a larger body of empirical evidence established by previous generations of researchers is integrated into a coherent whole (Pauly 2001). Studying the past is a key element in individual and group identity as well as the ability to imagine alternative futures that are more sustainable than the present.

When properly done, this has the ability to change the perceptions of what is the present and enables to establish more realistic objectives for the future. In other words, it changes the cognitive basis and the mental maps within which information about the past, present, and future is interpreted. Pulling together the evidence from diverse sources in a collaborative manner is a must today given the scale of the challenge. This type of voluntary cooperation is not only a need in terms of getting the "technical part" of the job done, but also has the added advantage of facilitating the process of recognising and legitimising the results, a key feature if they are to be used in societal or technological innovation or any form of negotiation. Indeed, in addition to the factual validation side of the content, the process is crucial to shorten waiting times until new knowledge and innovations are taken up (Moriarty et al. 2005; Nauen 2008). This is the result of building the trust necessary for uptake. The longer cooperation lasts, the more mature it becomes (Gyawali et al. 2006) and the higher the integration between the rational and emotional dimensions of knowledge and relations.

Back in 1982, the then European Development Commissioner, Edgard Pisani, underlined in a statement to the European Parliament that development was not merely a matter of building infrastructure, not even of transferring existing technologies to improve food security and meet basic health needs in developing countries, but that it was a matter of investing in people and local research capacity to develop the solutions suitable for the specific context in each country (European Commission 2008b). The group of African, Caribbean, and Pacific (ACP) countries, and even more specifically Africa, were a prime focus of these considerations (see also Galluccio 2007 and Aquilar and Galluccio 2008).

In other words, the analysis back in those days recognised that beyond the technicalities, there was a social, political and human factor that could not be reduced to technocratic action alone. This gave rise, in 1983, to the first European international scientific and technological (SandT) cooperation programme, called "Science and Technology for Development" (STD), the scope of which had been outlined in a modulated manner for different regions with which Europe intended to develop its SandT cooperation for mutual benefit (European Commission 1982a, 1983). Even though bi-regional dialogue and cooperation approaches are becoming more common since the 1990s, much of the reasoning even today reflects yesterday's world's perceptions of the importance of individual states. The scissions or outright break-ups of larger countries in the last 2 decades illustrate these perceptions in practice.

Thus, researching ways to enable greater inclusiveness at all levels is a key challenge for research to support sustainability. This sits well with the global nature of many public goods, across the wide spectrum from local, national, and regional to global issues, as well as the need to explore new ways to conceptualise their nature and adequate response so that existing institutions and social groups and networks can buy into them.

Implication of Some Recent Research Results from Different Branches of Science for a More Effective Engagement of Science with Societal Negotiation and Mediation Processes

Industrialisation and demographic growth in Western Europe in the last 200 years have required the rise of administrations with their emphasis on rules and entitlements. The long-term effect on the way people express their emotions in public is very visible if we compare what would have been perfectly normal in the early nineteenth century and how constrained our emotional expressions are today in many circumstances. Much of the management literature places the principal emphasis on rationality and streamlining behaviours along lines of efficiency and competitiveness. While even Confucius more than two millennia ago advocated putting learning and rationality first, scholars of the human condition and societies in the past recognised the power of emotions even if they could not rely on the biological sciences opening some first crude glimpses into the underlying mechanisms. Many, from the Greek philosophers to the Christian, Buddhist, Jewish and other thinkers over centuries devised rules ultimately intended to rein in socially undesirable behaviour fed by emotions and excessively egoistic drives.

Damasio (2003), building on LeDoux (1996) and many other leading neuropsychological scholars, explores the underlying biological functions in an attempt to help disentangle the complexities of individual and group behaviour. They show that emotions precede rational thought and decision-making. Also, emotions play an important part in memory formation. Individuals who lack emotions as a result of brain damage often have difficulties making decisions. Emotions are triggered when a competent stimulus is received in the amygdala of the temporal lobe or the ventromedial prefrontal cortex of the brain and transmitted to incite activity in other sites in the brain, such as the basal forebrain, the hypothalamus, or the nuclei of the brainstem. The amygdala react by default without inputs from the cortex, the thinking part of the brain. It is easier for the amygdala and the emotions to gain control over a person's action than for the cortex to keep the emotions in check. Emotions can be triggered even in the absence of cognition.

These insights are progressively being further substantiated by more recent brain and neuropsychological research results (e.g., Haxby and Gobbini 2007). Recent results of research into mirror neurons in the brain, which fire both when we do something and when we see someone else do something, suggest that the hypothesis that mirror neurons for motor functions and emotions are linked is correct (Enticott et al. 2008). These, and other results showing the importance of music in mobilising emotions and thus opening brain pathways, also give rise to the exploration of new approaches to helping emotionally constrained people.

Emotions have been closely linked to biological functions imparted to *Homo sapiens* by evolution. Given the fundamental role of fear for risk avoidance and survival, fear seems to be among the most basic and easiest to trigger (LeDoux 1998; Damasio 2003 and references therein). Fear seems to be governed by a different system than other emotions, such as joy and the amygdala and other involved brain structures show left-right differences in the triggering and processing of fear and joy.

Despite their deep biological roots and functions, within certain limits we might postulate that emotions and other biological reactions are amenable to modulation by social and cultural practices and norms. Thornhill and Palmer (2000) present quantitative and circumstantial evidence to interpret rape as an evolutionary survival strategy for males, who, because of low social status and other failures, would otherwise have difficult or no access to females for reproduction – a fundamental biological drive. The evidence also suggests that such socially undesirable behaviour can be reduced by education in conjunction with discouraging social behaviour. It has recently also been argued that culture may have effects on inheritance, in addition to our genes. The biological basis and mechanism proposed to support this interpretation of cultural build-up is, among others, the expansion of the working memory capacity in humans (Renfrey et al. 2008; Smith et al. 2008). In this conjunction work by Knoblich and Sebanz (2008) may constitute an interesting neurological result. In particular, the increase in size of memory, closely associated with emotions, seems to offer new room to interpret the range of empirical evidence about handing down traits, foremost through our genetic make-up, but not only. The relative roles of genetic versus epigenetic inheritance is very much a matter of debate, but the size of memory may be a mechanism to account for the ability to pass on some traits in addition to the genetic route. Neither should be misconstrued as a deterministic mechanism that creates a simplistic one-to-one causal link.

While the accumulated knowledge about patterns in human behaviour do translate into improvements, e.g., in education and capacity building as well as in setting up rules and processes, the identification and understanding of the material bases and causal networks (rather than chains) that link the structures and dynamics of brain functions to emotions and action remain extremely patchy.

The extent of modulability of social and cultural practices is very much a matter of debate and needs further research. A few concepts/findings are relevant to the ability to cooperate, in general, but particularly in international contexts where kin relations tend to be more distant than in communities closer by:

- There is a vast body of empirical experimental work on the propensity to cooperate. The fact that people engage voluntarily in costly cooperation and punishment of wreckers of such cooperation is well established, even when it concerns anonymous strangers unlikely to meet again. It has been documented by a range of teams and individual researchers over the last few decades.
- While there is much agreement on the observation of widespread human altruism, the interpretations of why this is so has been subject to much debate. This is also highly relevant for modern-day international relations and the way future institutions should be shaped to account for human nature in ways that encourage cooperation. Burnham and Johnson (2005) summarise and critically assess that literature and argue that such behaviour can best be explained by individual selection, but is maladaptive in today's context compared to the time it arose in

human evolution. They argue, "Today, the divergence between proximate and ultimate causes of behaviour is the source of much human strife. Proximate triggers continue to goad us into behaviour that no longer fulfills an adaptive function. Fortunately, knowledge of such mismatch provides the normative basis for co-opting cooperative mechanisms towards the public good. Because mechanisms can be fooled, it is possible to design institutions in which individuals gain emotional rewards for helping society even at personal cost. Institutions, negotiations and markets must harness incentives that resonate with our true human nature, targeting specific stimuli that trigger cooperative dispositions, such as cues for reciprocity or reputation" (p. 131).

- Interestingly, the mere thought of money has been shown in some experiments as making people more egoist and more prone to being cooperation spoilers: People in a sample survey who were induced to think about money showed significantly less willingness to cooperate than a control group (Vohs el al 2008), a fact that was also pinned down as a change factor in medical service (Hartzbrand and Groopman 2009). One may speculate that the fungibility of money reduces critical engagement and thus the propensity to cooperate, a perspective even shared by some bankers (e.g., B. Lietaer 2009, personal communication 2009).
- The wider debate about altruism versus selfishness continues, and more recently, it has been claimed that mathematical models can reproduce generosity that distinguishes winners from the less successful. The notion that winners don't punish, thus avoiding the cost of punishment (Trivers, 1971; Dreber et al. 2008; Novak 2008), even though enforcement (and punishment) is accepted as unavoidable for social organisations, also has some implications in terms of seeking organisational forms that minimise the need for punishment and external controls.
- The role of groups in human behaviour compared to purely individual trajectories has been subject to much speculation and stereotyping. Often "western cultures" are being portrayed as emphasising the individual over the group, leading to egoistic and unsocial behaviour. Conversely, "eastern cultures" are supposed to put the communal interest above the individual and thus encourage more responsible group behaviour at the expense of the individual. Some scepticism is in order in relation to schematising patterns in this way. On one end of the spectrum, the long search for picking either the winners or the villains based on genetic or other individual features has utterly failed and is now recognised even as impossible. On the other end of the spectrum, recent studies in the context of the long-term studies of a large social network suggest that such features as happiness and obesity are strongly influenced by such a social network (Christakis and Fowler 2007; Fowler and Christakis 2008).
- The importance of social networks and the trust that goes with them is also suggested in the psychology, political economy, and marketing literature suggesting that word-of-mouth (thus trust) appears often to be more effective than general publicity, both in different market related situations (jobs, products, services) as well as in the political arena. This would be resonant with findings of the IWRM review panel cited above (Gyawali et al. 2006) and a summary account of an ad hoc international working group on key parameters enabling increased research

impact, notably trust, perceived relevance, and ability to communicate (Nauen 2005).

Advancing the understanding of underlying mechanisms could be valuable because of the implications for devising and adapting institutions for sustainable societies in the twenty-first century without falling into the trap of determinism.

Our ability to cooperate is also mediated through the type of education available and dispensed. There are still great discrepancies in the generalised access to education between countries. While the last decades have seen progress, despite the huge increase in human populations, the advances have been differentiated in both quantitative and qualitative terms. The notion of a knowledge society, where all citizens can be at the same time users and providers of knowledge, implies much improved exchange and cooperation not only among the well-educated elites, including scientists. In order to counteract current inequalities and exclusion mechanisms the development of a sustainable knowledge society demands concrete efforts towards social inclusion and near universal access to knowledge. This is clearly not a zero-sum game.

By way of example, Latin American societies are characterised by still significant divisions, despite increased efforts in social and education policies. All countries have made substantial progress between 1960 and 2000. However, even if the Latin America education average is 6 years (generalised completion of the primary schooling cycle), this is considered insufficient for any ambition to graduate an economy from its dependency on natural resources towards a strongly knowledge-based one (Inter-American Development Bank 2006). Likewise, in Africa some progress has been made, but rapid population growth and underinvestment in education systems has meant that access to basic education is still not universal. Twelve countries out of the group for which estimates are available in the latest Human Development Indicators of UNDP have literacy rates of adults above the age of 15 below 50%, and 19 countries have school enrolment of young people below 50%. In many countries discrepancies between male and female access persist. It thus remains a formidable challenge to achieve at least basic literacy and numeracy for all and provide generalised access to basic school education in line with the second Millennium Development Goal. This is discussed by Naven and Hempel (2008) in relation to sustainable fisheries.

The doubling of the human population from three billion to more than 6.6 billion in the last 50 or so years is straining existing institutions. Despite considerable expansion of their scope, e.g., in education and health, demand for services of these institutions is beyond what they can deliver, not the least because the supports for teacher education and teaching materials cannot keep up with the scale and speed of change. So, despite much cooperation, the sense of competition for resources, not only in education and health, but also in terms of food, access to raw materials, and other types of resources, remains strong and, many would argue, is increasing. Meanwhile, the pervasive emphasis in many industrial countries and emerging economies on technological "solutions" is not necessarily yielding the expected results (Eco 2002; Jasanoff 2007). While admirable advances have been made in some fields, they have not been able to beat nature at its own game and come at a price. Moreover, increasingly sophisticated technologies require a skill level and physical and regulatory support systems that are prone to high risks of disruption from even small minority interests feeling left out from their benefits, as some of the more spectacular hacking incidents may illustrate. They illustrate the dilemma between striving for higher efficiency (thus reducing diversity) while not reducing diversity to the point where the resilience of the system (defined as the ability to bounce back as a result of a challenge) is lost.

In this context, Beck (2008) argues that over-reliance on technology fixes and administrative controls that often go with them might actually accelerate and increase risk and crises of truly global dimensions. Unwittingly, they might then undermine even the legitimacy and effectiveness of conventional institutions, mostly at national level. The difficulty, if not the impossibility of reining in and coming to grips with such risks arising from unintended consequences of high risk technologies or even intentional disruptions, produces a wide spectrum of reactions ranging all the way from denial to potential permanent anxiety, fear, and overreaction and much in between. At one extreme of the spectrum, denial may be based on blind belief in technological fixes or be religiously influenced. The now-ubiquitous fear of disaster striking – be it associated with unintended consequences of earlier human action (climate change is a case in point) or uncontrollable phenomena such as earthquakes or intentional acts including hacking or, worse, terrorism – poses challenges for which more than classic scientific investigation will be required as a response.

At the other extreme of the spectrum, Beck locates fear of uncertain futures, but also practical experience with denied recognition, let alone compensation (to the extent it would be possible), for damage suffered from unintended side effects or intended disruptions. According to the author, this creates or can create mistrust in the very institutions, public bodies, companies, and research centres unable to ensure human security and often suspected to contribute or even be the origin of the threats. This dynamic lays open unprecedented and intertwined risks for societal models based on liberal capitalism (and, one is tempted to say, sustainability of existing societies), but also fresh opportunities for a "new beginning." It obliges individuals and groups to revert to a higher degree of own activity in seeking to understand and regain some control, as delegation of responsibility to experts and institutions may not be a viable option. One is tempted to interpret this as a plea for democratic practice. In this context, J. Spangenberg (2005, personal communication) states that citizens are the experts of impact, though not necessarily of technologies, thus underlining the heightened importance of critical public participation.

Among the implications of exploring these new qualities of human societies and their relationship with nature and what that may mean for education systems and the need for defining concepts commensurate with these developments, it is quite clear that quantitative targets are very important for access to education and knowledge, but that quality matters just as much. It matters in terms of increasing performance of an educational system, e.g., reducing the numbers/percentages of pupils repeating classes or leaving prematurely without a certificate. Quality also plays a huge role in more subtle ways as recent research into some European and other school and life-long learning systems suggests. Here is not the place to elaborate on this vast literature. From the perspective of our discussion it may be sufficient to highlight some aspects, which result from observations in some education systems and in lifelong learning in many work places.

The first aspect to mention here is the notion that educational merit will open access to material wealth and more societal influence. That is the hypothesis of what is now often labelled as the "learning economy" in the instrumental terminology preferred by neoliberal economists, which reduces people to "human resources" in a mono-dimensional perspective. Tomlinson (2008 and references therein) shows that the empirical observations do not necessarily support such a linear generalisation. In some cases, research documents even higher stratification in practice, with middle classes seeing partial (increasing?) erosion of their ability for upward social mobility through education.

Similarly, Casey's (2005) comparative critique of research into lifelong learning in the work place, including small and medium sized enterprise (SME), casts doubt on the general validity of the "learning economy" notion in its prevailing articulation. She identifies trends in some countries and settings whereby elites steer the intensification of work, rationalisation, and intense managerialism, while large groups of the population are locked into low-knowledge jobs that discourage learning, such as call-centres, security, and some other low-end services). Holford (2006) also conveys a mixed message in relation to the ability of existing lifelong learning programmes to sustain broadly-based content not only geared at technical skills, but holistic citizenship. At the same time, these authors signal various efforts at bringing forward alternative models that satisfy a wider array of human and social (democratic) needs.

For our purpose, we may simply retain that one-dimensional emphasis on technical skills, be it in education systems or lifelong learning, including in the work place, may well produce results running counter to the very objective of increasing innovation capacity. This leads Lynch et al. (2007) to underscore the need for educational systems encouraging care-full citizens rather than only "rational economic actor" citizens. While increased rational skills are desirable and even necessary, a more balanced approach with attention to equivalent social and emotional capacity and empathy for others is of particular importance in today's interdependent world. The ambivalence of progress in some areas in the face of concomitant regression in others (often the result of unintended consequences of action within complex systems) shines through much of this literature and undermines the desire for greater security and predictability. All this militates for seeking to broaden the basis of scientific enquiry and compatibility between different ways of knowing, expanding cooperation well beyond what has been done in the past.

We will also need to direct scientific enquiry more explicitly at the formidable sustainability challenges of our age. While the diagnostic pioneering of the Intergovernmental Panel on Climate Change (IPCC) and the Millennium Ecosystem Assessment (MEA 2005) brought unprecedented international cooperation and give us a sense of the magnitude of the threats, a lot of higher resolution work at regional and smaller scales will be essential to provide inputs into societal negotiation processes about determining the direction of future developments. These large-scale exercises put the focus on much of the common pool resources and the changes human activity has already brought upon them. But depending on the context within which the exercises are interpreted, different people are drawing quite different conclusions.

What is becoming clearer, though, is that simple extrapolation of current trends of nature consumption is not a viable option. That also raises questions as to how we will be able to meet basic needs, produce and distribute enough high quality food without further degrading ecosystems, biodiversity and water resources; how we will extend health care and power development sustainably; and how we get information, education and training even into remote regions while being respectful of often rich local knowledge. Last but not least, bringing these strands together calls for inclusive institutions reconnecting the publics to democratically legitimised decision-making processes and their implementation under conditions of precaution, accountability and transparency.

Moreover, much of the operational capacity is at national and local levels and a multitude of responses matching conditions at these scales will need urgent exploration beyond the diagnosis. The way these challenges are being experienced varies widely, which is why emphasis on negotiation and dialogue-based cooperation is crucial. If this sounds utopian to some, it is the realistic alternative to coercion, societal and ecosystem collapse, and other unsustainable outcomes as illustrated, e.g., by the scenario development of the MEA and other analyses, such as the Stern review (2007) with its stronger economic perspective.

Under What Conditions Can International Scientific Cooperation Support Meeting the Challenges of the next Decades to Bring Human Societies in Line with Sustainability?

How can international scientific cooperation, scientific investigation, method and reasoning then become more effective in engaging critically with societal processes at such scales?

Within the growing community of sustainability researchers attempting to support more transparent and accountable processes, Bogliotti and Spangenberg (2005) propose a framework for developing and evaluating projects. They argue that sustainability science cannot succeed without explicit attention to ethics as a guiding external framework within which other forms of knowledge and the use of knowledge need to be negotiated.

Moreover, it has been shown that research findings in one field may have implications for others or enable applications well outside the initial intentions. A case in point is illustrated by Nauen (2006) in analysing a public web-based archive of scientifically validated information on all fish species known to science. The question was whether it was making a contribution to the implementation of the political decision at the 2002 World Summit on Sustainable Development to restore marine ecosystems and fish stocks to productive levels by 2015. The documented uptake by different user groups certainly showed that the originally targeted resource managers were reached and made use of the information system. The evidence did not show that the mandated reversal of earlier trends to ecosystem degradation was being achieved through the easier access to the information alone. There were, however, a lot of indications of use that had never been anticipated but helped, e.g., make better use of public resources in education and custom services as well as in business applications.

It is intuitively clear that some research findings that have taken years of painstaking work by trained scientists cannot be absorbed with all their implications in a few days or even hours of a final dissemination workshop with potential users. In a typical case potential users would need much more time to really assimilate the results and mull over what they could mean in their specific circumstances, including aspects the research project may not have covered. The closer the prior experience of the social actors is to the research with which they are confronted the easier it might be for them to make that assessment. This is being observed empirically in countless situations. The most common cases show that years if not decades may be required for the uptake of new knowledge, unless a combination of favourable factors speeds this process.

As a result, there is a rising interest in the practice of participatory research in relation to study of natural resources and their ecosystems. The water review panel advocated as much on a more systematic basis and the body of academic research into such approaches and their practice is rapidly growing. In the light of acute interest in the policy and development community, Warne (2006) suggests that multi-stakeholder platforms for integrated catchment management can be a useful institutional bargaining space, but that different stakeholders have different levels of expectations and engagement. Participatory forms of doing research are also gaining currency in relation to health, as is witnessed, e.g., by the movement of patient-influenced cancer research (Giles 2008).

Participatory forms of research do not imply that researchers become superfluous or that social actors need to give up all their other activities to follow the different research steps. Conversely, participatory research is more than responding to expressed demand in the form of some policy decision or international objective, such as the Millennium Development Goals adopted by the United Nations Millennium Summit in 2000. Participatory research should enable interaction between researchers and research users at certain points in the process with the triple objective of improving mutual understanding and alignment, increasing the transparency of the research process and facilitating access and uptake of results. Multi-stakeholder platforms and participatory forms of research thus have ingredients of a dialogue and negotiation process in which the parties can build trust and agree to use research as an input.

The above-mentioned conceptual approach with its underlying scientific method has perhaps as its principal advantage that the formulation of a hypothesis (sustainability, modernity theory) provides a handle for testing hypotheses and for the identification of gaps, which bottom-up approaches cannot deliver. A simple compilation of what is there without an overarching concept provides no objectivisable method of addressing missing areas of knowledge. Likewise, such a framework may also be used to approximate, what would be desirable areas of future research, provided a reasonable overview of existing knowledge is available.

Humankind is bound to reap major benefits from the construction of knowledge societies – clearly not a zero-sum game. Yet history tells us that many may be excluded from these benefits, unless specific counter measures are taken. This is why inclusion in the knowledge society (not to be confused with the more limited notion of the "learning economy") requires considerably reinforced cooperation in SandT, including economic and social partners able to make good use of the knowledge generated through science, research, and development as well as helping to steer the pursuit of knowledge. In the light of the above, when thinking about scientific and technological cooperation we must give priority to forms that privilege dialogue and involve different social groups and stakeholders and represent therefore more equitable ways of addressing shared problems and issues.

This brings us to expanding the initial point that in addition to sharing rational and instrumental knowledge more widely, the recognition of emotions and active promotion of social and ethical dimensions in international cooperation is needed to meet the sustainability challenges of today and tomorrow. Overcoming the separations between different fields of knowledge in cooperative ways is a necessary but insufficient condition. Such interdisciplinarity or even multi-disciplinarity is chronically difficult to achieve because different branches of study tend to operate their analyses at different scales. A variety of methodological approaches have been attempted to overcome this challenge. A promising approach is to use transects or other geographically based approaches forcing each disciplinary type of description and analysis to meet others when applied to a specific problem or challenge. When different branches of knowledge give compatible results, one may be more confident that the framing has been properly done. Conversely, incompatible or incongruent results may be a source of verification and correction, which might not otherwise have become visible and thus stimulate important advances in knowledge. Moreover, as we have seen above, some areas are not amenable to the types of scientific pursuit we know today and the unintended consequences of high-risk manipulations within our complex (societal and natural) systems cannot be fully anticipated. This adds weight to the proposed understanding and multi-actor approach to the knowledge society.

But as we have seen above, when first touching on the impact of scientific research and knowledge, we need more than knowledge to act. When analysing the conditions under which research and science and technology may accrue their impact on society, an international ad hoc reflection group identified a number of key features, which were distilled from a cross-section of empirical observations in international scientific cooperation (Nauen 2005). The group identified the following three basic features as indispensible conditions for societal impact:

- *Perceived relevance* of the new knowledge, not so much from the perspective of the researchers themselves, but rather of those individuals, organisations, and institutions capable of using such knowledge in their activities, be these for products or processes, for regulatory processes or in private undertakings.

- *Trust* in the messenger was underscored as a major factor in the acceptability of the new knowledge. The younger readers may have themselves experienced a situation where they make a very good proposal in a meeting which, frustratingly to themselves, is entirely passed over, while the same proposal uttered by an established member of the group finds acclaim. A variation of such situation may be that if the trusted adviser (gate keeper) to a political leader or CEO "buys" into the new knowledge, it may be heard and seriously considered, while it will not even be taken notice of otherwise. Such dynamics are well documented in, e.g., political economics, including the phenomenon that on the way to establish a new structure there is greater openness to new knowledge and connections that may be marshalled in support, while once established, the demand for new knowledge retreats and emphasis moves to maintenance, rather than change. In all cases, trust and the emotional states that go with it is a fundamental need for constructing and keeping up relations and organisations.
- *The capability to communicate* scientific results in an understandable manner for non-specialists is a third important feature influencing uptake or otherwise of new knowledge. As already mentioned above, this assumes that some communication takes place (i.e., there is willingness to listen on both sides). This skill was not necessarily a standard feature of scientific training. "Too much" effort into communication has sometimes been frowned upon by the scientific community, because of the risk of oversimplification or distortion of the scientific process of whittling out the most reliable interpretation of the observed facts, or sometimes even loss of privileged access. However, in today's context, when governments set ambitious targets for huge public (and private) investment into scientific research, it is only normal that the public should expect to see how these resources have been utilised and what benefits they bring to the public. This is why there is more emphasis on considering communicating science as being part of the role of a scientist (Winston 2009).

Moreover, the impact on society not only depends on the supply side at a primary level, but even more so on demand and the degree to which those in need of the new knowledge have their demand organised and connected with a capacity to act. At this higher level, many more conditions need to be met, including normally enabling policy environments, access to infrastructure, and other resources, including people and finance. Because of the multitude of factors, one needs to be cautious in attributing societal effects alone or predominantly to science (e.g., Baur et al. 2001).

In today's overcrowded planet in crisis – how can international scientific cooperation contribute to building trust and empathy? How can we share the analyses of the complicated and interconnected challenges without overtaxing human comprehension and capacity? After all, one case of a human, economic, or environmental disaster generates empathy; 100,000 are a statistic.

To some extent, we are already witnessing how the media are picking up some of the biggest scientific and political stories of our time, such as climate change, water and biodiversity, poverty, and others. In doing so, they do make use of scientific results and weave them into a narrative that engages the public much more than was the case only a few years ago. But it is also clear that we need other forms of bringing together various ways of knowing on an unprecedented scale. We also need to strengthen the enabling environment for international cooperation for mutual benefit – of particularly critical importance in the next few decades until world population stabilises and then starts decreasing.

There are well-tested principles of such practice, based on more than 25 years of international scientific and technological cooperation by the European Union. Among the most important for today's context, we may mention:

- Cooperation based on mutual respect and benefits, looking at the whole, people and institutions with their emotions and rationality
- Accepting that benefits may be of different types for different cooperation partners, but still worthwhile
- Emphasising transparency, shared responsibility, accountability, and the long-term nature of the relationships
- Building human and institutional capacity at local, national, regional, and international levels to allow for expansion of cooperation and wider use of its results
- Recognising historical pathways, difference in culture and sensitivities as a critical first step
- Recognising the importance of diversity for overall resilience of systems, even at the expense of some efficiency ("better to do the right thing a little less badly than the wrong thing perfectly – and efficiently")
- Creating shared practice and mutual discovery as a way to build up sustainable trust – long-term relations based on dialogue, institutionalisation, and critical engagement
- Expanding the practice significantly because it is not enough to have some specialists, researchers, and other well-trained people cooperate. Instead involve large cross-sections of societies in the process in tune with the principles of the knowledge society and in order to spread the benefits much more widely and equitably
- Seeking to increase the effectiveness and impact of SandT cooperation for sustainability explicitly by combining scientific excellence with greater responsiveness to the demand from governmental and non-governmental actors.

Living up to the sustainability challenges will require huge changes in the way we do business in most parts of the planet. In a context where the major direction and goals meet with consensus in the existing UN and other existing international fora, but the concrete intermediary steps to get there, and even part of the bigger goals, are steeped in uncertainty, and there is insufficient trust among the parties on how to share the cost and the benefits equitably, time for progressive adjustment and continuous dialogue are essential to move forward. Social networking using a variety of IT platforms is opening new opportunities to address some of the gaps in novel and more inclusive ways. Many of these forms of interaction could benefit from insights into psychological processes derived from a combination of objective conditions and perceptions as are commonly encountered in negotiation situations

(Aquilar and Galluccio 2008), but have analogous relevance in less formal settings.

We will have to accelerate waste reduction and increase resource use efficiency in industrialised countries, while opening up human development in developing and emerging economies. Some have also suggested that the global financial crisis illustrates the extent of interdependence across the globe, but also the enormous risks of aggravating inequalities. To be able to build a larger consensus around the goals aiming at more sustainable societies and relationships and the many intermediary steps that need to be taken, we will want to rebalance aspirations and place more emphasis on intellectual, social, environmental, and spiritual values at the expense of certain types of material goods, particularly money, as the (only or predominant) exchange convention, which are even cited by some as an impediment to happiness (e.g., von Schönburg 2005). We will want to increase international cooperation and concrete action towards assuring dignified livelihoods to humanity in all parts and refuse to accept current trends of increasing hunger and abject poverty affecting a huge percentage of fellow citizens.

Davis (2009) puts a finger on the tension caused by rational cognition of extremely worrisome indicators of environmental, social and financial unsustainability in the way people in industrialised countries relate to nature and to other societies. At the same time he expresses the need for utopian hope to harness the knowledge and cooperative will across all traditional boundaries for peaceful and dignified living on planet Earth. This is not only a scientific agenda, it is foremost a political one, but one which could benefit from harnessing diversified scientific cooperation for its ends. Reconstructing past states and developing narratives around them will be essential for the ability to determine and sharpen societal objectives compatible with sustainable futures and build the social and political consensus around them that will enable their achievement.

Concluding Remarks

The train of thought in this chapter has the contribution of international science cooperation to sustainability of human societies as its red thread. In the attempt to provide indications for both its need and feasibility, it touches on a quite disparate range of fields of enquiry in search of compatible elements.

An underlying message is that human behaviour is rooted in the physiology of the individual and conditioned by reactions to surrounding social and environmental systems of which the individual is part. In other words, behaviour and emotions have a material base. Scientific understanding has just started to scratch at the surface but has already shown that the relationship is neither mechanistic nor deterministic. Pharmacological and nutritional research explores ways of restoring health or enhancing well-being through molecular or micro-level interventions, while at the same time opening up large and diverse areas of often unintended other effects resulting from multi-functionalities and the complexity of the structure and dynamic functioning of the body system.

On a different scale, social and environmental systems (some may even say that social systems are a subset of nature) show a reduced buffer capacity and resilience largely as a result of human intervention. As a result, the interactions are becoming more visible, immediate and diverse – the unintended consequences as well. The confidence in "easy" technological or rational fixes is shrinking, and more prudent, iterative approaches that allow assessment of the expected and unexpected effects should gain currency. Iterative approaches also have advantages in terms of harnessing a greater diversity of action and possible responses to perceived challenges and opportunities. While greater diversity may not be the most efficient way of achieving an objective, it certainly is the most sustainable and robust way, particularly under conditions of change. Monocultures, whether in farming, forestry, or social environments, are not sustainable, though they may have superior efficiency for a while.

Some speculative connections are made here between vastly different scales, borrowing a principle from scale-less network theory, which suggests that focus on the critical nodes (at whichever scale) is the most parsimonious way to connect distant elements within a complex system. The price for stringing together such diverse elements is, inevitably, that none of the elements can be discussed in any great depth and that important, even major, publications from each field remain unquoted. It is hoped, however, that at least some of the contours of international cooperation in sustainability science have become clearer and that the importance of combining excellence in the pursuit of knowledge be combined with multi-stakeholder dialogue across societies in critically engaged ways. This is another way of searching for a balance between diversity and efficiency that will be robust in our changing conditions.

International scientific cooperation and the scientific diplomacy that goes with it has very good potential to contribute such steps towards a transition to sustainability. But to realise this potential, nothing short of a new deal with society will be required. While excellence in science requires independence from political interference, sustainability science is enriched by critical interaction with groups of social actors and attention and respect for other ways of codifying knowledge, from traditional knowledge and the arts, all of which may make consonant contributions to addressing the great multiple transformations of our societies, towards more sustainable and equitable modes.

Acknowledgement The author is grateful for the encouragement by Mauro Galluccio. Without his prodding this chapter would not have been written.

References

Aquilar, F., & Galluccio, M. (2008). *Psychological processes in international negotiations. Theoretical and practical perspectives*. New York: Springer.

Baur, H., Bosch, M., Krall, S., Kuby, T., Lobb-Rabe, A., Schuetz, P. T., et al. (2001). *Establishing plausibility in impact assessments*. Eschborn, DE: Gesellschaft für Technische Zusammenarbeit mbH (GTZ).

Bazerman, M. H., & Hoffman, A. J. (1999). Sources of environmentally destructive behavior: Individual, organizational and institutional perspectives. *Research in Organizational Behavior, 21*, 39–79.
Beck, U. (2008). *Weltrisikogesellschaft*. Frankfurt M: Suhrkamp.
Bogliotti, C., & Spangenberg, J. (2005). A conceptual device for framing sustainability in project development and evaluation. In A. Kungolos, C. A. Brebbia, & E. Beriatos (Eds.), *Second international conference on sustainable development and planning. Sustainable development and planning II* (Vol. 1, pp. 347–358). Boston: WIT Press.
Burnham, T. C., & Johnson, D. D. P. (2005). The biological and evolutionary logic of human cooperation. *Analyse and Kritik, 27*(2005), 113–135.
Casey, C. (2005). Work and workers in the learning economy: Conceptions, critique, implications. In M. Kuhn, M. Tomassini, & R.-J. Simons (Eds.), *Towards a knowledge based economy? Knowledge and learning in European educational research.* (pp. 149–170). New York: Peter Lang.
Christakis, N. A., & Fowler, J. H. (2007). The spread of obesity in a large social network over 32 years. *The New England Journal of Medicine, 357*, 370–379.
Damasio, A. (2003). *Looking for Spinoza. Joy, sorrow and the feeling brain.* New York: Harvest.
Davis, M. (2009). Wer wird die Arche bauen? Das Gebot utopischen Denkens im Zeitalter der Katastrophen. *Blätter für deutsche und internationale Politik, 2*, 41–59. German version of the speech delivered 11/12/2008 in acceptance of the "Kulturpreis" of the Münchener Universitätsgesellschaft.
Dörner, D. (2003). *Die Logik des Mißlingens. Strategisches Denken in komplexen Situationen.* Reinbek bei Hamburg: RoRoRo.
Dreber A, Rand D, Fundenberg D, Novak MA. (2008). Winners don't punish. *Nature, 452*, 348–351.
Eco, U. (2002). Science, technology and magic. Speech first given in Rome in November 2002 at an International Scientific Conference (on information in science) chaired by Umberto Veronesi. In *Turning back the clock. Hot wars and media populism* (pp. 103–111). London: Vintage Books.
Enticott, P. G., Johnston, P. J., Herring, S. E., Hoy, K. E., & Fitzgerald, P. B. (2008). Mirror neuron activation is associated with facial emotion processing. *Neuropsychologia, 46*(11), 2151–2854.
Estrella Santos, N., & Nauen, C. E. (Eds.) (2008). Catalogue of synopses of International SandT Cooperation (INCO) projects on challenges in fisheries, coastal zones, wetlands and aquaculture. ACP-EU Fish Res Rep 17:309 P.
European Commission. (1982a). The Community's development policy. Commission memorandum transmitted to the council on 4 October 1982. COM (82) 640 final, 27 p. Brussels, European Commission.
European Commission. (1982b). Food strategies. A new form of cooperation between Europe and the countries of the Third World. Europe Information Development, DE 40:22. Brussels, European Commission.
European Commission. (1983). A community research policy for development. Europe Information Development, DE 44:23. Brussels, European Commission.
European Commission. (2004). REACH in brief. Brussels, European Commission, Enterprise Directorate General and Environment Directorate General. Brussels, 18 p.
European Commission. (2005). International scientific cooperation with developing countries (INCO-DC), Framework Programme 5 – European Commission-funded projects. Luxembourg: Office for Official Publications of the European Communities.
European Commission. (2007). International cooperation in FP6 – project synopses. Luxembourg: Office for Official Publications of the European Communities.
European Commission. (2008a). International cooperation with Africa in FP6. Luxembourg: Office for Official Publications of the European Communities.
European Commission. (2008b). The ASEM aquaculture platform. sustained supply, finding solutions, bridging the divide (3:28). Luxembourg: Office for Official Publications of the European Communities.

European Commission. (2008c). Responding to global challenges: The role of Europe and of international scientific and technological cooperation. Workshop Proceedings, October 4–5, 2007. Luxembourg: Office for Official Publications of the European Communities.
European Environment Agency. (2001). Late lessons from early warnings 1896–2000. Copenhagen: European Environment Agency, Environmental Issue Report.
Fowler, J. H., & Christakis, N. A. (2008). Dynamic spread of happiness in a large social network: longitudinal analysis over 20 years in the Framingham Heart Study. *British Medical Journal, 337*: a 2338. [10.1136/bmj. a2338]
Galluccio, M. (2007). *Cognitive psychotherapy and international negotiation: An overview*. Paper presented at the V World Congress of Behavioural and Cognitive Therapies, Barcelona, July 2007, Spain.
Giles, J. (2008, October 25). Patients doing it for themselves. *New Scientist*, pp. 34–35.
Gyawali, D., Allan, J. A., Antunes, P., Dudeen, B. A., Laureano, P., Luiselli Fernández, C., et al. (2006). *EU-INCO water research from FP4 to FP6 (1994–2006). A critical review*. Luxembourg: Office for Official Publications of the European Communities.
Hartzbrand, P., & Groopman, J. (2009). Money and the changing culture of medicine. *The New England Journal of Medicine, 360*, 101–103.
Haxby, J. V., & Gobbini, M. I. (Eds.) (2007). The perception of emotions and social cues in faces. *Neuropsychologia 45*(1), 1–206.
Holford, J. (2006). The role of lifelong learning in building citizenship: European Union approaches in the light of British and colonial experience. *International Journal of Lifelong Education, 25*(3), 321–332.
Hollingsworth, J. R., Müller, K. H., & Hollingsworth, E. J. (2008). The end of the science superpowers. *Nature, 454*, 412–413.
Inter-American Development Bank. (2006). *Education, science and technology in Latin America and the Caribbean*. Washington, DC: A statistical compendium of indicators Inter-American Development Bank.
Jasanoff, S. (2007). Technologies of humility. *Nature, 450*, 33.
Kaul, I. (2008). Responding to global challenges: Re-thinking public economics and finance. Proposal for an international research project of the European Commission. In: European Commission (2008c) Responding to global challenges: The role of Europe and of International Scientific and Technological Cooperation. Workshop Proceedings, 4–5 October 2007. Office for Official Publications of the European Communities, Luxembourg, pp. 167–176.
Knoblich, G., & Sebanz, N. (2008). Evolving intentions for social interaction: From entrainment to joint action. *Philosophical Transactions on the Royal Society B, 363*(1499), 2021–2031.
LeDoux, J. (1996). *The emotional brain: The mysterious underpinnings of emotional life*. New York: Simon & Schuster.
LeDoux, J. (1998, May 5–6). Discovering our selves: The science of emotion. Executive summary. Closing session "The future of the study of emotion." The Decade of the Brain 1990–2000. Rockville: National Institute of Mental Health.
Lynch, K., Lyons, M., & Cantillon, S. (2007). Breaking silence: educating citizens for love, care and solidarity. *International Studies in Sociology of Education, 17*(1–2), 1–19.
Maddison, A. (2001). *The world economy. A millennial perspective*. Paris: OECD.
Millennium Ecosystem Assessment. (2005). www.millenniumassessment.org.
Mittelstrass, J. (2004, April 25–28). The Europe of knowledge 2020. A vision for university based research and innovation. Parallel Session Number 4 "A new paradigm for relations between higher education and research." A contribution to the discussion by Professor Dr. Jürgen Mittelstrass, Liège, p. 8.
Moriarty, P., Fonseca, C., Smits, S., & Schouten, T. (2005). *Learning Alliances for scaling up innovative approaches in the water and sanitation sector*. Delft: IRC.
Nauen, C. E. (Ed.). (2005). *Increasing the impact of the EU's international scientific cooperation for the transition towards sustainable development*. Luxembourg: Office for Official Publications of the European Communities.

Nauen, C. E. (2006). Implementing the WSSD decision of restoring marine ecosystems by 2015 – scientific information support in the public domain. *Marine Policy, 30*, 455–461.
Nauen, C. E. (2008). Ten years of international scientific cooperation in fisheries, aquaculture and coastal zones: some preliminary lessons. *Environment, Development and Sustainability, 10*(5), 605–622.
Nauen, C. E., & Hempel, G. (2006, May 2). Science and capacity building for sustainable development in fisheries. Presentation at the International "Thinking Big" Symposium, Fisheries Centre, UBC, Vancouver, Canada p.11.
Novak, M. A. (2008). Generosity: a winner's advice. *Nature, 456*, 579.
Pauly, D. (1995). Anecdotes and the shifting baseline syndrome. *Trends in Ecology & Evolution, 10*, 430.
Pauly, D. (2001). Importance of the historical dimension in policy and management of natural resource systems. In Feoli, E. & Nauen, C. E. (Eds.), *ACP-EU Fisheries Research Initiative*. Proceedings of the INCO-DEV International Workshop on Information Systems for Policy and Technical Support in Fisheries and Aquaculture, Los Baños, Philippines, 5–7 June 2000. ACP-EU Fish Res Rep (8):135 pp. 5–10.
Regalado, A. (1995). Multiauthor papers on the rise. *Science, 25*(268), 785–786.
Renfrey, C., Frith, C., & Malafouris, L. (Eds.) (2008). The sapient mind: archeology meets neuroscience. *Philosophical Transactions of the Royal Society B, 363*(1499), 1935–2061.
Smith, K., Kalish, M. L., Griffiths, T. L., & Lewandowsky, S.S. (Eds.) (2008). Cultural transmission and the evolution of human behaviour. *Philosophical Transactions of the Royal Society B, 363*(1502), 3469–3603.
Sobel, D. (1996). *Longitude. The true story of a lone genius whole solved the greatest scientific problem of his time*. London: Fourth Estate.
Stern, N. (2007). *The economics of climate change. The Stern review*. Cambridge: Cambridge University Press.
Thornhill, R., & Palmer, C. R. (2000). *A natural history of rape. Biological bases for sexual coercion*. Cambridge: MIT Press.
Tomlinson, S. (2008). Gifted, talented and high ability: selection for education in a one-dimensional world. *Oxford Review of Education, 34*(1), 59–74.
Trivers, R. (1971). The evolution of reciprocal altruism. *The Quarterly Review of Biology, 46*(1), 35–37.
Vohs, K. D., Mead, N. L., Goode, M. R. (2008). Merely activating the concept of money changes personal and interpersonal behavior. Current Directions in Psychological Science, 17(3): 208–212. doi: 10.111/j.1467-8721.2008.50076x.
Von Schönburg, A. (2005). *Die Kunst des stilvollen Verarmens. Wie man ohne Geld reich wird*. Berlin: Rowohlt.
Warne, J. F. (2006). More sustainable participation? Multi-stakeholder platforms for integrated catchment management. *Water Resources Development, 22*(1), 15–35.
Wilson, E. O. (1999). *Consilience, the unity of knowledge*. New York: Vintage Books.
Winston, R. (2009). Why turning out brilliant scientists isn't enough. *New Scientist, 2993*, 22–23.
Wuchty, S., Jones, B. F., & Uzzi, B. (2007). The increasing dominance of teams in production of knowledge. *Science, 316*, 1036–1039.

Chapter 10
Representative Decision Making: Constituency Constraints on Collective Action

Daniel Druckman, Esra Çuhadar, Nimet Beriker, and Betul Celik

Overview

This chapter focuses on the role of group and national identity in various types of collective actions. It features the decision to take action and asks about factors that influence that decision. Thus, our perspective is from the standpoint of the decision-maker who usually represents a collectivity (group, organization, nation). The interest is less about those decision-makers' *own* identities and attachments than about various *drivers and constraints* on their decisions to act.

People responsible for developing organizational and national policies often think in terms of futuristic scenarios. They ask about options in the form of "what … if," and turn alternative stories around in their mind. They play out some implications of alternative futures – with regard to such problems as the stability of regimes, the mobility of elites, negotiating tactics, and peacekeeping operations. This study takes advantage of this familiar kind of thinking about policy and action. We ask: What if a situation was like this? What would you do? We then continue the questioning in an attempt to tease out the reasons for the decision, in this case various collective actions. We add an analytical dimension to scenario decision-making. By administering the scenarios to a large population of respondents, we can systematically vary several aspects of both situations and actions. By using a simple rating task, we can produce scales – like temperature scales – that distinguish more ("hotter") from less ("cooler") important elements in decision-making. This is a new approach to the study of decision-making in an international context.

D. Druckman (✉)
10509 Gainsborough Road, Potomac, Maryland 20854, USA
e-mail: dandruckman@yahoo.com

F. Aquilar and M. Galluccio (eds.), *Psychological and Political Strategies for Peace Negotiation*, DOI 10.1007/978-1-4419-7430-3_10,

Background

We define collective action as a situation in which a group member (in our case this group member is a decision-maker) acts as a representative of the group and where the action is directed to the group as a whole (Wright et al. 1990; Wright and Tropp 2002). We construe decision-makers as negotiating representatives. As in many negotiations, they must be responsive to their constituencies or principals. Referred to as a boundary role, this responsiveness must be balanced with the demands made by the opposing negotiators or national decision-makers. Demands may take the form of threatened violence from a neighboring nation, internal protests of administration policies, or pleas for humanitarian aid for nations in crisis. The decision taken in response to these demands is influenced by various features of national constituencies. This influence process has been modeled as an information-processing problem, where decision-makers weight the features in terms of their impact on decisions (Druckman 1977). This study applies this negotiation model to several types of collective action decisions.

Our framework identifies five aspects of "constituencies" that may drive or constrain decisions to take action on behalf of the group or nation: These aspects are motivation, efficacy, type of identity, durability of identity, and spread of identity. The motivational and efficacy variables resemble those developed by Gurr and Davies (2002). The identity variables are based on a three-factor theory of national identity proposed by Druckman (2001).

The work done by Gurr and his colleagues on ethno-political conflicts inspired this project. However, there are important differences between the projects. Their research focuses on the action itself, coded as events (dependent variables). We are concerned with the decisions to take action. We do not focus specifically on ethnic groups, although the distinction between national and ethnic identities is often blurred. They explore the impacts of 19 variables on violent collective actions: These are organized into the categories of incentives for action, group identity, group capacity, and domestic and international opportunity factors. We consolidate these variables into three categories, motivation to act, efficacy in acting, and group identity.

Our motivational variable is similar to their international opportunities for collective action but also includes the severity of the threat. Our efficacy variable is similar to their group organization and territorial concentration indicators but also includes readiness to take action. Our political system variable, a part of group identity, incorporates their repression, restrictions, and autocratic or mixed polities indicators. We define it specifically in terms of type of political system, as autocratic or democratic. The other two parts of identity are not included in their set but derive from theoretical work on national identity as discussed in the social-psychological literature. Even though Gurr and his colleagues have taken into consideration the "perceived" nature of deprivation, their identity variables did not capture the underlying psychological processes that enhance the likelihood of collective action. Yet these psychological processes, such as the strength of in-group identification, are essential to our understanding of identity (Tropp and Wright, 1999). Our durability variable refers to the strength of citizen identity, distinguishing between strong and weak ties to the nation. The spread variable is defined in terms of the amount of citizen support for actions as indicated in public opinion polls (see Druckman 2001).

In an article on negotiating identities, Druckman (2001) proposed three dimensions of identity formation and change. One refers to the extent to which identities are subject to being negotiated or are coerced: Thus, identities are likely to be chosen in democracies but largely involuntary in autocracies. Another dimension is the durability of identities, ranging from fluid to durable: Durable identities are resistant to change with altered circumstances. A third dimension is spread of identities, ranging from wide to limited: Limited spread refers to little sharing of a national identity across the population. These dimensions were shown to influence the flexibility of negotiating representatives. Coerced, durable, and widespread identities pose a constraint on decision-making. The author also illustrated how various African countries (Morocco, Libya, Tunisia, Algeria) are situated in this three-dimensional space.

Another important difference between the projects is that unlike the Gurr-Davies project – and most studies of political and ethnic violence – we do not limit the focus to violent actions. We examine several types of collective actions. These include violent, non-violent, and humanitarian actions. We know little about the decisions for non-violent protests and probably less about why nations (or other groups such as NGOs) participate in humanitarian missions in other countries. It will be interesting to learn whether the same (or different) variables that influence decisions to act violently also influence decisions to act in non-violent ways. For instance, democratic peace theory suggests that regime type constrains or prevents states from going to war in both the monadic (Maoz and Abdolai 1989; Rummel 1995) and dyadic versions of the theory (Russett 1993). The theory provides a single factor explanation for decisions to go to war and limits the focus to one type of collective decision, violent actions.

At the heart of this project are questions about identity. These questions have been largely ignored in the literatures on causes of international conflict. Those studies focus mostly on the characteristics of the international system such as alliances and polarity, power capabilities of states, and geopolitics (Singer et al. 1972; Bremer 1980; Bueno de Mesquita 1981; Maoz 1989, Waltz 1990).

On the other hand, identity is taken into account in the civil war/internal conflict literatures. These literatures deal with identity in two ways. First, some of the studies that consider grievance as a key factor take identity into consideration as part of the *motivation* for collective action (e.g., Gurr 1993, 2000; Reynal-Querol 2002). According to this view, grievances about unjust treatment are shared by group members and reflected in their cultural identity, which serves as a motivator for collective action (Aquilar and Galluccio 2008; Gurr 1993). Second, other studies take identity or grievance into consideration but downplay the importance of it in relation to such factors as structural and organizational efficacy or resource mobilization (Collier and Hoeffler 2001; McCarthy and Zald 1977; Tilly 1978).

Further, regardless of the degree of importance they attribute to identity in explaining violent collective action, many of these studies focus attention only on broad categories such as ethnic group or religion. More importantly, while measuring identity, these studies primarily look at grievance-causing indicators as proxies to identity, such as economic inequality, denial of political rights, ethnic polarization, and ethnic dominance (e.g., Collier et al. 2005). To our knowledge, no previous study has examined the strength of citizen identification with an identity group. An attempt is made in this study to unpack the identity variable by examining three components posited to influence decisions to act.

In sum, the emphasis of the most studies in the international and internal conflict literatures is on motivation and efficacy for taking violent actions. We know more about how actions spring from intentions and assets than from the way citizens identify with their nation, particularly the durability and spread of those citizen identities. This is due in part to the tractability of these variables: Stated intentions and assets are easier to measure than is identity.

The decision-making focus of this project is also mostly missing from the earlier research. The international relations studies discussed in the previous paragraphs deal with the acts or events of violent collective action rather than the factors that are taken into consideration by decision-makers before engaging in collective action. An exception is Lichbach's (1990, 1994) game theoretic model, which highlights an individual's dilemma of choice about participating in violent collective action. He regarded collective action to be a matter of individual decision, in which rational actors choose not to rebel when it works against their own interests.

Several studies in the social-psychology literature on collective action focus attention on decision-making as well. These studies distinguish between individual action and collective action and elaborate on the underlying conditions for each (see Turner et al. 1987; Hogg and Abrams 1988; Wright and Tropp 2002; Ellemers 2002). An individual seeks action to achieve personal outcomes when her identity is salient and when she perceives permeability between inter-group boundaries. On the other hand, a person seeks collective action for social change when social identities are salient and inter-group boundaries are perceived as being impermeable. Thus, these studies suggest strength of in-group identification as an essential factor in predicting collective action regardless of the degree of perceived grievance, which is a motivational factor.

However, although the studies deal with decision-making regarding collective action, they primarily examine an individual's decision to participate in the action. They do not specifically take political decision-makers/negotiating representatives acting on behalf of nations into consideration. This study attempts to fill this gap in understanding conflict. Specifically we learn about:

1. The decisions that precede and precipitate actions.
2. The calculations of decision-makers in the role of group representative.
3. The way that different kinds of conflict situations impact on decisions.
4. The way that the same set of contextual and identity variables influence different types of decisions to act – violent, non-violent, and humanitarian actions.

There are two ways of construing the relationship between identity and the contextual variables of motivation and efficacy. One approach addresses the issue of relative importance of these factors. Each factor is regarded as an independent variable: In other words, identity variables are regarded as being orthogonal to contextual variables. It captures the idea of weighting the importance of one type of factor against another: Do decision-makers emphasize citizens' identity more or less than citizens' motivation and readiness for action? Which aspect of identity or context is most important? This approach is suited to the study of the way decisions are made and guides the study drocussed in this chapter.

Another approach examines interactive effects: With regard to motivation, strong identities can intensify the motivation to act. On efficacy, strong identities enhance group cohesion, which, in turn, contributes to performance. This interactive approach is suited to the study of group action or performance, where the dependent variables are the actions themselves. It guides the next phase of our research on collective actions.

A framework for the project is shown in Fig. 10.1. Both independent and interactive effects are depicted. The former asks about relative impacts of the five variables (shown in the smaller boxes) on each of the three types of collective action decisions. The latter asks about whether identity variables mediate the relationship between context and collective action. Mediating effects are depicted by the arrows between the larger boxes.

The study design is a static, comparative analysis. It is static because it assesses decisions at a point in time. It is comparative because it explores different situations and collective actions. The methodology is designed to tease out the influences and to evaluate their impact on judgments. And, it is intended to connect to the next phases of the project, where actual actions are taken in selected or sampled cases. It will be interesting to discover whether the key influences on decisions to act are also the primary indicators of the actions taken.

Relatively undeveloped theory on these problems, as we note above, encourages us to approach the topic in an exploratory fashion rather than as an evaluation of theoretically-derived hypotheses. The results will distinguish between more and less important influences on decisions. They contribute to the development of a theory of decision-making for collective action by offering a set of hypotheses induced from the findings. Although this is a descriptive project, it may also have value for practitioners by alerting them to the way decisions about collective actions are made by other countries or groups (rather than the way they should be made by our own country). We turn now to a discussion of the research design.

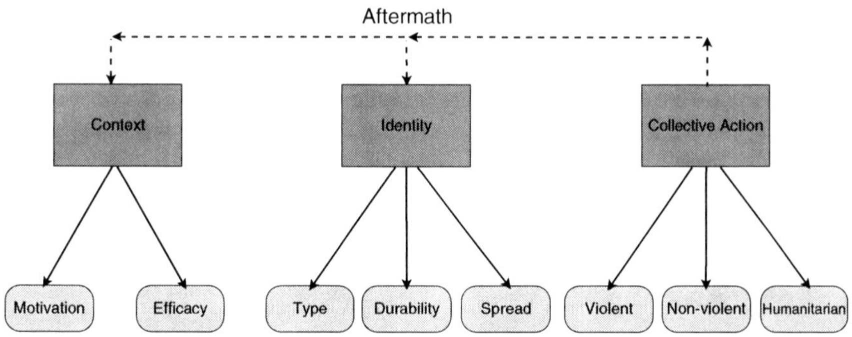

Fig. 10.1 Framework of influences on collective action decisions

Research Design

For each type of collective action (violent, non-violent, humanitarian) four scenarios were written. They differ in terms of direction of the five variables. The variables either encouraged or discouraged taking action, or they were mixed with contextual (or identity) variables encouraging action and identity (or contextual) variables discouraging action. In one scenario, both the contextual (motivation, efficacy) and the identity (political system, durability, spread) variables were geared in the direction of taking action: For the violent scenario, these are severe threat, high readiness, an autocratic regime, widespread support, and durable nationalist identities. An example is the war between the armed forces of Iraq and Iran lasting from September 1980 to August 1988 (efficacy). The autocratic regime of Iraq (political system) viewed the Pan-Islamism and revolutionary Shia Islamism of Ayatollah Khomeini and the Islamic Republic of Iran as a substantial threat (motivation). Saddam Hussein's regime used Arab nationalism (durability, spread) to rally population support for the September 22, 1980, attack on Iran. Hussein's pretext was an alleged assassination attempt on Foreign Minister Tariq Aziz in southern Iraq.

In another scenario, these variables were geared toward inaction: for example, a moderate threat, low efficacy, a democratic system, limited support, and fluid internationalist identities. An example is the sinking of the docked Rainbow Warrior by the French in New Zealand in 1985. The New Zealand Greenpeace vessel, a boat used to peacefully protest the nuclear tests at the French Muraroa Atoll, was blown up by the "action" branch of the French foreign intelligence services. This was not seen as a substantial threat (motivation) by the democratic New Zealand government (political system), and New Zealand's relatively weak military forces did not go to war with France. Support for action was not widespread, nor were New Zealand's citizens deeply nationalistic. The French bombers were treated in accordance with international law and a trial was held.

Similarly, examples can be given for the non-violent and humanitarian scenarios. Contrasting examples show the difference between situations that encourage either non-violent action or inaction. Following the 2002 Israeli Operation Defensive Shield, an enraged Syrian public was encouraged by the autocratic regime (political system) to boycott American goods (motivation). Widespread public support (spread) from a nationalist citizenry (durability) provided additional impetus to effectively organize the demonstrations (efficacy).

Despite a robust trading relationship between Canada and the USA (democratic political systems), issues arise on occasion. Recent disputes over softwood lumber and the beef trade have provided an impetus for protest. However, low threat (motivation) combined with limited support (spread) from an international public (fluid identity) has discouraged action. Limited experience with non-violent demonstrations further discouraged the Canadian public to rally around these issues.

Peacekeeping serves as a context for humanitarian missions. With regard to action, Canadian peacekeeping provides an example. Widespread popular support for Canada's participation in UN missions combines with internationalist and multilateral policies (motivation and durability) to provide strong incentives for active involvement. A well-trained peacekeeping force makes Canada a valued partner in most peace operattions. By contrast, Iran proves an example of inaction. This autocratic government (political system) has been reluctant to participate in UN missions. Limited popular support (spread) combines with nationalist and unilateral policies (motivation and durability) to provide strong disincentives for participation. A poorly trained military further discourages involvement, both from the vantage point of Iranian regimes and the UN (efficacy).

The other two scenarios were mixed such that the contextual variables were geared toward action (or inaction) while the identity variables were geared toward inaction (action). However, the meaning of "geared toward action or inaction" depends on the type of collective action considered. For example, autocratic regimes with nationalist populations are geared toward taking violent action. Democratic regimes with internationalist populations are geared toward committing to humanitarian missions. These different meanings were taken into account in the construction of the scenarios.

The key variables are underlined in each scenario as shown in the Appendix example of decisions to take humanitarian actions, where the variables were geared toward taking those actions. The research design captures the framework shown above in Fig. 10.1: It permits comparisons among the four configurations of the variables and the three types of actions. It is referred to as a four (types of scenarios) by three (types of collective actions) design. The comparisons are made among scaled weights for each of the five variables by scenario and by type of collective action. Questions asked are: Do the weights change for the different types of situations for each collective action? Do the weights change for the different types of collective action? For example, is motivation more or less important than efficacy in situations where both are geared to taking action? Is spread more or less important than durability as an influence on decisions to promote humanitarian missions?

Data Collection and Analysis

Data were collected from large classes at the University of Queensland in Brisbane, Australia, and from two universities in Turkey, Bilkent in Ankara and Sabanci in Istanbul. A total of 64 scenarios were distributed at each university, divided into roughly 16 per condition (scenario) for each of the three types of collective actions. There were a total of 179 respondents, assigned randomly to the violent (65), non-violent (54), and humanitarian (60) scenarios.

A random-numbers table was used to order the questionnaires before dissemination in the classes. This satisfies the requirement of random assignment to condition. For most role players the task took between 15 and 20 minutes to complete. There were no apparent problems with understanding the situations or the rating task.

After reading about the situation, role-players were asked to make a decision. For the violent scenario: "Based on the information you received above, will you mobilize your army for action against your neighbor or only put them on readiness alert?" For the non-violent scenario: "Based on the information you received above, will you organize your citizens and NGOs around the country to demonstrate against your neighbor or will you wait for further indications of their intentions before encouraging mass demonstrations of protest from your citizens?" For the humanitarian mission scenario: "Based on the information you received above, will you send your military and civilian peacekeepers to Asghania or not take any action at all?"

The role-players were then asked to complete a pair-comparison exercise. This consisted of comparing each variable with each of the other variables, resulting in ten judgments of "more or less importance in influencing your decision." Judgments were made in the following format:

A more or less important factor in your decision than:

	Your economy/ historical record	Your peacekeeper's readiness	The spread of citizen support	The strength of citizens' identity within your nation
Is your political system	More/less	More/less	More/less	More/less
Is your economy/ historical record		More/less	More/less	More/less
Is your peacekeepers' readiness			More/less	More/less
Is the spread of support				More/less

Role-players were told to make decisions by circling "more" or "less" for each comparison without leaving any blank. The method of pair comparisons produces values on a psychological scale. The procedure gives the number and proportion of times each element is judged as being more important than each of the other elements. This produces a proportions matrix, which is then converted into areas of the normal curve. The result is an interval scale.

Based on Thurstone's law of comparative judgment, the procedure is suited especially for *similar* elements such as colors judged for pleasantness, samples of handwriting judged for excellence, or vegetables judged for taste. We take some license for this task. Here we are asking respondents to judge *different* elements for importance. To the extent that the comparisons can be made, we have confidence that the resulting scales are meaningful. We have reason to believe that the five variables can be ordered and, thus, compared in pair-wise fashion. An advantage of the procedure is that it allows for direct comparisons of situations and actions, which is the goal of this project. For technical details of computation, see Guilford (1954). For an application of the procedure in the context of a simulated international negatiation, see Druckman (1993).

Results

The resulting weights for each of the four scenarios by type of collective action are presented in this section. For each scenario, the five factors are ordered in terms of the size of the weights. The higher the weight, the more important the factor is judged in that scenario. The scaled weights are shown in Tables 10.1–10.3. Spacings between factors are rough indications of distance between the weights.

The weights for the violent action scenarios are shown in Table 10.1. They are summarized as follows:

1. Threat – the motivational variable – is the strongest factor in the first scenario (high threat/readiness, high nationalism). It remains strong as well for each of the other scenarios.
2. One identity variable, spread, is judged as being very strong in scenarios 2, 3, and 4.
3. The political system variable is moderately strong in the fourth scenario.
4. The efficacy factor is only moderately strong in each of the scenarios.
5. Durability is weak in all four scenarios.

Table 10.1 Violent action scenarios[a]

All variables geared toward action (n = 16):	
Threat	2
Readiness/efficacy	1.63
Spread	1.17
Durability	1.11
Political system	0.70
All variables geared toward inaction (n = 17):	
Threat	1
Spread	0.95
Readiness/efficacy	0.62
Political system	0.54
Durability	0.34
Context geared toward action, identity toward inaction (n = 16):	
Spread	1
Threat	0.98
Readiness/efficacy	0.58
Political system	0.17
Durability	0
Context geared toward inaction, identity toward action (n = 16):	
Spread	1
Threat	0.92
Political system	0.69
Readiness/efficacy	0.69
Durability	0.47

[a]All the scales are inverted in order to present the variables in a descending order of importance from higher to lower weights. Each calculated weight is subtracted from 1 or 2.

These results suggest that, for decisions about taking violent collective action, spread of support is as important as the threat and more important than efficacy. Strength of identity (durability) is a relatively unimportant consideration in these sorts of decisions, irrespective of whether it is high (primary identity) or low (one of several identities). It seems that the severity of the threat and spread of support are the primary drivers or sources for these decisions. We turn now to the results for the non-violent action scenarios.

The scaled weights for non-violent actions are shown in Table 10.2. The key findings are summarized as follows:

1. Durability of identity is most important in the two scenarios where identity variables are geared toward encouraging non-violent protests.
2. The severity of the threat is most important in the two scenarios where the context variables are geared toward taking non-violent actions.
3. The other three variables, readiness, spread, and political system, are inconsistent from one scenario to another.

This is the only type of collective action where durability of identity is a strong influence on decisions. When the constituent population consists mostly of patriots,

Table 10.2 Non-violent action scenarios[a]

All variables geared toward action (n = 13):	
Durability	1
Threat	0.84
Spread	0.51
System	0.33
Readiness	0.29
All variables geared toward inaction (n = 12):	
Spread	1
Readiness	0.78
Durability	0.60
Threat	0.42
System	0.05
Context geared toward action, identity toward inaction (n = 16):	
Threat	1
Spread	0.88
System	0.87
Readiness	0.54
Durability	0.22
Context geared toward inaction, identity toward action (n = 13):	
Durability	1
Readiness	0.84
System	0.80
Threat	0.54
Spread	0.46

[a]Each calculated weight is subtracted from 1 in order to present a descending order of importance, from higher to lower weights.

decisions are based primarily on this information. As in the other types of collective actions, threat is important, but only in the scenarios where the threat is serious. Spread is less important in these scenarios than it is for the other types of actions. However, the effects of spread, like readiness and political system, are inconsistent. We turn now to the results from the humanitarian action scenarios.

The weights for the humanitarian action scenarios are shown in Table 10.3. The key findings are as follows:

1. The motivational variable (economy) is consistently strong.
2. Spread is also consistently strong, and is very strong in scenario 4.
3. Readiness is inconsistent, it flip flops from being strong in scenarios 1 and 2 (geared either toward or away from taking action) to be generally weak in the mixed scenarios 3 and 4.
4. Durability and political system are relatively weak in each of the scenarios.
5. The largest split between the variables occurs in scenario 1 but an interesting split occurs also in scenario 4, where spread sits alone at the top.

These results on humanitarian actions are more remarkable for their similarities than for their differences to those obtained with the violent-action scenarios.

Table 10.3 Humanitarian action scenarios[a]

All factors geared toward action (n = 15):	
Readiness/efficacy	2[a]
Economy	1.80
Spread	1.73
System	0.91
Durability	0.62
All factors geared toward inaction (n = 15):	
Economy	2
Readiness/efficacy	1.93
Spread	1.87
Durability	1.73
System	1.63
Context geared toward action, identity geared toward inaction (n = 15):	
Economy	2
Spread	1.92
System	1.68
Durability	1.65
Readiness/efficacy	1.50
Context geared toward inaction, identity geared toward action (n = 15):	
Spread	2
Economy	1.70
System	1.58
Readiness/efficacy	1.55
Durability	1.44

[a]Each calculated weight is subtracted from 2 in order to present a descending order of importance, from higher to lower weights.

In both, the motivational variable is consistently strong, whether defined as a threat (violent scenario) or in terms of the economy (humanitarian scenario). Spread is consistently strong for both types of actions, with the strongest effects in the mixed scenarios 3 and 4. Readiness is similarly inconsistent for both types of collective action, but is stronger in scenarios 1 and 2 than in 3 and 4.

Discussion

The purpose of this study is to discover patterns in decision making for collective action. The patterns emerged from judgments made by a large number of respondents, each of whom played a role of policy maker in 1 of 12 constructed situations (four configurations for each of three types of collective actions).

The pattern highlights three of the five variables: motivation, spread of support, and durability of identity. Motivation and spread are the primary drivers of decisions for both violent and humanitarian actions. These variables have dominant effects across the four scenarios, whether they are geared toward action (severe threat, widespread support) or inaction (modest threat, limited support). These findings suggest a general, *two-factor theory of action.* Further experimentation by the authors showed that these variables are the key influences on action decisions taken in external conflicts. Both the violent and humanitarian action scenarios involved external problems. This suggests that decision-makers may be responding primarily to the external feature of these problems, rather than to their source.

Durability plays an important role in decisions to take non-violent actions. This variable is dominant when it is geared in the direction of taking action (primary identity for a patriotic population) but not when it is geared toward inaction (one of several identities, a population of internationalists). Similarly, motivation, defined as severity of the threat, is a strong influence on decisions only when the threat is severe. These findings suggest a contingency theory of action: Durability and motivation are drivers *under some circumstances*. Further experimentation by the authors showed that durability and threat were the primary drivers on decisions to act within the nation. Thus, the key distinction for actions may be between external (violent and humanitarian scenarios) and internal (non-violent scenario) actions.

The condition of severe threat makes identity variables less important or not important at all. This finding is corroborated by findings from studies on crisis decision-making. These studies show that in crisis situations (i.e., severe threat to one's existence) there is a contraction in the decision-making unit (Hermann 1972; Lebow 1981). This implies that during such times decision-makers largely ignore their constituencies' preferences. This may be the reason why identity variables were trumped by motivation in most of the scenarios. Future research should explore this link in real life settings. Another important implication of this finding is that severe threat may increase or interact with the strength of group identification and thus lead to stronger support for violent collective action.

These findings suggest the following set of hypotheses:

1. Motivation in the form of threat will drive decisions about taking violent actions against the source of threat.
2. Motivation in the form of economic development and experience will influence the decision to participate in humanitarian missions.
3. Spread in the form of population support for action will drive decisions about taking violent actions against the source of the threat.
4. Spread in the form of population support for humanitarian missions will influence the decision to undertake those missions.
5. Durability in the form of primary identity will influence decisions to organize for non-violent protests.
6. Motivation in the form of severity of threat will drive decisions to organize for non-violent protests.
7. Type of political system (as democratic or authoritarian) will be a less-important influence on decisions to take violent, non-violent, and humanitarian collective actions.

The seventh hypothesis is worth elaborating further, especially in light of the arguments advanced on democratic peace theory. Contradicting the arguments from this theory, we found that political system/regime type was not ranked as a primary constraint on decision-making. Although we did not conduct interviews, we can suggest possible reasons for this finding. One explanation is that only in dyadic relations, democracies constrain decisions for violent collective action (Russett 1993). Since we did not describe the political system of the target of decision in our study, this may be the case. Alternatively, our findings may be supporting those studies that challenge the democratic peace theory based on the argument that the theory overlooked instances of coercive actions short of formal war. Hermann and Kegley (1995) suggest that there are numerous incidents of democratic states intervening with military force against other democracies. Since our scenarios deal with the decision for taking violent action rather than the act itself, this may be plausible. In any case, our finding encourages further inquiry on this matter. The inquiry will contribute to the scholarly debate regarding the factors that prevent democratic states from going to war with each other.

A final hypothesis is as follows:

8. Readiness for action will be a less-important influence on decisions to take violent, non-violent, or humanitarian actions.

With regard to the importance of identity variables, spread of support appears to be the key driver (along with motivation) of decisions. Durability comes into play but only in a contingent way for non-violent actions. We would conclude that the role played by some identity variables is as significant as that played by some context variables, and is a more important influence on decisions than readiness to act. However, there remains much to be learned about these variables.

The findings can also be interpreted in terms of levers for action. Policy-makers can energize their own populations by manufacturing severe threats and rallying citizen support. They may provoke other nations by posing a severe threat to those with strongly patriotic populations. The Iraq wars are examples. But, they may also encourage support from other nations for their own plight by appealing to developed countries with a history of, and widespread support for, aid. The Tsunami crisis is an example.

The issue of relevance is addressed in terms of a familiar process of thinking about policy and action. The idea of "what…if" futuristic thinking was introduced at the beginning of this chapter. An attempt was made in this study to reproduce this form of thinking in the context of scenarios. Relevance – or verisimilitude – to real-world decision-making is enhanced to the extent that we have captured this process. This can be known only by comparing results reported here with data collected from foreign policy decision-makers. Similar results would support relevance. However, it would be interesting to know whether our linear model captures the way they process the scenario information. Questions about how the information was used in arriving at action decisions would be helpful. It would also be interesting to know what other types of information about populations influence their decisions: Is our distinction between context and identity relevant? Are these the key contextual and identity variables? Answers to these questions would contribute to revisions in our framework and to the content of the scenarios.

The relevance question also turns on our conception of decision-makers as negotiating representatives. In this role they are responsive to the preferences of constituents. Preferences are expressed in the form of motivation to act, durability, and spread of identity. The motivation and spread variables were shown to influence decisions in the violent and humanitarian action scenarios; durability influenced non-violent action decisions. The other variables – efficacy and type of political system – had less impact. These results suggest that the role-players were influenced more by constituents' preferences to act or restrain from acting than by organizational and systemic factors. They highlight the representational role features of decision-making, and, thus, the relevance of negotiation models. Whether these models also depict decisions made by the actual policy-makers remains to be investigated.

More practically, the findings have implications for the interface between constituents (or stakeholders) and their representatives. One implication is for the monitoring function in negotiation. Information about motivation and identities helps to formulate negotiation strategies. They also insure that decisions (or concessions) made will resonate with the represented populations. Another implication is for mobilization. Popular collective action decisions facilitate the task of mobilizing citizens to take action, whether military, non-violent, or humanitarian. However, these types of actions may present different mobilization challenges.

A number of next steps are suggested by the findings. One question to be asked concerns the sequencing of decisions: In what order is the information about these variables processed on the way to making decisions? This can be assessed with a decision task where respondents are asked to report on how they use the information in making decisions. Another question concerns interactive or correlated effects: Does a severe (non-severe) threat serve to mobilize (discourage) support for an action? Is widespread (limited) support easier to mobilize with nationalistic (internationalist) populations? This can be discovered with a factorial design that allows for all combinations of the key variables.

The scenario results alert us to focus on the motivational and spread variables. Cases can be selected in each of four combinations of these variables: high on motivation, high on spread; low motivation, low spread, and the two mixed combinations. These variables can also be explored with a large sampling of cases. Emphasizing the generality of findings, a broad sampling of cases can also be used for modeling.

The generality issue can be addressed with other types of populations. It would be advantageous to recruit policy makers and/or experts to respond to the same scenarios. The policy makers are those with experience in foreign policy departments of governments. The experts are academics specializing in problems of international collective action. An advantage of our approach to data collection is that judgments can be made in a short amount of time. A problem is that we will not have the captive population of respondents provided by university classes. To an extent, this problem can be overcome by administering all the scenarios and actions to each expert. The data would be analyzed as repeated measures, providing us with similar comparisons to those made with the large student population. Of interest is the question of whether the motivational and spread variables are also judged by them to be the key drivers of action decisions.

Appendix

The Situation

You are a national decision-maker from Canasia, which has a democratically elected government where citizens are encouraged but not required to show loyalty to the State. You are faced with the following situation and must make a decision.

A far away country, Asghania, is a failed state and relies on the support of the international community, including your country, to provide security and to distribute humanitarian aid to its impoverished people, whose survival is threatened by the local warlords in the country. Your country is a well-developed nation, which historically has been a contributor to international peacekeeping and humanitarian operations. Your military and civilian support agencies are well-trained in peacekeeping and humanitarian operations. Public opinion polls show that there is widespread support among your citizens for sending your peacekeepers on a humanitarian mission to Asghania, and most of your citizens regard their national identity as one of their several group identities. The majority of your citizens regard themselves as internationalists.

You must now decide whether you want to send your peacekeepers on a costly humanitarian mission to Asghania that aims at providing security and humanitarian assistance to the people there. Based on the information you received above, will you send your military and civilian peacekeepers to Asghania or not take any action at all? (Circle one).

You will notice that there are five underlined elements in this situation. These must be taken into account in making your decision: *your nation's political system, the economic situation and the historical record of your country, the training and readiness of your peacekeepers, the spread of support throughout your population for your actions, and the strength of your citizens' identity within the nation.* We ask you to compare these features of the situation in terms of their relative importance in influencing your decision. This is done with the following procedure.

The matrix below lists each of the elements along the side and at the top. You will compare each element with each of the other elements as a pair-wise comparison. For example, if you think that your nation's political system is a more important influence on your decision than the economic situation and historical record of the country, circle *more*; if the peacekeeper's readiness is less important than the spread of support, circle *less*. Please make a decision of more or less influence on your decision for each of the ten comparisons. Remember you are being asked to compare the row factor with each factor in the four columns.

References

Aquilar, F., & Galluccio, M. (2008). *Psychological processes in international negotiations: Theoretical and practical perspectives*. New York: Springer.

Bremer, S. (1980). National capabilities and war proneness. In J. D. Singer (Ed.), *The correlates of war II: Testing some realpolitik models* (pp. 57–82). New York: Free Press.

Bueno de Mesquita, B. (1981). Risk, power distributions, and the likelihood of war. *International Studies Quarterly, 25*, 541–68.

Collier, P. A., & Hoeffler, A. (2001). *Greed and grievance in civil war. World Bank policy research working paper 2355*. Washington: World Bank.

Collier, P., Hoeffler, A., & Sambanis, N. (2005). The Collier-Hoeffler model of civil war onset and the case study project research design. In P. Collier & N. Sambanis (Eds.), *Understanding civil war: Evidence and analysis*. Washington: World Bank.

Druckman, D. (1977). Boundary role conflict: Negotiation as dual responsiveness. *Journal of Conflict Resolution, 21*, 639–662.

Druckman, D. (1993). The situational levers of negotiating flexibility. *Journal of Conflict Resolution, 37*, 236–276.

Druckman, D. (2001). Negotiation and identity: Implications for negotiation theory. *International Negotiation, 6*, 281–291.

Ellemers, N. (2002). Social identity and relative deprivation. In I. Walker & H. J. Smith (Eds.), *Relative deprivation: Specification, development, and integration*. Cambridge: Cambridge University Press.

Guilford, J. P. (1954). *Psychometric methods*. New York: McGraw-Hill.

Gurr, T. R. (1993). *Minorities at risk: A global view of ethnopolitical conflicts*. Washington: US Institute of Peace.

Gurr, T. R. (2000). *Peoples versus states: Minorities at risk in the new century*. Washington: US Institute of Peace.

Gurr, T. R., & Davies, J. (2002). Dynamics and management of ethnopolitical conflicts. In J. Davis & E. Kaufman (Eds.), *Second track/citizens' diplomacy*. New York: Rowman & Littlefield.

Hermann, C. (1972). *International crises: Insights from behavioural research*. New York: Free Press.

Hermann, M. G., & Kegley, C. W., Jr. (1995). Rethinking democracy and international peace: Perspectives from political psychology. *International Studies Quarterly, 39*, 511–534.

Hogg, M. A., & Abrams, D. (1988). *Social identifications: A social psychology of intergroup relations and group processes*. London: Routledge.

Lebow, R. N. (1981). *Between peace and war: The nature of international crises*. Baltimore: Johns Hopkins University Press.

Lichbach, M. (1990). Will rational people rebel against inequality? Samson's Choice. *American Journal of Political Science, 34*, 1049–1076.

Lichbach, M. (1994). What makes rational peasants revolutionary? Dilemma, paradox, and irony in peasant collective action. *World Politics, 46*, 383–418.

Maoz, Z. (1989). Power, capabilities, and paradoxical conflict outcomes. *World Politics, 41*, 239–66.

Maoz, Z., & Abdolai, N. (1989). Regime types and international conflict, 1816–1976. *Journal of Conflict Resolution, 33*, 3–35.

McCarthy, J., & Zald, M. (1977). Resource mobilization and social movements: A partial theory. *American Journal of Sociology, 82*, 1212–1241.

Reynal-Querol, M. (2002). Ethnicity, political systems, and civil war. *Journal of Conflict Resolution, 46*, 29–54.

Rummel, R. J. (1995). Democracies are less warlike than other regimes. *European Journal of International Relations, 1*, 457–479.

Russett, B. M. (1993). *Grasping the democratic peace: Principles for a post-cold war*. Princeton: Princeton University Press.

Singer, J. D., Bremer, S., & Stuckey, J. (1972). Capability distribution, uncertainty, and major power war, 1820-1965. In B. Russett (Ed.), *Peace, war, and numbers* (pp. 19–48). Beverly Hills: Sage.

Tilly, C. (1978). *From mobilization to revolution*. Reading: Addision-Wesley.

Tropp, L. R., & Wright, S. C. (1999). Ingroup identification and relative deprivation: An examination across multiple social comparisons. *European Journal of Social Psychology, 29*, 707–724.

Turner, J. C., Hogg, M. A., Oakes, P. J., Reicher, S. D., & Wetherell, M. S. (1987). *Rediscovering the social group: A self categorization theory*. Oxford: Blackwell.

Waltz, K.N. (1990). Realist thought and meorealist theory. *Journal of International Affairs, 44*, 21–37.

Wright, S., & Tropp, L. (2002). Collective action in response to disadvantage. In I. Walker & H. J. Smith (Eds.), *Relative deprivation: Specification, development, and integration*. Cambridge: Cambridge University Press.

Wright, S., Taylor, D. M., & Moghaddam, F. M. (1990). Responding to membership in a disadvantaged group: From acceptance to collective protest. *Journal of Personality and Social Psychology, 58*, 994–1003.

Chapter 11
Ideal Negotiator: A Personal Formula for the New International System

Victor Kremenyuk

Since the advent of the notion of "practical negotiator" (Zartman and Berman 1982) the majority of those who work in the field of negotiation analysis have been using this concept as the mainstream of thinking. A "practical negotiator" is not necessarily one who fanatically preaches negotiation; he/she simply understands the importance of an agreement and is ready to undertake necessary steps to achieve a negotiated solution.

This is quite understandable if one remembers the time and strategic conditions under which the concept was born: the Cold War at the moment when, due to the unbridled arms race, both superpowers had achieved a rough parity in their enormous destructive capabilities and, at the same time, the legitimate questions on the controllability of these capabilities appeared. Were the human systems controlling the weapons or, this time, was it the weapons that controlled the human decision-making? Under these conditions, understanding the necessity to search for negotiated solutions looked absolutely logical, and the conclusion was: Whether you like to negotiate or not, you have to look for practical negotiable solutions as a means to avoid disaster.

The whole culture of the study of international negotiations was born on the basis of this principle. In essence, it was an implementation of T. Schelling's postulate, which did not exclude negotiation as an instrument of strategy in conflict under conditions where the use of force was either counter-productive or irrelevant (Schelling 1960). In this case negotiation was not so much a desirable or a preferable means to resolve a conflict but more an unavoidable choice. Following this conclusion, a "practical negotiator" was one who understood the necessity to negotiate as a means of a strategy in conflict without sharing the values of non-violence. Negotiation was recognized and legitimized, parallel to coercion, as an appropriate strategy for winning a conflict.

This reasonable and ethically appropriate idea was in essence a development of the age-old approach which dominated at that time human thinking and human relations.

V. Kremenyuk (✉)
Institute for USA and Canada studies, Russian Academy of Sciences, Russian Federation
Moscow 12399, Khlebny pereulok 2/3
e-mail: vkremenyuk@gmail.com

F. Aquilar and M. Galluccio (eds.), *Psychological and Political Strategies for Peace Negotiation*, DOI 10.1007/978-1-4419-7430-3_11,

Due to the specifics of human nature and human history violence was traditionally considered an "ultimo ratio" as a solution to a disputable problem. Though the teachings of the Holy Bible and hundreds of cases testified against the use of force and gave direct evidence that violence was leading only to a protracted struggle rather than to peace and prosperity, still the types of authority which dominated preferred violence and not negotiation as a means to promote their interests.

Pleas by the Messiah or people like Immanuel Kant to change this mindset and to recognize the relevance of agreement as a full-size alternative to violence were falling on deaf ears. It was only under the threat of an all-out nuclear war that the leaders and thinkers have turned to the idea of negotiation as an equal, and even preferable, tool of national strategy. From this point of view the concept of "practical negotiator" has played a role as a bridge between the position in which violence acquired the role of ultimate arbiter and the policy in which negotiation has become preferable in strategic interaction.

In the real world this turn was associated with the US President Richard Nixon Doctrine (1969–1974), which declared an "era of negotiations" as one of the major tools of US policy in relations with the USSR, China, Cuba, and other former enemies. The concept of "practical negotiator" has helped adherents of the power policy to swallow the bitter lesson of the nuclear stalemate and to agree that in the long run negotiation was "not worse" than weapons. And then something unexpected happened to the "era of negotiations." Soviet–US negotiations on managing the risk of inadvertent nuclear war and arms control, attempts to find peaceful solutions to the long-term conflicts in Korea, the Middle East, the Indian Sub-continent, and the former Yugoslavia have revealed that the "practical negotiator" approach was rather ineffective.

It helped to identify problems, it helped to achieve a common understanding of the issues to be solved but, at the same time, it didn't lead to durable solutions. Relations between the USA and Russia, the USA and China, the state of major regional conflicts, issues born of NATO enlargement in Europe did not bring robust solutions and were on the brink of a reversal back to the Cold War. There were dozens of explanations for these facts and among them, as the issue to be studied in this paper, the inadequacy of the "practical negotiator" approach. The is a need to look for something more appropriate, maybe the concept of the "ideal negotiator," which has appeared both as a practical and a theoretical task. And to a certain extent it demanded a thorough reappraisal of the existing experience rather than simply suggesting an alternative idea.

Two Sides of Negotiation

H. Raiffa from the Harvard University School of Business Management in his book on negotiations identifies two sides of the subject: art and science of negotiation (Raiffa 1984). He speaks of negotiation as an "art," a creative activity with a hardly predictable outcome, based on human inspiration and divine guidance, an act of "virtue." At the same time he perceives negotiation as "science," as a result of a systematic study that leads to the accumulation of knowledge, identification of regularities, and achievement of verifiable results. Actually he echoes some thinkers of the past, such as Niccolo Machiavelli or Phillippe de Commines, who supposed that a human being, having an immortal soul and mortal substance, has a dual nature: the ability for creativity, which comes from the divine father, and common sense inherited from his or her earthly parents. Both are demonstrated in the process of negotiation.

Russian poet Alexander Pushkin, in one of his "little tragedies," studies the distinction between inspiration and labor. Mozart and Salieri, two opposing types of creators, identify the duality of the human artistic performance. Mozart has a divine-inspired talent; his music comes from the heaven. He is an instrument of God. The people feel happy when they hear his music. Antonio Salieri, a man of virtue who studied music all his life, who "analyzed the music like mathematics" and worked hard for many long days to create even a small musical piece. Two dramatically different types of creativeness in which one, that of the divine origin, always wins over in human inspiration while the other, being a result of hard work, will always be second ("There is no justice on earth," says Salieri. And then continues: "And even higher, in the heavens, it also does not exist"). This "injustice," as Salieri puts it, has to be corrected, and that is why he decides to kill his friend. He takes the job of correcting the "mistake" of the God. But Mozart before his death tells him something that destroys all Salieri's chances for justice: "A genius (if he is a creation of God) cannot be evil."

The dual nature of human creativity has a direct application to negotiation. Negotiation, as any other type of human performance or thinking in general, comes into the realm of creative human activity. It is based to a large extent on the search for a creative solution because theoretically there may be two different types of outcomes in any negotiation: a symmetrical outcome, based on equality of the parties, which finds an algorithm to balance their interests (usually we call it a "just solution"), and an asymmetrical outcome in which one side, using its assets, forces the other to agree to the proposed solution, ignoring the necessity to respect the interests of the other side. From this point of view, negotiation must acquire the qualities of creativity in order to produce an agreement that will survive the understandable challenges to its relevance once the agreement is concluded.

It is hard to split negotiation into two separate parts following its dual nature. They are in negotiation as hydrogen and oxygen in water: Both are there, but if you separate them water disappears. What can and may take place in the understanding of the two sides of negotiation is the ratio between the two parts, art and science – the proportion in which they are mixed. If creativity prevails, the negotiation acquires a certain quality of genuine arbiter between the two contending parties to the general satisfaction. If the other quality – rationality – prevails then the negotiation may very easily become a tool of injustice simply because very often the participants have different understandings of rationality.

The real problem for those who study and teach negotiation is, first, how to identify these two sides and, second, how to manage them every time the dosage of each of the two elements changes, depending on the type of problem, type of partners, and the type of process. This is not something that may be directed administratively or through a prescription. You may teach people how to write and to read, but in order to make them poets something else is needed. The same happens with negotiators: You may teach the students basics of this profession, but only experience, inspiration, and spiritual guidance will make them creative diplomats. This means, at least, that in order to make negotiation an acceptable and effective management tool one has to recognize the scope and character of the problem on which effective negotiation depends.

Scope and character are conditioned by the basic fact that negotiation is, first of all, an element of governance of relations between sovereign entities – be they individuals, companies, institutions, or nations – and a certain way of interaction which has, as its ultimate goal, to settle disputes and other differences through a joint agreement. All of these elements can be studied and explained since they do not demand anything supernatural. While the situation between the interacting parties develops along regular lines it may be dealt with through the use of regular means. And it is a totally different thing when, due to various reasons, the situation develops in a critical way that demands mobilization of all possible resources and knowledge.

In international relations these situations happen rather often, reflecting the inequality of the actors, their ethical standards, and their doctrines. Negotiation has to play the role of "equalizer," making the two or more sides interested in a joint decision, but in reality, reflecting an aggressive and incessant human desire for domination, it suffers the consequences of the inequality and inability of those who are weak to resist the pressure of the stronger. And here the necessity of a good and skillful negotiator becomes critical. As an example, the case of the famous French diplomat Charles Talleyrand may be quoted as well as his magnificent negotiation skills, which permitted him to defend the legitimate interests of the defeated France at the Vienna Congress in 1815. The art and inspiration of Talleyrand defeated the rude power of the winners.

So, contrary to many statements by those who preach power and coercion, negotiation may acquire the qualities of a true power if used appropriately and in relevant conditions. This is not the "power of the weak"; it is the "power of the wise." This is the game of chess-players – not of boxers. But to make it a powerful weapon for the defense of one's legitimate interests and of the truth, negotiation has to be carefully studied and applied to different human psychological qualities. First of all, it should be understood that the "practical negotiator" approach ceases to be useful and applicable in this case. Both students and practitioners of the negotiation must go much further in understanding the essence of negotiations and the performance of the person who is engaged in this activity and wants to master it. Something like the refresher course "Getting to Yes" (Fisher and Ury 1981) plus additional psychological training are needed (Aquilar and Galluccio 2008).

Three Dimensions of Negotiation as the Beginning

A thorough analysis of negotiation gives an interesting picture of three different dimensions that constitute together a process of negotiation as such. First, negotiation plays a role as a tool of a strategy of conflict resolution. Second, negotiation plays the role of a decision-making procedure in which two or more actors are involved. And third, negotiation plays the role of a channel of communication between the actors engaged in negotiation. This assessment of the process of negotiation has already been described (Kremenyuk 2005) and includes both a new vision of the negotiation and new possibilities for its study. It also provides a chance to explore depths of the negotiation analysis that were not open for scrutiny until now. What was traditionally known about negotiation was that it was a part of the diplomatic skill set. What has been added to it now is that it is a much more universal process of human interaction in which different aspects of activity join each other in one process.

When negotiation is regarded as a tool, an instrument in the implementation of a certain strategy of conflict resolution, it gives a better explanation of several things: participants (who are to be engaged), issues in question (what is to be discussed) and desirable outcome (what is to be achieved). It establishes a logical relation between two points of departure: first, the initial stage at which involved parties agree to begin contacts with the purpose of finding a solution to the disputed problem and, second, the last stage at which they agree that what they have come to is the last possible collective solution ("how to make an agreement possible").

At the initial stage they agree to negotiate the issue where their interests come into conflict and where no one can count on a unilateral solution. At the concluding stage they agree that the outcome is the best that they can produce together even if the "child" of this "marriage" is "ugly" – that is even if the agreement they have come to is worse than any unilateral solution.

When negotiation is regarded as a decision-making process (an "interactive" process as H. Raiffa calls it) it provides another chance to analyze the process as such. First of all, the negotiation strategies are to be identified and studied: The priorities of each side, the "rate of exchange" between different components of the negotiation position, a sequence of actions in the process of bargaining, the shape of a possible agreement. This point of the negotiation is one of the most important in the whole endeavor: It may and will help to understand the process of making a deal in negotiation, explaining the difference between the "ideal" solution that could be theoretically suggested by the experts as the goal of the strategy of solution and the "real world" solution, which may be achieved between contenders who are torn between the desire to win as much as possible and not to lose an opportunity to negotiate a deal.

The third part of the process we call a "channel of communication." Here there may be a disagreement because in some negotiation cultures, for example in American culture, the priority is given unequivocally to the deal, to the result: "If there is an agreement the negotiation is considered successful, if not – it failed." This is a rather widespread argument by American experts who share completely the values of their negotiation culture mainly based on business experience rather than on the experience of diplomacy. In business, more that in any other sphere of human relationship, the value of the contract is the highest: no contract – no negotiation.

In older diplomatic cultures (in Europe it is Italian or French, in Asia it is Chinese) the essence of the negotiation is not so much concentrated on the outcome but on the process itself. It permits to establish closer and more fruitful links between the partners, or give a chance to become friends (or at least to know each other better), to create a certain "monde," a world of people who live in one sphere of interests and profession, who find a pleasure in diplomatic games, who sometimes really achieve the possibility of working together to give each other a chance to win and a chance to be friends. Negotiation combines all of these different aspects of diplomatic or business activity. What is interesting for the purposes of research is both to identify these dimensions and to establish the way they come together in one process. Here the type of culture (in both senses – a general culture of civilization and the culture of diplomacy) becomes crucial.

All these aspects depend on the type of administrative and political regime back at home: In a democracy the processes that shape the negotiation behavior and changes in position are totally different from those in a totalitarian system where very often one person decides the final shape of the position of the nation. It also depends on the tradition and previous experience of the nation: As one example of the negotiation position former Soviet foreign minister Andrei Gromyko (Mr. Nyet) may be quoted. His typical behavior was to meet any initiative of the West with skepticism, even when it was for the benefit of all (as it was in the Helsinki process). As a result, one may see the elements of the "nyet" approach in the negative response by the Russian military and diplomats to US proposals on the anti-missile system in Europe, which is supposed to defend European cities against possible terrorist launches that threaten Russian cities no less than the European.

The process of pre-negotiation (preparation of the negotiation, identification of the initial process, of the priorities, and even of the negotiations) rather substantially describes the beginning of the negotiation and of the way its different dimensions are shaped: type of decision-making at home, type of historical traditions and type of diplomatic culture. What it does not explain and does not prescribe is the type of negotiator, which is needed for a successful outcome, and the type of behavior of the negotiator – in short, the "homo negotiatus" (the negotiating man) who can implement both recommendations of science and demands of diplomacy.

This is one of the problems that is not easily solved because there are two different approaches to the subject. On one hand, there is a rather popular position which states that "anyone can be a negotiator" once he/she is trained appropriately. This is the axiom of the authors of "Getting to Yes." W. Ury and R. Fisher wrote their book with the conviction that it opens a way to everyone who wants to become a negotiator. This is understandable because the market economy of the West and availability of resources provide a possibility for ordinary people to acquire abilities to negotiate their jobs, their salaries, their homes, their purchases, their insurance, and many other aspects of their lives, which is still rather unknown in countries with limited resources (and they constitute the vast majority of the planet's six billion population). I had a chance to mention all that in the introduction to the Russian translation of their book.

But this level of understanding problem somehow overshadows the real importance of the negotiation process. In the globalizing world, which is sharply divided into "haves" and "have-nots," where the resources, industrial as well as natural, are spread unequally, where the ideas of equality and equity have became dominant, the negotiation has acquired a totally new quality. Traditionally, search for power by the monarchs and democratic leaders was justified by the necessity to correct the divine "injustice" whereby some nations possessed enormous resources because of their geography while the others, rather hardworking and industrious, had almost no resources and had to import vitally needed articles – from fuels to food. The evolution of the world in twentieth century has given a good example of the futility of attempts to correct this "injustice" through the use of force. Instead, it suggested the use of negotiation if people want to change conditions: The case of OPEC is good evidence of the triumph of negotiation over violence in the redistribution of income, which flows into the countries rich in energy resources.

When negotiation is raised to the level of global (or almost global) governance, it is clear that the whole approach to it has to be changed: operationally, fundamentally, and even psychologically. "Practical negotiator" ceases to satisfy the demand and something new has to be introduced. This "new" has to relate to a perfection of the planning procedure in working out an appropriate strategy to solve the disputed problem. Since negotiation is a tool born of the realization of such a strategy it must have, instead of a double-use (for both violent and non-violent cases), a new one, oriented only to non-violent, negotiable, mutually acceptable, and cooperative strategy. This strategy has to formulate clearly what has to be negotiated and what should be the outcome (with possible variations of the outcome).

Equally, the decision-making procedure at the negotiation has to be re-identified. One of the most crucial elements of this aspect is the relation between the negotiator and decision-maker back at home, a "double-decked structure" (Putnam 1988). The negotiator who is supposed to follow prescriptions from his government must have a certain freedom of action in order to contribute to the process of negotiation and to the shape of the final agreement. For different reasons, including the spirit of solidarity, the contents of the final agreement may be different from what was originally formulated by the national decision-makers. The negotiator must see sufficient possibilities to avoid a permanent feeling that his actions are constrained by unnecessary controls (in addition to that he is actively supervised by the media and an interested expert community). There should be some definite rules that establish the division of labor and responsibility between a negotiator and his or her bosses.

Finally, the process of communication has also to be reassessed. It is one thing when actors representing the same cultural or civilizational background come to negotiations: They have a common frame of reference. Very often when even such seemingly hostile actors as the Communists (while the Communist world existed) and their Western partners were negotiating some cultural proximity helped them to understand each other (in the long run, Marxism was the product of the Western Christian thinking). But what to say of current times when in international affairs the agents of completely different cultures and civilizations meet as equal partners?

And the problem is not only in the differences in negotiating styles; this was more or less studied at the appropriate time (Binnendijk 1987). The problem is in the fact that different civilizations with sometimes opposite values and absolutely unequal historical backgrounds meet and try to find a common ground. That is a real problem of today's governance and world integrity.

Some New Elements of the Setting

The end of the Cold War has produced significant changes in the structure of the world community, in the scope of issues, which acquire additional importance, and in the ways nations communicate. There is a vast group of developed "rich" nations, headed by the United States as their senior ally and integrated into various alliances among themselves: NATO as a mechanism of security in the Euro-Atlantic zone; the European Union as a mechanism of economic and political integration on the European continent; alliances between the United States and some important nations of the Asian-Pacific zone (Japan, the Republic of Korea, Taiwan, Australia, New Zealand); the Organization of American States in the Western hemisphere. All of these nations have gone rather far in the process of integration, and negotiation has become a part of their day-to-day lives, for example in the European Union (Cede and Meerts 2004). This does not mean that they do not need any perfection in their decision-making mechanism, but it definitely means that in their part of the world negotiation is something working, regular, and a part of the social psychology.

There is a vast group of the so-called "transitional" states that have chosen to pursue economic and social reforms and try to find a solution to their domestic problems (food, housing, transportation, communication, education, health) through modernization and intensification of their advancement rather than through wars and violent acquisitions. These nations have a double-type contact with the outside world: First, they want to learn from the experience of the developed nations and to borrow from it for their purposes, including investment, technology transfer, and access to markets; and, second, they want to acquire their "legitimate" place in the contemporary world and its institutions where the West continues to play the dominant role: the World Trade Organization (WTO), the Organization of Economic Cooperation and Development (OECD), and G-8.

Besides, they have numerous subjects for negotiation among themselves because the state of their relations may be clearly characterized as a conflict-cooperation model: conflict because of competition for foreign resources and cooperation in their desire to change the existing rules of the world market and world policy in their favor. As a result, they have two major negotiation areas: with the developed nations and among themselves. Both areas are very intensive and important for the future prospects of these nations. Depending on the results of their interaction they may either make a breakthrough comparable to the economic and social success of Germany, Italy, and Japan after World War II and, thus, join the group of developed nations, or create an international group comparable to NATO or OECD that will defend their legitimate interests in confronting the West.

There are also two other groups of nations: "traditionalist" (mainly the countries of Islam) and "failed," sources of illegal immigration, drug production and traffic, and terrorism. The most outstanding partner for negotiation among them is of course the Islamic nations. The oil-producing Islamic nations, members of OPEC, are the long-time negotiation partners of the West, and this part functions regularly. But some other areas of negotiation in this part of the world are far from being satisfactory and, on the contrary, demonstrate a rigid and stable refusal to accept the negotiation that the West tries to impose as a solution of their problems. First of all, it is the Arab–Israeli conflict over Palestine, but it is also the issues of Iran, India–Pakistan, as well as the issue of non-proliferation of weapons of mass destruction.

These are four major groups of nations that have problems to negotiate, both inside each group individually and among all of them. In the conditions of the globalizing world and growing interdependence they constitute potentially stable and identifiable areas of negotiation that demand recruitment of professional and devoted negotiators.

The general conditions for negotiations have also changed since the end of Cold War. First, it is the diminishing importance of the global balance of strategic weapons. Both the United States and Russia still possess enormous arsenals of these weapons and even declare readiness to develop new types. In reality the importance of strategic weapons in the current world has changed: While in North–North relations it is fixed at a certain level and has even gone down, in the South its importance grows. India and Pakistan have become a nuclear dyad threatening to unleash a war one day. Iran and North Korea are actively interested in acquiring nuclear capabilities. All in all, it creates a certain perspective for negotiations between different actors in strange constellations: "six" on the Korean nuclear program (the United States, China, Russia, Japan, and the two Koreas); five permanent members of the UN Security Council and Germany on the Iranian nuclear program; Russia and the United States on monitoring the production and distribution of nuclear fissile materials, and so on.

Second, is the general attitude toward the use of military force. It may seem strange but it was the experience of the great powers, the USA and the Soviet Union, which has already raised the questions of relevance to the power policy. Both superpowers were defeated militarily in Vietnam (USA) and Afghanistan (USSR). Both tried to explain their failures by the indirect intervention of the other side and its assistance to the enemy. But the case of Iraq has cleared up this conclusion almost completely: Under current conditions even a striking asymmetry in the military capabilities does not necessarily lead to victory. Something has happened with the role of the military force, and its traditional niche in the governance of events has to be filled by some other means.

Third, the role of international law was expected to grow while the power policy was losing its attractiveness. But, instead, it has revealed that the current law in which the role of sovereignty has played such a pivotal concept also needs changes. The most evident example is the case of "failed" states. They simply need assistance in governance like bankrupt companies. Someone – the UN, NATO, developed states – has to take care of their security, economy, finance, administration, health, education, etc., disregarding the fact that they are considered sovereign states. The feeling of morality does not permit the more developed nations to watch what is happening in these countries without an attempt to interfere. In a more general way, the state of human rights and freedoms, which have been declared by UN Charter to be universal values, and their abuse in individual countries, also raises the issue of the relevance of current norms of international law.

Fourth, while the above-mentioned changes happened, there is a growing sense of planetary solidarity and global values. The majority of the nations, including "transitional" and "traditionalist," want development and social progress. Vast sums are invested in these countries' futures: infrastructure, education, human capital, and development strategies. They need and want free access to the common values of humankind, to the fruits of culture and science, to the information technologies. And that creates a new agenda for discussions and a new set of demands that have to be satisfied in the interests of all.

All these aspects elevate the importance of negotiation as a major tool in the governance of the global issues.

The Structure of the International Negotiations (A System)

As it seems the solution of the major issues of security, development, human needs, and rights, preservation of natural environment demands a common global strategy because many issues cannot be solved through unilateral efforts and individual national strategies which have, as a common base, the interests of the human race but are built on a solid base of national traditions and culture. Both formulations of global strategy and individual strategies are already a subject for negotiation: in global institutions, like the UN, WTO, "Kyoto protocol," other international regimes and systems; in regional organizations, such as the EU, Asian-Pacific Cooperation Council, Commonwealth of Independent States, Organization of American States, Organization of African Unity, League of Arab States, Organization of Islamic Conference, etc.; and in functional groups, such as OPEC, IAEA, and others. All this constitutes a vast and endless agenda for negotiation among the nations – provided they are interested in solving immediate problems by searching for solutions to common problems.

The existing four-level structure of the world is the result of two interrelated processes: one is the ability of a group of nations (due to specifics of their origin and culture) to achieve progress on their territories due to their own effort, but also due to domination over other nations and acquisition of their wealth (colonialism), and the other is the process of transferring the experience and achievement of the more developed nations to the less developed. It concerned both the nations of Europe (in which the leading Anglo–Saxon nations were paving the way for the development of the others) and of the rest of the world in which nations like Russia, Japan, Turkey, Iran, and China were eager to borrow from the European experience in order to defend their independence and to develop a European-type world on their soil. In history this process very often was accompanied by wars of competition and resource redistribution. But now, with the existence of strong limitations on the use of power, of the possibilities to solve issues of development through the spread of transnational cooperation, of the advent of the philosophy of common destiny, there exists the possibility of arranging the swift flow of development assistance from the top (OECD) to the bottom on a non-violent, manageable basis.

It means construction of a comprehensive and organized structure of negotiations that should incorporate the possibility of changing the nature of the international system to share the assets of the "haves" with the needs of the "have-nots," but not in the most primitive way of putting the poor nations on the payroll of the rich (see the interesting research on the EU–ACP negotiation process in Aquilar and Galluccio 2008). The words of Confucius: "If you give a fish to someone you will feed him once; if you teach him to fish he will feed himself all his life." The point of strategy in negotiations is to give a chance to the poor to learn how to feed themselves. Of course, this is a Herculean task because too many people on both sides of the barrier between rich and poor are not interested in the solution to the problem of development. They are interested in power. That is why the real role of "transitional" nations is so important: They give an example of "turning the swords into ploughshares," of changing psychology from belligerence to hard-working ethics. These are huge and potentially strong nations, and they can very easily, especially having nuclear weapons in their arsenals, change the emphasis in their development strategy from acquisition of foreign know-how, technology, investment, and markets, to acquisition of foreign resources and territories (like Saddam's Iraq in Kuwait 1990).

But the realities of the current world demonstrate that acquisition of foreign experience is much more profitable than wars. Consider the example of Japan, which, in the search for prosperity opened by the Revolution of Meidzi (1866–1868), made a journey to imperialism, colonialism, and ultimate defeat in World War II, and finally chose the strategy that has led it to prosperity. Nations such as the Republic of Korea, the Republic of China (Taiwan), Singapore, Malaysia, Thailand, the Philippines and a few others have also traveled the same pattern and provided impressive results. The accumulated conclusion from these examples is the collective desire by the poor part of the humankind to achieve a sustainable and strong path of development, which is another agenda for negotiation in addition to security (negotiation both in the UN and regional organizations), preservation of health, environment, human rights, and many others.

The agenda for a global system of negotiations is more or less ready. It is not officially approved (only some parts of it have become subject to approval by governments), but there is a vast consensus on what should be negotiated and by whom. The next task for the global community is to work out a comprehensive strategy for negotiation, indicating general purposes, participants, locations, rules of conduct, and desirable outcomes. Among different influential international bodies the G-8 has taken care at least to identify issues for global concern and their priorities. This body has no formal powers, but everyone knows the importance of its judgment on issues of the global strategy.

One of the subordinate problems for the implementation of this strategy will be organization and realization of a system of governance that may lead to the realization of this task and, first of all, a system of international negotiations. As a first task, this system has to be constructed and acquire a legal status. It cannot be completely independent from the nations, which are the bearers of sovereignty, but it also must receive some sort of sovereignty in order to avoid the transformation of negotiations into a struggle among states. The system of negotiations will inevitably be integrated into the structure of global governance together with the rulings of individual states and decisions of the international organizations.

What will acquire a primary importance when this system is activated is the education and promotion of a staff of professional negotiators who will take the responsibility for governance. They will need appropriate training. They will need appropriate status. They will need special preparation beginning with psychological selection and training (Aquilar and Galluccio 2008). An "ideal" negotiator is not simply a highly trained person with knowledge of the latest analyses and findings. It is a certain psychological type: an open, intelligent nature, capable of listening to the others and understanding their grievances, dedicated to the ideas of compromise and agreement – in other words, the "ideal" person for making negotiations not simply a "job" (as the ideas of "practical negotiator" prescribe) but a way of life, a credo, a certain vision of the human contact.

There is one thing that has acquired outstanding importance recently. On one hand, it is the importance of sovereign nations as the basic elements of the current international structure. On the other hand there is a need to bring nations together, to create conditions for the avoidance and even prevention of conflict (a task set by the UN), and to suggest instead means and ways to establish a system of mutual cooperation and collective solutions to the existing problems: peace, development, human rights, and respect for cultural inheritance. In order to achieve this purpose some new and advanced tasks should be introduced and accepted – among them, the concept of the "ideal negotiator," which will help humankind realize the most vital decisions of the global community without hurting the legitimate feelings of national identity. In the long run much will depend on the psychological framing of the activities of negotiators and their ability to prove to national decision-makers that negotiable solutions are "not worse" than unilateral ones and may be even better.

References

Aquilar, F., & Galluccio, M. (2008). *Psychological processes in international negotiations: Theoretical and practical perspectives*. New York: Springer.

Binnendijk, H. (Ed.). (1987). *National negotiating styles*. Washington DC: Center for the Study of Foreign Affairs, Foreign Service Institute, US Department of State.

Meerts, P., & Cede, F. (Eds.). (2004). *Negotiating European union*. Chippenham/Eastbourne: Antony Rowe Ltd.

Fisher, R., & Ury, W. (1981). *Getting to yes: Negotiating agreement without giving in*. Boston: Houghton Mifflin.

Kremenyuk, V. (2005). Negotiation paradigm: Three in one. In G. O. Faure (Ed.), *La negociation: Regards sur sa diversite. Premiere Biennale internationale de la negociation, sous la direction de Guy Olivier Faure*. Paris: Publibook.

Putnam, R. (1988). Diplomacy and domestic politics: The logic of two-level games. *Internal Organization, 42*(1), 427–460.

Raiffa, H. (1984). *The art and science of negotiation*. Cambridge: Harvard University Press.

Schelling, T. C. (1960). *The strategy of conflict*. Cambridge: Harvard University Press.

Zartman, I. W., & Berman, M. R. (Eds.). (1982). *The practical negotiator*. New Haven: Yale University Press.

Chapter 12
How It Looks When Negotiations Fail: Why Do We Need Specific and Specialized Training for International Negotiators?

Olivera Zikic

It would be nice to be capable of anticipating events, particularly those negative ones that happen to everybody during their lifetime. Then, we would be able to better prepare for their coming and fight the potential consequences. Unfortunately, fortune-telling is not one of the skills we have available to us as human beings. We can only rely on our up-to-date experience and available information. It is even worse if such events happen somehow, suddenly and unexpectedly (Aquilar and Galluccio 2008). Just that happened to ordinary Serbians during recent decades. Probably, there were a certain number of those who could have anticipated the future sequence of events, but ordinary people had not even thought that something like that could have happened to us and our country. It is possible that "blindness" to future events originated from the fact that for years we had been living in a country (Yugoslavia) where we had every day confirmations that we were living in harmony and love with other nations and ethnic minorities, as well as of our good relations with neighboring countries and almost all countries of the world. We were proud of the fact that, in historical terms, we had always been on the side of justice and the winners, that we mutually considered each other as friends and allies. At least, it seemed to be so. We were proud because, wherever we may have travelled, we were greeted warmly, with a smile and the loudly spoken words of our hosts: "Friends, Tito, Yugoslavia." Our solid economic situation, as well as the possibility of schooling, traveling, and meeting with other cultures made us feel wealthier and satisfied that our lives were of better quality, among other things.

However, it was not enough for a happy ending. In the 1990s a process started that brought a lot of evil to the whole region and the Serbian people as well. Everything started with the decomposition of old Yugoslavia and the secession of its republics. The consequence of compromise failure during negotiation processes

O. Zikic (✉)
Medical Faculty, University of Nis, Department for Psychiatry.
e-mail: okac55@gmail.com

F. Aquilar and M. Galluccio (eds.), *Psychological and Political Strategies for Peace Negotiation*, DOI 10.1007/978-1-4419-7430-3_12,

led to the start of a civil war among peoples who had lived together for many years. What followed were civil wars in Croatia and Bosnia and Herzegovina, UN sanctions imposed on Serbia lasting 3½ years, enormous inflation, and finally the conflict in Kosovo and 3 months of bombardment. Huge changes brought suffering that affected everybody. Maybe the most important negotiation process for Serbia was that one in Rambouillet in France. It was a climax of unsuccessful negotiations between Serbian and Albanian delegations with international delegates as mediators. The two delegations engaged in the conflict didn't even meet each other in Rambouillet. At the start, none of the sides accepted the agreement. And, the most terrifying part of our lives in recent history started after the failure of negotiations in Rambouillet. The consequences of this failure were far reaching for the whole nation, both during the 3-month period of bombardment and afterward.

Consequences

An old saying tells us that in terms of love and quarrel, respectively, it is necessary to have two persons involved. The same rule may apply to negotiations, where the futures of entire nations may be decided (Fisher et al. 1991). Blocked readiness for a compromise or lack of skills during the negotiation process generally lead to failure and far-reaching consequences (Aquilar and Galluccio 2005). Probably, the causes of such happenings are many and very complex, starting from historical events in previous periods and centuries, via the current political situation, to the very people who participated in policy creation and negotiations of that time. It is difficult to say with certainty which was the determining factor, and perhaps each conflict participant has his or her own truth (Galluccio 2008). However, what seems to be certain and cannot be denied by anyone is the fact that due to the failure to reach a common solution during negotiations, many lives were lost, many families and towns disappeared, the future of many young generations was destroyed, and advancement and prosperity were disabled.

Material Damages

It is not necessary to emphasize that any war entails destruction and suffering. It has been estimated that economic damage from bombardment come to US$30 billion (Lečić-Toševski and Bakalić 2004). During the bombardment there were many bridges, roads, industrial facilities, civil and public structures, and companies destroyed, as well as religious monuments (such as churches and monasteries), airports, electrical and waterworks plants, etc. Let us not neglect the damage to the natural environment wrought by bombs, which were charged with depleted uranium and other poisonous substances that were released from hit structures, such as transformation stations.

Migrations

Although the material damages are huge, they, for sure, cannot be compared to human casualties and their destinies, which are hard to describe. Hard times resulted in huge migrations of populations, either of immigration to or emigration from Serbia. UN sanctions lasted 3½ years, and their consequences are immeasurable. The war and economic difficulties caused migrations of around 300,000 people, who found residence in various European countries as well as countries outside Europe.

The war in the neighborhood brought about the mass migrations of population. Depending on data sources, the estimates of the number of refugees and Internally Displaced Persons (IDPs) in Serbia have varied from 350,000 to 800,000. According to the United Nations High Commissioner for Refugees Agency (UNHCR) data, there are 650,000 refugees currently living in Serbia. More than 200,000 of them are Kosovo refugees, or so-called internally displaced persons. That number represents a significant percentage of the total population of Serbia (around 7.5 million), and it is quite enormous for a country with big economic problems (Lečić-Toševski and Bakalić 2004; Web site of Serbian Government, 2004 a,b).

During the crisis in the Balkans, a huge number of Serbs from the ex-Yugoslav republics moved to Serbia and continue to live here. During 1990 and 1991, at the time war broke out in Croatia and later in Bosnia and Herzegovina, hundreds of thousands of Serbs from Croatia and Bosnia and Herzegovina left their homes, and most of them found refuge in Serbia. A similar thing happened in 1995, after the operations of the Croatian Army, called "Bljesak" (Flash) and "Oluja" (Storm), when practically the entire Serbian population from Krajina moved to Serbia in an endless caravan of vehicles. The climax of the conflict was the period of NATO bombardment (March 24–June 10, 1999). During that period, a phenomenon of mass migrations (motivated either by fear of war or pressure threatening) reached its climax. The war, which lasted 78 days, ended on June 10, 1999, with the end of NATO bombardment, the signing of the Military and Technical Agreement in Kumanovo, and the adoption of UN Resolution No. 1244, which guaranteed Yugoslav sovereignty over Kosovo. All Yugoslav armed and security forces left Kosovo, and NATO troops entered Kosovo. Albanian refugees returned to their homes, and more than 200,000 non-Albanian Kosovo inhabitants left their homes on the way to the territory of central Serbia and Vojvodina, in most cases (Human Rights Watch 2003; Radovic 2004; Web site of Serbian Government, 2004b).

Today, as a result, Serbia has 649,980 refugees, war-affected, and internally displaced persons, making it the country with the greatest number of refugees in Europe. While the return of refugees who originate from Croatia and Bosnia and Herzegovina is giving some, quite modest results, there is no return of Kosovo Serbs to Kosovo, and it is completely uncertain when (and if at all) these citizens will get back to their homes (Radovic 2004).

Civil Casualties

Bombardment that lasted 11 weeks in the spring of 1999 represented an intensive acute stress, which was added to already existing chronic stress. People became anxious, apathetic, helpless, and hopeless. It is stated that there were 1,200 civil casualties; among them – 79 children, while 5,000 people were wounded and became disabled. Let us not forget about 1,300 people who became missing in Kosovo, whose fate no one knows. Their families are under chronic stress because they cannot organize a funeral or express their mourning, which negatively impacts their mental and physical health. Most refugees experienced multiple, high intensity stresses. Several thousand persons who stayed in detention camps in Bosnia and Croatia live in Serbia now. Many of them were subjected to various kinds of psychical and physical abuse, which left a deep trace, both in mental functioning of the very victims, and in the lives of their families (Lečić-Toševski and Bakalić 2004). In these situations, emotional and cognitive processes are impaired and the feeling of being powerless could bring in a majority of persons a felt or real impossibility to act insofar inducing loss of motivation and severe phenomena of disorganizations and dissociation of consciences (Frijda, 1987, 2004; Liotti, 2007).

Subsequent Consequences

Consequences of negotiation failure during the after-war period are enormous, too. The consequences of prolonged stress on mental health are significant. We could say that our mental health deteriorated and that we have an increase in prevalence of mental and behavior disorders. For instance, in the period from 1999 to 2002 the prevalence of mental and behavior disorders increased by 13.5%. This means that mental disorders became second largest public health problem (Žikić et al. 2004).

One of the important issues for a psychiatrist and a psychologist is linked to the psychological consequences within the refugee population (Beck 1999). The most reliable data come from research conducted by regional psychiatric institutions and specialized centers, such as the Trauma Centers in Belgrade and Nis. The most frequent are the huge percentage of chronic Post-traumatic Stress Disorders (PTSD) (29.2%) and adjustment disorders (40%).

There are also data from refugee associations. According to these associations, the greatest number of suicide attempts and suicides were in refugee centers. Additional data come from international Red Cross programs for psychosocial help. They noticed that the most prominent psychiatric problems within refugee population are depressive states, reactive states, and adjustment disorders.

When we generally talk about PTSD, we find the highest percentage of PTSD patients among the group of persons that were in detention camps (74.8%). If we talk about refugees and PTSD, the highest percentage of PTSD is found among sexually abused persons (Žikić et al. 2004).

It has been shown that PTSD was frequent but not the only consequence of severe stress and trauma (Lečić-Toševski and Bakalić 2004). There are other disorders such as depression, somatoform disorders, and certain anxiety disorders. In addition, there have been some changes in personality traits. We noticed an increase in substance abuse and drug abuse, as well as an increase in the prevalence of suicide.

Morbidity and mortality caused by psychosomatic and somatic diseases have increased as well. It is very unrealistic to expect that somebody could count the exact number of late and silent victims of psychosomatic diseases caused by stress. In an attempt to establish that partially, at least, a group of experts was formed, which was included in the IAN (International Aid Network) Project – the goal of which was to investigate the frequency and kind of somatic diseases in clients of the Torture Victims Rehabilitation Center (for clients affected during war conflicts on the territory of ex-Yugoslavia, in the period from 1991 to 1999). The clients included had complained about somatic health discomforts, and were referred by IAN psychiatrists and psychologists. Also included were torture victims from refugee camps visited by doctors during their field work. The project covered 730 patients in all. In 63% of patients, the first and most important diagnoses established involved cardiovascular diseases. Of those 82% were diagnosed with arterial hypertension, and 5.2% – coronary disease. Second place, in terms of prevalence, was assigned to endocrine gland diseases (11.8%). Of that number 67.4% suffered from diabetes mellitus. It was confirmed that clients of the Torture Victims Rehabilitation Center represent a population at high risk for somatic disease development (Otaševic et al. 2004).

Other, very upsetting data, refers to the frequency of oncological diseases. Until 1999, in Serbia there were registered between 15,000 and 20,000 new cancer cases a year; in 2004 the number had soared to 30,000 new patients.

Burnout syndrome and chronic fatigue syndrome are frequent states, especially among medical doctors, psychiatrists, and psychologists. Of course, all this impacts the quality of life for many persons.

The war and long-lasting political whirling brought about social disintegration and increased delinquency, aggression, and violence. Social transition also contributed to the genesis of numerous psychological problems of population, and the continuous stress adds to anomie, alienation, helplessness, and uncertainty. The war, refuge and torture caused the degradation, poverty, dehumanization, and death of many persons.

Conclusions

This was the dark side of the Serbian negotiation process in recent years. But, I have to say that within the last few years we have seen a new diplomatic era, characterized by a different approach to negotiation processes. Currently, our diplomatic actions are based on other rules, such as a win–win approach, respect for the other side, lack of labeling, and avoiding language of hate. As a result, some positive changes have occurred in the last few years. We have better relationships with other countries in the region and especially with the European Union, and something that is very important for a wounded country, we have re-established our connections with European and world economic institutions.

And, finally, this presentation was not about the war even if it looks like it. This presentation is a vote for peace. We presented all of this only to emphasize how important it is to give even a small contribution to prevent such disaster. Psychiatrists and psychologists are not politicians, but professionals who deal with human psychology and, among other things, with cognitive and behavioral therapies, and communication skills (A. Beck, 1988; J. Beck, 1995). If there is something in our knowledge and skills that could be added as, at least, one brick in the wall to maintain peace, then it is our duty, as professionals and intellectuals, to contribute to it. Cognitive and behavioral psychology and psychotherapy-focused techniques could help us find several tools to open the door for a better understanding of psychological interdependent dynamics within the realm of international negotiation and for a far more cooperative way to try to resolve common shared problems (Aquilar and Galluccio 2008). Certainly, we cannot eliminate the entire spectrum of arbitrary conclusions or stereotypical interpretations, but we could work at the modification of dysfunctional attitudes and thoughts, thus helping to bring about "a virtuous cognitive process." It seems to me that Aquilar and Galluccio's theoretical framework and their action plan focused on specialized and efficient training for international negotiators and mediators is very relevant. Their work on trying to establish a bridge between two apparently distant disciplines, international relations and negotiation and cognitive psychology and psychotherapy, is of great value and has important operational consequences. These two authors have been developing an analysis of the cognitive and emotional processes identifiable in negotiation and mediation experiences and applying the results of this analysis to propose and to delineate a project of specific training for negotiators and mediators delineated in their previous book (Aquilar and Galluccio 2008; see also Aquilar's and Galluccio's chapters in this volume), which in a limited period of time would allow participants to acquire the ability to understand their interlocutors and to master one's emotions (useful to improve the quality and, hopefully, also the results of negotiation). It is our wish that their very important work represents a stimulus in the right direction toward making the world, through peace negotiations, a much safer place.

References

Aquilar, F., & Galluccio, M. (2005). *International negotiation: A new challenge for cognitive psychotherapy*. Paper presented at the 35th congress of the European association for behavioural and cognitive therapies (EABCT), Thessalonica, Greece, 21–24 September 2005.

Aquilar, F., & Galluccio, M. (2008). *Psychological processes in international negotiation*. New York: Springer.

Beck, A. T. (1988). *Love is never enough*. New York: Harper & Row.
Beck, A. T. (1999). *Prisoners of Hate*. New York: Harper Collins.
Beck, J. S. (1995). *Cognitive therapy: Basics and beyond*. New York: Guilford.
Fisher, R., Ury, W., & Patton, B. (1991). *Getting to yes. Negotiating an agreement without giving in*. London: Random House.
Frijda, N. H. (1987). Emotions, cognitive structure and action tendency. *Cognition Emotion, 1*, 115–143.
Frijda, N. H. (2004). Emotion and action. In A. S. R. Manstead, N. Frijda, & A. Fischer (Eds.), *Feelings and emotions* (pp. 158–173). Cambridge: Cambridge University Press.
Galluccio, M. (2008). *Cognitive approaches to international relations: Perspectives and prospects of international negotiation*. Paper presented at the 6th international congress of cognitive psychotherapy, Roma. Abstract: Psicoterapia Cognitiva e Comportamentale 14(2), 54.
Human Rights Watch. (2003). Po naredenju: ratni zlocini na Kosovu [Under orders: War crimes in Kosovo]. Samizdat B92, Beograd.
Lečić-Toševski and Bakalić J. (2004). Protiv torture—put ka zdravlju pojedinca i društva: Centar za rehabilitaciju žrtava torture—IAN Beograd. In Ž. Špirić, G. Knežević, V. Jović, & G. Opačić (Eds.), *Tortura u ratu, posledice i rehabilitacija. Jugoslovensko iskustvo*. Beograd: Centar za rehabilitaciju žrtava torture International Aid Network, 91–100.
Liotti G. (2007), "Internal working models of attachment in the therapeutic relationship," in: Gilbert P., Leahy R.L., eds., *The therapeutic relationship in the cognitive behavioral therapies*, New York: Routledge.
Otaševic, P., Mitrovic, K., & Mitrovic, P. (2004). Somatske bolesti klijenata Centra za rehabilitaciju žrtava torture: Jednogodišnje iskustvo MEDIAN-A. In: Špirić Ž, Knežević G, Jović V, Opačić G (eds) *Tortura u ratu, posledice i rehabilitacija. Jugoslovensko iskustvo*. Beograd: Centar za rehabilitaciju žrtava torture International Aid Network, 163–175.
Radovic, B. (2004). Jugoslovenski ratovi 1991–1999 i neke od njihovih društvenih posledica. In Ž. Špirić, G. Knežević, V. Jović, & G. Opačić (Eds.), *Tortura u ratu, posledice i rehabilitacija. Jugoslovensko iskustvo*. Beograd: Centar za rehabilitaciju žrtava torture International Aid Network, 25–68.
Web site of Serbian Government (2004a). Facts about Serbia: Population, Language and Religion. http://www.arhiva.serbia.gov.rs/cms/view.php?id=1015.
Web site of Serbian Government (2004b). Facts about Serbia: Refugees in Serbia. http://www.arhiva.serbia.gov.rs/cms/view.php?id=1017.
Žikić, O., Grbeša, G., & Lečić-Toševski, D. (2004). *Mental health care in Serbia and Montenegro: The problem of refugees*. International congress of the world psychiatric association – Treatments in psychiatry: An update, Florence, 2004.

Chapter 13
Cognitive Therapy in National Conflict Resolution: An Opportunity. The Lebanese Experience

Aimée Karam

A.T. Beck (1976) years ago emphasized a conceptualization of the human mind, putting forth an intimate link between emotions, cognition, and behavior. He has detected the importance of and profit in working with schemas' constellation in our attempt to understand, formulate, and modify dysfunctional cores that are maintaining mental health disorders such as depression, anxiety, eating disorders, etc. This has been and is still one of the most robust platforms, allowing the field to evolve tremendously with remarkable input from researchers and clinicians who also are movers and shakers in the evolution of Cognitive–Behavioral Therapy (CBT) (Alloy et al. 2006; Wells 2000). A particular effort is constantly made to validate the foundation of CBT and the scope of its efficacy in treating disorders through an emphasis on the essential role of mediators such as contents and cognitive styles that underlie the way people build meanings and relate to their experience with self, others, and the world (Beck 2004).

Recently, the idea of exploring the implementation of cognitive therapy principles in enhancing its use and efficacy in the area of conflict resolution and political negotiation has been actively disseminated. Authors like Francesco Aquilar and Mauro Galluccio (2008) have been particularly active in initiating team reflection, workshops, seminars and research in this area. I have been solicited by my friend and colleague, Francesco Aquilar, to participate in two seminars on conflict resolution. The first one during a Congress of the European Association for Cognitive and Behavioral Therapies (EABCT), held in September 2005 in Thessaloniki, Greece, where I had the great opportunity to meet Mauro Galluccio (a political scientist and psychologist), who is one of the most active and innovative persons in the field of integrating CBT principles into the art and science of international negotiation. The second gathering was during the World Congress of Cognitive and Behavioral Therapies (WCBCT) in July 2007, in Barcelona, Spain.

The following chapter represents an update of the work I presented at these two congresses. The *first part* aims at addressing the following points:

A. Karam (✉)
Department of Psychiatry and Clinical Psychology, Saint George Hospital University Medical Center, Beirut, Lebanon
e-mail: aimeekaram@hotmail.com

F. Aquilar and M. Galluccio (eds.), *Psychological and Political Strategies for Peace Negotiation*, DOI 10.1007/978-1-4419-7430-3_13,

1. What have we learned so far from the CBT principles that we could apply in the area of conflict resolution?
2. How do we benefit from CBT principles to better prepare negotiators and better read the situation?
3. New challenges.

Review of the Basic Principles of CBT

One of the main focuses of cognitive therapy is to highlight the intimate relation between thoughts, emotions, and behavior – in particular how they are interrelated and keep influencing each other. One major outcome of this constellation is cognitive formulation (Beck 1995):

1. Early experience and its implications for self, world, and future.
2. Basic core beliefs and their enduring perspective on self, world, and future.
3. Conditional, dysfunctional assumptions in terms of rules, standards, and guidelines that one puts on himself or herself and expects from others.
4. Critical incidents like events occurring which map onto original experiences or with negative implications for self.
5. Activation of beliefs/assumptions and processing biases operated through components such as attention, perception, interpretation and memory.

All of these concepts allow us to not only understand part of the natural functioning of the human brain, but they also shed light on specific faulty thinking patterns that perpetuate dysfunctional attitudes and detrimental outcomes: overgeneralization, dichotomous thinking, selective abstraction, personalization, tunnel vision etc. These are all examples of faulty thinking, maintaining dysfunctional attitudes and beliefs. Additionally, the meta-cognitive model (Wells 2000) offers an interesting option of focus when one is attempting to understand and help achieve better emotional management. The emphasis is mainly on the cognitive attention system mediated by one's met cognition, which means the beliefs about an interpretation of worry itself; the main work is on the attributed meaning of a thought rather than on the content of the thought, per se. Also the work on personality disorders (Beck 2004) could serve as an interesting avenue to keep in perspective when analyzing interactions between people, specifically when they interfere in conflict resolution and negotiation. Also, schemas' contents are full of dysfunctional beliefs that are constantly displayed in the process of negotiation and interpersonal relations resulting in a partial or absolute mismatch in communication that limits or ends the efficacy of these procedures.

How Do We Achieve This?

The above formulation is put in practice through a session of a specific format. Typically, the structure of a session goes this way (Young and Beck 1980):

1. Agenda setting:
   - Pinpointing the target problem(s)
   - Setting priorities
2. Eliciting feed-back
3. Understanding
4. Interpersonal effectiveness
5. Collaboration
6. Pacing and efficient use of time
7. Guided Discovery
8. Focusing on key cognitions and behaviors
9. Strategy for change
10. Applications of CBT
11. Homework

Formatting a session is useful for standardizing, assessing, and measuring the way CBT is applied and conducted. In parallel, it could be inspiring to try the same structure when conducting an intervention oriented towards conflict resolution.

The Principles of Negotiation (Young and Beck 1980) Involve Principally

1. People
2. Position versus interest
3. Possibilities and solutions
4. Objective criteria

Types of Conflict Situations

Negotiation always occurs in a conflict situation, which means disagreement around something. The types of conflict situations (killing, rape, rupture in pride, properties, power, etc.) are major factors determining the content of a negotiation. The cultural backgrounds imply multiple meanings that need to be elucidated and carefully examined in order to reach a common basic ground. Questions such as: "What do we have to lose or win" determine the motivation for and engagement in the process of negotiation. There is a marked difference if the answer to these questions is "nothing more" or "a lot." The socio-economic status of countries is a major point to consider as well: poverty of countries and their capacities, and whether basic rights were violated, as well as disruption or loss of basic support and the feeling of being underprivileged. The types of emotions involved, such as rage, humiliation, losing the sense of trust, safety, or security are important parameters to consider in determining the type of conflict situations. Past history and background, prior dramatization, and previous community history are data to gather when negotiating.

The Lebanese Experience

Although the Lebanon Wars ended more than a decade ago, Lebanon is far from having achieved a stable peace. National politics remain deeply affected by ethnic and religious sectaries, which are kept alive by an entrenched sense of prejudice and distrust among the different communities. Below are some examples undergone by local initiatives to achieve conflict transformation and reconciliation, what we call Post-War Community Building. We have focused on three regions of Lebanon: A, B, and C. The goal was to reconcile communities, facilitate dialogue, and rebuild a healthy cohabitation. The common situation in the three villages was a severe conflict between two different religious groups, including civil crimes, assassination of political leaders, displacement, and dishonor.

Region A

A previous history of basic trust existed and was completely shattered due to catastrophic crimes, resulting in human losses and humiliation.

Distal condition:
No implicit or explicit political decision was taken in favor of reconciliation.

Negotiation tools:

- Several trials were made to put conflicting parties together. They resulted in the breaking off of communication and "no shows."
- The negotiators were not in full control of the situation, nor were the concerned communities because the real decision makers were unknown and "underground."

Results:
No reconciliation, impossible mediation, unresolved situation.

Region B

A previous history of basic trust existed and was completely shattered because of the occurrence of a dramatic, extreme event: People were killed while praying inside the church. This traumatic situation was followed by a dramatic escalation of the conflict. Additionally, the notion of territory was poorly defined for each community.

Distal conditions:
The political decision to solve the problem was to pay all involved parties in order to compensate for damages.

Negotiation tools:

- Several trials to put people together and bring them to meet failed because of money receipt.
- A constant diversion from the core problems kept people away, and only very superficial subjects were approached.
- Very poor work was performed on involved emotions, core beliefs, and main interests.

Results:
Complete failure in reconciliation process. The concerned communities lived *near one another* but not *with* each other. Feelings of unresolved grudge remained.

Region C

A previous history of positive cohabitation existed. The community is composed of highly educated people, highly exposed in both involved communities. Also, Village C is geographically close to Beirut (the city). This village is a symbol of successful cohabitation and enrichment that was gained through interaction. During the conflict, more material losses than human ones occurred.

Distal conditions:
Exceptional leaders. Clear and explicit desire towards problem solving.

Negotiation tools:

- Young adults were heavily involved, not only more senior people. The renovation of the village was quickly initiated, engaging people in work of common interest and value systems, such as renovation of historic sites with an emphasis on preserving the traditional architecture. A particular emphasis was placed on the cultural specificities of the village through conferences, concerts, and national meetings.

Results:
Absolute success in achieving reconciliation and remarkable development of the village. Successful cohabitation and acceptance of each other.

How Could Negotiators Benefit from CBT to Be Better Prepared in Situations Such as A and B?

- Understanding how the perception of a given situation is assimilated through specific schemas and underlying assumptions. Also, how reality could be wrongly processed because of faulty thinking.
- Being aware of issues such as beliefs, identity definitions, emotions involved, preferred style of thinking, faulty thinking (catastrophizing, selective abstraction, dichotomous thinking, to name but a few).

- Using guided discovery and collaborative work to reach a meaningful formulation of the conflict and the reasons of its maintenance. Addressing the key cognitions and emotions (dignity of people, pride, shame and betrayal).
- Eliciting lots of feed-back and reformulation from both parties in order to ensure an effective work with them and prioritize the core issues that are involved.
- Recognizing the interpersonal dimension between the negotiators themselves and the parties involved in the negotiation are of particular importance and require caution since prejudices have a detrimental effect on outcomes.
- Making negotiators aware of the importance of having concerned communities as owners of the process and part of collaborative planning rather than subject to models planned for them.
- Training in cognitive models of various personality structures can be extremely informative and may prevent pitfalls while managing people in the process of negotiation.
- Getting familiar with procedures aimed at increasing resilience in the face of adversity would serve as a good tool in the face of disappointment and severe conflict management when working with negotiation and conflict resolution.

New Challenges for CBT

It would be helpful for negotiators to have a handy and instrumental way of addressing emotions in extremely hostile situations when emotions like anger, hostility, sadness, humiliation, and shame are involved (Aquilar and Galluccio 2008). This would imply a deep understanding of how these emotions are maintained, as well as the various cognitive assumptions in which they are embedded. Understanding the cultural value of several types of emotions seems to be an important matter in the process of negotiation, in the sense that for some communities, for example, pride is extremely valued, while in others property, and still others, fairness.

Pinpoint the limitations: Who is the decision maker, and where is the power? At times, people who are negotiating are not free in their decision(s). Ambiguous and multidimensional conflicts caused through successive historical facts, context, and political data variables, require availability and commitment of negotiators in charge and necessitate a rigor in meeting schedules and refined professional skills, especially when people involved in negotiation in a country like Lebanon might themselves suffer from having been in extreme situations of loss and threat, causing at the time long-term suffering and handicaps. These very preliminary reflections imply the benefits of putting together a well defined and comprehensive cognitive model for conflict resolution in national and international negotiation processes while, simultaneously, working towards putting together a training program with clear objectives, principles of supervision, and follow-up for those who are interested in developing into effective negotiators (Aquilar and Galluccio 2008).

This *second part* is an example of how cognitive therapy principles could be applied in difficult negotiations, both their benefits and limitations. The national dialogue in 2006 has brought together all key Lebanese political factions – the "majority" and the "opposition" – in the broadest gathering since the end of the Lebanon war in 1990. The 14 Christian and Muslim leaders met to forge a compromise over a host of conflict issues that have paralyzed the government and led to a level of sectarian polarization not seen since the 1975–1990 Lebanon wars. The dialogue, which spanned many months, was convened to discuss the following:

1. United Nations Security Council Resolution 1559, which is a resolution adopted by the United Nations Security Council on September 2, 2004. It called upon Lebanon to establish its sovereignty over all of its land and called upon "foreign forces" (generally interpreted as referring but not limited to Syria) to withdraw from Lebanon and to cease intervening in the internal politics of Lebanon. The resolution also called on all Lebanese and non-Lebanese militias to disband and declared support for a "free and fair electoral process."
2. Setting up an international tribunal to try the suspects in former Prime Minister Raffia Hariri's assassination.
3. Presidential elections.
4. Redefining the future of Syrian–Lebanese relations (Syria withdrew its troops from Lebanon in April 2005, ending 29 years of military occupation).

It is important to keep in mind that the national dialogue was held within the following context:

National conflicts:

Divisions inside the Lebanese community, which have the value of a proximal factor. These divisions reflect as well the broader rifts emerging in the Middle East pitting an alliance of a powerful order (USA–France) and its allies against the regional ambitions of another powerful order (Iran–Syria) and its allies. This regional and international atmosphere that surrounds Lebanon has the value of a *distal variable*. The national dialogue resulted in a failure to reach negotiation and a rupture in the dialogue.

Methodology:

We have selected six key political representatives who participated in the national dialogue as members of four different major political groups. We conducted a one-to-one interview with each person of 60–120-min duration and asked them the following:

1. Why do you think the "national dialogue" failed?
2. What are the basic beliefs of your group, the most prominent feelings and their expression in your behavior as a group?

Objectives:

1. Identify each group's causal attributions of the breakdown.
2. Identify their basic beliefs, emotions, and strategies.
3. Discover how Cognitive Therapy Interventions (CTI) could be used by negotiators to facilitate the dialogue.
4. Understand the limitations of CTI in this case.

Causal Attribution of Rupture as per Analysis of the Interviews

Parties highly dependent on external influences:

1. All parties were commanded or highly influenced by international and regional agendas.
2. The leaders in the national dialogue were instructed to wait for better timing, which led to the dilution of the emergency and necessity to solve the problems immediately (See summary in table below, Group D).
3. A variety of regional events was occurring simultaneously, causing a shift of focus away from national matters (See summary in table below, Group D).

Lack of trust in motives, credibility, and political weight of people:

1. Some parties in the dialogue were perceived as having a "double standards" in dealings.
2. Hegemony of one group: there was an acute self-perception of leadership among parties involved in the dialogue, which goes against the concept of democracy (See table below, Group B).
3. An unresolved past history of strong and negative mutual emotions and atrocities among groups was still present at the time of the dialogue.

Maladaptive strategies of players:

1. Different belief systems:
   - One belief system was passionate, seeking common values among people.
   - Another one realistic and seeking common interest that would ensure the right outcome (See table below, Group B).
2. Priming of a conflict mode following this prototype: "I will say what I want, and if it does not work, let the conflict stay."
3. Discussions were not oriented towards problem solving but rather expressing opinions.
4. People couldn't distance themselves from their cause to reach objectivity (See table below, Group B).
5. There were large variations in political weight of players.
6. Lots of dichotomous thinking on the part of some players (See table below, Group D).

Unclear agenda and processes:

1. There was no preliminary consensus among parties to achieve a compromise.
2. Difference in priorities to discuss and an absence of agreement on major topics (See table below, Group B).
3. No common grounds were established preliminary to this national dialogue (e.g., legitimacy of the current government; definition of Lebanese identity). This has impacted the level of "readiness" of people in discussing some topics (See table below, Group C).

Cognitive Factors

Group A

	Relevant behavior	Emotions	Behavior
1	We believe that ideology tradition, thoughts, and emotions of people are important	Anger	No real alliance with the rest of the parties
2	We feel under pressure to protect our people and what they believe in	Hatred	Search for a powerful external protector
3	External powers are interfering with our internal matters	Unfairness	Legitimacy of transgressing established rules and laws
4	We are marginalized and our rights are not being recognized		
5	No equal chances are given to all		
6	This unfairness is perpetuated by an unfair and hypocritical government		
8	Resistance is our right		

Group B

	Relevant behavior	Emotions	Behavior
1	We are fair	Flat affect	Activist: behavioral activation: creation of national slogan: i.e., "I love life," "Lebanon first"
2	We can set the model against violence and political conflicts	Denial of others' concerns	
3	We want peace		Think outside your confessional affiliation
4	We recognize our errors		
5	Democracy is the solution		Think democracy, "Lebanon first"
6	The perpetrator should be punished		Focus on the future
7	Set an intellectual and economical model for the whole region		
8	Reinforce the Lebanese identity		
9	Create Social programs		
10	Evolutionary perspective		
11	We should stay in power		
12	Emphasize laicism versus religion		

Group C

	Relevant behavior	Emotions	Behavior
1	We are an independent nation		– Alliance with powerful entities
2	Alliance should be based on common interest not common affiliations	Surviving	– Realistic, non passionate strategies
3	We should apply tolerance and realism; they are the path to follow	Resilience	– Tolerance of others
4	Preserve a personal identity (affiliation religion) but the minimum requested.	Wisdom	– Adaptive attitudes toward the reality of the situation where pluralism should be accepted
5	Ideologies should be tempered		
6	The opponents are liars. They do not declare their convictions and their fundamental refusal of the basics		– Emotional regulation achieved between past memory and current reality

Group D

	Relevant behavior	Emotions	Behavior
1	I know better than the people, and they should listen to me	– Guilt towards own people	– Not flexible
2	I know best what is in the interest of the group. I will protect them	– Irritability – Anger, rage	– Doesn't use negotiation methods – Use persuasion
3	My people are martyrs, I owe them	– Unfairness	– Assumes unpopularity
4	I did a lot for the nation and have sacrificed a lot, so…	– Neglect – Insecurity	– Didactic approach
5	I deserve what I am asking for, because I sacrificed the most	– Frustration	– Independent steps: surprising and unexpected
6	Principles, ideology, and ethics are the basics. They are equal to values		
7	Because we are honest, we have the right to decide and the right to govern	– Deprived from their rights and what they deserve	– High level of commitment to their decisions
8	Pride is essential	– Pride: "We are ethically superior"; "I was right when all were wrong." "What I told you will happen, or happened"	– Very difficult to shift to "realism"
9	We are the only ones who are honest and dedicated, not others		– Daring to resist in order to reach what they want
10	If it does not work for us, nobody else deserves better, so we won't let it work for anybody		

Identification of Some Cognitive Biases as per Analysis of the Interviews

1. Arbitrary inference: "I did a lot for the nation and have sacrificed a lot."
2. Overgeneralization: "Democracy is the solution."
3. Dichotomous thinking: "We are the only ones who are honest and dedicated, not others."
4. Absolute, categorical cognitions: "Resistance is our right."
5. Ideologies and prejudices: "Principles, honesty, integrity are our foundation; we have values. They don't."
6. Distortions in self-concept representation: "I know better what is good for them, and they should listen to me."

Summary of Emotions

Anger	Hatred
Feeling treated unfairly	Protection of one's own people

Limited Emotions	Denial of other's Issues
Internal Sorrow	

Surviving	Wisdom
Resilience	

Guilt towards one's own people	Feeling treated unfairly
Anger, rage, irritability	Neglected, pride

Examples of Cognitive Conceptualization

1. View of self:
   We are the only ones who are honest and dedicated, not others.
2. View of others:
   Corrupt.
3. Relevant beliefs:
   If it doesn't work for us, nobody else deserves better.
4. Consequent strategies:
   We won't let it work for anybody.

5. Activated Mode:
   Confrontative and conflictual.
   We could identify two main types of reasons for rupture:

Organizational factors:
Lack of clear definitions and expectations: objectives, decision process, conflict resolution means, timing constraints, etc.

Cognitive and emotional factors:
Causing an atmosphere not conducive to agreement, especially in the absence of the above definitions.

How Cognitive therapy interventions could have increased the chance of success:

1. As inputs into organizational factors.
2. As facilitators to reduce impact of cognitive, behavioral differences among the players.

Organization

1. Specify the agenda and clear up objectives.
2. Set up the process by:

   - Limiting the impact of harmful assumptions, prejudices, and emotions such as mistrust, for example
   - Limiting the undesired activated mode
   - Correcting the identified faulty thinking style
   - Staging the interventions by first ensuring the basics then going into more complexities
   - Orienting people towards constructive thinking rather than deconstructive thinking
   - Use of problem solving strategies rather than conflicted and or ruminative strategies
   - Search for and highlight cognitive commonalities that can facilitate the task and provide a framework for conflict resolution between parties
   - Establish consensus to rank priorities in dialogue.

CTI as a Facilitator, Aiming at Reducing the Impact of Cognitive-Behavioral Differences

1. Identify and address the cognitive representation and resulting polarized thinking that activate "the right to fight" assumption.
2. Identify and address distrust when it is experienced: Mind reading used to understand the antagonist's thinking is much more difficult when distrust is activated.
3. Identify the displayed emotions and their inevitable consequences on the behavioral dimension and the coping strategies.

4. Emotions such as anger, hatred, and unfairness seem to lead more easily to an instrumental type of violent behavior which states: "The end justifies the means" (Aquilar and Galluccio 2008).
5. When threat and insecurity are experienced in such a context, watch the emergence of a confrontative/fighting mode rather than avoidance.
6. An overvalued emotion such as pride seems to facilitate the "right to do as I believe" assumption and consequent behavior.

Conclusions

CTI tools may be very promising for high-level conflictual negotiations as they allow for the possibility to operate within a specific, rigorous structure. CTI tools permit practitioners to profile, which means detect and minimize the impact of harmful cognitions, emotions and modes. They set up processes, distinguish perceptions and expectations, set up adaptive strategies and mediate. Of course, some parameters impede on CTI capacities. The impact of regional and international political alliances on priming the existing national conflicts and vulnerabilities is a powerful obstacle in the process of CTI. Also, resolving prejudices despite the squeal of past conflicts between parties, as well as reaching consensus over such a diverse definition of identity, are also limitations for the CTI. Working with personality components and inducing changes within a national or international conflict resolution context is a big challenge, as is reaching a compromise when power struggle is an issue that is not based on well- and clearly defined criteria. The creation of new clinical models and the implementation of valid antidotes to particular dysfunctional cognitive schemas emerging within this field are highly needed. Also needed is formal cognitive behavior training, directed at training negotiators and mediators in the process of national and international negotiation and conflict resolution. Aquilar and Galluccio's (2008) Cognitive-Motivational Model and the tailored training for negotiators and mediators foresees the development of an interdisciplinary approach to the study of international relations and, specifically, to the study of interpersonal negotiations, as the main mechanism for managing conflicts (Galluccio 2007). This is welcome and timely because in today's international political context pulling together new comprehensive interpretative angles might open new opportunities for a better understanding of conflicts and their resolution through peace negotiations.

References

Aquilar, F., & Galluccio, M. (2008). *Psychological processes in international negotiations: Theoretical and practical perspectives*. New York: Springer.

Alloy, L. B., Abramson, L. Y., Whitehouse, W. G., Hogan, M. E., Panzarella, C., & Rose, D. T. (2006). Prospective incidence of first onsets and recurrences of depression in individuals at high and low cognitive risk for depression. *Journal of Abnormal Psychology, 115*, 145–156.

Beck, A. T. (1976). *Cognitive therapy and the emotional disorders*. New York: New American Library.

Beck, A. T., Rush, A. J., Shaw, B. F., & Emery, G. (1979). *Cognitive therapy of depression*. New York: Guilford Press.

Beck, A. T., Freeman, A., & Davis, D. D. (2004). *Cognitive therapy of personality disorders*. New York: Guilford Press.

Beck, J. S. (1995). *Cognitive therapy: Basics and beyond*. New York: Guilford Press.

Fisher, R., Ury, W., & Patton, B. (1991). *Getting to yes. Negotiating an agreement without giving in*. London: Random House.

Galluccio, M. (2007). *Cognitive Psychotherapy and International Negotiation: An overview*. Paper presented at the 5th World Congress of Behavioural and Cognitive Therapy, 11–14 July, Barcelona, Spain.

Wells, A. (2000). *Emotional disorders and metacognition: innovative cognitive therapy*. New York: Wiley.

Young, J. A., & Beck, A. T. (1980). *Cognitive therapy scale rating manual*. http://www3.hku.hk/psychodp/students/graduate/passing_out_system/CTS_Rating_manual.pdf

Chapter 14
Transformative Leadership for Peace Negotiation

Mauro Galluccio

> ...The most important topic on earth: world peace (...) I am talking about genuine peace, the kind of peace that makes life on earth worth living, the kind that enables men and nations to grow and to hope and to build a better life for their children—not merely peace for Americans but peace for all men and women—not merely peace in our time but peace for all time (...) Let us focus instead on a more practical, more attainable peace—based not on a sudden revolution in human nature but on a gradual evolution in human institutions—on a series of concrete actions and effective agreements, which are in the interest of all concerned. There is no single, simple key to this peace, no grand or magic formula to be adopted by one or two powers. Genuine peace must be the product of many nations, the sum of many acts. It must be dynamic, not static, changing to meet the challenge of each new generation (...) For peace is a process—a way of solving problems.
>
> President John F. Kennedy, Washington, D.C., 10 June 1963

Introduction

This chapter takes an interdisciplinary approach to the study of international relations and specifically to interpersonal negotiations, as the main mechanism for managing and transforming conflicts. The literature on psychology applied to international negotiation has been progressing at a theoretical level, but we know much less about how to really master interacting cognitive and emotional processes to shape judgments and decisions in providing "operational connections" between different disciplines. The psychological cognitive-motivational approach applied in our theoretical framework (Aquilar and Galluccio 2008), together with contributors' work in this book, could help in widening, and improving, through specific tailored training programs, the understanding of negotiating beliefs and relational behavioral abilities of negotiators to face conditions of uncertainty and ambiguity, and in helping to reduce the risks of negotiation failure in related contextual situations.

Mauro Galluccio (✉)
European Association for Negotiation and Mediation (EANAM),
Square Ambiorix 32/43 B-1000 Bruxelles, Belgium
e-mail: mauro.galluccio@eanam.org

F. Aquilar and M. Galluccio (eds.), *Psychological and Political Strategies for Peace Negotiation*, DOI 10.1007/978-1-4419-7430-3_14,

Everybody agrees that peace processes cannot be nurtured by force. They can be better achieved by a process of mutual understanding. It was Gian Battista Vico who said, "For when man understands, he extends his mind to comprehend things; but when he does not understand, he makes them out of himself, and by transforming himself, becomes them" (Vico 1744, 1999, p. 160). Unfortunately, the world today is more complex and difficult to understand. We, therefore, need complex cognitive tools to face these realities. The challenges to peace that lie ahead of us have been, in some cases, unresolved from many decades. The world is geopolitically fragmented and the "division" of the great powers' areas of influence is an "ordered memory" of the past. It is difficult to think globally while facing challenges at a micro level capable of influencing the macro level, including regional disorders that do not display clear "situated" enemies and targets. This "confused" situation is reinforced by a modern paradox: an exponential and incontrollable growth of bulimic political communication tools that have been developing at the expense and detriment of an anorexic human communication modality and in general of a correct information flux around the world. As a result, politicians often seem to be caught by surprise by the way that events unfold, as well as their speed. Unfortunately, maybe because of the general complex and ambiguous international framework in which events unfold, international actors seem to display a lack, or rigidity of leadership (Keller 2009; Reicher et al. 2007). We are witnessing difficulties to master and shape international events through this "mysterious" political construct called *global governance*, where main international actors seem to have worries about negotiating the "common translation and interpretation" of it (Eco 2003). This brings discordant and asymmetric beliefs and behaviors on how to structure international institutions, to set up mechanisms to handle the complexity of political relations, to give stability to working relationships, and to facilitate negotiating processes in order to "regulate" common international interests among states and other international actors.

Even most enduring alliances in the field of international relations are under strain because of events and policies (sometimes absence or lack of cooperation) and tools deployed to face them. A part of this discrepancy between the reality and governance could also be due to a reduced meta-cognition (Wells 2000) and to a specific lack of meta-cognitive and meta-representative mental functions of governors, advisers, diplomats, and policy makers (Aquilar and Galluccio 2008). These mental functions are useful in humans to improve the mastery of an appropriate and timely ability to control events and face reality as it is (Falcone et al. 2003; Dimaggio et al. 2007). It is useful to clarify that meta-representative functions deficit is neither related to a deficiency of intelligence nor to poor public communication skills. Training and improved awareness about (also but not only) this deficit could start from the top (people who should lead and their advisers) through innovation and educational political strategies that can bring an improvement of cognitive and emotional resources of diplomats, governors, and negotiators in a way to spread this knowledge to populations as well. Thinking is understood to be an embodied process: We know things not just through our heads, but also through our actions and our bodily felt experience. Thinking, feeling, and acting are embodied, and all essays to understand behaviors without taking into account the cognitive and emotional processes could be deemed to fail in the international arena, as well in all other contexts. This should be considered as a main political priority to be pursued in this century in the field of international relations if we want to improve the cognitive well-being of populations around the globe. As President Kennedy (1963) stated in his famous speech mentioned above, no nation is able to impose peace, no matter how strong it is. Peace must instead be the product of many nations (without, however, sidelining direct concerned actors). Could we enter a new era of conscious compassionate multilateralism? Maybe it is too early to speak of sustainable multilateralism until the main international actors reach a cognitive and political awareness, and can "digest" this multi-polar world in which we all live. A world as it is now, and not as it should be, or could have been.

On the international scene, for instance, I consider the new American President Barack Obama is demonstrating a talented, compassionate, and transformative leadership. His new, seemingly unstructured, doctrine (which, however, is well structured instead) seems to be based on a "win-win" political negotiating approach in applying problem solving modalities through global negotiations. It is certainly a strong merit of President Obama to have been talking in a transformative and inspiring way to the world since his mandate began (even before) (Obama, 2008, 2009a, 2009c, 2009d, 2009e, 2009f, 2009g, 2009h, 2009i, 2009j, 2009m, 2009n, 2009o). His cooperative and open minded attitude in "pushing" international actors to face and tackle the difficult common challenges of the 21st century could explain in part why he has been awarded the Nobel Prize for Peace. The ripeness of his negotiating beliefs, attitude, and behavior is timely, appropriate, and characterized by a natural touch of awareness. He has called for a time of shared responsibility, a world where all the international actors are called upon to do their part in the interest of all humanity. In a time where there is a void of international leadership, President Obama's inner relational capacity and ability to understand, and I would say remember "the other" viewpoint, shows his mental ability to master the important meta-cognitive function of *decentering*. This is the ability to assess interactive sequences, to assume (and remember) someone else's point of view in the relational context (Aquilar and Galluccio 2008, 2009; Falcone et al. 2003; Dimaggio et al. 2007). Understanding others' values and opinions gives him a cognitive and emotional advantage (I think his great experience with communities in his country has allowed him to develop his mental capital and now it is helping him a lot as president of the USA). He has been giving a sense of hope and psychological strength to people around the globe since the beginning of his presidential mandate. Moreover, President Obama is "preaching" cooperation among nations, men, and women, as a way forward nowadays to build peace processes. The important message President Obama has been trying to pass on, and that is the core of his political doctrine, is that everybody from the bottom to the top of the pyramid of power should be engaged in interpersonal negotiations to achieve a common ground from which to negotiate and mediate, with respect, mutual interests. President Obama has based his international strategic leadership on moving, for example, towards a world free of nuclear weapons, and delivered the message to the world through his famous speech given in Prague on 5 April 2009 (Obama 2009d) that could be seen as a natural complement of the speech given on 24 July 2008 in Berlin

(Obama, 2008) during his electoral campaign. Making poverty history is another of his firm intentions, together with other political issues Obama (2009h, 2009i). But the United States cannot solve problems alone on the global stage (Nye 2004; Moïsi 2009). The reality is that they badly need "friends," and friends badly need the United States (Kagan 2003). The world is interdependent, and we need to be able to manage the interdependence through peace negotiations, with political and psychological strategies, in strengthening international cooperation in order to solve common international problems. Alliances' capacity building is more important in this historical period than ever before, and international negotiations should also help to build up sustainable working relationships. The way political leaders, negotiators, and mediators will manage these relationships is of great importance in order to foster international integrated cooperation and common coordinated problem-solving behaviors. Otherwise, peace will continue to lose precisely its most important operational modality: that of solving problems. In the world there are still too many people suffering or dying for causes that are easily treatable or through violent conflicts. Ending conflicts is just one of the moral imperatives to be achieved through international global negotiations. But until we all help to resolve problems around the globe, we will continue to be selectively and morally disengaged from the real world in which we all live (Bandura 2002, 2004).

International Organizations as Medium to bring Nations and People closer together

In this particular historical period an illusion is coming to an end: that of controlling a world that by nature cannot be controlled anymore because it is a deeply uncertain and ambiguous world. A major challenge the great powers have before them is still that of negotiating and mediating the end of wars and violent conflicts in general, or even better, their prevention, and starting inclusive peace processes together with other international actors. This also means managing power with cognitive and emotional competence unfolding cooperative synergetic leadership in building alliances and restructuring common international institutions improving their problem-solving attitudes and behaviors. Indeed, until the moment we unfold strategies to help to resolve real problems we will not be able to start mindful and "healing" peace processes among people and nations as well. This institutionalization could stabilize expectations in many ways (Nye 2003) and foster international socialization (the European Union, through the performed functions of its institutions, is a "unique" and most advanced example of it) (Cooper 2004). The process could help to face the anxiety provoked by the uncertainty that characterizes world politics, providing better shared information and more structured communication, increasing mutual trust and general credibility, insofar improving international cooperation (Keohane 2005). Moreover, this institutionalization could help to improve the quality of political relations and stability through working relationships by providing international contexts where peace negotiations will be a part of the culture of such kinds of forums.

President Obama is aware that the United States of America (USA) can anymore to longer wage any kind of wars and nurture leadership alone in an isolated context:

If the USA were to do it, its destiny would probably be that of a "lonely stressed superpower" as seems to have been the case since the fall of the Berlin Wall. The past is no longer here (analogies may endanger decision-making processes) and the future is not real (the *worst case scenario*, which was the basis of the "famous" doctrine of 1% coined by former President George W. Bush and his vice president, Dick Cheney, is not tenable anymore) (Sunstein 2007). It is far better to live in present times having a strategic vision of the future, to handle with care, where policy-makers would need to carefully differentiate between their mental states and perceived future scenarios, understanding the latter as representations of reality instead of as reality in itself – therefore potentially wrong and at best probabilistic. The world is growing multipolar, and negotiating alliances' capacity building could represent powerful strategic processes to solve common and shared international problems. The USA needs other international actors on its side (and they need the USA), to better manage the interdependence of modern times. Among alliances, the strengthening of the partnership with the European Union (EU) seems to represent a part of a strategic choice. It is also equally strategically important that the bureaucracy and decision-making procedures of leading international organizations could leave room for maneuvers for an improved institutional problem-solving attitude. It could be "interesting" to understand how international organizations' contexts may psychologically influence their officials and to propose plans and training to handle and heal dysfunctional situations.

International organizations are fundamental pillars of the international architecture, but it also seems that they could need to improve their cognitive and emotional resources potential, whom could then support their members to better consider the importance of inclusiveness in decision-making processes and the intimate link between mental health and well-being when developing policies and designing interventions on global scale (Beddington et al. 2008). Any sort of exclusion or discrimination in international negotiations of real actors playing on that contextual stage runs the risk of gathering "around the table" people who are not directly involved in those discussed issues, and who may be not "legitimately appointed" to decide upon real problems. Talking about AIDS and climate change with powerless representatives from concerned developing countries would be meaningless; or having Middle-East and Afghanistan peace talks and operating a division between bad and good guys (leaving bad guys outside the door) could invalidate the best intentions in order to pave the road for reality-based compromises. The sad and frustrating reality is that, sometimes, we have international bodies that are paralyzed by their members' negotiating behaviors, decision-making processes, internal procedures, and cultural closure, and hence their actions could be socially impotent, with actors overwhelmed by events and unable to transfer the negotiated results to the field.

Leaders around the world (and especially the USA) seem to be concerned with the difficult task of negotiating, in national and transnational contexts, inclusive strategies in a way to cede "absolute power," to attract other countries. Sharing powers on the world stage means also sharing consequential responsibilities, looking for mutual interests, and resolving common problems: Peace is a way of solving problems, and it should be done by all the actors, and not just by quartets, six party meetings, and G2 gatherings. It also means a proliferation of actors and a new geography of powers, with a consequential proliferation of pacific tools to handle international conflicts, where global negotiation and mediation will be playing decisive roles. Situations of structural uncertainty, an absence of effective authority and decision rules, and stalemates in unilateral means of solving problems and resolving conflicts are all conditions that call for negotiating alliances among main actors on the international scene (Bercovitch and Jackson 2001). This increases the social interest in managing conflicts in sustainable ways with scientific issues likely to provide the knowledge that will lead to more constructive conflicts resolution tools (Deutsch 2002; Kelman and Fisher 2003) and a better mastery of human interactions. If conflicts can be caught early on and managed effectively, they could be better contained and transformed. Strategic integrated process approaches used to solve problems is deemed of great importance as "The balance between war and peace may be a matter not of the nature of the differences that divide us but of *the process we use to resolve these differences*" (Raiffa 2002, p. 9).

Small and Flexible Teams of Negotiators Within International Institutional Frameworks: The Case of the European Union

Peace negotiation represents, as never before, major tool to try to build up an implemented international cooperation around the globe. However, in order not to "amplify" the asymmetry in the negotiation contexts (poor countries with unskilled negotiating actors vs richer countries with experienced negotiating actors), there is a need to increase the cognitive and emotional resources of all actors, empowering their skills through integrated tailored training available for all of them (Galluccio, 2005a, 2005d). If negotiators are trained with all the available techniques and methods for them "to play the counterpart," this will just produce or multiply asymmetric negotiations with consequential loss of hope and "disturbance" of social peace. Instead, inclusive negotiation strategies could be encouraged so as to foster and nurture working relationship capacity building through:

1. The establishment of international minimum training standards for negotiations.
2. The improvement of communication and meta-communication tools.
3. The mastery of mass-media tools and ability to channel communication but avoiding political propaganda.
4. The awareness of the powerful relational *momentum* represented by breakdown points in negotiation processes.
5. The ability to create *momentum* within negotiation processes and to channel them to the press and media in general (Aquilar and Galluccio 2008).

In thinking globally we should take care to develop operational, flexible mental and technical cognitive tools to also handle specific and complex locally based situations. Nowadays, conflicts have changed their nature (Aquilar and Galluccio 2009; Kaldor 2006). Today, around the world, there is not a prevalence of conflicts between states anymore, but rather intra-state violent ethnic conflicts. As environments and general political frameworks have changed, or are changing, roles international actors might play have been changing as well. Transnational corporations may be involved in local conflicts, and states may be confronted with more or less structured terrorist groups. The metaphor of the story of *David and Goliath* has never been more topical than today.

International organizations and their institutions could help to facilitate this role playing change process by implementing the capability to throw out their influence and cognitive-strategic thinking to try to help better face, negotiate, and resolve some of the problems of this multipolar world, where different centers of power may not always have cooperative attitudes (Galluccio, 2008). It could be useful to set up flexible teams of negotiators, mediators, and advisors, who are cognitively oriented and able to move back and forth (within the received negotiated mandate) with a certain degree of "intellectual" autonomy from the bureaucracy and procedures of international structures. International organizations could create inside their premises small, flexible, and structured teams of negotiators and mediators. Moreover, they could create training centers, composed by cognitive psychologists and psychotherapists, as well as political scientists, sociologists, negotiators, and mediators, to provide and coordinate different kinds of integrated and tailored specialized training courses for "carefully" selected subjects. At the same time, such centers could also play an important role as "guardians" with technical and cognitive competence (belonging to the organization and institutions) in assessing the work and proposals of external trainers and experts who could have contacts with these organizations. For instance, the European Commission, the European Parliament and the Council of the European Union spend each year considerable amounts of money to train their officials on negotiation theory and techniques and related intrapersonal and interpersonal skills enhancing courses. Why do not create, instead, special cells for interpersonal negotiation and mediation training? Why not set up a team of specialized negotiators and mediators having received a specific integrated training in order to join negotiating delegations on different issues? To negotiate a ceasefire, or sit on a panel for investigating hidden dumping suspicions are two different issues, but both should be handled with care and compassionate competence with the aim of trying to build up working relationships.

International organizations and their institutions could also liaise/cooperate with specific external teams of negotiators and mediators, but they could do it with a different "cognition of cause." Synergies will be mastered and assessed by public international institutional powers, which could also help more easily to avoid or limit general or sectorial "gaming the system" risks. Even in cases of violent conflicts, e.g., terrorist groups, such teams might be able to apply a sustainable communication back-channels strategy in a way to really influence the peace process in a politically proactive way by avoiding dangerous bureaucratic-political untimely standstills.

The European Union, for instance, sends European representatives with different regional competencies around the world to facilitate political dialogue and conflict prevention or resolution. The kind of teams we have been describing could also be put at disposal to assist representatives with their tasks. The European Union Special Envoys and their advisers, if cognitively and emotionally empowered, could acquire added value as mediators of the organization and its institutions. The political and psychological process of transforming the conflict consists also of accompanying measures and techniques that can help to:

- Increase the cognitive and emotional resources of parties
- Challenge cognitive-behavior abilities and enhance cognitive-behavior modification
- Pave the way for reconciliation
- Monitor peace processes

These teams could be aiming to build trust through reciprocated knowledge among themselves and between the parties they are supposed to work with. They need patience and goodwill to manage endless negotiation processes and never-ending conflict mediations. They should have the modesty of being *super partes*, neutral, supranational, and to keep their size small, and be reliable cells within the European Union's larger institutional framework, and their credibility will be built and monitored by "the citizen." The European Union seems to be fit to perform this great task and lead by example because negotiating political strategies should comprehend:

1. Long term commitment without being guided by "political-business principles" (you know when you start the process, but you do not know when it will be ended).
2. Long term presence on the ground (we have the European Union delegations around the world, and this is a vital logistic element that is important for this strategy).
3. Moral and ethical authority based on a body of common high principles and values now also enshrined in the Treaty of Lisbon.
4. A soft and mindful power, whose main tool is represented by *moral suasion,* able to mobilize third parties and build up working relationships and attract other international actors (nations, international organizations, NGOs, think tanks, universities, civil society as a whole, etc.). This way will enhance the ability to mobilize human network potential and institutional webs to help, through cooperative efforts, conflict resolution, and peace processes implementation.

The European Union and US Negotiating Behaviors

The European Union has undoubtedly important negotiating and mediating skills and a great and invaluable internal experience in alliance capacity building, and it seems well "positioned" to lead on this international path in tandem with its member States. The "community method" oriented toward sustainable compromises within the European Union has been greatly improved and implemented, and it has helped to construe internal coexistence and policy coherence. However, it seems as there is still something missing: an external global political recognition as "full" global player. This could be the right moment to rise and play a leading role on the international stage that President Obama seems to be offering to the United States' special allies. It is time to act, because missing this political opportunity would be sad and frustrating, especially for the "European citizen." The interdependence and interaction of two strategic partners, as the USA and the EU, through an improved cooperation process could bring fruitful results to the international community as a whole. Again, this is an historical period to face international challenges together instead of closing "external doors" and concentrating on domestic problems. Events unfold notwithstanding our willingness, but at the same time they prepare the field for seizing the opportunities globalization has brought for social structures as well. The USA can no longer guarantee international security and stability on its own because in order to address global threats it will need the legitimacy that Europe can provide (Kagan 2003). The EU could lead by example (that's a rare art in politics) through open dialogue and shared common ground (its great internal experience). It could "export" the European Union Governance based on a sound institutional framework and political and economic solidarity between member states through peaceful negotiations and mediation processes. But talking about hard, soft, smart, and intelligent powers may well be wishful thinking if the EU member states lack the political will to go ahead. For the EU member States not to rethink and redefine the EU political role on the international scene would be politically myopic in that it would fail to prepare for the future and could condemn the organization to remain but a hybrid between an incomplete political union and a big economic free trade zone.

On the other side of the Atlantic Ocean, President Obama's administration has achieved a real breakthrough in diplomacy and negotiating attitude and behavior. The president has been showing a rare political coherence on the international stage between his electoral campaign and ongoing presidency even if he is "pressured" by internal issues. He is offering to establish diplomatic working relationships with all international actors: with friends and especially with foes of the USA, towards whom, instead, President George W. Bush's administration had taken rigid political stances and shown rigid and inflexible negotiating behavior. The great US negotiator Robert Gallucci (2002) said during an interview: "One of the things that's very difficult, and I haven't quite figured it out yet, and this (Bush) administration is not helping me figure it out, is how to bring the American people along to believe that negotiations can be an honorable way to deal with the national security issues."

The history of international relations teaches us that negotiations and mediation have always been the most useful political and diplomatic mechanisms to solve international disputes (Bercovitch and Jackson 2001). The illusion of isolating adversaries in order to make them accept democratic rules:

1. Triggers rage (and other negative emotions).
2. Reduces trust and reciprocal knowledge.
3. Fosters hostility.

4. Freezes political positions and stances.
5. Increases the production of "Prisoners of Hate" (Beck 1999, 2002).

The ending of the cold war was characterized by two fundamental kinds of *momentum:* (1) the start of diplomatic relations between China and USA in the 1970s (despite China backing the USA foes during the Vietnam war), when former President Nixon took a decision to open the USA relations with China; and (2) the change of political attitudes between Reagan and Gorbachev in the 1980s. Moreover, both kinds of *momentum* were led by two US Republican presidents, and Mr. George Bush was a vice-president during Reagan's presidency period. Also, what was the most important momentum for peace in the Middle East region? Considering former Egyptian President Anwar el-Sadat and his journey to Jerusalem, or former Israeli Prime Minister Yitzhak Rabin and his pursuit of the Oslo accords: Did they do the right thing in trying to negotiate a peace process? An attentive observer might point out that the two leaders in the Middle-East paid for the opening of peace negotiation processes with their lives, and Mr. Gorbachev left office under political pressures before the end of his term.

My sincere hope is that President Obama continues to look forward to negotiating and mediating on the international stage. I am here defending an attitude of negotiating and mediating common grounds for resolving international problems all together with shared responsibilities. If he will be able to reflect Kennedy's view of peace processes he really might continue a dream President Kennedy had; and we will see whether it works. President Obama is spreading a culture of dialogue even in the most complicated and complex international political situations in some parts of the world. His remarks at the Pentagon Memorial, Arlington, Virginia on September 11, 2010 (Obama, 2010): "As Americans we are not – and never will be – at war with Islam. It was not a religion that attacked us that September day" demonstrate cognitive, emotional, and political rare qualities for an international leader. The strategy of inclusion is more difficult and uncertain than that of isolating enemies, but it can give a real chance to peace processes through negotiations. To think, feel, and act straightforward and to cultivate a culture of hope instead of a culture of fear, or even worse a culture of hate, represents a main breakthrough that could be able to mitigate this terrible love human beings seems to have for war (Hillman, 2004). Giving hope to our counterparts is better that strategically humiliating them by behaving in a way to make them fear us, which seems to be a politically unsustainable illusion likely to backfire more often than not.

Interpersonal Negotiations

Negotiating sustainable alliances among different international actors is a formidable task for leaders and their advisers around the world. However, it seems especially a test for Mr. Obama's presidency, measuring the degree of achievement or failure of his foreign policy, whose main doctrine seems to be based on the awareness of the inadequacy of the zero-sum beliefs, a precursor of the zero-sum game, and instead on the doctrine of a "win-win" game to *negotiating without losers*. Throughout, the meaning of this "win-win" strategy needs to be specified in operational terms and discussed with all international partners. In fact, if it were (mis) interpreted unilaterally as a sort of masked zero-sum game it could cause even more damage among "friends and foes" by creating disagreement and disillusion. This in turn will determine a "preventive failure" of the strategy to negotiate a comprehensive, coherent, and inclusive global partnership to manage international cooperation among nations. The strategy will be a paying one if we are instead able to negotiate what is really at the core of all negotiations: reciprocal trust and confidence among the international community actors. The USA will be facing the hardest choice between the need to manage the power and the dilemma of relying on partnerships to ensure their homeland security as well. It should be honestly recognized that great powers may have common interests, but each of them have their own interpretation of what common interest means. Being aware of this anthropological, psychological, and political fact will help actors to adopt respectful positions and also sometimes *to agree to disagree* in a peaceful way, bearing in mind that their negotiating behavior may be perceived as aggressive and could prompt fear, rage, hatred, and consequential reactions from the other side (Aquilar and Galluccio, 2005).

"We are stronger when we act together!" This is the message President Obama carried on throughout his trip to Europe in the springtime of 2009. However, his most difficult task will be that of negotiating a common ground with his partners where duties and rights, joy and pain, charges and burdens, in one word, responsibility, will be equally shared, in order to define conflicting interests as a mutual problem to be satisfyingly resolved (Deutsch 2002), but where partners will be assured to be active subjects in political decision-making processes.

President Obama has received a Nobel Prize on a sort of blind faith for achievements, but we think also on courage showed in talking to the world the way he is doing (he will run for another presidential mandate within 2 years). However, the president in the near future could be more influenced, while talking to the world, by this dynamic of internal consensus. The world is characterized by a growing complexity, and the development of complex intrapersonal and interpersonal cognitive-emotional skills and of mental states mastery could be precious tools in leaders' "hands" to manage this complexity. Investing in human capital through a specific cognitive training program could be part of a common strategic aim to improve alliance capacity building and coordinate international problem solving modalities.

Individual and Social Cognitive Mechanisms Influencing Decision-Making Processes

> "We of the Kennedy and Johnson's administrations who participated in the decisions on Vietnam acted according to what we thought were the principles and traditions of this nation. We made our decisions in light of those values. Yet we were wrong, terribly wrong (...) I truly believe that we made an error not of values and intentions, but of judgement and capabilities."
>
> McNamara and Vandemark (1995: xvi)

President Obama's (2009n) Nobel lecture transcript shows clearly his awareness of certain "thinking errors" that could be harmful for the information system and affect political decision-making processes. He specifically speaks of "gaming the system," referring to some foreign nations: "...But it is also incumbent upon all of us to insist that nations like Iran and North Korea do not game the system." "Gaming the system" is an information manipulation strategy through which high level government decision-making could be guided by some members of government teams. They could selectively frame the information, or distort the type of different opinions of advisors through a proactive manipulation in order to misguide and voluntarily bias the information that will be allowed to a decision-making process. This behavior could be strictly linked to the phenomenon observed and described first by Janis (1982) as "groupthink," in which some persons from the team of decision-makers can act as *mindguards* in a way to opt, in the process of decision making, for a sort of secrecy of the information to the point of excluding experts, mass-media, and outside critics in order to retain unity and *esprit de corps*. Both in "gaming the system" and "groupthink," what seems to be in danger is the final decision about a certain issue that could be defective, because there is an incomplete survey of information endangering the decision making process and alternative courses of action. However, groupthink has been studied and found application first to US governments, especially during Kennedy's and Carter's presidencies (Aquilar and Galluccio 2008; Janis 1982). Gaming the system instead has been better assessed by the 2008 Pulitzer winner, Barton Gellman (2008), in a book on the US vice presidency of Dick Cheney, who apparently seemed to have this constant behavioral attitude in gaming the system.

Leaders and politicians in general should also be careful of cognitive distortions (thinking errors), in themselves and their counterparts, such as dichotomous thinking, selective abstraction, overgeneralization, arbitrary inference, labeling, tunnel vision, to name but few of them extensively treated in our previous book (Aquilar and Galluccio 2008; Beck 1988, 1995, 1999). Moreover, they should be aware of human cognitive interpersonal cycles (Aquilar and Galluccio 2008; Galluccio 2004, 2007; Safran 1984, 1998; Safran and Muran 2000; Semerari 2006); meta-cognitive and meta-representational functions deficit (Aquilar and Galluccio 2008; Dimaggio et al. 2007); the social mechanisms of selective moral disengagement (Aquilar and Galluccio 2009; Bandura 2002), applied also to the terrorism and counter-terrorism actions (Bandura 2004); the Lucifer effect where common and usually peaceful people may develop a tendency to display harmful behaviors towards others, hurting them if "pushed" in this sense by an authoritative person (Zimbardo 2007; See Chapter by Francesco Aquilar, this volume); the phenomenon of the intoxication of power caused by the "Hubris Syndrome" described by David Owen as when "power has gone to political leaders and governors' head," wherein to many political leaders the very experience of holding office and substantial power for a certain length of time seems to infect them and undermine their mental stability and behaviors (Owen 2007).

Aware Leadership for the Future

The importance of having in each political cabinet, or negotiating team, professionals and advisers cognitively oriented with characteristics and training briefly described along this chapter could represent a major tool to better assess final decisions (See Aquilar and Galluccio 2008). Professionals who know the importance of sustaining and advising leaders in decision-making processes, as for instance, to practically be concentrated on the present time, but be able to divide present situations from apparently similar analogous past situations (Houghton 1998; See Chapter by Don Meichenbaum, this volume). They could help to develop a timely and purposeful political strategy that is psychologically oriented, to aim to support leaders and decision-makers to master uncertainty and ambiguity present in international relations.

In our vision, these professionals could help to facilitate political processes by trying to implement cooperative attitudes and behaviors among international actors. This represents a powerful means to build and implement peace processes through interpersonal negotiations. Each negotiation should not be an end in itself. It should be rather a tool to develop processes of awareness and understanding of the other part's spoken and written words (Eco 2003), needs and actions in nurturing working relationships and creating security and stability in international relations. The personal traits and negotiating styles and behaviors of main actors, cognition, emotions, motivations, ways to comm-unicate, values, principles, all have a direct impact on the negotiation processes and likely outcomes. As Bob Leahy timely states in this volume, "If we attempt to understand, empathize, validate, and find common ground we may find more than we bargained for: We may find peace." This should be the main and very difficult task of governors and their political advisers. But peace is not a static concept. It is rather a very dynamic and changing state of mind. How could we find peace and help others to benefit from it?

As I noted beforehand, the world has become a "global village," challenges and opportunities that lie ahead are complex and interdependent, and learning processes should continue throughout lives and careers. Those countries able to capitalize on their citizens' cognitive and emotional resources are countries that will prosper more and could help other countries to do the same (Beddington et al. 2008). Howard Gardner, of Harvard University and a distinguished contributor to this book, is concerned in his professional life also with the kinds of minds that people will need to develop if they – if we – are to thrive in the world during the eras to come. To meet this new world on its own terms, we should begin to cultivate these capacities now.

Gardner's (2006) five minds for the future are here summarized:

1. *The disciplinary mind*: Mastery of major schools of thought (including science, mathematics, and history), and of at least one professional craft.
2. *The synthesizing mind*: Ability to integrate ideas from different disciplines or spheres into a coherent whole and to communicate that integration to others.
3. *The creating mind*: Capacity to uncover and clarify new problems, questions, and phenomena.

4. *The respectful mind*: Awareness of and appreciation for differences among human beings.
5. *The ethical mind*: Fulfillment of one's responsibilities as a worker and a citizen.

   To these minds we would like to add two important ones, the sixth conceptualized by Paul Gilbert (2009) (see Aquilar 2008a):
6. *The compassionate mind*: Because cruelty can flourish when our capacity for compassion is turned off, especially in specific environments.

   The seventh one takes a stake from Buddhist tradition:
7. *The mindfulness*: We are part of a society with peoples and nations that seem to be concentrated on future time, losing sight that their present time will be the past of those who will come after them. Political advisers could make efforts to raise awareness among their leaders and staff in general of the importance of social-skills nurturing and resilience (in the face of stress) development, and collaborative-aware exploration of interpersonal behaviors, on "what is going on," *here and now*. This is a different, enlarged, and optimistic perspective, where the attention is on present states of mind, activating problem-solving modalities, and focusing on possible solutions, instead of recriminating on past interactions, or of dreaming too much in detail about the future that by definition it does not yet exist (Safran and Muran 2000).

Negotiating Working Relationship

Internal and external peace, within and among negotiating teams, requires also human and technical skills to sense, detect, and master impairments, or minor "disturbances," in the quality of working relationships between actors involved in negotiation processes, with a particular attention to events such as agreements and breakdowns in negotiation. Now onwards, the attention will be focused on the latter because we think that the first has instead received more attention in the specialized literature (Fisher et al. 1991; Kremenyuk 2002; Raiffa 1982; Thompson 2006; Watkins and Rosegrant 2001). Each negotiating breakdown is characterized by a certain contextual environment, timing, intensity, duration, endurance, and particular history, depending on the issues at the stake. But it is also "influenced" by the mentality and personality of actors who are involved into the negotiation process, and by the working relationships, for the bad or the worse, they have been able to build up. Cases where a part may blatantly express strong emotions to the other part or even, precipitately leave the negotiating room are not so rare. Moreover, there are times where minor perturbations in the quality of working relationships may be extremely difficult to detect even for a skilled negotiator; nevertheless it is important to learn how to address them in a way to prevent, or transform conflicts. A working relationship building process may consist of three independent elements: (a) the relational bond between different parties; (b) the tasks and structure of the negotiation (i.e., the specific issues and actions in which parties are required to engage in); and (c) the goals to be achieved by the negotiation (i.e., final outcomes different actors would like to achieve). The quality of negotiating relationships may be structured in function of the degree of agreement between parties about the goals and tasks of the negotiation. However, the quality of the relational bond between parties could also be affected by intrapersonal and interpersonal dimensions of the actors involved into the process (Argyle 1994; Safran 1998; Safran and Segal 1990).

The significance I give to a sound working relationship might lead some to conclude that negotiating techniques, tactics, and strategies are less important than the relational aspects. The complexity and subtlety of negotiation processes cannot be reduced to a set of disembodied techniques, because techniques gain their meaning, and in turn, their effectiveness from the particular interaction of individuals and issues involved in that particular contextual environment. The mutual impact of the different actors' behaviors into the process could ultimately be understood in terms of actors' mutual perception of interpersonal negotiating behaviors, and this perception could also be determined by the unique learning story of each single actor. One and the same negotiating behavior by an actor may thus be interpreted very differently by two or more different counterparts. While a party may perceive it in a way that promotes the negotiating working relationship, another one may perceive it in a manner that impedes it. This is because an actor's perception of the meaning of other's people actions is organized around interpersonal schemas that are based on past experience and generalized expectations about self-other interactions (Dimaggio et al. 2007; Guidano and Liotti 1983; Safran 1984; Safran and Segal 1990; Semerari 2006). These interpersonal schemas may be dysfunctional and may activate "negative" cognitive interpersonal cycles in which, for example, the expectations of an actor may lead to a negotiating behavior on her part that is likely to elicit predictable interpersonal cycles that may confirm her dysfunctional negotiating beliefs (Aquilar and Galluccio 2008). Instead, if the counterpart with her responses is able to avoid being "entrapped" in the other side's interpersonal modality web, the latter could experience a positive "cognitive dissonance" in maybe challenging her dysfunctional expectations.

Here comes to the fore the importance of focusing attention on negotiating breakdowns, which could also occur at the moment where the counterpart's negotiating behavior and actions confirm the other actor's dysfunctional interpersonal schema (Aquilar and Galluccio 2008; Safran 1998). Hence, they are important events that may occur during negotiation processes, which demands a particular awareness and appropriate tools and techniques for fruitful investigations. A specific cognitive training programme, able to implement awareness on how to continue the negotiation, while "repairing" breakdowns, should provide actors with suitable cognitive and emotional skills. These acquired social skills could allow negotiators to better understand counterparts' negotiating behaviors in perhaps exploring together expectations, needs, beliefs, cognitive distortions, emotions, and appraisal processes that play a central role in an actor's dysfunctional cognitive-interpersonal cycles (Safran 1998; Safran and Segal 1990). The successful resolution of a negotiating breakdown can be one of the most influential means of transforming the conflict between actors to improve the quality of relationships, and could be a catalyst for sustainable individual and collective social changes. Instead, failure to adequately resolve a breakdown could lead to poor outcomes in negotiations and put relationships under serious strains.

Cognitive and emotional skills could also have the potential to improve the sustainability of negotiation processes by helping actors in some cases, for example, to clarify whether they really have been targets of a counterpart's "malevolent" action aimed at humiliating, demeaning, or patronizing them; or to put it another way, they have perceived and *felt feelings* of having been humiliated, demeaned, or patronized.

Breakdown Resolution and Alliance Building: Training Elements

The mastery of meta-communication processes and improvements of meta-cognitive and meta-representative functions are powerful cognitive tools that could improve breakdown resolution chances. The human communication tool called meta-communication stands for talking about the communication, in other words, talking about what is taking place during the negotiation process. This strategic communication is, of course, a main tool to be unfolded in any interpersonal approach in our lives and it should be largely used in all negotiation and mediation processes. However, meta-communication becomes very useful in critical contextual moments, as when we have negotiating breakdown impairments. We will emphasize those aspects of a meta-communication process strategy that could be important to master in the process of breakdown resolution (Aquilar and Galluccio 2008; Safran 1998; Safran and Muran 2000), highlighting useful meta-cognitive functions and related abilities to be improved (Aquilar and Galluccio 2008; Falcone et al. 2003; Dimaggio et al. 2007):

- *Attending to breakdowns in the negotiating relationship.* The process of resolution cannot begin until the breakdown has been perceived as such by all involved actors. The correct perception of what is going on is essential and should not be underestimated. For example, diplomatic negotiators could be reluctant to communicate negative attitudes, emotions, or behaving accordingly (while feeling different emotions from what they are showing). This is because emotions are governed by "social norms" or should we say social expectations, and both reflect and sustain the social structures in which they develop (Parkinson et al. 2005; Thoits 2004). Hence, to notice working relationship impairments in advance and to try to prevent breakdowns can be problematic. A perceptual readiness should be nurtured through cognitive-oriented training to provide for an "early warning" system as a way to detect even the threat of a breakdown. Breakdown markers could facilitate the systematic identification of such threats and hopefully enhance conflict resolution possibilities (i.e., verbal and nonverbal communication/expression of emotions; indirect communication of hostility; rigidity in disagreeing about goals or tasks; presence of dysfunctional beliefs and cognitive distortions that could be manifested through avoidance maneuvers; "compulsive" self-esteem-enhancing operations; systematic non-cooperative attitude; etc.).

Here comes to the fore the importance of the meta-cognitive function called "integration," which is the ability to reflect on emotional and mental states; to consciously organize them in an ordered sequence; to structure a thought's hierarchy (by importance). This way, behaviors will have the consistency necessary for adaptation and the pursuit of goals "guided" by defined coherent individuals' identity;

- *Implementing intrapersonal and interpersonal emotional competence.* This is a fundamental step to be carefully assessed during the training program because cognitive and emotional competence represents a useful "human compass" for a better "orientation" at negotiators' disposal to be deployed all along the negotiation process. The ability of actors to recognize, express, and modulate emotions may provide important interpersonal information that could help implement the communication process. Moreover, the identification of one's own emotions is an important part of the process of accepting responsibility. It represents a useful tool to appraise the situation with "open eyes," and could bring an objective admission that this situation has been originated by the intrinsic interdependence of main actors. Unfortunately, if negotiators are not able to accurately recognize their own emotions at the least (notwithstanding that of the other side), their actions will be biased by factors outside their consciousness. Emotional awareness offers a flexibility of responses based on the particular history of interactions with the environment (Galluccio 2004). For example, a negotiator who is angry at his counterpart but is avoiding displaying that anger may nevertheless communicate it in subtle ways through his nonverbal language. In this view, situational determinants may determine emotional arousal; but these cannot be separated from the role an individual's cognitive processes may play, not only in interpreting the situations but also in generating many of them (Safran and Segal, 1990).

Here comes to the fore the importance of the meta-cognitive function called "identification," which is the ability to appropriately recognize one's own and others' emotions; and identifying links between cognition (thoughts) and emotions (I feel inadequate because I think I am not well prepared to face certain issues in this negotiation); or between intrapersonal and interpersonal dimensions (I feel outraged because he is trying to patronize me);

- *Accepting responsibility.* One of the most important components of awareness in resolving a relational breakdown and implementing peace negotiations consists of the negotiator acknowledging his or her role in the interactional process. The reason for this importance is that often when there is a breakdown, negotiators may become locked into a negative cognitive interpersonal cycle in which they are both trying to defend their actions and "justify" their negotiating behaviors. Instead, this situation could be unlocked if the negotiator is able to transform the conflict, by transferring it from a competitive to a cooperative playground. This is a collaborative activity and should include oneself in the description of the interaction in assuming responsibility for the role played and contribution given to the process of interdependence. This way, the situation could begin to shift from one in which there is a sense of "me against you," to one in which there is a sense of "we-ness" (Safran 1998). If the breakdown begins to be perceived as "our problem," a sense of connectedness may begin to develop (Galluccio 2004, Galluccio 2007a).

Here comes to the fore the importance of the meta-cognitive function called "differentiation," which is the ability to understand the mental states as representations of reality, therefore potentially wrong and at least probabilistic (distinguishing between reality and wishful thinking);

- *Assessing interactive sequences with empathy.* Awareness of one's own responsibility and contributions to the interdependence is very important. However, it could also be extremely fruitful for a negotiator to timely communicate empathic and compassionate feelings about what has been "detected" from the counterpart's experience. This way, the counterpart may feel understood and could start a common exploration process to find out what is going on in the interaction. However, even if often the process of conflict resolution could be facilitated by this empathic communication, sometimes it could instead inhibit it. Our experience and direct observation on the spot has been that this negative dynamic of inhibition tends to happen when the counterpart feels patronized by the other part's empathic response (which could be missing compassion) (see Paul Gilbert in this volume).

Here comes to the fore the importance of the meta-cognitive function called "decentering," which is the ability to assess interactive sequences, being able to assume (and remember) someone else's point of view in the relational context. Decentering refers to acquired mental skills that allow individuals to see the perspective from which others relate to the world and to realize that their negotiating behavior may be "guided" by values, principles, and goals that could differ from ours and could also not be directly related to our interpersonal relationship dynamics;

- *Mastering Uncertainty.* Addressing a breakdown could be a difficult task because you intervene to open up a scenario of crisis. This is a huge responsibility, even if it is intended as a step forward to implement the quality of the alliance between different actors. As experience shows, human beings attach different meanings to the same words. For example, our counterpart could have an emotion of fear just thinking about the word "crisis." Sometimes, instead, addressing a "hidden" breakdown to try to prevent conflict escalation could be embarrassing, uncomfortable, and possibly a threatening experience because you know when you start to address it but you do not know: (1) if you will be able to handle it; (2) if it will work; (3) and when it will be ended. One should not allow uncertainty of the present time to make her/him uncertain on a long-period as well.

Here comes to the fore the importance of the meta-cognitive function called "mastery," which is the ability to intentionally intervene on one's own thoughts, mental states and emotional states, in order to solve tasks, or master problematic states, in a way to adequately face complex situations. This could be seen as an improved cognitive and emotional awareness of oneself in the process of coping with distress in general and stressful interpersonal contexts, where reflective efforts are required to avoid feeling impotent (powerless) and giving up chances to actively contribute to ongoing interactions.

Often leaders, diplomats, and negotiators may try to avoid open rifts by behaving as if nothing happened, even against the evidence. In doing so, they risk being moulded into the quicksand of a difficult meta-communication modality without addressing the relational core of the rift and facilitating, on the contrary, the entrapment of actors into maladaptive interpersonal cognitive cycles. Instead, if they focus and are able to master a breakdown resolution they could have a better opportunity to enhance their relational competence and improve interpersonal negotiation skills, and they may gain confidence and hope that they could do it again in another negotiating context.

A Cognitive Oriented Political Strategy

Our political and psychological strategy for peace negotiation puts forward four mutually reinforcing priorities:

- *Aware negotiations*: developing integrated training courses based on techniques, knowledge, and innovation; fostering cognitive and emotional resources, creative, analytical and social skills, and resilience improvement. Such training should be made available for all parties in order to master more balanced negotiation processes;.
- *Sustainable negotiations*: promoting more cooperative, efficient, and ethical negotiation processes;.
- *Inclusive negotiations*: fostering a broad framework for all actors involved in different issues; delivering, through interpersonal negotiations, socially cohesive results;.
- *Balanced negotiations*: negotiating within alliances a common approach to problem solving that should be careful without being paranoid.

This strategy should be implemented through specific training tailored to different subjects involving governors, rulers, advisers, negotiators, etc., in order to:

(a) Increase theoretical as well as experiential knowledge of cognitive and emotional dynamics within negotiation processes.
(b) Encourage analytical reflection on negotiation processes that affect the quality of public life.
(c) Enhance awareness of preferred as well as habitual negotiating styles and behaviors.
(d) Encourage experimentation with negotiation methods that can be used to advance high-priority interests and values while protecting working relationships.
(e) Support the formulation of strategies for improving interpersonal negotiation skills and managing international conflicts through peace negotiations.

Our far-reaching proposals for training politicians, negotiators and mediators aim to challenge and improve their cognitive-behavioral abilities. This could enable them to act as catalysts for social change, bringing sustainable benefits for individuals, societies, and nations. A cross-governmental approach might be beneficial. This could bring substantial changes in the nature of governance, taking into account the intimate link between mental health and well-being of peoples, when developing policies and designing interventions (Beddington et al. 2008). A specialized training at the heart of policy-making could provide benefits to citizens and nations alike.

Conclusions

US President Obama's doctrine is based on a "win-win" approach, but this doctrine seems to lack a theoretical framework that defines techniques for "cognitive-behavioral modification" that is able to nurture mental changes in leaders, rulers, negotiators, mediators, and public opinion. An example of "cognitive-behavioral modification" could be that of using techniques based on cognitive psychology and psychotherapy to modify a political adviser's "war mentality."

President Obama's main political and human qualities can be summarized as follows:

1. No cognitive egocentrism;
2. No US-centrism;
3. Not excessively simplifying the world, unlike George W. Bush and Tony Blair, who both tried to simplify the world and seem to have displayed cognitive distortions and deficits with regard to meta-cognitive and meta-representative functions (Aquilar and Galluccio 2008);
4. Taking care of more underprivileged categories of citizens (from national health reform in the USA to policies in favor of poor people around the globe);
5. Seeking interpersonal negotiations without losers. This represents a basic element of our project. The only losers should be anti-democratic forces, criminals, and spoilers (foes and friends);
6. Using a gradual transformative approach to problem-solving. This approach, seems appropriate in order to avoid upsetting the economic and political equilibrium, and causing dangerous political imbalances worldwide;
7. Showing a calm and coherent anti-racist attitude that is strongly felt and mastered, which is a real and not rhetorical attitude;
8. Paying more attention to substance than form: President Obama is a remarkably informal leader.

In this context, from an outside viewpoint, a contribution to improving these skills might include:

1. Contextualizing issues for domestic audiences. President Obama's speeches at West Point and Brookings Institution (Obama, 2009l, 2009m), for example, could have been focused more on the interdependence of the actual world and on the necessity to implement cooperative strategies to manage this interdependence all together. A word about the "external world," even for these types of domestic speeches, could enhance cognitive awareness that the USA is no longer alone on the world stage when it comes to facing international problems.
2. Making changes at a reasonable pace. Although the US presidency lasts 8 years at most, sometimes President Obama could act with even more audacity ("the audacity of Hope", 2006) and show a bit more firmness towards certain interlocutors (foes or friends) without fearing internal lobbies.
3. Taking care of the explicit psychological aspects of interpersonal negotiations and including experts in cognitive psychology in his political staff. President

Obama is a politician who knows how to do his job and has a good knowledge of the political-legal system. He is also surrounded by skilled people. If he could enrich his staff with advisers who are familiar with cognitive psychology and psychotherapy, he would gain better tools for cognitive-behavioral modification, to influence the thinking of both his supporters and his opponents and pass on his political messages.

4. Helping to set up, together with all other international actors, a committee on international negotiation and mediation, to establish international shared rules on negotiations, and minimum training standards (with the help of cognitive psychologists, psychotherapists, sociologists, and political scientists).
5. Creating a space on President Obama's staff for advisers experienced in "predicting" trends and innovative thinking. As Howard Gardner loves to recall, at this historical stage human ideas change faster than before. This process of innovation does not just concern goods and services. It also applies to views and opinions (see Howard Gardner, this volume) including those of leaders, rulers, and negotiators, as well as public opinions. It could also help to change negative image representations through which certain nations perceive each other (see Olivier Faure, this volume).

Professionals' and political advisors' contribution to sustaining and "counseling" leaders in decision-making processes might include:

6. Helping political leaders to master the uncertainty of the modern era and to develop the cognitive and emotional mental health of nations.
7. Refining political and psychological techniques of persuasion to elicit and implement a peace-oriented attitude in public opinions, especially in non-democratic countries. Political control over non-democratic countries should not only come from the deterrence of weapons, but also from an "educated" public opinion within that country. Social psychotherapy can help populations in democratic countries (see Francesco Aquilar, this volume), but perhaps even more so in non-democratic countries, improving the mental resources of communities across the world.
8. Helping to choose the right negotiators, at the right time, for the right situation. We need "anthropologically appropriate" negotiators and mediators who can understand the thinking and the culture of their interlocutors.
9. Ensuring that the information and communication process is as transparent as possible. Civil society should be better informed if we want it to be more engaged in pressing governments for change and creating democratic societies based on diversity, tolerance, and equality.

Peace processes are largely a matter of cooperation and partnership between different actors (especially those directly involved in the conflict), who must play their own proactive roles among other actors in order to achieve mutually satisfying and sustainable negotiated results.

The future requires leaders who can actively influence peace processes through negotiation and implement the final results. However, we need to make sure that negotiators are playing the same "game." Unfortunately, today, often international negotiations resemble a situation where some of the actors are playing football, others rugby and others handball. The rules and timing are completely different, and finding common ground represents a virtually insurmountable challenge for those involved. That is also why we need minimum training standards for negotiators and mediators. It would be better to reach an awareness that all the actors in the negotiation process are interpersonally linked and play an active role in shaping working relationships. Believing negotiating behaviors improve without individual efforts could be *wishful thinking*. Believing that working relationships can deteriorate just because of the counterpart could sometimes be a demonstration of cognitive egocentrism and a lack of emotional competence.

Most of all, we need new methods and techniques for training leaders, negotiators, and mediators. This could have a significant impact on conflict resolution, helping to build a sustainable and lasting peace.

References

Aquilar, F. (2008a). *Cognitive and emotional training for politicians and negotiators: Practical perspectives*. Paper presented at the 6th international congress of cognitive psychotherapy, Rome, 19–22 June 2008.

Aquilar, F., & Galluccio, M. (2005). *International negotiation: A new challenge for cognitive psychotherapy*. Paper presented at the 35th congress of the European association for behavioural and cognitive therapies (EABCT), Thessalonica, Greece, 21–24 September 2005.

Aquilar, F., & Galluccio, M. (2008). *Psychological processes in international negotiation*. New York: Springer.

Aquilar, F., & Galluccio, M. (2009). Negoziazioni interpersonali. In F. Aquilar & M. Galluccio (Eds.), *La negoziazione internazionale come processo psicologico*, pp. 15–20. Milano: Franco Angeli.

Argyle, M. (1994). *The psychology of interpersonal behaviour*. London: Penguin.

Bandura, A. (2002). Selective moral disengagement in the exercise of moral agency. *Journal of Moral Education, 31*(2), pp. 101–119.

Bandura, A. (2004). The role of selective moral disengagement in terrorism and counterterrorism. In F. M. Mogahaddam & A. J. Marsella (Eds.), *Understanding terrorism: Psychological roots, consequences and interventions* (pp. 121–150). Washington, DC: American Psychological Association.

Beck, A. T. (1988). *Love is never enough*. New York: Harper and Row.

Beck, J. S. (1995). *Cognitive therapy: Basics and beyond*. New York: Guilford.

Beck, A. T. (1999). *Prisoners of hate*. New York: Harper Collins.

Beck, A. T. (2002). Prisoners of hate. *Behaviour Research and Therapy, 40*, 209–216.

Beddington, J., Cooper, C. L., Field, J., Goswami, U., Huppert, F. A., Jenkins, R., et al. (2008). The mental wealth of nations. *Nature., 455*, pp. 1057–1060.

Bercovitch, J., & Jackson, R. (2001). Negotiation or mediation? An exploration of factors affecting the choice of conflict management in international conflict. *Negotiation Journal, 17*, 59–77.

Cooper, R. (2004). *The breaking of nations*. London: Atlantic.

Deutsch, M. (2002). Social psychology's contributions to the study of conflict resolution. *Negotiation Journal, 16*, 307–331.

Dimaggio, G., Semerari, A., Carcione, A., Nicolò, G., & Procacci, M. (2007). *Psychotherapy of personality disorders*. New York: Routledge.
Eco, U. (2003). *Mouse or Rat? Translation as negotiation*. London: Phoenix.
Falcone, M., Marraffa, M., & Carcione, A. (2003). Metarappresentazione e psicopatologia. In G. Dimaggio & A. Semerari (Eds.), *I disturbi di personalità. Modelli e trattamento* (pp. 43–76). Bari: Editore Laterza.
Fisher, R., Ury, W., & Patton, B. (1991). *Getting to yes. Negotiating an agreement without giving in*. London: Random House.
Gallucci, R. (2002). *Interview: Conversations with history*. UC Berkeley: Institute of International Studies, 11 February 2002.
Galluccio, M. (2004). *International negotiation: Cognitive, emotional and communicative aspects*. Paper presented at the 27th annual scientific meeting of the international society of political psychology, Lund, Sweden, 15–18 July 2004.
Galluccio, M. (2005a). *Addressing cognitions and emotions in the negotiation and mediation practices. A research project on how European commission's officials negotiate with developing countries*. Paper presented at the 28th annual scientific meeting of the international society of political psychology, Toronto, Canada, 3–6 July 2005.
Galluccio, M. (2005d). *Emotional competence as a compass to facilitate the negotiation process*. Paper presented at the second international biennale on negotiation, Paris, 17–18 November 2005.
Galluccio, M. (2007a). *Cognitive psychotherapy and international negotiation: An overview*. Paper presented at the V world congress of behavioural and cognitive therapy, Barcelona, Spain, 11–14 July 2007.
Galluccio, M. (2008). *Cognitive approaches to international relations: Perspectives and prospects of international negotiation*. Paper presented at the 6th international congress of cognitive psychotherapy, Rome, 19–22 June 2008.
Gardner, H. (2006). *Five minds for the future*. Boston: Harvard Business School Press.
Gellman, B. (2008). *Angler: The Cheney vice presidency*. New York: Penguin.
Gilbert, P. (2009). *The compassionate mind*. London: Constable and Robinson.
Guidano, V. F., & Liotti, G. (1983). *Cognitive processes and emotional disorders*. New York: Guilford.
Hillman, J. (2004). *A terrible love of war*. New York: Penguin.
Houghton, D. P. (1998). Historical analogies and the cognitive dimension of domestic policymaking. *Political Psychology, 19*(2), 279–303.
Janis, I. L. (1982). *Groupthink*. Boston: Houghton Mifflin.
Kagan, R. (2003). *Paradise and power*. London: Atlantic Books.
Kaldor, M. (2006). *New and old wars*. Cambridge: Polity Press.
Keller, J. W. (2009). Explaining rigidity and pragmatism in political leaders: A general theory and a plausibility test from the Reagan presidency. *Political Psychology, 30*(3), 465–498.
Kelman, H. C., & Fisher, R. (2003). Conflict analysis and resolution. In *Political psychology* (pp. 315–353). New York: Oxford University Press.
Kennedy, J.F. (1963). Speech given at American University, Washington DC, 10 June 1963.
Keohane, R. O. (2005). *After hegemony. Cooperation and discord in the world political economy*. Princeton, NJ: Princeton University Press.
Kremenyuk, V. A. (Ed.). (2002). *International negotiation. Analysis, approaches, issues*. San Francisco: Jossey-Bass.
McNamara, R. S., & Vandemark, B. (1995). *In retrospect: The tragedy and lessons of Vietnam*. New York: Times Books.
Moïsi, D. (2009). *The geopolitics of emotions: How cultures of fear, humiliation, and hope are reshaping the world*. New York: Doubleday.
Nye, J. S., Jr. (2003). *Understanding international conflicts*. New York: Pearson Addison Wesley.
Nye, J. S., Jr. (2004). *Soft power*. New York: Public Affairs.
Obama, B. (2006). *The Audacity of hope*. New York: Random House.

Obama, B. (2008). Speech given at the Victory Column, Berlin, DE, Tiergarten Park, Germany, 24 July 2008.
Obama, B. (2009a). Speech given at the United States Capitol, Washington DC, USA, 24 February 2009.
Obama, B. (2009b). Speech given at the Dwight Eisenhower Executive Office Building, Washington DC, USA, 27 March 2009.
Obama, B. (2009c). Speech given at Strasbourg Town Hall, Strasbourg, France, 3 April 2009.
Obama, B. (2009d). Speech given at Hradcany Square, Prague, the Czech Republic, 5 April 2009.
Obama, B. (2009e). Speech given at Turkish Grand national Assembly Complex, Ankara, Turkey, 6 April 2009.
Obama, B. (2009f). Speech given at Cairo University, Cairo, Egypt 4 June 2009.
Obama, B. (2009g). Speech given at the New Economic School Graduation, Gostinny Dvor, Moscow, Russia, 7 July 2009.
Obama, B. (2009h). Speech given at the Ghanaian Parliament in Accra, Accra, Ghana, 11 July 2009.
Obama, B. (2009i). Speech given at the United Nations General Assembly, New York, USA, 24 September 2009.
Obama, B. (2009j). Speech given at Suntory Hall, Tokyo, Japan, 13 November 2009.
Obama, B. (2009k). Speech given at the Museum of Science and Technology, Shanghai, China, 16 November 2009.
Obama, B. (2009l). Speech given at the United States Military Academy at West Point, New York, USA, 1 December 2009.
Obama, B. (2009m). Speech given at the Brookings Institution, New York, USA, 8 December 2009
Obama, B. (2009n). Nobel Lecture, Oslo, City Hall, Norway, 10 December 2009.
Obama, B. (2009o). Presidency Inaugural Address, Washington, DC, USA, 21 January 2009.
Obama, B. (2010). Remarks by the President at the Pentagon Memorial, Arlington, Virginia, USA, 11 September, 2010.
Owen, D. (2007). *The hubris syndrome: Bush, blair and the intoxication of power*. London: Politico's.
Parkinson, B., Fischer, A. H., & Manstead, A. S. R. (2005). *Emotion in social relations*. New York: Psychology Press.
Raiffa, H. (1982). *The art and science of negotiation*. Boston: Harvard University Press.
Raiffa, H. (2002). Contributions of applied systems analysis to international negotiation. In V. A. Kremenyuk (Ed.), *International negotiation* (pp. 5–21). San Francisco: Jossey-Bass.
Reicher, S.D., Haslam, S.A., & Platow, M.J. (2007, August/September). The new psychology of leadership. *Scientific American Mind*, pp. 22–29
Safran, J. D. (1984). Assessing the cognitive-interpersonal cycle. *Cognitive Therapy and Research, 8*, 333–348.
Safran, J. D. (1998). *Widening the scope of the cognitive therapy*. North Bergen: Jason Aronson.
Safran, J. D., & Muran, J. C. (2000). *Negotiating the therapeutic Alliance*. New York: Guilford.
Safran, J. D., & Segal, Z. V. (1990). *Interpersonal process in cognitive therapy*. New York: Basic Books.
Semerari, A. (2006). I cicli interpersonali e i disturbi metacognitivi nella relazione terapeutica. In S. Sassaroli, R. Lorenzini, & G. M. Ruggiero (Eds.), *Psicoterapia cognitiva dell'ansia*. Milano: Cortina.
Sunstein, C. R. (2007). *Worst-case scenarios*. Ann Arbor MI: Caravan Books.
Thoits, P. A. (2004). Emotion Norms, Emotion Work, and Social Order. In A. S. R. Manstead, N. Frijda, & A. Fischer (Eds.), *Feelings and emotions*. New Haven: Cambridge University Press.
Thompson, L. L. (Ed.). (2006). *Negotiation theory and research*. New York: Psychology Press.
Vico, G.B. (first published in 1744; 1999). *New science*. London: Penguin.
Watkins, M., & Rosegrant, S. (2001). *Breakthrough international negotiation*. San Francisco: Jossey-Bass.

Wells, A. (2000). *Emotional disorders and metacognition. Innovative cognitive therapy.* Chichester: Wiley.
Zimbardo, P. (2007). The Lucifer Effect. London: Rider.

Chapter 15
Social Cognitive Psychotherapy: From Clinical Practice to Peace Perspectives

Francesco Aquilar

> *As a long-time psychotherapist, (…) I have naturally given considerable thought to the use of psychological and psychotherapeutic principles to achieve and preserve peace (…). I shall present some of the products of this thought in this paper – without any promises of panaceas or final solutions.*
>
> Albert Ellis, 1992

Introduction

In order to define the functions and applications of social cognitive psychotherapy, it could be helpful to begin with some simple questions I have been asked during interviews following the publication of our previous volume titled *Psychological Processes in International Negotiations* (Aquilar and Galluccio 2008).

1. Why do some people become "sympathizers," supporters, or active followers of terrorism?
2. How people sometimes "change" their character because of particular situations and within certain "political systems"?
3. Why is the "military war culture" so rooted in the world, and why is indifference to this problem so pervasive?
4. Why are peace organizations and supranational organizations like the United Nations (UN) not always able to get the desired results from their international actions?
5. What could really be done (by public opinion and the media in particular) to help and contribute to peace negotiation processes?

F. Aquilar (✉)
Center for Cognitive Psychology and Psychotherapy Via Guido de Ruggiero 118, 80128, Napoli, Italy
e-mail: francescoaquilar@tiscali.it

F. Aquilar and M. Galluccio (eds.), *Psychological and Political Strategies for Peace Negotiation*, DOI 10.1007/978-1-4419-7430-3_15,

6. What contradictions came up in awarding US President Barack Obama, chief of the world's most powerful army, the Nobel Prize for Peace 2009?
7. To what extent do international negotiations (on war, terrorism, trade, energy, climate, environmental pollution) affect ordinary people?
8. What awareness and training might be needed by Governors, politicians, and their staffs to shape decision-making processes and to improve negotiated results?
   *Political scientists, psychologists, and psychotherapists have already tried to answer these questions (Aquilar and Galluccio, 2005). Several studies and research projects have been very useful; and specific operational projects of "social psychotherapy" have been developed (Aquilar, 1994, 1996, 2000, 2006a). However, an "operational connection" between the two disciplines – political and diplomatic sciences, psychology, and psychotherapy – is still missing. Aquilar and Galluccio (*2008*) attempted to try to fill the gap, since the two authors have theoretical and practical expertise in each field previously mentioned. Unfortunately, the use of means of mass communication to disseminate this information is still missing (Aquilar, 2006b, 2008).*
9. What makes peace negotiations so difficult?
10. How can a seemingly simple objective, that of achieving peace, so strongly desired by most actors in the field, in fact turns out to be so difficult to implement?
11. Why is a "war solidarity" easy to achieve within groups while a "peace solidarity" among different groups is much more difficult to achieve?
12. Could we find any real opportunity to try to change a modality (that of war) that has seamlessly characterized human history from its origins?

   Philosophers and politicians have been dealing with these problems throughout the centuries (Petrini, 2008). Many of them have proposed solutions. Sometimes, long periods of peace have characterized certain areas of the world. Often, the aftermath of war still influenced the fate of these areas.

13. How, then, can cognitive psychotherapists change such a solid trend?
14. And with how many chances of successful results?

I will try to answer some of the above mentioned questions through this chapter. Targets of our communication are primarily "people of culture" interested in peace processes; secondly, governors and politicians; and thirdly, professionals with expertise in communication issues. I will try to be as clear as possible, by avoiding technical language and defining core issues of relevant importance to the topic of this chapter. Then, I will examine reasons, motivations, and research for which certain conclusions are proposed in order to implement and develop effective political and psychological strategies for peace negotiations. At a second stage, I will provide references, which are the basis of the ideas developed along the chapter, taking care of other key targets of this book: scholars and students from the fields of psychology and psychotherapy and political and diplomatic sciences.

From Clinical Practice to Peace Perspectives

Three specific areas of reference (Zimbardo 2007) could help to improve the general understanding of war and peace actions. They are the following: (a) The psychobiological structure of human beings; (b) the context in which they act; and (c) the system that determines the rules of each environment. Concerning the psychobiological structure of human beings, we can consider four well-documented and heuristic theoretical frameworks: (1) cognitive and cognitive-behavioral psychotherapy; (2) the attachment theory of John Bowlby and his colleagues; (3) the multi-motivational theory of Giovanni Liotti; and (4) the meta-cognitive functions described by Antonio Semerari and his colleagues. These theoretical frameworks were born within psychotherapy as clinical practice and not as an explanation of the reasons for war and peace. However, they seem particularly useful for understanding social processes in helping to change some socially dangerous phenomena (Aquilar and Galluccio 2008, 2009).

The general framework of cognitive and cognitive-behavioral psychotherapy, although articulated in different schools of thought, is characterized by several elements: (a) It is built on the value of research, both on psychological and neuroscience fields, and therefore it is in permanent evolution; (b) it focuses the attention on the observable behavior and on the characteristics that determine it; (c) it assumes the prevalence of cognitive schemas on behaviors; (d) it identifies a set of inadequate cognitive processes (dysfunctional ideas, pathogenic beliefs, cognitive distortions, automatic thoughts) related to the emotional experience and to psychopathological disorders, and defines models for their modification; (e) it tracks down for each individual's disorder a "history of learning" that generates the disorder and maintains it (Aquilar and Del Castello, 1998; Aquilar, Del Castello and Esposito, 2005). Briefly stated, this general framework studies and applies the knowledge about human emotions to human activity in relation to individual, couple, and group processes with a focus on meaningful relationships (see: Gilbert and Leahy 2007).

> According to this framework, some political leaders seem to think and act through the biased lens of cognitive distortions and dysfunctional cognitive processes, maybe because inadequate early learning of interpersonal schemas centered on violence and oppression. Even if this way of thinking seems "irrational" it could "coagulate" in some contexts the approval of social or military groups.
>
> (Ellis 1992; Beck 1999)

John Bowlby and his collaborators' attachment theory (Bowlby 1969, 1988; for an update, see Pallini 2008) is concerned with affectional bonds, and it is built on a valuable research paradigm (especially longitudinal research). It describes the making and breaking of affectional bond modalities, and in particular it specifies the long-term effects of childhood trauma, separation, loss, mourning, and abuses of individuals. The attachment theory was born within the psychoanalytical context. Then, it was included within the paradigm of cognitive and cognitive-behavioral psychotherapy through the major contribution of two Italian scholars (Guidano and

Liotti 1983). This has powerfully enhanced the clinical and predictive efficiency of cognitive and cognitive-behavioral psychotherapy.

The attachment theory explains some additional reasons for which, through personal and particularly dramatic development stories, some people can develop a tremendous desire for retaliation and revenge, at any cost, to try inappropriately to heal emotional wounds of their past. But it also indicates the need to provide a series of individual psychological and physiological development aids on behalf of society, especially during childhood, in a way to prevent violent and dangerous interpersonal modalities.

The Multi-Motivational Theory of Giovanni Liotti (Liotti 1994/2005, 2001, 2007; Liotti and Monticelli 2008) is also built on the basis of extensive neuro-scientific research, and it represents an extension and deepening of the attachment theory. It basically states that humans, in order to make and keep relationships with each other, are driven by some biological motivations that are necessary for the survival of species. These motivations can be summarized in five main categories, plus two additional ones:

a) Attachment system, i.e., the innate drive to seek help in case of difficult times (sickness, hardship, etc.) from those who appear stronger or wiser;
b) Caregiving system, i.e., the innate drive to provide help to people who ask for it, especially if they are your descendants or affiliates;
c) Procreative sexual system to establish relationships that enable the conception of offspring and a safe environment in which to bring up children;
d) Competitive system to establish a rank between humans of the same group, and to regulate the access (and the order of access) to limited resources;
e) Peer cooperative system to temporarily erase differences of rank, to achieve together a common goal that could be unattainable without uniting individual efforts;

The two additional motivational systems (Liotti and Monticelli 2008) are the following:

f) Affiliation to the group;
g) Social game;

These systems use mechanisms similar to those of the peer cooperation system, even if they are shaped through more sophisticated "neocortical" modalities.

It is possible to imagine the interaction of the five main systems in human beings, and a specific architecture of motivations provided for this interaction (and consequently of emotions that result from the attainment or failure of goals). In abstract terms, a balance between individual motivational systems is important to achieve a satisfactory life cycle. But in practice, everybody's life ups and downs could alter the interaction of each original psychobiological structure with a relative disparity of a certain motivational system to the detriment of others. In some way, the original architecture of human motivation could be modified by life events with a consequential structural and plastic reorganization of the relation between the motivational systems and the relative amplitude of each of them (Liotti and Monticelli 2008).

In this sense, the war would progress through the basis of the agonistic-competitive motivational system, with an individual (and his group) psychobiologically "pushed" to dominate others to assert their superiority and their power.

But secondly, the war would also move through the cooperative system: Without cooperation between and among many people on policies proposed by their rulers, it would not be possible to achieve any objective of war. Other "war motivations," therefore, would originate from dysfunctional architecture of motivations in some of the leaders and power groups.

Another heuristic topic of clinical and psychosocial interest is represented by meta-cognition, i.e., the complex rules and abilities on which thought is developed. It is defined by Semerari and colleagues (Semerari 2006; Dimaggio and Semerari 2003; Dimaggio et al. 2007) as consisting of three fundamental characteristics: self-reflection, others' mind understanding, and mastery. More specifically, we can describe five meta-cognitive or meta-representational functions as more or less developed in each individual, which may be displayed in certain contextual environments (Falcone et al. 2003; Dimaggio et al. 2007). These functions are: (a) identification, namely the ability to appropriately recognize one's own emotions and those of others; (b) decentering, or the ability to assess external reality, keeping in mind not only one's own point of view but also that of other persons, accepting and giving value to it; (c) differentiation, the ability to distinguish between mental representation and external reality (and by extension, between situations that seem similar); (d) integration, the ability to remember the various, even contradictory, elements and experiences, that have happened or are happening at a given time; d) mastery, the ability to exert mastery over one's own behavior regardless of emotions felt at that moment. The study on so-called personality disorders, and on three of them in particular – narcissistic, borderline and paranoid – have revealed a systematic dysfunction of some meta-cognitive mechanisms in individuals. These dysfunctions are neither related to a deficiency of intelligence nor to a lack of public communication skills.

Some political leaders could be strongly characterized by disturbed personalities without being undermined in their ability to proselytize or spread their beliefs in a convincing manner. Another set of "war motivations" would then be composed by leaders characterized by meta-cognitive dysfunctions associated with great intellectual and persuasive abilities.

Cognitive Approaches to Peace

Albert Ellis (1992), in the article from which the epigraph to this chapter is excerpted, provided the first structured and best example of cognitive psychotherapy application to the construction of peace processes. Essentially, Ellis' stance identifies the possibility of psychotherapy to help patients and their relatives and affiliates to develop peaceful attitudes and behaviors first towards themselves (see also Gilbert 2005, and in this volume), then towards their families and their neighbors, and finally towards different ethnic, political, and foreign groups (Ellis 1992, p 79). In this way, psychotherapists can indirectly influence, through their patients, many social processes in which the patients are themselves leading actors or are instead able to influence leading actors.

In applying Ellis' principles (1992, 2008) to try to resolve domestic and international conflicts, individuals, peoples, and governments can choose either peaceful methods of interaction and negotiation or combative methods. They can focus on vulnerability, defensiveness, anger and hostility, or they can develop empathy and hope for the future. Or instead, they can learn to overcome depression, despair, and rigid and absolutist thinking. This could be true and possible for people who undertake the psychotherapy proposed by Ellis (REBT: Rational-Emotive-Behavioral Therapy). Individuals who, through psychotherapy, have acquired a "rational" modality in order to facilitate changes of their thought-emotion-action schemas, could extend this modality to different contextual environment (Ellis, 2008). Such a modality could also be employed to help military actors overcome the stress of war experience. However, this can hardly influence foreign governments not used to these cognitive modalities.

The focus of Aaron T. Beck (1999, 2002) on this theme is instead mostly centered on the origins, prevention, and maintenance of terrorism, and on functional strategies to prevent or reduce it. From his studies, we can isolate three basic tips: (a) Strategic tolerance, which should be exercised towards beliefs that collide with one's own beliefs (or with those of one's own group); (b) hostility processes, which should be monitored (including predisposition, precipitation, and reaction to certain events) to try to prevent or stop violence escalation; (c) interlocutor's potentially aggressive basic beliefs, which should be identified to respond with strategic maneuvers. This could reduce the probability that he could draw arbitrary inferences from one counterpart's public peaceful communication.

*Beck's viewpoint (*1999, 2002*) concerns terrorism from a Western perspective, specifically the American perspective. He defines terrorists as "prisoners of hatred" and notes a number of strategies to cope with the situation. Moreover, the timely identification of cognitive errors, from both the Western side and that of terrorists, could help to reduce the risk of conflict escalation. But even in this case, the extrapolation from the context of war and peace of fundamental cognitive psychotherapy acquisitions is difficult to apply in practice. It could* represent *a trend, a comprehensive and enlightening analysis, but we are still missing extensive potential applications of the model to the realm of peace studies.*

Ellis and Beck's models are particularly articulated, and they have been extensively discussed elsewhere (Aquilar and Galluccio 2008).

Selective Moral Disengagement

Albert Bandura (1986, 2002) is also a pioneer in the application of cognitive psychology to social issues. Through his "social cognitive approach" in psychotherapy he has explored the construct of selective moral disengagement. Why is it some people, even if they own an ethical system of values, can be induced to commit, tolerate, or line up with morally reprehensible attitudes and behaviors that promote violence? This could happen through a temporary and selective-based inhibition of moral rules, which is activated under certain circumstances and through different human mechanisms. Bandura called this phenomenon selective moral disengagement and identified eight specific mechanisms of the *selective moral disengagement*. We will list them using the synthesis proposed by Dario Bacchini (2004, pp 57–60; see also Aquilar and Galluccio 2009):

1. Moral justification: The damage done to others is justified in the name of the highest moral values (e.g., "It is good to use force against anyone who offends your family").
2. Euphemistic labeling: Violent or illegal actions are "cleaned" through semantic processes by using a different name (e.g., "ethnic cleansing" instead of "extermination").
3. Advantageous comparison: Blameworthy actions seem to be reappraised when compared to other worst actions (e.g., "Accepting a small 'bribe' is nothing compared to the billions of dollars stolen by some people").
4. Displacement of responsibility: placing on others, regarded as more "authoritative" persons, the responsibility for reprehensible actions (e.g., "If kids are not well educated at home, it is not their fault if they behave violently").
5. Diffusion of responsibility: supporting individual irresponsible behaviors through the insistence that "everybody is like that" (e.g., "One cannot blame those who use violence because in his group this is normal").
6. Distortion of consequences: pushing people to believe that the consequences of their violent actions are less serious than might appear (e.g., "Sexual relationships with children are normal in that culture; to those children there will not be any consequences at all").
7. Dehumanization of victims: seeing people subjected to violence or abuse as subhuman (e.g., "Some people deserve to be treated like animals").
8. Attribution of blame to the victim: considering and emphasizing an alleged "provocation" by those who suffered damages or aggressive behavior (e.g., "Kids who are ill-treated usually deserve it").

Selective moral disengagement (Bandura 2002) appears to be strongly linked to a shedding of responsibility of citizens, and it is subject to certain problematic conducts, both in individual social behavior (as in case of bullying) and in areas directly and indirectly linked to international terrorism and war. In the latter, it appears of particular importance to develop abilities in a way that builds up a critical social consciousness capable of examining (and later on, influencing peaceful attitudes) both the communication among peoples, and especially the explicit and implicit messages generated by means of mass communication. As matter of fact, this kind of cognitive influence oriented to overpowering exasperated competition, enhanced by the mechanisms of selective moral disengagement, may have substantial effects on social views, and especially on visible and hidden behaviors of rulers and negotiators.

The Psychological Effects of Power

Philip Zimbardo (2007), after a long study of psychosocial phenomena reported in his book titled *The Lucifer Effect: How Good People Turn Evil,* draws the conclusion that "evil is power" in certain contexts and within specific systems. Ordinary peaceful people may tend to have harmful behavior towards others and could hurt them if pushed in this sense by authoritative people. This behavior could be strengthened if individuals are "trained" to not feel responsible for the pain or humiliations inflicted on others. If the "aggressive behavior" is taught gradually the result is improved (Zimbardo 2007). The suggestion brought forward by Zimbardo is to reduce the chance for "ordinary" people to be driven to commit injurious or humiliating acts towards others through constant attention to their freedom to oppose unjust authoritative orders. Therefore he suggests a number of strategies to resist negative influences the power could exert on some people, especially in specific contexts (stressful and/or isolated contexts) and within specific systems (political, military, prison, sectarian, or communicative). These strategies can be summarized as follows (Zimbardo 2007, pp 614–622, Italian edition):

1. To learn how to recognize one's own mistakes and share this awareness with others: This reduces the likelihood of persisting with inappropriate behaviors.
2. To keep the attention alive: This helps to keep people from acting on the basis of non-critical automatic behaviors.
3. To retain responsibility for one's actions.
4. To maintain one's individual identity.
5. To differentiate between good and bad authority.
6. To maintain independent opinions (although it is legitimate to desire social acceptance).
7. To pay special attention to framing events and actions: Sometimes harmful actions may be disguised as seemingly noble intentions.
8. To position situations in one's own life continuum in order not to cut and fix oneself in contexts of "expanded present" without rules.
9. To give priority to individual and civil freedom, rather than to illusions of safety and security.
10. To remember that one can hinder unfair systems.

Zimbardo's contribution to this field is conceived to help ordinary people avoid committing to harmful violent and/or humiliating acts on other people: Thus, they could avoid becoming torturers, and sometimes instead acting as heroes simply by implementing the above mentioned strategy suggestion. In other words, the invitation is not to transform oneself into evil actors just because an "authority" has ordered or allowed it. Isolated environments without external controls require even greater vigilance and resistance to social mechanisms of selective moral disengagement.

Psychological Effects of Leadership

Up to now, we have been taken into account elements of moral weakening of ordinary people, especially if they are empowered by the situation. What happens, instead, when we look at personality transformations associated with the holding of political powers for a long period of time? In what way does power tend to negatively transform leaders?

David Owen (2008), after thorough study and research into the characteristics and personal developments of heads of states and governments during the last 100 years, proposed the possibility that holding power for long periods of time tends to elicit an "inebriation syndrome" (hubris syndrome), which involves a series of behavioral symptoms. The author identifies 14 symptoms, which can be summarized as follows (Owen 2008, pp xxvi–xxvii):

(a) Narcissistic tendency to see the world as an arena in which to exercise power and seek for glory, with a tendency to take actions in order to put themselves at the center of attention
(b) Identifying themselves with the nation, with the consequent tendency to talk about themselves in the third person or to use the collective "we"
(c) Excessive confidence in themselves and in their own abilities, with contempt for criticism, considering themselves above human judgment
(d) Systematic lack of rest with worsening impulsivity
(e) Loss of contact with reality, often associated with progressive isolation
(f) Preventive overestimation of moral rightness and effectiveness of one's own decisions, ignoring the negative aspects, costs, risks, and consequences
(g) Inability to change ideas, resulting in continuous progressive incompetence

This framework, derived from a meticulous historical analysis, is rather alarming. The phenomenon seems to involve leaders and the duration of the exercise of power: The more time one has spent in a position of power, the greater the effect of "inebriation *syndrome." Simultaneously, it is possible that those "ordinary" people who in turn exert a power originating, more or less, from that of the leader, have been infected by the "Lucifer effect" described by Zimbardo (2007). We can imagine that in leaders the synergy between the Lucifer effect and the Hubris syndrome could help events to unfold in directions of war or terrorism (of course, along with historical, economic, social, political, and military factors to name a few).*

Countermeasures

What kind of countermeasures could be devised? Why might this historic period be favorable for the modification of a hyper-agonistic competitive structure that has been running humanity until now? Maybe it is because the objectives of motivational systems are guided by a biological goal in favor of the human species; hence, the current possibility of the human species' extinction as a result of actual military power can disable the rank system that had been built by evolution to protect the species (Gilbert, 2009). This is one of the reasons why it could be easy to obtain, in this period, general attention to social peace explanations as well as a chance for a highly successful social persuasion strategy to bring about active participation in peace processes, at least in the Western world (Aquilar and Ascolese, 2008). A second factor worth considering is represented by the spread of the Internet and the possibility for people worldwide to communicate directly and in real time over large distances. Public opinion, fueled by an increased individual awareness of the ability to manage the exchange of ideas free from government control, would challenge governments' actions more effectively, monitoring, choosing and influencing – especially in times of crisis – the conduct of staff decision-makers. Moreover, historical and political studies and research suggest, among other things, how to increase democratic control (Chomsky 2005, 2009); strategies to combat the indifference of citizens (Kanaan 2002); and new possible institutional functioning modalities focused on strengthening results achieved by supranational organizations (Kennedy 2006). Many contributions have also originated from psychology and psychotherapy studies and research, some of which have hitherto been summarized. However, two additional sectors are deemed indispensable to support actions for peace: mass communication means and training in the broadest sense.

However, the search for meaning is so disruptive in periods of crisis that terrorism is able to "convince" some people to sacrifice their life for a deeper and absolute goal (from the perspective of the terrorists). Terrorists, supporters, and tolerant observers who "cover" terrorism in some way appear convinced that terrorists have been taking good, ethical, and necessary actions. This position needs to be changed by a social action for peace. However, we must act to ensure that individuals, leaders, and people overcome cognitive egocentrism; and we should put pressure on governments to meet the needs of all peoples in order to avoid or encourage the recruitment of more terrorists or supporters.

Integrating Viewpoints

For peace negotiations to be efficient and without losers, it could be important to "enlarge the pie," taking into account all participants' viewpoints in the negotiation (and also of "involved" outsiders), to aim to improve their personal situation (Aquilar and Galluccio 2008). In this respect, we should consider the following viewpoints (and the powerful emotions associated with them). That of:

1. People who feel trampled in some of their fundamental rights
2. Governors and politicians: both of whom wish to maintain power and who wish to develop welfare states
3. Journalists, the press or television, who have the power to directly influence (in some parts of the world) public opinion
4. Ordinary citizens, who must simultaneously struggle with different stages of their life cycle: growing up, finding a job, raising a family, organizing an acceptable daily life, etc.
5. Negotiators, who are at the forefront of international negotiations and who should respect the assigned mandate and try to establish an atmosphere of collaboration with interlocutors
6. Sociologists, who study the evolution of society and could offer new solutions, outlining possible future scenarios in advance
7. Psychologists and psychotherapists, who are studying possible applications of their knowledge in a perspective of peace and global prosperity

8. Finally, anti-democratic subjects, who focused their efforts on immediate gain (economic, political, or linked to the power) with an "advantageous" perspective to someone (including themselves) but seriously harming others

In-depth study of anti-democratic subjects' viewpoints, in order to identify in advance possible aggressive actions, and try to neutralize them, could be one of the goals of social and cognitive psychotherapy. This knowledge may be included in cognitive-oriented training programs for politicians and negotiators. An example of such a program has been described elsewhere (Aquilar and Galluccio 2008). The presence of anti-democratic subjects makes all but inevitable the creation and careful management of a defensive army to protect principles and actions for peace. This situation allows us to integrate the apparent contradiction of a Nobel Peace Prize given to the chief of the most powerful army in the world, as was done to US President Barack Obama in 2009. However, a permanent and effective action of social control on power management is necessary, and it could also be applied through specific psychological strategies.

Psychological Strategies

Psychological strategies for peace negotiation can be divided into two broad categories:

(a) *Intervention on the citizens and the followers/supporters of terrorism.* It regards war and terrorism prevention, management, and recovery from it. This area is not only concerned with actions of persuasion and social awareness of the reasons for peace; but also with a specific system of techniques designed to deter, dissuade, and retrieve individual followers or supporters from war, or from terrorist organizations;

(b) *Intervention on governments, politicians, and negotiators.* It regards psychological cognitive-oriented interventions on leaders, politicians, negotiators, mediators. These interventions aim at rationalizing a scientific approach to some specific problems that governments and diplomats should resolve.

More specifically, in this second area some issues can be summarized as:

1. *The behavior of crisis units.* The rulers/governors and their advisers may be forced, by crisis emergency, to commit some cognitive-emotional errors, already identified by research, such as the so-called "groupthink" (Janis 1982; Aquilar and Galluccio 2008) or the Lucifer effect (Zimbardo 2007). A team of psychologists in support to crisis units could reduce these distortions.
2. *The factors involved in negotiations and mediations.* Negotiation dynamics have been studied, particularly with regard to certain factors, including: a) *Breakdown* (timing and differences: right time to strategically interrupt negotiations; how long the breakdown should last; and how and when to restart negotiations); b) *threats-retaliations* (where it seems useful to make a threat and/or a retaliation, and under what circumstances, instead, this strategy could be harmful); c) *negotiation styles*

(which aspects may promote specific positive results and which ones may prevent them: such as deceit, aggressiveness, empathy). The results of these studies and their operative meta-analysis could be made available to decision-making teams (See Aquilar and Galluccio 2008).

3. *Negotiators' personal skills.* Negotiators' behavioral, cognitive, emotional, and communication competencies could be enhanced by psychologically cognitive-oriented training. In particular, their ability to pay attention, to tolerate frustration, to be self-reflective, to understand others' minds, and to exhibit self-mastery could be specifically implemented.
4. *The predictions of counterparts' behaviors.* Effective analysis of cognitive-emotional processes of the counterpart may allow actors to predict in advance actions that could be undertaken. This could be helpful in anticipating possible interpersonal peaceful actions. This area covers the possibility of detecting in counterparts cognitive processes characterized by narcissistic, borderline, and paranoid cognitive egocentrism.
5. *The psychology of organizations.* People working in organizations are submitted to a series of constraints that may distort the positive results that each individual could carry on. A systematic correction of cognitive distortions raised by the organizational context could be implemented with the assistance of psychologists (Argentero, Cortese and Piccardo, 2009).

A Model of Social Psychotherapy

These psychological strategies, in order to gain effectiveness, require an action plan, a sustainable dissemination policy, and a wide social application. Moreover, they need a variety of means through which they can effectively influence political-decision making processes.

Articulated hypothesis of a psychological strategy application could be put into action through three main channels:

(a) Universities
(b) Public opinion
(c) Political/diplomatic world

The means by which this intervention could be developed would respectively be:

1. Targeted dissemination of studies and research results
2. A conscious use of means of mass communication
3. A series of specific training programs for politicians and negotiators

Then, it would become possible to outline three synergetic assumptions for a socio-political influence:

(a) Influencing universities through the research process. Universities could help to influence national governments and supranational organizations through actions of counseling.

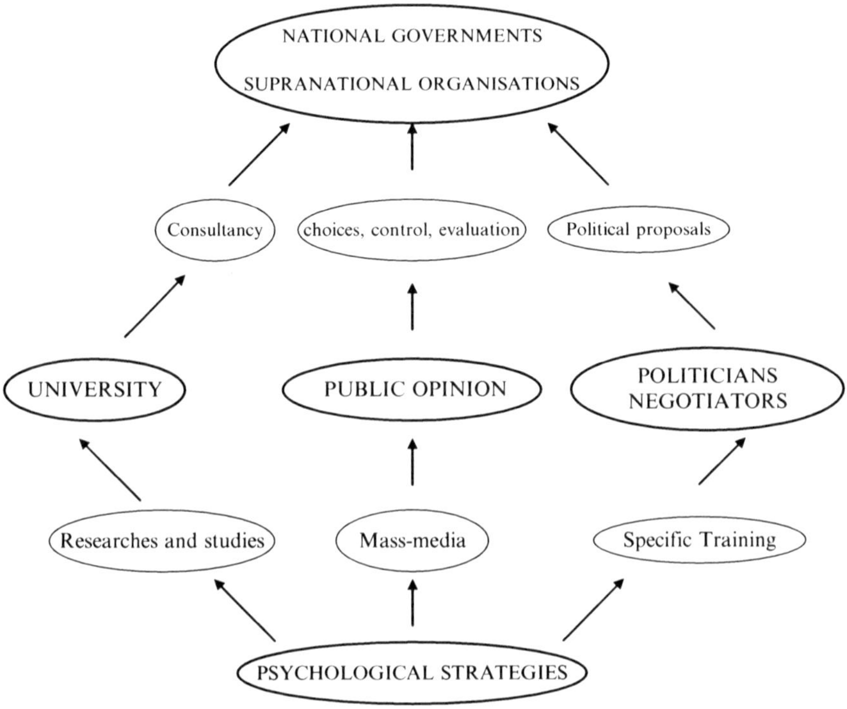

Fig. 15.1 Operative implementation model

(b) Targeting public opinion and social attitudes through mass media. This could provoke changes towards an operational concept of peace. Public opinion might in turn influence national governments (and supranational organizations) through a more careful process of action, control, and evaluation of people appointed to public powers (and on the actions performed by these people).
(c) Targeting policy-makers and negotiators through specific training programs. Such influence could be directly intended to modify and streamline the choices and behaviors in the direction of peace.

Fig 15.1 sketches the plan of *psychotherapeutic* intervention on governments and on society:

Conclusions

Some psychological strategies for peace negotiations have been underlined in this chapter, and significant elements have been highlighted. The psychological motivations underlining war, terrorism, and guerrilla warfare could be understood (and hopefully changed) taking also into consideration the:

1. Psychobiological nature of human beings;
2. History of individual attachment;
3. Mechanisms that regulate their behavior;
4. Cognitive schemas and different viewpoints of those involved;
5. Meta-cognitive abilities (and the interaction between their meta-cognitive dysfunctions);
6. Negotiating skills (which may be implemented);
7. Contexts in which their cognition and actions are developed;
8. Communication and political system in which people grow up;

Some of these individual factors, contexts, and systems can deeply affect the ethical values of people and their behaviors. In particular, the management and the exercise of power at different levels seem to be linked to possible negative consequences that could be spread to the highest levels.

In this context (from clinical practice to psychosocial intervention) the social-cognitive psychotherapy contribution may concern:

a. A special focus cognitive psychotherapy may give to the social life of patients, taking into account the importance of the social dimension of consciousness, emotions, and personal relationships;
b. A wide dissemination of psychotherapy acquisitions (making them operational) for as many people as possible. This knowledge should not remain a privilege of a few people – as happened with the hygiene standards at the end of the nineteenth century – but should be socially broadened;
c. An implemented collaboration between social psychologists, sociologists, political scientists, and mass-media professionals to try, through the knowledge derived from psychotherapy, to influence social processes (including negotiations, wars, terrorism, and peace), which are, in fact, fundamentally reverberating in people's daily lives;
d. Specific social-cognitive training programs, to be prepared and set up in collaboration and cooperation with all professionals above mentioned, reserved for specific categories of people;

In particular, in relation to psychological and political strategies for peace negotiations, social cognitive psychotherapy could help to build up a meaningful context through influencing: (a) politicians, rulers/governors, and their family members (Ellis 1992); (b) political decision-making staff and negotiating staff through specific training programs (Aquilar and Galluccio 2008); (c) public opinion, with the collaboration of mass-media, with particular attention to the need of an early detection of selective moral-disengagement processes (Bandura 2002); (d) legislators, in a way for them to provide corrective factors for uncontrolled power consequences at various levels (Zimbardo 2007; Owen 2008). Finally, we have introduced a model for operative implementation of this project of social cognitive psychotherapy.

Needless to say, further specific research is necessary and urgent, and it must help differentiate between operative modalities and efficient techniques against these objectives. However, the large amount of theoretical, clinical, and experimental studies available in specialized literature brings us a positive, optimistic hope for a better future.

References

Aquilar, F. (1994). Psicoterapia per la pace. *Il tetto, 31*(182), 158–169.

Aquilar, F. (Ed.). (1996). *La coppia in crescita*. Assisi: Cittadella.

Aquilar, F. (2000). *Riconoscere le emozioni*. Milano: Franco Angeli.

Aquilar, F. (2006a). *Psicoterapia dell'amore e del sesso*. Milano: Franco Angeli.

Aquilar, F. (2006b). *Le donne dalla A alla Z*. Milano: Franco Angeli.

Aquilar, F. (2008, June 19–22). *Cognitive and emotional training for politicians and negotiators: Practical perspectives*. Paper presented at the 6th international congress of cognitive psychotherapy, Rome.

Aquilar, F., & Ascolese, R. (2008, June 19–22). *Social cognitive psychotherapy, attachment based approach and modification of society*. Paper presented at the 6th international congress of cognitive psychotherapy, Rome.

Aquilar, F., & Del Castello, E. (Eds.). (1998). *Psicoterapia delle fobie e del panico*. Milano: Franco Angeli.

Aquilar, F., Del Castello, E., & Esposito, R. (Eds.). (2005). *Psicoterapia dell'anoressia e della bulimia*. Milano: Franco Angeli.

Aquilar, F., & Galluccio M (2005, September 23) International negotiation: A new challenge for cognitive psychotherapy. Paper presented at the 35th Congress of the European Association for Behavioural and Cognitive Therapies, Thessaloniki, Greece

Aquilar, F., & Galluccio, M. (2008). *Psychological processes in international negotiations: Theoretical and practical perspectives*. New York: Springer.

Aquilar, F., & Galluccio, M. (2009). Negoziazioni interpersonali. In F. Aquilar & M. Galluccio (Eds.), *La negoziazione internazionale come processo psicologico*, pp.15–20. Milano: Franco Angeli.

Argentero, P., Cortese, C. G., & Piccardo, C. (2009). *Psicologia delle organizzazioni*. Milano: Cortina.

Bacchini D. (2004). Educare alla legalità: modelli e strumenti nell'ambito della psicologia dello sviluppo, in: Bacchini D., Boda G., De Leo G., eds., Promuovere la responsabilità, Franco Angeli, Milano.

Bandura A. (1986). Social foundations of thought and action: a social cognitive theory, Prentice Hall, Englewood Cliff

Bandura, A. (2002). Selective Moral Disengagement in the exercise of Moral Agency, *in Journal of moral Education, 31*(2).

Beck, A.T. (1999). *Prisoners of hate*. New York: Harper Collins.

Beck, A.T. (2002). Prisoners of hate. *Behaviour Research and Therapy, 40*, 209–216.

Bowlby J. (1969). Attachment and loss: I. Attachment, Hogarth Press, London

Bowlby J. (1988). A secure base, Routledge, London

Chomsky, N. (2005). *Government in the future*. New York: Seven Stories Press.

Chomsky N. (2009). Quattro Nobel non meritati, *Internazionale*, 17(828), 29.

Chomsky, N. (2010). Quattro Nobel non meritati. *Internazionale, 17*(828), 29.

Dimaggio, G., Semerari, A., Carcione, A., Nicolò, G., & Procacci, M. (2007), *Psychotherapy of personality disorders*, New York: Routledge.

Ellis, A. (1992). Rational emotive approaches to peace. *J Cog Psychot, 6*(2), 79–104.

Ellis, A. (2008). Foreword. In F. Aquilar & M. Galluccio (Eds.), *Psychological processes in international negotiations: Theoretical and practical perspectives*. New York: Springer.

Falcone, M., Marraffa, M., Carcione, A. (2003), Metarappresentazione e psicopatologia, in: G. Dimaggio & A. Semerari, A., (Eds.). I disturbi di personalità, Laterza, Roma-Bari

Gilbert, P. (Ed.). (2005). *Compassion*. London: Routledge.

Gilbert, P. (2009). *The compassionate mind*. London: Constable and Robinson.

Gilbert, P., & Leahy, R. L. (Eds.). (2007). *The therapeutic relationship in the cognitive-behavioral psychotherapies*. London: Routledge.

Guidano, V. F., & Liotti, G. (1983). *Cognitive processes and emotional disorders*. New York: Guilford.

Janis, I.L. (1982). *Groupthink*. Boston: Houghton Mifflin Company.
Kanaan, J.-S. (2002). *Ma guerre à l'indifférence*. Paris: Laffont.
Kennedy, P. (2006). *The parliament of man: The past, present and future of United Nations*. New York: Vintage Random House.
Liotti, G. (1994/2005). La dimensione interpersonale della coscienza. Rev edn. Carocci, Roma.
Liotti, G. (2001). *Le opere della coscienza*. Milano: Cortina.
Liotti G. (2007). Internal working models of attachment in the therapeutic relationship, in: P. Gilbert & R.L. Leahy (Eds.), The therapeutic relationship in the cognitive behavior psychotherapies, Routledge, London
Liotti, G., & Monticelli, F. (Eds.). (2008). *I sistemi motivazionali nel dialogo clinico*. Milano: Cortina.
Owen, D. (2008). *In sickness and in power*. London: Methuen.
Pallini, S. (2008). Psicologia dell'attaccamento, Franco Angeli, Milano
Petrini, C. (2008). *Madre terra*. Milano: Mondadori.
Semerari A. (2006). I cicli interpersonali e i disturbi metacognitivi nella relazione terapeutica, in: S. Sassaroli R. Lorenzini & G.M. Ruggiero, *Psicoterapia cognitiva dell'ansia*, Milano: Cortina
Zimbardo, P. (2007). *The Lucifer effect. How good people turn evil*. New York: Random House.

Chapter 16
Conclusions

Francesco Aquilar and Mauro Galluccio

This book on psychological and political strategies for peace negotiation has two essential features: peer cooperation and practical operational application. Without these two elements, the ideas we have developed, and the contributions from a range of distinguished and influential authors, might appear to be simply good intentions.

Research in the area of cognitive psychology and psychotherapy can help support political negotiations for peace, although we should not underestimate the influence of other variables (anthropological, economic, and power-based). This approach is neither psychologically self-centered nor cognitively egocentric, and it complements historical-diplomatic analysis, political science, and the practical field experience gained by negotiators and statesmen. The synergy between cognitive psychology/ psychotherapy and political science could make a very real contribution to improve real people's lives in this difficult and sometimes tragic period for the human species.

The applications of this operational hypothesis pass through a precise strategic "chain" of influencing national governments and supranational organizations, as described in the text, which includes the establishment of a participatory and informed public opinion, as well as a series of strategic maneuvers through specific information and training (initially and especially permanently updated) of citizens, negotiators, politicians, and governors/rulers.

Three aspects could be drawn as final conclusions: a legitimate hope, a risk, and an intention.

F. Aquilar (✉)
Center for Cognitive Psychology and Psychothorapy, Via Guido de Ruggiero 118, 80128, Napoli, Italy
e-mail: francescoaquilar@tiscali.it

M. Galluccio (✉)
European Association for Negotiation and Mediation, Square Ambiorix, 32/43, B-1000, Brussels, Belgium
e-mail: mauro.galluccio@eanam.org

F. Aquilar and M. Galluccio (eds.), *Psychological and Political Strategies for Peace Negotiation*, DOI 10.1007/978-1-4419-7430-3_16,

1. The *legitimate hope* is that, from this attempt, prompt and effective action could be taken and that this would be beneficial to increase peace through "negotiations without losers." In this context, mass communication tools and public opinion should not represent external noise of minor importance, but rather two industrious arms through which we can build and keep peace.
2. The *risk* could be represented by the fact that what remains at the end of the day is just words, maybe even beautiful words, but destined to become at best the object of reflection for most experts in the field, or at worst, just chatter and waste paper with no real consequences.
3. The *intention* is not to stop with theory or abstract modeling, however valuable these may be, but to continue operationally in the project of building a possible peace perspective that could be realized and implemented over time.

The power of ideas can transform people, meanings, things, relationships, and partially also the world. We have gathered a large number of distinguished experts around our project, which aims to develop synergy between cognitive psychology/psychotherapy and political science for peace. Strengthened by this collaboration, we will continue to involve people who are interested in changing peace negotiations and international relations, and who are committed to the achievement of civil, democratic, and peaceful coexistence for everyone, both within each state and among states. If through this project even one human life could be saved, our effort will not have been useless.

Index

F. Aquilar and M. Galluccio (eds.), *Psychological and Political Strategies for Peace Negotiation*, DOI 10.1007/978-1-4419-7430-3,

Breinigsville, PA USA
30 December 2010
252275BV00001B/7/P

9 781441 974297